THE DOMINIE

Thesaurus

FOR YOUNG WRITERS

Published by

Dominie Press, Inc.

1949 Kellogg Avenue
Carlsbad, California 92008 USA
(800) 232-4570

ISBN 0-7685-2298-6

www.dominie.com

THE DOMINIE
Thesaurus
FOR YOUNG WRITERS

Vera Dobson Gould
Patricia J. Hughes

Dominie Press, Inc.

What Is a Thesaurus?

The word *thesaurus* comes from a Greek word meaning *treasury*. In other words, a thesaurus is a treasury of words. Unlike a dictionary, which gives you definitions of words, a thesaurus provides you with synonyms, or words with the same meanings. It also lists antonyms, which are words with opposite or contrasting meanings.

Why Do I Need a Thesaurus?

A thesaurus improves your writing

- A thesaurus helps you find the right words to say what you want to say.
- It also helps you avoid using the same words all the time.
- Your writing becomes clearer and more interesting when you use appropriate words. For example, many writers use the word *good* to describe almost everything. If you look up *good* in this thesaurus, you will find there are many different words with similar meanings. So, instead of saying, "She is a good skater," you could say, "She is a skillful skater."

A thesaurus expands your vocabulary

Regular use of a thesaurus will expand your vocabulary. Learning, thinking about, and using more words will boost your comprehension skills. In this thesaurus, there are more than 7,000 entry words, 20,000 synonyms, and 15,000 antonyms!

A thesaurus develops your language skills

In this thesaurus, each entry word (and its extended form) is accompanied by a sample sentence that uses the word in a meaningful context. Parts of speech for each word are listed in italics. By reading the sentences, you will be learning the correct way to use each word. In this way, you will be improving your language skills, which are an important part of all literacy tests that you will be taking throughout your school years.

Parts of speech

A noun	*is the name for people, animals, things, or places*
A verb	*is an action word that tells you what someone or something is doing*
An adjective	*is a describing word that tells you more about a person, thing, animal, or place*
An adverb	*tells you more about a verb or action*
A preposition	*tells you where things or people are or how they are related*
A conjunction	*joins two words, phrases, or clauses in a sentence*

The   brown   dog   barked   loudly   and   the   cat   scampered   up   the   tree.

adjective   noun   verb   adverb   conjunction   noun   verb   preposition   noun

Thesaurus Sample Page

Entry words are listed alphabetically in the color bar on the left side of each page.

The guide word helps you find the word you are looking for. On a left-hand page, the guide word is the first entry word on that page. On a right-hand page, the guide word is the last entry word on that page.

Synonyms, or words with similar meanings to the entry words, are listed here.

The sample sentence is a vital feature of this thesaurus. The sample sentence helps you to understand the meaning of the entry word, and it also shows you how the word is commonly used.

Should the entry word have another use related to its meaning, this part of speech is listed in *italics,* followed by a sentence using the word in a meaningful context.

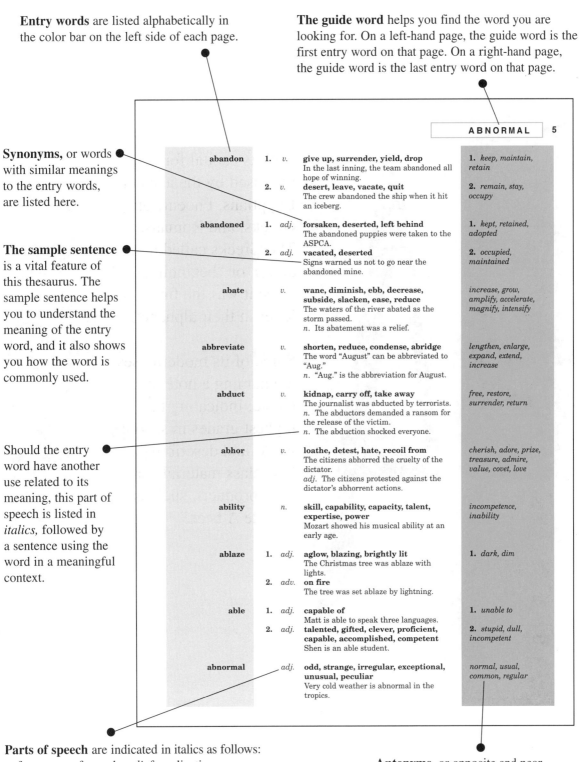

ABNORMAL   5

abandon	1.	*v.*	**give up, surrender, yield, drop** In the last inning, the team abandoned all hope of winning.	1. *keep, maintain, retain*
	2.	*v.*	**desert, leave, vacate, quit** The crew abandoned the ship when it hit an iceberg.	2. *remain, stay, occupy*
abandoned	1.	*adj.*	**forsaken, deserted, left behind** The abandoned puppies were taken to the ASPCA.	1. *kept, retained, adopted*
	2.	*adj.*	**vacated, deserted** Signs warned us not to go near the abandoned mine.	2. *occupied, maintained*
abate		*v.*	**wane, diminish, ebb, decrease, subside, slacken, ease, reduce** The waters of the river abated as the storm passed. *n.* Its abatement was a relief.	*increase, grow, amplify, accelerate, magnify, intensify*
abbreviate		*v.*	**shorten, reduce, condense, abridge** The word "August" can be abbreviated to "Aug." *n.* "Aug." is the abbreviation for August.	*lengthen, enlarge, expand, extend, increase*
abduct		*v.*	**kidnap, carry off, take away** The journalist was abducted by terrorists. *n.* The abductors demanded a ransom for the release of the victim. *n.* The abduction shocked everyone.	*free, restore, surrender, return*
abhor		*v.*	**loathe, detest, hate, recoil from** The citizens abhorred the cruelty of the dictator. *adj.* The citizens protested against the dictator's abhorrent actions.	*cherish, adore, prize, treasure, admire, value, covet, love*
ability		*n.*	**skill, capability, capacity, talent, expertise, power** Mozart showed his musical ability at an early age.	*incompetence, inability*
ablaze	1.	*adj.*	**aglow, blazing, brightly lit** The Christmas tree was ablaze with lights.	1. *dark, dim*
	2.	*adv.*	**on fire** The tree was set ablaze by lightning.	
able	1.	*adj.*	**capable of** Matt is able to speak three languages.	1. *unable to*
	2.	*adj.*	**talented, gifted, clever, proficient, capable, accomplished, competent** Shen is an able student.	2. *stupid, dull, incompetent*
abnormal		*adj.*	**odd, strange, irregular, exceptional, unusual, peculiar** Very cold weather is abnormal in the tropics.	*normal, usual, common, regular*

Parts of speech are indicated in italics as follows: *n.* for noun; *v.* for verb; *adj.* for adjective; *adv.* for adverb; *prep.* for preposition, and *conj.* for conjunction.

Antonyms, or opposite and near opposite words, are listed in the color bar on the right side of each page.

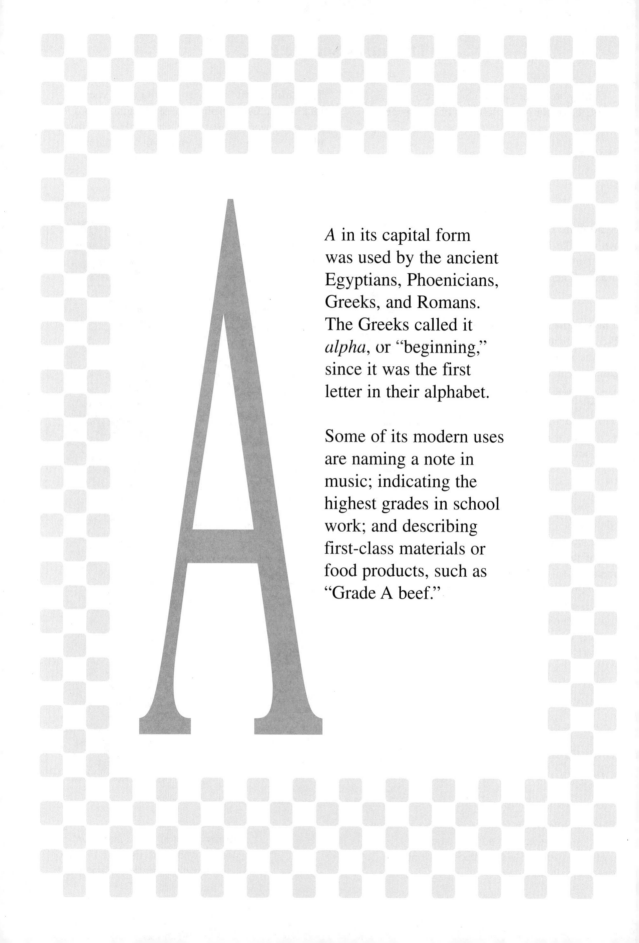

A in its capital form was used by the ancient Egyptians, Phoenicians, Greeks, and Romans. The Greeks called it *alpha*, or "beginning," since it was the first letter in their alphabet.

Some of its modern uses are naming a note in music; indicating the highest grades in school work; and describing first-class materials or food products, such as "Grade A beef."

abandon	1.	*v.*	**give up, surrender, yield, drop** In the last inning, the team abandoned all hope of winning.	1. *keep, maintain, retain*
	2.	*v.*	**desert, leave, vacate, quit** The crew abandoned the ship when it hit an iceberg.	2. *remain, stay, occupy*
abandoned	1.	*adj.*	**forsaken, deserted, left behind** The abandoned puppies were taken to the ASPCA.	1. *kept, retained, adopted*
	2.	*adj.*	**vacated, deserted** Signs warned us not to go near the abandoned mine.	2. *occupied, maintained*
abate		*v.*	**wane, diminish, ebb, decrease, subside, slacken, ease, reduce** The waters of the river abated as the storm passed. *n.* Its abatement was a relief.	*increase, grow, amplify, accelerate, magnify, intensify*
abbreviate		*v.*	**shorten, reduce, condense, abridge** The word "August" can be abbreviated to "Aug." *n.* "Aug." is the abbreviation for August.	*lengthen, enlarge, expand, extend, increase*
abduct		*v.*	**kidnap, carry off, take away** The journalist was abducted by terrorists. *n.* The abductors demanded a ransom for the release of the victim. *n.* The abduction shocked everyone.	*free, restore, surrender, return*
abhor		*v.*	**loathe, detest, hate, recoil from** The citizens abhorred the cruelty of the dictator. *adj.* The citizens protested against the dictator's abhorrent actions.	*cherish, adore, prize, treasure, admire, value, covet, love*
ability		*n.*	**skill, capability, capacity, talent, expertise, power** Mozart showed his musical ability at an early age.	*incompetence, inability*
ablaze	1.	*adj.*	**aglow, blazing, brightly lit** The Christmas tree was ablaze with lights.	1. *dark, dim*
	2.	*adv.*	**on fire** The tree was set ablaze by lightning.	
able	1.	*adj.*	**capable of** Matt is able to speak three languages.	1. *unable to*
	2.	*adj.*	**talented, gifted, clever, proficient, capable, accomplished, competent** Shen is an able student.	2. *stupid, dull, incompetent*
abnormal		*adj.*	**odd, strange, irregular, exceptional, unusual, peculiar** Very cold weather is abnormal in the tropics.	*normal, usual, common, regular*

aboard	*prep.*	**on** There were three people aboard the yacht.	*ashore, off*
abolish	*v.*	**eliminate, put an end to, terminate, quash, stamp out, stop** The government abolished smoking in public places.	*retain, keep, hold, maintain, continue, renew, create, promote, restore*
about	1. *prep.*	**concerning, regarding** He spoke about his plans for the future.	
	2. *prep.*	**around, in** The tourists wandered about the ruins of the historical site.	
	3. *adv.*	**around, nearly, approximately, almost** We are about the same size.	3. *exactly, precisely*
above	1. *adj.*	**preceding, previous** How are you? The above statement is a question.	1. *following, next*
	2. *prep.*	**higher than** Her apartment is two floors above mine.	2. *below, beneath*
	3. *adv.*	**overhead, aloft** Planes flew above.	3. *underneath*
aboveboard	*adj.*	**fair, honest, straightforward, open** This company is aboveboard in all its dealings.	*deceitful, dishonest, crooked*
abroad	1. *adv.*	**at large, in circulation** Strange rumors are abroad.	1. *contained*
	2. *adv.*	**out of one's country, overseas** Our family went abroad last summer.	2. *at home*
abrupt	1. *adj.*	**sudden, hasty, unexpected** . The car screeched to an abrupt stop at the lights. *adv.* He left abruptly without saying good-bye.	1. *gradual, expected, slow*
	2. *adj.*	**very steep** My old car couldn't make the abrupt climb up the hill.	2. *gradual*
	3. *adj.*	**curt, sharp, blunt, to the point** His abrupt manner offended us.	3. *diplomatic, gentle, polite*
absent	1. *adj.*	**away, not present** Sue is absent from school today because she is ill.	1. *present*
	2. *adj.*	**lacking** Trees are absent in the tundra region.	2. *existing, present*
absent-minded	*adj.*	**forgetful, inattentive, preoccupied** The absent-minded boy forgot his books.	*attentive, interested, alert*
absolute	*adj.*	**perfect, entire, complete, total, whole** At the trial the witness swore to tell the absolute truth. *adv.* The evidence proved that she was absolutely right.	*limited, incomplete, imperfect*

absorb	*v.*	**soak up, suck in, drink in** A sponge absorbs water.		*exude, eject, discharge*
absorbed	*adj.*	**preoccupied, engrossed** She was so absorbed in her book that she forgot the time.		*distracted*
abstain	*v.*	**forgo, refrain from, hold back, avoid** Everyone should abstain from cigarettes.		*indulge, yield*
absurd	*adj.*	**silly, foolish, ridiculous, nonsensical, preposterous, bizarre, senseless** Cows fly? What an absurd idea! *n.* Do not bother me with such an absurdity!		*wise, sound, logical, sensible, reasonable, rational*
abundance	*n.*	**plenty, full supply** There is an abundance of fruits in the summer.		*scarcity, shortage*
abundant	*adj.*	**profuse, plentiful, rich, luxuriant, copious** Abundant vegetation grows in the tropical rain forests. *adv.* Tropical foliage grows abundantly.		*sparse, lean, meager, scant, skimpy*
abuse	**1.** *v.*	**injure, mistreat, damage, harm, hurt** The man abused his dog. *n.* There are laws against the abuse of animals.		**1.** *care for, protect, treat kindly, shield*
	2. *v.*	**misuse, exploit** The dictator abused her power by arresting all those who opposed her.		**2.** *enhance, respect, sustain*
accelerate	*v.*	**speed up, hurry, hasten, quicken** The plane accelerated before takeoff.		*retard, hinder, impede, slow down*
accent	**1.** *n.*	**inflection, tone, manner of speech** The visitor spoke English with a Spanish accent.		
	2. *n.*	**emphasis** The room was decorated with an oriental accent.		
	3. *v.*	**emphasize, heighten, intensify** Woofers accent the bass sound in stereos.		**3.** *detract from, lower, diminish*
accentuate	*v.*	**emphasize, stress** Her big smile accentuated how glad she was to see us.		*de-emphasize, minimize*
accept	*v.*	**agree to, consent to, receive** We accepted the invitation to the party. *n.* We sent the host a letter of acceptance.		*refuse, reject, decline*
acceptable	*adj.*	**agreeable, satisfactory, appropriate, fitting, suitable** The two families arrived at a mutually acceptable solution to their problem.		*unacceptable, inappropriate, unsuitable*

access	1.	*n.*	**approach, entry** There is a hidden access to the cave.	*1. exit*
	2.	*v.*	**open, enter, reach** I forgot my password and could not access my files on the computer.	
accessory	1.	*n.*	**assistant, partner, helper, accomplice** Two people were convicted as accessories to the crime.	*1. opponent, adversary*
	2.	*n.*	**extra, addition, appendage** A cellphone is a useful accessory.	*2. necessity*
accident	1.	*n.*	**misfortune, mishap, crash** He was injured in a skiing accident.	*1. good fortune*
	2.	*n.*	**chance, coincidence, fluke** We met by accident at the mall.	*2. design, plan*
accidental		*adj.*	**unexpected, unintentional, unplanned** Our meeting was an accidental one. *adv.* The vase broke when I accidentally dropped it.	*deliberate, intentional, on purpose*
acclaim	1.	*n.*	**approval, praise** This new book received much acclaim.	*1. blame, criticism*
	2.	*v.*	**hail, applaud, recognize** The firefighter was acclaimed a hero for saving the child.	*2. condemn, blame, criticize*
accommodate	1.	*v.*	**house, hold, contain** This room accommodates forty people.	*1. be inappropriate*
	2.	*v.*	**oblige, help, cater to** The hotel staff accommodated the guest's request for a quiet room.	*2. hinder, displease*
accommodation		*n.*	**lodging, housing, shelter, room** We had poor accommodations on our trip.	
accompany		*v.*	**escort, attend, go with** I accompanied my mother to the store.	
accomplish		*v.*	**achieve, complete** Min accomplished her goals through hard work.	*fail*
accomplished		*adj.*	**expert, masterly, proficient, adept, skilled, able, superb, talented** She is an accomplished violinist.	*unaccomplished, raw, rough, deficient*
accomplishment		*n.*	**attainment, achievement, feat** Her parents are proud of her accomplishments.	*defeat, failure*
accord	1.	*n.*	**agreement, harmony** The argument was settled in accord.	*1. disagreement, discord, conflict*
	2.	*v.*	**grant, concede, allow** Our teacher accorded us extra time to complete our homework.	*2. withhold, refuse*

account	1.	*n.*	**narrative, report, explanation, story** Marco Polo wrote interesting accounts of his travels.	
	2.	*n.*	**reason, motive** Do not go near the dumpsite on any account.	
accumulate		*v.*	**collect, gather, assemble, hoard** If you do not clean the house regularly, the dust will accumulate.	*scatter, distribute, disperse, spend, lose, throw out, get rid of*
accumulation		*n.*	**collection, store, mass, heap, stock** An accumulation of books filled the shelves.	*dispersion, dispersal, scattering*
accurate		*adj.*	**precise, exact, truthful, sure, reliable, dependable** The eyewitness gave police an accurate description of the suspect. *adv.* The witness accurately reported what he saw.	*doubtful, vague questionable, inaccurate, misleading, unreliable*
accusation		*n.*	**charge** The accusation that she was lying proved to be false.	
accuse		*v.*	**charge, blame, indict** The clerk accused the girl of shoplifting.	*clear, acquit, vindicate, exonerate*
accustom		*v.*	**become used to, familiarize** We soon accustomed ourselves to the new school.	
accustomed		*adj.*	**usual, regular, ordinary, familiar** The jogger followed his accustomed route in the park.	*unusual, strange, unaccustomed*
ace		*n.*	**expert** As a golfer, Tiger Woods is an ace. *adj.* His many victories indicate that he is an ace golfer.	*beginner, learner, novice, tyro*
achieve		*v.*	**accomplish, fulfill, get, win, gain** Peter achieved his goal after many years of hard work.	*fail, forsake, give up failure, blunder*
achievement		*n.*	**accomplishment, deed, feat** It was a great achievement when Neil Armstrong landed on the moon in 1969.	
acid		*adj.*	**sour, sharp, biting, pungent, tart** The salad dressing had an acid taste.	*sweet, smooth*
acknowledge	1.	*v.*	**admit, grant, concede, accept, declare** The candidate acknowledged his defeat in the election. *n.* His acknowledgement of defeat was broadcast on the evening news.	1. *deny, refuse, decline*

	2. *v.*	**recognize, notice, hail** The world acknowledged Marie Curie as a leading scientist.	**2.** *ignore, disregard, reject, spurn*
acme	*n.*	**height, peak, apex, summit, crown, top, zenith, pinnacle, high point** The acme of an athlete's career is winning an Olympic gold medal.	*bottom, depth, base, nadir, low point*
acquainted	*adj.*	**known to, familiar** They were acquainted with each other from dance class. *n.* Jose is an old acquaintance of mine.	*unknown, strange*
acquire	*v.*	**get, gain, win, receive** David acquired fame and fortune after his book was published.	*lose, give*
acquit	*v.*	**clear, free, release, discharge, exonerate** The jury acquitted the accused man.	*convict, condemn*
acquittal	*n.*	**discharge, deliverance** Her name was cleared when she received an acquittal in court.	*conviction, condemnation*
acrid	*adj.*	**bitter, pungent, sour, acid** The stale food produced an acrid smell.	*sweet, pleasant, fragrant*
act	**1.** *n.*	**deed, feat, accomplishment** Mother Teresa was admired for her acts of kindness.	
	2. *v.*	**do, execute, operate, respond** The lifeguard acted quickly to save the swimmer who was in trouble.	**2.** *halt, cease, rest, refrain, ignore*
	3. *v.*	**perform, impersonate, pretend, play, portray** She acted the role of Lady MacBeth in the school play.	
action	**1.** *n.*	**deed, feat, accomplishment, activity, movement, response** The firefighters' quick action stopped the fire from spreading.	**1.** *inactivity, idleness, rest*
	2. *n.*	**battle** Uncle Sam died in action in World War II.	**2.** *peace*
active	*adj.*	**alert, quick, sharp, lively, spry, busy, energetic, vigorous** Grandma is an active eighty-year-old.	*idle, slow, inactive, dormant*
actual	*adj.*	**genuine, authentic, real** The diamond is an actual gem. *adv.* Are you actually leaving before the party is over?	*counterfeit, false, unreal, bogus, fictitious*
acute	**1.** *adj.*	**sharp, severe, intense** Joe felt an acute pain in the chest.	**1.** *dull, mild*

	2.	*adj.*	**penetrating, piercing, shrill, high** An acute blast from the factory siren halted all work.	**2.** *low, soft*
	3.	*adj.*	**keen, sensitive** Dogs have acute hearing.	**3.** *dull*
adamant		*adj.*	**determined, firm, set, unbending** Mom is adamant that I complete my homework before watching TV. *adv.* She adamantly sticks to the rule.	*yielding, pliable, submissive, lax*
adapt	**1.**	*v.*	**adjust, suit, fit, comply** We have adapted to the customs of our new country.	
	2.	*v.*	**alter, change, modify, remodel** Jack adapted the box to make a wagon.	
add	**1.**	*v.*	**increase, enlarge, extend, attach, affix, append** We added another room to our house. *n.* The addition of another room made the house more comfortable.	**1.** *reduce, decrease, remove*
	2.	*v.*	**total, calculate, tally** We added up the bill after the meal.	**2.** *subtract, deduct*
addict		*n.*	**enthusiast, fan, devotee, buff** Kelly is a television addict.	
addicted		*adj.*	**hooked on, dependent on, obsessed with** Lucy is addicted to chocolate. *n.* She is trying to end her addiction.	
additional		*adj.*	**more, extra** When I heard you were coming too, I ordered an additional ticket.	*less, fewer*
address	**1.**	*n.*	**location** Write your address on the envelope.	
	2.	*n.*	**speech, talk, oration, lecture** The graduation address was inspiring.	
	3.	*v.*	**greet, speak to, deliver a speech** The President addressed the nation on television.	
adept		*adj.*	**skillful, proficient, expert, able** Glenn is an adept carpenter.	*clumsy, unskilled, awkward*
adequate		*adj.*	**enough, sufficient, ample** Was there adequate food for all of you? *adv.* She is paid adequately for the job.	*insufficient, inadequate, lacking, deficient*
adjacent		*adj.*	**adjoining, neighboring, bordering, next** I can hear music in the adjacent room.	*distant, far, detached, remote*
adjust	**1.**	*v.*	**regulate, alter, change** Dad adjusted the TV to make it brighter.	**1.** *disarrange, jumble*

2. *v.* **adapt, accustom, condition, get used to**
Our friends from Singapore finally adjusted to the winter.

admirable *adj.* **worthy, excellent, noteworthy**
The audience applauded the singer for her admirable performance.
adv. She sang admirably.
unworthy, disgusting, mediocre, displeasing

admiration *n.* **praise, appreciation, respect, approval, esteem**
We were filled with admiration for the firefighters' courage.
disapproval, contempt, disregard

admire **1.** *v.* **enjoy, appreciate**
We stopped to admire the scenery.
1. *dislike*
2. *v.* **revere, respect, value**
We admire the surgeon's skill.
2. *condemn, despise*

admirer *n.* **suitor, lover, fan, follower, devotee**
Jen's admirer sent her flowers.

admit **1.** *v.* **confess, acknowledge, disclose**
Be honest and admit your mistakes.
1. *deny, reject*
2. *v.* **allow, permit, receive**
This ticket admits one to the show.
2. *disallow, bar*

adolescent **1.** *n.* **youth, teenager, teen, minor**
An adolescent is a person who is between 13 and 18 years of age.
1. *grown-up, adult*
2. *adj.* **juvenile, childish, immature**
Throwing spitballs in class is adolescent behavior.
2. *mature, grown-up, adult*

adopt *v.* **choose, take, assume, accept**
The Smiths adopted a baby.
n. The adoption of the baby pleased everyone.
reject, repudiate

adore *v.* **worship, cherish, love, idolize**
The whole family adored the baby.
n. The teenagers gazed in adoration at the rock star.
adj. The baby was adorable.
hate, detest, abhor, dislike, loathe, revile

adrift *adv.* **unfastened, untied, loose**
The boat is adrift in the lake.
moored, tied, fastened

adult **1.** *n.* **grown-up**
The adults watched over the children while they were swimming.
1. *child, baby, juvenile, adolescent, minor*
2. *adj.* **mature, full-grown, developed**
The young man has an adult attitude toward work.
2. *childish, immature, young*

advance **1.** *v.* **go ahead, proceed, continue**
The troops advanced toward the border.
1. *withdraw, retreat*

	2. *v.*	**improve, progress** The students passed their exams and advanced to the next level.	**2.** *decline, worsen*
advanced	**1.** *adj.*	**modern, latest, sophisticated** We bought an advanced computer system.	**1.** *obsolete, out-of-date*
	2. *adj.*	**higher level, complex, difficult** Matteo was promoted to the advanced French class after his excellent test.	**2.** *basic, elementary*
advantage	*n.*	**benefit, gain, bonus, boon, blessing** Height is an advantage for basketball players.	*hindrance, drawback, disadvantage, obstacle, burden*
adventure	*n.*	**feat, thrill, challenge, escapade** Skydiving was an adventure for us.	
adventurous	*adj.*	**bold, brave, daring, fearless** The adventurous woman sailed around the world alone.	*timid*
adversary	*n.*	**opponent, rival, competitor, enemy** I beat my adversary in the election by just three votes!	*ally, friend, associate, colleague*
adverse	*adj.*	**contrary, unfortunate, unfavorable** The adverse weather conditions made driving dangerous. *adv.* The umpire's decision affected the team adversely.	*favorable, desirable, agreeable*
adversity	*n.*	**bad luck, misfortune, distress, trouble, hardship** During their flight to safety, the refugees faced adversity with courage.	*good fortune, prosperity, good luck*
advertise	*v.*	**promote, publicize, plug, announce** The store advertised a special sale. *n.* The advertisement appeared on TV. *n.* The advertiser was pleased with the response to the promotion.	*conceal, suppress, hide*
advice	*n.*	**counsel, guidance, direction** If you have a problem, go to your teacher for advice.	
advise	*v.*	**counsel, recommend, instruct, direct** Dad advised me not to quit school.	*misdirect, lead astray*
affair	**1.** *n.*	**occasion, event, function, do** The charity ball was a splendid affair.	
	2. *n.*	**concern, business, responsibility** Don't meddle with my personal affairs.	
	3. *n.*	**incident, matter, episode** The argument turned into a messy affair.	
	4. *n.*	**relationship, romance, involvement** Jill and Bob kept their affair a secret.	

affect	1.	*v.*	**influence, have an effect on** The cold weather has affected my health.	
	2.	*v.*	**move, touch, stir** We were affected by the sad news.	**2.** *leave unmoved*
	3.	*v.*	**pretend, assume, feign** Kyli affected an air of innocence after spilling the milk.	
affected		*adj.*	**pretentious, artificial** Affected manners irritate people. *n.* Drop your affectations and be yourself.	*regular, ordinary,* *down-to-earth, sincere*
affection		*n.*	**attachment, fondness, tenderness,** **goodwill, love, devotion** Biz has a deep affection for her sister. *adj.* She is an affectionate sister.	*dislike, hatred,* *aversion, indifference,* *antipathy*
affirm		*v.*	**assert, declare, claim, ratify** We affirmed our support for the cause. *n.* Our affirmation was cheered.	*deny, disclaim, reject,* *veto, rescind*
afflict		*v.*	**distress, trouble, torment, plague** The plague afflicted thousands. *n.* Many people died from the affliction.	*relieve, comfort*
affluent		*adj.*	**rich, wealthy, prosperous, well-off** All the homes in this affluent neighborhood have a security system.	*poor, needy, destitute,* *impoverished*
afraid		*adj.*	**timid, scared, frightened, fearful,** **alarmed, terrified** Are you afraid of snakes?	*brave, gallant, bold,* *courageous, reckless*
again		*adv.*	**over, another time, anew** I dare you to do that again.	*once, never*
age	1.	*n.*	**time, era, span, period** This is the age of space exploration.	
	2.	*n.*	**years of life, span of life** What is your age?	
	3.	*v.*	**grow feeble, decline, fade, deteriorate** After his wife died, he aged overnight.	
aged	1.	*adj.*	**old, elderly, senior** We cared for our aged aunt. *n.* She moved into a home for the aged.	**1.** *young, youthful*
	2.	*adj.*	**mature, mellow** The aged wine fetched a high price.	**2.** *immature*
aggravate	1.	*v.*	**worsen, intensify, magnify** Their quarrel aggravated the problem.	**1.** *improve, help,* *calm, soothe, relieve*
	2.	*v.*	**irritate, bother, annoy, irk, pester** Loud noise aggravates most people. *n.* Noise is an aggravation.	**2.** *please, delight*
agile		*adj.*	**nimble, spry, dextrous** The agile gymnasts impressed us. *n.* Agility comes with years of training.	*awkward, clumsy,* *stiff*

agitate		*v.*	**excite, disturb, upset, unnerve, stir up**	*calm, soothe, relieve, relax*
			The loud siren agitated the children.	
			n. They screamed in their agitation.	
agony		*n.*	**torment, anguish, torture**	*joy, delight, pleasure*
			Rani was in agony with a toothache.	
			adj. She suffered agonizing pain.	
agree	1.	*v.*	**consent, approve, accept**	**1.** *refuse, oppose*
			My friend agreed to help me.	
	2.	*v.*	**concur, coincide, match, conform**	**2.** *disagree, differ, contradict*
			I'm glad your ideas agree with mine.	
agreeable	1.	*adj.*	**pleasing, pleasant, inviting**	**1.** *unpleasant, disagreeable*
			Billy has an agreeable personality.	
	2.	*adj.*	**willing, approving**	**2.** *against, unwilling*
			Mina nodded to show she was agreeable to the suggestion.	
	3.	*adj.*	**suitable, appropriate**	**3.** *inappropriate, unsuitable*
			NASA waited for agreeable weather before launching the satellite.	
agreement	1.	*n.*	**contract, treaty, promise, bargain**	
			The two nations signed a trade agreement.	
	2.	*n.*	**accordance, harmony, conformity, correspondence**	**2.** *disagreement*
			We are both in agreement about these proposals.	
ahead		*adv.*	**in advance, before, forward**	*behind, backward*
			The children walked far ahead of us.	
aid	1.	*n.*	**help, assistance, support**	**1.** *hindrance, opposition*
			We sent food in aid of the famine victims.	
	2.	*v.*	**help, assist, support**	**2.** *hinder, block, injure, impede*
			He aided the new student in English.	
ailment		*n.*	**sickness, illness, disorder, malady**	*health, fitness*
			Kirk suffers from a heart ailment.	
aim	1.	*n.*	**goal, objective, ambition, plan**	
			Her aim is to be a pilot.	
	2.	*v.*	**point at, direct, focus**	
			Vince aimed carefully before shooting the ball into the basket.	
aimless		*adj.*	**pointless, purposeless, haphazard**	*planned, purposeful*
			Bob was told to take charge of his aimless life and act responsibly.	
air	1.	*n.*	**atmosphere, sky**	
			The plane climbed high into the air.	
	2.	*n.*	**appearance, style, look, aura**	
			Her easy manner gave her an air of confidence.	
	3.	*n.*	**breeze, draft, wind**	
			The cold air made us shiver.	

4. *v.* **ventilate**
We aired the cabin as soon as we arrived.

airy
1. *adj.* **light, fluffy, delicate**
The sponge cake was so airy it melted in my mouth.
  1. *heavy, dull*

2. *adj.* **lively, joyous**
Their airy laughter filled the room.
  2. *dull, dreary*

3. *adj.* **breezy, ventilated, open**
The high ceiling made the room airy.
  3. *stuffy, confined, stale*

alarm
1. *n.* **warning, alert**
We were awakened by the fire alarm.

2. *n.* **fear, fright, terror, dread, panic**
The gunshots caused much alarm.
  2. *calm, peace*

3. *v.* **frighten, agitate, disturb, excite**
The gunshots alarmed everyone.
adj. There have been an alarming number of burglaries lately.
  3. *calm, soothe, quiet*

alert
1. *n.* **warning, alarm**
The boaters hurried to shore when they heard the storm alert over the radio.

2. *adj.* **watchful, attentive, vigilant**
The alert ranger noticed the smoke.
  2. *drowsy, inattentive*

3. *adj.* **sharp, quick, active, nimble, lively**
Grandma still has an alert mind.
  3. *sluggish, slow, inactive, lethargic*

alibi
n. **excuse, defense**
The defendant had a foolproof alibi.

alien
1. *n.* **foreigner, newcomer, stranger**
Many people claim to have seen aliens from other planets.
  1. *native, citizen*

2. *adj.* **foreign, different, strange**
Boris soon adapted to the alien customs of his new country.
  2. *familiar, native, known*

alike
adj. **identical, similar**
Michelle and Lisa look alike.
  different

allegiance
n. **devotion, faithfulness, loyalty**
Pledge allegiance to your country.
  disloyalty, treason

alliance
n. **connection, pact, union, league**
The three neighboring countries formed a close alliance.
  separation, opposition

allocate
v. **apportion, assign, earmark**
The school allocated funds to the teams.
n. It was a fair allocation.
  deny, refuse

allot
1. *v.* **assign, give, allocate**
The teacher allotted the students a week to write the essay.

2. *v.* **divide, distribute, award**
The school allotted books to the students.
n. We received our allotment of books.
  2. *keep, retain, withhold, withdraw*

allow	*v.*	**permit, let, grant, consent** Mom allowed us to stay up late on New Year's Eve.	*deny, refuse, forbid, restrain, disallow*
allowance	*n.*	**pocket money, wage, salary** May receives a weekly allowance from her parents.	
alone	1. *adv.*	**by oneself, solo, singly** All his friends were busy, so he went alone.	1. *accompanied, escorted*
	2. *adj.*	**solely, only** He alone was left.	2. *numerous, many, several*
aloof	1. *adj.*	**unsympathetic, cool, distant** His aloof manner told me he was upset.	1. *sympathetic, warm, sociable*
	2. *adv.*	**apart, at a distance** The stranger stood aloof at the party.	2. *nearby, close*
also	*adv.*	**besides, too, in addition, likewise** My friends were going, so I also went.	
alter	*v.*	**change, modify, vary, adjust** The tailor altered the coat to fit me. *n.* The coat fit better after the alterations.	*preserve, keep*
alternative	*n.*	**option, choice** What are the alternatives in this matter?	*obligation*
always	1. *adv.*	**constantly, regularly, perpetually** Mike is always late for school.	1. *never, seldom, rarely*
	2. *adv.*	**forever, for all time, eternally** He promised to love her always.	
amateur	1. *n.*	**nonprofessional** Amateurs compete in sports for the love of it, not for the money.	1. *professional*
	2. *n.*	**novice, beginner, trainee** For an amateur, she knows a lot about painting. *adj.* The amateur skier twisted her ankle on the ski slope.	2. *expert, ace*
amaze	*v.*	**overwhelm, surprise, astonish, astound** The magician's tricks amazed us. *adj.* Making her assistant disappear into thin air was an amazing trick.	
amazement	*n.*	**surprise, astonishment, wonder, shock, bewilderment** The tourists stared in amazement at the pyramids in Egypt.	*boredom, coolness, calmness, composure*
ambition	*n.*	**desire, aspiration, enterprise, goal, aim** Her ambition was to lead the nation. *adj.* She works hard because she is ambitious.	*laziness, indifference, indolence*

ambitious	*adj.*	**purposeful, driven, forceful** The ambitious student worked very hard and won a scholarship.	*aimless, unambitious*
amend	*v.*	**improve, better, correct, reform** The government amended the law to make it fairer. *n.* The amendments were well-received by the people.	*harm, impair, spoil, injure*
amiable	*adj.*	**engaging, genial, good-natured, agreeable, pleasant, kindly** We enjoyed babysitting the amiable child.	*grouchy, irritable, ill-tempered, troublesome, sullen*
amount	1. *n.*	**total, full value, sum** What is the amount of the bill?	
	2. *n.*	**quantity, supply, number** There was a large amount of food at the party.	
ample	*adj.*	**enough, abundant, copious** No one went hungry as there was ample food.	*insufficient, inadequate, scant, meager, sparse*
amplify	*v.*	**enlarge, increase, make louder** A microphone amplifies sound. *n.* An amplifier increases the sound.	*reduce, shorten, lessen, curtail*
amuse	*v.*	**entertain, interest** The circus clowns amused the crowd. *adj.* The clown's big red nose was an amusing sight.	*bore, tire, annoy, vex*
amusement	*n.*	**fun, diversion, entertainment** We watch movies for amusement. *adj.* Children love the rides in amusement parks.	*boredom, monotony*
anarchy	*n.*	**chaos, disorder, tumult** The war brought years of anarchy to the region.	*law and order*
ancient	*adj.*	**very old, aged, antiquated** The ruins of the ancient pyramid were fascinating.	*modern, up-to-date, current, recent, young*
anger	1. *n.*	**rage, fury, ire, wrath** The beast's anger was frightening. *adv.* The lion growled angrily at the hunter.	**1.** *mildness, patience, peace, calm, contentment*
	2. *v.*	**irritate, vex, annoy, provoke, enrage** Lee's rude behavior angered his mom.	**2.** *calm, please, soothe, delight*
angle	*n.*	**viewpoint, approach, position, slant, perspective** Let's discuss the problem from a different angle.	

angry		adj.	**furious, livid, mad, annoyed, irate** The angry crowd booed the speaker.	*pleased, happy, content*
anguish		n.	**agony, misery, torture, extreme pain, suffering, woe** The fire victim suffered great anguish from his burns.	*ease, comfort, relief*
animal	1.	n.	**beast, creature** We went to the zoo to see the animals.	
	2.	adj.	**bestial, brutish, untamed, wild** In a fit of animal anger, he smashed the vase.	*2. tamed, cultivated*
animate	1.	adj.	**living, live** Plants and animals are animate.	*1. inanimate, lifeless*
	2.	v.	**activate, stimulate, energize, rouse** The spectators animated the team with their loud cheers.	*2. deactivate, suppress*
annihilate		v.	**destroy, ruin, exterminate, eradicate** The earthquake annihilated the town. n. The annihilation of the town was complete.	*spare, preserve, save*
announce		v.	**proclaim, make known, tell, notify, advertise, reveal, report, declare** The couple announced their engagement. n. The engagement announcement was printed in the newspaper. n. Radio announcers must speak clearly.	*keep silent, conceal, hide, withhold*
annoy		v.	**aggravate, irritate, bother, pester, irk, badger, trouble** He annoys everyone with his constant complaining. n. The dog's persistent barking was an annoyance. adj. Pushy salespeople are annoying.	*soothe, calm, help*
annual		adj.	**yearly** Valentine's Day is an annual event. adv. Summer holidays occur annually.	
another		adj.	**additional, one more, different** Let's run another race after this one.	*same*
answer	1.	n.	**solution, explanation** I know the answer to the riddle.	*1. problem, question*
	2.	n.	**reply, response, reaction** What was your answer when he asked you for a favor? v. We answered the letter right away.	*2. request, question, inquiry*
antagonize		v.	**repel, offend, annoy, alienate** She antagonized us with her rudeness. n. We showed our antagonism by ignoring her.	*pacify, ingratiate*

anticipate		*v.*	**expect, predict, foresee** We canceled the picnic as we anticipated that it would rain. *n.* I took my umbrella in anticipation of rain.	*be surprised, doubt*
antique		*adj.*	**ancient, quaint, old-fashioned, timeworn, antiquated, very old** The antique jewelry was donated to the museum. *n.* Antiques are priceless because they represent a piece of the past.	*new, modern, recent, up-to-date, stylish, fashionable, current*
anxiety		*n.*	**concern, uneasiness, worry, anguish** Kit's illness caused us much anxiety.	*ease, contentment, peace*
anxious	1.	*adj.*	**troubled, worried, uneasy, concerned** Dad was anxious when we were late returning home.	1. *calm, relieved, unconcerned*
	2.	*adj.*	**desirous, fervent, eager** Derek was anxious to get a new car. *adv.* Sue waited anxiously for the test results.	
apart		*adv.*	**aside, separately** Place those cups apart from the rest.	*together, side by side*
apathy		*n.*	**indifference, unconcern, passiveness** The environment has been damaged because of public apathy. *adj.* We must change our apathetic attitudes before it is too late.	*concern, interest, care, zeal*
apex	1.	*n.*	**pinnacle, summit, peak, top** The mountaineers reached the apex of Mount Everest.	1. *base, foot, bottom*
	2.	*n.*	**climax, high point, zenith, acme** Winning the trophy was the apex of the team's career.	2. *depth, low point, nadir*
apparent		*adj.*	**obvious, probable, likely** The apparent cause of the fire was carelessness. *adv.* The accident was apparently the driver's fault.	*unlikely, doubtful*
appeal	1.	*n.*	**request, entreaty, petition** The prisoner's appeal for a new trial was granted.	1. *denial, refusal*
	2.	*v.*	**beg, plead, ask, pray, entreat** The police appealed to eyewitnesses for help.	2. *deny, refuse*
	3.	*v.*	**interest, engage, charm** Traveling appeals to many people. *n.* Traveling has great appeal for many.	3. *disgust*
appealing		*adj.*	**enticing, attractive, charming** Her appealing personality won her votes.	*unattractive, unpleasant, repulsive*

appear	1.	*v.*	**come into view, emerge** The sun appeared from behind the clouds.	*1. disappear, vanish*
	2.	*v.*	**seem, look** Judging by his hearty appetite, the patient appears to be recovering. *n.* His healthy appearance cheered everyone.	
appetite		*n.*	**hunger, craving, longing** The aroma of freshly baked cookies whetted my appetite.	*aversion, dislike, distaste*
appetizing		*adj.*	**appealing, enticing** An appetizing aroma came from the kitchen.	*repulsive, distasteful*
applaud	1.	*v.*	**clap, cheer** The audience applauded wildly after the performance. *n.* The applause was deafening.	*1. boo, deride, jeer*
	2.	*v.*	**approve, praise, acclaim** The press applauded the government for its new healthcare policies.	*2. disapprove, criticize*
apply	1.	*v.*	**use, practice, employ** Paul applied his knowledge to the project.	
	2.	*v.*	**dedicate, direct** She applied herself to the job and finished it quickly.	
	3.	*v.*	**refer, fit, pertain** Safety rules apply everywhere.	
	4.	*v.*	**spread on, put on** We applied wax to the floor.	*4. remove, take off*
	5.	*v.*	**make an application, request** Will you apply for a job this summer? *n.* I mailed my university application yesterday.	
appoint	1.	*v.*	**name, select, nominate** The committee appointed its new president.	*1. dismiss*
	2.	*v.*	**arrange, set, decide on** We appointed the date for the next meeting. *n.* I have an appointment tomorrow to see my dentist.	*2. cancel, change*
appreciate	1.	*v.*	**be thankful for, welcome, enjoy** Jan appreciated her friend's kindness. *n.* She sent flowers to express her appreciation.	*1. object to*
	2.	*v.*	**understand, realize, comprehend** It is difficult to appreciate the cost of education today.	
	3.	*v.*	**improve, inflate, rise in value** Property values have appreciated greatly in the last few years.	*3. depreciate, devalue, deflate*

apprehend	*v.*	**arrest, capture, seize, catch** The police apprehended the robbers at the scene of the crime.	*free, release, let go*
apprehension	1. *n.*	**capture, seizure, arrest** We were relieved to hear of the apprehension of the kidnappers.	**1.** *release*
	2. *n.*	**trepidation, foreboding, dread, fear** Deanna was filled with apprehension about her driving test. *adj.* She was apprehensive about the test.	**2.** *calm, peace*
approach	1. *n.*	**access, entrance, path** The approach to the cabin is hidden by trees.	**1.** *exit, departure*
	2. *v.*	**move toward, come near** The delivery person approached the growling dog cautiously.	**2.** *leave, recede, depart, retreat*
appropriate	*adj.*	**suitable, fitting, proper, apt** Leave an appropriate tip for the waiter. *adv.* Dress appropriately for the party.	*inappropriate, improper, unsuitable*
approval	*n.*	**sanction, permission, assent** They asked for the committee's approval to proceed with the project. *v.* The committee approved the project.	*disapproval*
approximate	*adj.*	**estimated, near** The approximate time of arrival is two o'clock. *adv.* The tree was approximately twice my height.	*correct, exact, accurate, precise*
arduous	*adj.*	**trying, heavy, tiring, exhausting** Pushing the stalled car up the hill was arduous work.	*easy, effortless*
argue	1. *v.*	**squabble, bicker, quarrel** The children argued over their toys. *n.* Mom stopped the heated argument.	**1.** *agree, concur, assent*
	2. *v.*	**dispute, debate** The students argued against extra homework.	
arid	*adj.*	**parched, dry, barren** Crops don't grow well in arid areas.	*well-watered, lush, moist, verdant, damp*
arms	*n.*	**weapons, munitions** Soldiers use arms in battle. *v.* The soldiers armed themselves for battle. *adj.* Armed robbers held up the bank.	
aroma	*n.*	**smell, fragrance, odor, scent** The aroma of freshly baked bread came from the bakery. *adj.* Roses are known for being aromatic.	

arouse	*v.*	**awaken, stir up, excite** Ken's curiosity was aroused when he heard his friends whispering.	*calm, soothe, dampen*
arrange	1. *v.*	**adjust, group, sort** Arrange these words in alphabetical order.	*1. scatter, jumble, disarrange*
	2. *v.*	**plan, determine, prepare for** The caterers will arrange everything for the party. *n.* The arrangements for the party are going smoothly.	
array	1. *n.*	**display, arrangement, formation** There was a splendid array of jewelry in the museum.	
	2. *v.*	**dress, outfit, clothe, attire** The queen was arrayed in a magnificent gown.	
arrest	1. *v.*	**catch, detain, capture, hold, nab** The police arrested the suspects. *n.* Excellent police work led to the arrest.	*1. release, set free, let go, discharge*
	2. *v.*	**stop, check, halt, suspend** The new drug arrested the spread of his cancer.	*2. promote, foster, encourage*
arrive	1. *v.*	**come, approach** They will arrive on the next flight. *n.* We will meet them on their arrival.	*1. go, leave, depart, embark, withdraw*
	2. *v.*	**reach, attain** After much discussion, the students arrived at a decision.	
arrogance	*n.*	**vanity, contempt, conceit, self importance** His arrogance made him unpopular. *adj.* The arrogant boy refused to admit he had made a mistake.	*simplicity, humility, modesty, shyness*
art	*n.*	**skill, craft** She has spent years developing the art of quilt-making.	
artificial	1. *adj.*	**imitation, synthetic, fake** These artificial pearls look real.	*1. real, natural, genuine*
	2. *adj.*	**pretended, phony, affected** Her artificial smile showed she was insincere.	*2. honest, sincere*
artist	*n.*	**creator, author, musician, dancer, composer, painter, sculptor** A painter is one type of artist.	
ascend	*v.*	**rise, climb, scale, mount** The plane ascended suddenly to avoid the mountaintop. *n.* The ascent of the mountain tired us.	*descend, go down*

ashen	*adj.*	**pale, wan, pallid** Ian looked ashen after his illness.	*flushed, rosy*
ask	1. *v.*	**inquire, question** The police asked many questions about the accident.	**1.** *tell, answer, inform*
	2. *v.*	**request** The hospital asks for your support in its charity drive.	**2.** *demand, order, require*
	3. *v.*	**require, demand, charge** This store asks high prices.	**3.** *give*
assemble	1. *v.*	**put together, combine, construct** She assembled the model jet in a day.	**1.** *take apart, detach, dismantle, break*
	2. *v.*	**gather together, meet, convene** A crowd assembled outside the theater. *n.* The school has a weekly assembly of all the students.	**2.** *scatter, disperse*
assert	*v.*	**claim, declare, insist** He asserted that the accident wasn't his fault. *n.* He will have to prove his assertion of innocence.	*deny*
assessment	1. *n.*	**rate, appraisal, evaluation** According to the jeweler's assessment, my ring is worth one thousand dollars.	
	2. *n.*	**tax, charge, fee** Each property owner must pay a new assessment for sewers.	
assign	*v.*	**allot, appoint, give** The teacher assigns homework daily. *n.* Our homework assignment is to research a famous inventor.	
assist	*v.*	**help, aid** He assisted the old man across the road. *n.* She came to my assistance when I had a problem.	*hinder, delay, oppose, obstruct*
associate	1. *n.*	**partner, colleague, ally** He is meeting with his associate to discuss a business deal.	**1.** *competitor, rival, opponent*
	2. *v.*	**socialize, fraternize, work with** I prefer to associate with people who have a positive attitude.	**2.** *avoid, ignore*
	3. *v.*	**link, connect, relate, correlate** Cats learn to associate the sound of a can opener with mealtime.	**3.** *disconnect, separate*
association	*n.*	**union, society, body, group, club, company, organization** I joined a writer's association.	

assorted	*adj.*	**mixed, various, different** Assorted clothes were collected for the refugees. *n.* There was a wide assortment of food at the banquet.	*identical, uniform*
assume	*v.*	**suppose, think, believe, guess** He never called back so we assumed he wasn't interested in our proposal. *n.* He told us later that our assumption had been correct.	*know, prove*
assumed	*adj.*	**false, phony** The author wrote under an assumed name to protect his identity.	*actual, real, true*
assurance	*n.*	**confidence, self-reliance** The experienced pilot flew the plane with assurance.	*nervousness, insecurity, doubt*
assure	*v.*	**promise, guarantee, pledge** The babysitter assured us that she would take good care of the baby. *n.* We were relieved to hear this assurance.	*deny, refute*
astonish	*v.*	**surprise, amaze, shock, astound** The young violinist's performance astonished the audience. *adj.* It was an astonishing performance. *n.* Her musical talent caused much astonishment.	
astound	*v.*	**shock, amaze, astonish** The news of the tragedy astounded us. *adj.* The pilots performed astounding flying feats at the airshow.	
atomic	*adj.*	**small, minute, infinitesimal, molecular** A powerful microscope is used to see atomic objects.	*enormous, gigantic, huge*
attach	1. *v.* 2. *v.*	**fasten, connect, join, unite, combine** We attached the trailer to the bumper of the car. **add, append, link** I attached my essay to my e-mail. *n.* My professor received the attachment with my e-mail.	*1. sever, detach, disconnect, cut, separate*
attachment	*n.*	**friendship, love, affection, devotion** There was a strong attachment between the friends.	*animosity, dislike, indifference*
attack	1. *n.*	**invasion, assault, charge** The army made a surprise attack on the rebel camp. *v.* The army attacked the enemy at dawn.	*1. retreat, surrender, withdrawal*

	2.	*n.*	**sudden occurrence** He had an attack of the flu.	
attain		*v.*	**get, gain, obtain, arrive at, accomplish, earn, reach** After much hard work, she attained her goal. *adj.* She set herself an attainable goal.	*lose, fail, give up, surrender*
attempt		*v.*	**try, endeavor, strive** She attempted to jump over the high bar. *n.* It took her three attempts before she succeeded.	*avoid, shirk*
attend	1.	*v.*	**be present at, go to** Students must attend school regularly. *n.* The teacher recorded the class attendance.	1. *miss, be absent*
	2.	*v.*	**care for, look after** The nurse attended to the injured student.	2. *neglect, ignore, disregard*
attention	1.	*n.*	**care, thought, consideration** The patient received the best medical attention.	1. *neglect, unconcern*
	2.	*n.*	**heed, notice, observance** Pay attention to the teacher.	2. *disregard*
attentive	1.	*adj.*	**alert, intent** The attentive audience listened to everything the speaker had to say.	1. *inattentive, unconcerned*
	2.	*adj.*	**courteous, polite, thoughtful** The attentive waiter received a large tip.	2. *impolite, careless, rude*
attire	1.	*n.*	**dress, apparel, clothing, clothes** I changed into comfortable attire for the picnic.	
	2.	*v.*	**dress, array** The clown was attired in brightly colored clothing.	2. *undress, disrobe, strip, bare*
attitude	1.	*n.*	**outlook, disposition, view** He has a positive attitude toward work.	
	2.	*n.*	**position, pose, stance, manner** Kim's forlorn attitude told us he had lost.	
attract		*v.*	**draw, interest, lure, appeal to, captivate** The show attracted a large crowd. *n.* The robot was a great attraction.	*offend, disgust, repulse*
attractive		*adj.*	**charming, lovely, pleasant, alluring** These new fashions are quite attractive.	*ugly, unpleasant, repugnant*
attribute		*v.*	**credit, blame, accredit** The FBI attributed the bomb blast to a terrorist attack.	*dissociate*

audacious	1.	*adj.*	**brave, plucky, daring, bold, fearless** The audacious mountain climber made it to the summit.	1. *timid, cowardly, frightened*
	2.	*adj.*	**reckless, risky, daring** The acrobats performed audacious feats on the tightrope.	2. *careful, cautious*
audible		*adj.*	**clear, distinct, loud, detectable** The patient's voice was barely audible.	*faint, muffled*
augment		*v.*	**expand, add to, increase** The baseball team augmented its funds by selling candy.	*reduce, shrink, decrease*
austere		*adj.*	**severe, strict, stern, cold, forbidding** The teacher's austere expression made students nervous.	*kindly, easy, gentle*
authentic		*adj.*	**true, real, genuine, legitimate** Experts established that the signature was authentic and not a forgery.	*counterfeit, false, fictitious*
authority	1.	*n.*	**control, command, power, mandate** Does he have the authority to do this?	
	2.	*n.*	**scholar, specialist, expert** Jacques Cousteau was an authority on underwater research.	
automatic	1.	*adj.*	**involuntary, reflex, spontaneous** Blinking is an automatic action.	1. *planned, intended*
	2.	*adj.*	**mechanical, self-operating** The automatic door swung open as I walked toward it.	2. *manual*
auxiliary	1.	*n.*	**helper, aid, assistant, supporter** The parents' auxiliary helps at the school.	1. *adversary, antagonist*
	2.	*adj.*	**helping, supporting** The auxiliary motor on the boat enables it to go faster.	2. *main, chief, primary*
available		*adj.*	**obtainable, handy, free** We had to stand as there were no available seats.	*unavailable, taken, occupied*
average	1.	*n.*	**mean, standard, norm** Her grades are above the class average.	
	2.	*adj.*	**normal, ordinary, usual** The study showed that the average family has two children.	2. *unusual, exceptional, extraordinary*
aversion		*n.*	**dislike, hatred, disgust** We have an aversion to violence.	*affection, fondness*
avert		*v.*	**prevent, avoid, ward off** The driver's quick action averted a serious accident.	*cause*

aviation	*n.*	**flying, flight, aeronautics** The Wright brothers are very important in the history of aviation.	
avid	*adj.*	**keen, eager, devoted** Marilyn is an avid reader of mysteries.	*unwilling, reluctant*
avoid	*v.*	**shun, evade, escape, dodge** He avoided her by crossing the street. *n.* The avoidance of a problem doesn't solve it.	*confront, meet, face, invite*
award	1. *v.*	**give, grant, accord** The judges awarded the gold medal for figure skating to Anu.	1. *deny, refuse*
	2. *n.*	**prize, honor, trophy** Kevin won the award for Best Golfer at the tournament.	
aware	*adj.*	**informed, knowledgeable, mindful, conscious of** I became aware of the fire when I smelled smoke.	*unaware, ignorant, oblivious*
away	1. *adj.*	**absent, gone, not present** The boss is away until three o'clock.	1. *present, here*
	2. *adv.*	**aside, at a distance** Please go away and don't bother me.	2. *near*
awe	*n.*	**fear, reverence, wonder, marvel** Our first sight of the Great Wall of China filled us with awe. *adj.* It is an awesome sight.	
awful	*adj.*	**dreadful, horrible, terrible, alarming, horrendous, shocking, frightful** The awful accident shocked everyone.	*wonderful, terrific, pretty, delightful*
awkward	1. *adj.*	**ungainly, gawky, clumsy** The circus bear's awkward movements amused the children.	1. *graceful, artful, easy, nimble*
	2. *adj.*	**uncomfortable, embarrassing** There was an awkward silence when the results were announced.	2. *comfortable*
	3. *adj.*	**inconvenient, difficult, troublesome** It will be awkward to fit four people in the small car.	3. *convenient, easy, handy*

B

The Greeks made use of the Phoenician word *beth* and changed it to *beta*, from which comes the Roman letter *B*. Our alphabet gets its name by combining the Greek words for the first two letters, *alpha* and *beta*.

babble   *n.*   **chatter, jabber, prattle, murmur**
The excited babble of the crowd drowned out the music.
v. Babies babble before they learn how to talk.

baby   1.   *n.*   **babe, infant, tot, toddler**   1. *adult, grown-up*
Dad rocked the newborn baby to sleep.
2.   *n.*   **offspring**
Animals protect and feed their babies.

bad   1.   *adj.*   **evil, vile, corrupt, wicked**   1. *honest, good*
In fairy tales the bad characters are often punished in the end.
2.   *adj.*   **rotten, foul, putrid, rancid, tainted**   2. *fresh, pleasant, clean, pure, delicious*
The smell of bad fish made me ill.
3.   *adj.*   **defective, deficient, inferior, awful**   3. *superior, excellent, correct*
No one can read her bad handwriting.
4.   *adj.*   **ill, diseased, ailing, sick**   4. *well, healthy, hearty*
Ravi missed the trip because he felt bad.
5.   *adj.*   **harmful, damaging, dangerous**   5. *good, helpful, beneficial*
Smoking is bad for one's health.
6.   *adj.*   **unfavorable, unfortunate, distressing**   6. *good, favorable, fortunate*
Did you hear the bad news about the car accident?

baffle   *v.*   **puzzle, bewilder, confound, confuse, perplex**   *clarify, clear up*
His strange behavior baffled us.

balance   1.   *n.*   **scales, weighing machine**
The butcher weighed the meat on the balance.
2.   *n.*   **equilibrium, equivalence, symmetry, steadiness, stability**   2. *imbalance, instability*
May lost her balance and fell off the bike.
v. She balanced herself carefully on the bike and rode off.
3.   *n.*   **cash on hand, credit, surplus**   3. *deficit*
She had a bank balance of five hundred dollars.
4.   *n.*   **remainder**
I intend to take things easy for the balance of the year.

balmy   *adj.*   **soft, soothing, gentle, mild, summery**   *harsh, unpleasant, severe, inclement*
The balmy spring weather melted the snow.

ban   *v.*   **forbid, prohibit, outlaw, bar**   *allow, permit, encourage*
The government banned smoking in public places.
n. There is a ban on smoking in elevators.

band   1.   *n.*   **group, flock, herd, collection**   1. *individual, one*
The band of wild dogs roamed the plains searching for food.

2.   *n.*   **strip, stripe, ribbon, sash, belt**
She wore a red band in her hair.

3.   *v.*   **unite, gather, join**
The angry citizens banded together to
protest the new taxes.

      3. *disband, disperse,
divide, separate*

bandit   *n.*   **thief, robber, outlaw**
The bandits escaped in a van after they
robbed the bank.

banish   *v.*   **exile, dismiss, expel, evict, eject**
The court banished the spy.

      *welcome, harbor,
accept, admit, retain*

bar   *v.*   **obstruct, block, restrain, keep out,
prevent, exclude, ban**
He was barred from the examination
because he was caught cheating.

      *permit, allow, admit,
welcome, accept,
harbor, invite*

bare   1. *v.*   **disclose, divulge, reveal, make known**
The actor bared the facts of the scandal in
his memoirs.

      1. *keep secret, hide,
cover*

2. *adj.*   **uncovered, naked, unclothed,
exposed, unprotected**
At the campground mosquitoes attacked
my bare arms and legs.

      2. *clothed, covered,
protected*

3. *adj.*   **simple, unadorned, modest, plain,
unpretentious**
Jin decorated the bare walls of her room
with bright posters.

      3. *ornamented,
adorned, decorated,
pretentious, fancy*

4. *adj.*   **empty, barren**
The hungry kids were dismayed to find a
bare refrigerator.

      4. *full, well-stocked*

barely   *adv.*   **hardly, just, scarcely**
We left late and barely caught our train.

      *amply, sufficiently,
adequately*

bargain   1. *n.*   **pact, agreement, deal, contract,
promise**
We made a bargain to help each other
with our homework.

2. *v.*   **haggle, negotiate**
He bargained with the salesperson for a
better deal.

barren   *adj.*   **sterile, unproductive, unfruitful**
Modern irrigation techniques have
transformed barren deserts into farmland.

      *fertile, fruitful,
productive, prolific,
luxuriant*

barrier   *n.*   **obstacle, hindrance, impediment,
block, restriction**
For many people, fear can be a mental
barrier to adventure.

      *entrance, opening,
thoroughfare, way,
path*

base   1. *n.*   **bottom, foot, foundation, support**
The statue stood on a base of marble.

      1. *summit, top, crest*

2. *v.*   **establish, found**
Juri based his opinions on thorough
research.

3. *adj.* **contemptible, mean, vile, despicable**
The base acts of the terrorists disgusted everyone.

3. virtuous, noble, superior, esteemed, refined, lofty

bashful *adj.* **shy, timid, retiring, reserved, modest, timorous**
The bashful student would not speak in public.

conceited, bold, forward, impudent, brazen, pert

basic *adj.* **essential, primary, central, principal, fundamental, necessary, required, indispensable, key**
Food and shelter are our basic needs.

dispensable, unnecessary, trivial, secondary, extra

bat **1.** *n.* **stick, club**
Try to hit the ball with a bat.
2. *v.* **hit, strike, sock, whack**
Dan batted the ball across the field.

battle **1.** *n.* **fight, combat, conflict, clash, strife, contest, engagement, encounter**
The battle ended in a truce.
2. *v.* **fight, struggle**
The accident victim battled for her life.

1. peace, harmony, agreement, truce, armistice
2. give in, quit, yield, succumb, surrender

beam **1.** *n.* **rafter, plank, girder**
The construction worker riveted the steel beam into place.
2. *n.* **ray, gleam, glow**
The laser beam is used in medical procedures and in warfare.
3. *v.* **transmit, give out, send, broadcast**
Satellites beam television signals around the world.
4. *v.* **laugh, grin, smile brightly**
Nida beamed when she saw her gift.
adj. The beaming child opened the gift eagerly.

3. receive

4. frown, scowl, glower

bear **1.** *v.* **carry, transport, convey**
Donkeys can bear heavy burdens.
2. *v.* **support, hold up**
This small chair bears the weight of an adult.
3. *v.* **suffer, endure, tolerate, shoulder**
The injured person bore the pain quietly.
adj. The heat was more bearable after I changed into my shorts.
4. *v.* **yield, produce, generate**
The apple tree bore delicious fruit.

1. leave behind

2. drop, let go, collapse

3. succumb, give in

4. wither, be barren

beast *n.* **brute, savage, creature**
The wild beast lunged at the hunter.

beat **1.** *v.* **hit, strike, punch, whack, thump, pummel, thrash, pound, flog**
Thugs brutally beat the old man.
n. The police saved him from the beating.

2. *v.* **defeat, conquer, surpass, overcome**
After a long struggle, Yun beat Nick in
the chess game.

2. surrender, give in

beautiful *adj.* **handsome, pretty, good-looking,
attractive, lovely, splendid, exquisite**
Uri's beautiful photograph of a sunset
won him a prize.
adv. The bride smiled beautifully.

unattractive, ugly

beauty *n.* **loveliness, charm, splendor**
The beauty of the tulip fields in Holland
is world-renowned.

*ugliness,
unattractiveness*

because *conj.* **on account of, owing to, since, as**
I put on my raincoat because it was
raining.

becoming **1.** *adj.* **fitting, proper, suitable**
Shouting and pushing is not becoming
behavior.

*1. unsuitable,
improper, unbecoming*

2. *adj.* **pleasing, attractive, flattering**
Chris complimented Ray on his becoming
suit.

*2. unattractive,
hideous, ugly*

before **1.** *adv.* **previously, earlier, sooner, heretofore**
I recognized the place because I had been
there before.

*1. in the future,
afterward*

2. *prep.* **in front of, ahead of**
There are many people before me in the
line.

*2. behind, after,
at the rear of*

3. *prep.* **in advance of, previous to**
I went to the dentist the day before
yesterday.

3. after, following

befriend *v.* **help, favor, assist**
The family befriended their new
neighbors.

hinder, impede

beg **1.** *v.* **beseech, implore, entreat, plead, ask**
The prisoners begged for mercy at their
trial.

*1. insist, require,
demand*

2. *v.* **ask for charity, ask for alms**
The starving children begged for money
on the streets.
n. Tourists gave the beggars some money.

*2. give, endow,
donate*

begin *v.* **commence, start, launch**
We began our homework after dinner.

*finish, end, stop,
complete, terminate*

beginner *n.* **novice, learner, amateur, trainee, tyro**
A beginner in swimming should not go far
from the shore.

*expert, ace,
professional*

beginning *n.* **start, opening, origin, outset, source,
commencement**
I was late, so I missed the beginning of
the movie.

*end, finish, close,
completion, closing,
conclusion,
termination*

behavior		n.	conduct, manners, deportment, actions, bearing The children were on their best behavior at the concert.	*misbehavior, misconduct*
behind	1.	adv.	in the rear, aft, at the back The animal's tail hung behind.	1. *in the front, fore, at the front*
	2.	adv.	farther back The slower walkers lagged behind.	2. *ahead*
	3.	adv.	slow, late, not on time, tardy The train should arrive soon, unless it's running behind.	3. *on time, on schedule, fast, ahead of schedule*
	4.	prep.	at the back of, in the rear of The child hid behind the door.	4. *in the front of*
	5.	prep.	later than The mail delivery is behind schedule today.	5. *earlier than, ahead of schedule*
	6.	prep.	in support of, for My friends will stand behind my actions.	6. *against, anti*
believe		v.	accept, think, have faith I believe that you are telling the truth. *n.* It is my belief that you are telling the truth.	*doubt, deny, suspect*
bellow		n.	howl, cry, roar, shout loudly Lou let out a bellow of pain when he fell. *v.* The lumberjack bellowed a warning as the tree began to fall.	*whisper, whimper*
belongings		n.	property, possessions All their belongings were lost in the fire.	
below	1.	adv.	beneath, underneath I looked over the balcony and spotted my friend below.	1. *above, on top, overhead*
	2.	prep.	lower than, under It gets cold when the temperature falls below 32 degrees Fahrenheit.	2. *above, higher than*
	3.	prep.	unworthy of, beneath Cheating is below contempt.	3. *worthy of, deserving of*
bend	1.	n.	curve, turn The car went out of control on the sharp bend in the road.	1. *straightaway*
	2.	v.	curve, turn, twist The electrician bent the wire around the base of the lamp.	2. *straighten, unwind, extend*
	3.	v.	submit, yield The people refused to bend to the dictator's demands.	3. *defy, resist, disobey*
beneath	1.	prep.	under, below, underneath, underfoot We picnicked beneath a huge tree.	1. *above, on*
	2.	prep.	unworthy of, undeserving of, below Such a cruel dictator is beneath contempt.	2. *worthy of, deserving of*
benefit	1.	n.	advantage, profit, favor, help A good coach is a benefit for any team.	1. *disadvantage, loss, detriment*

	2.	*v.*	**help, aid, assist** Extra practice will benefit this team's game.	*2. hurt, harm, hinder, damage*
bent	**1.**	*adj.*	**determined, inclined** She is bent on winning a scholarship. *n.* With her bent for hard work she will most likely succeed.	*1. disinterested, indifferent*
	2.	*adj.*	**twisted, distorted, curved, crooked** The car had a bent fender from the accident.	*2. rigid, straight, erect*
bet		*n.*	**wager, gamble, stake** The gambler placed a bet at the casino. *v.* How much money did he bet?	
bewilder		*v.*	**puzzle, perplex, confuse, mystify, confound** His strange illness bewildered the doctors.	*inform, guide, instruct, enlighten*
bias		*n.*	**preference, leaning, partiality** We have a bias for the home team.	*impartiality, fairness, objectivity*
big		*adj.*	**huge, large, great, grand, vast, immense, enormous, bulky** The stadium was big enough to hold 60,000 people.	*small, little, petite, tiny, lean, minute, microscopic*
bind		*v.*	**fasten, tie, secure, truss** We bound the package with a cord. *adj.* A contract is a binding document.	*loosen, unfasten, free, untie*
biting	**1.**	*adj.*	**bitter, piercing, penetrating, sharp, intense, harsh** The biting wind prevented us from skating outdoors.	*1. soft, gentle, soothing*
	2.	*adj.*	**pungent, stinging, sharp, tart, bitter, astringent** Pickles have a biting taste.	*2. bland*
	3.	*adj.*	**sarcastic, cutting** The debater resorted to biting remarks about the opposing team.	*3. kind, gentle, complimentary, flattering*
bitter	**1.**	*adj.*	**biting, sour, sharp, pungent, tart, astringent** Spoiled nuts have a bitter taste.	*1. sweet, pleasing*
	2.	*adj.*	**harsh, cruel, unbearable** We all complained about the bitter winter.	*2. mild, gentle, kind*
blame	**1.**	*n.*	**fault, guilt, condemnation, liability** Industries have to take the blame for some environmental pollution.	*1. credit, praise, commendation*
	2.	*v.*	**accuse, condemn, criticize, charge** Police blamed the drunk driver for the accident.	*2. praise, commend, credit*
bland	**1.**	*adj.*	**mild, soothing, gentle** A warm spring breeze is bland.	*1. severe, harsh, bitter, biting*

2. *adj.* **affable, polite, agreeable**
The police officer's bland manners helped us relax.

3. *adj.* **uninteresting, dull, flat**
Kit disliked the hospital's bland food.

2. *rude, abrasive, disagreeable, abrupt, harsh, severe*
3. *exciting, spicy, hot, tasty, delicious*

blank **1.** *n.* **void, empty space, hollow, opening**
Fill in the blanks on the form.

2. *adj.* **expressionless, vague, vacant, impassive**
The blank look on his face told us he was daydreaming.

3. *adj.* **unused, empty, fresh**
Write your answers on a blank page.

2. *excited, expressive, alert*

3. *used, inscribed*

blaze *v.* **flame, flare, burn**
The forest fire blazed for days.
n. The firefighters had a difficult time extinguishing the blaze.

bleak *adj.* **dismal, desolate, dreary, dull, barren**
Bleak winter days can be very depressing.

balmy, pleasant, cheerful

blemish **1.** *n.* **flaw, defect, imperfection**
A pimple is a blemish on the skin.

2. *v.* **hurt, harm, injure, mar, spoil**
Tim's illness blemished his perfect attendance record.

1. *perfection, impeccability*
2. *enhance, help*

blend **1.** *n.* **mixture, combination**
The sauce was made from a blend of ten different spices.

2. *v.* **mix, combine, mingle, unite, merge**
Blend these ingredients together to make the pudding.
n. Use the electric blender.

2. *separate, divide, split*

bliss *n.* **joy, ecstasy, rapture**
The bride and groom were in a state of bliss on their wedding day.
adj. The ceremony was a blissful occasion.

misery, woe, suffering, unhappiness

block **1.** *n.* **hindrance, obstruction, obstacle, barrier, restriction**
The plumber cleared the block in our pipes.

2. *v.* **close off, obstruct**
Huge snowdrifts blocked the mountain pass.

1. *opening, aid*

2. *clear, open up*

bloom *v.* **flower, blossom**
Tulips bloom in the spring.
n. Tulip blooms come in many colors.

decay, wilt, shrivel, wither, fade

blossom **1.** *v.* **flower, bloom**
Fruit trees blossom in the spring.
n. Cherry blossoms are a sign of spring.

2. *v.* **develop, grow**
José blossomed into a fine writer.

1. *wither, fade, decay, wilt, shrivel*

2. *deteriorate, decline*

blot	1.	*n.*	**spot, stain, smudge, smear, blemish** The spilled coffee left an ugly blot on my shirt.	
	2.	*v.*	**dry, absorb, soak up** We blotted the spilled milk with paper towels.	*2. wet, soak*
blow	1.	*n.*	**hit, knock, rap, cuff, stroke, bang** A boxer suffers fierce blows to the body.	
	2.	*n.*	**misfortune, loss, disaster, calamity, catastrophe** The loss of her cat was a blow to Nan.	*2. blessing, comfort, relief*
	3.	*v.*	**fling, whirl, sweep, waft, flutter** The flags blew in the wind.	*3. remain still*
	4.	*v.*	**puff, exhale, pant** Take a deep breath and blow out the candles.	*4. inhale, breathe in*
bluff		*v.*	**fool, mislead, trick, deceive** Hal tried to bluff his way into the show without a ticket. *n.* The usher saw through his bluff and refused to let him in.	
blunder	1.	*n.*	**error, mistake, oversight, slip** The careless cashier made costly blunders. *v.* The careless cashier blundered in the addition of my bill.	*1. correction, reparation*
	2.	*v.*	**stumble, trip, fall** The tired boy blundered down the stairs.	
blunt	1.	*adj.*	**dull, unsharpened** The scissors were too blunt to cut the fabric.	*1. sharp*
	2.	*adj.*	**outspoken, curt, frank, abrupt** Blunt remarks can hurt people's feelings.	*2. diplomatic, gentle, polite, tactful, subtle*
blur		*v.*	**obscure, dim, shadow, cloud, screen** The driver slowed down when the fog blurred her view. *n.* Everything was a blur in the fog.	*clear, focus*
boast		*v.*	**brag, show off** Richard boasted about his new convertible. *adj.* He was a boastful person.	*be humble*
body	1.	*n.*	**frame, physique, form, figure, build** Exercise builds strong bodies.	
	2.	*n.*	**corpse, remains, cadaver** Police found the victim's body in the bush.	
	3.	*n.*	**expanse, mass, area** An ocean is a large body of water.	
	4.	*n.*	**organization, corporation, group, association** The student body met with the principal about the new rules.	

bogus		*adj.*	**fake, artificial, phony, fictitious, counterfeit, sham, false** The bogus five dollar bill was difficult to detect.	*real, legitimate, genuine*
boisterous		*adj.*	**noisy, loud, rowdy, disorderly, unruly** The boisterous crowd at the football game was told to calm down.	*quiet, reserved, restrained, calm*
bold	1.	*adj.*	**daring, brave, fearless, intrepid, courageous, valiant, adventurous** A team of bold astronauts blasted off into space.	*1. timid, shy, cowardly, retiring*
	2.	*adj.*	**brazen, saucy, impudent, rude, impertinent** The bold child made faces at us.	*2. polite, courteous, well-behaved, mannerly*
boon		*n.*	**blessing, help, benefit, advantage** Thermal underwear is a boon in winter.	*hindrance, handicap, disadvantage*
boost	1.	*n.*	**shove, push** "Give me a boost over the wall," shouted Sheila.	*1. pull, haul, tow*
	2.	*v.*	**raise, improve, increase, enhance** The good news boosted our morale.	*2. decrease, lower, decline*
boot up		*v.*	**turn on, warm up** I'm waiting for my computer to boot up.	*shut down*
border	1.	*n.*	**fringe, trim, edge, margin** Put a border along the hem of the dress.	*1. center, inside, interior*
	2.	*n.*	**boundary, frontier** Canada and the United States share an undefended border.	*2. interior*
bother	1.	*n.*	**nuisance, irritation, annoyance** It's such a bother to work in this heat.	*1. assistance, aid, help*
	2.	*n.*	**worry, fuss, trouble** He makes a big bother out of everything.	*2. joy, delight, pleasure*
	3.	*v.*	**pester, worry, badger, fuss, irritate, trouble** Don't bother me while I'm busy.	*3. help, aid, assist*
bound	1.	*v.*	**leap, jump, spring, vault** Deer bound through the forests.	
	2.	*adj.*	**obliged, obligated, compelled** We are legally bound to pay taxes.	*2. free*
	3.	*adj.*	**certain, sure** You're bound to be in trouble if you come home late.	*3. uncertain*
boundless		*adj.*	**endless, unlimited, limitless, infinite** Outer space is boundless.	*limited, finite, restricted, confined*
brave	1.	*v.*	**face, defy, oppose** Christopher Columbus braved the mutiny among his crew.	*1. hide, run from*

	2.	*adj.*	**fearless, bold, valiant, heroic, daring, courageous, adventurous, dauntless** It takes a brave person to overcome a physical challenge.	**2.** *cowardly, frightened, timid, cringing, fearful*
bravery		*n.*	**courage, valor, daring, gallantry, fearlessness** She was commended for her bravery in rescuing the drowning child.	*cowardice, fearfulness*
brazen		*adj.*	**impudent, rude, impertinent, saucy, forward** His brazen behavior shocked us.	*polite, retiring, shy, reserved, modest, withdrawn*
break	1.	*n.*	**crack, gap, split, rupture, rift, schism, fracture** The seal emerged through the break in the ice.	
	2.	*n.*	**rest, interval, pause** We have a half-hour break for lunch.	
	3.	*v.*	**crack, smash, shatter, split** The plate broke into many pieces when it fell on the floor.	**3.** *mend, join, attach, fasten, bind*
	4.	*v.*	**injure, damage, ruin, destroy** The baby broke his sister's toy.	**4.** *restore, repair, fix, enhance*
	5.	*v.*	**reveal, disclose, make known** Radio, television, and the Internet break the latest news to the public.	**5.** *conceal, hide, shield*
	6.	*v.*	**interrupt, stop** A loud crash broke my train of thoughts.	**6.** *continue*
	7.	*v.*	**soften, lessen, diminish** The soft snow broke her fall so she wasn't injured.	**7.** *increase, worsen*
breakable		*adj.*	**fragile, delicate, frail, weak, brittle** China plates are breakable.	*durable, strong, tough*
breakdown		*n.*	**collapse, disruption, stoppage** A computer breakdown caused the bank to close for the day.	*recovery, renewal*
brief	1.	*n.*	**summary, outline** The lawyer compiled a brief on the case.	**1.** *tome*
	2.	*adj.*	**short, terse, concise** A brief announcement of the event was made on television.	**2.** *lengthy, wordy, detailed*
	3.	*adj.*	**skimpy, small, slight, insufficient** Jen's brief bikini attracted attention.	**3.** *large, ample, sufficient*
bright	1.	*adj.*	**brilliant, shining, gleaming, glowing, lustrous, scintillating, sparkling, twinkling** Stars seem bright on clear nights. *adv.* Jewels shine brightly.	**1.** *dark, dull, clouded, gloomy, opaque, dreary*
	2.	*adj.*	**clever, brilliant, intelligent, alert** She is full of bright ideas.	**2.** *stupid, dull, unintelligent*
	3.	*adj.*	**promising, favorable, auspicious** Lisa has a bright career ahead of her.	**3.** *obscure, doubtful, dubious*

brim
1. *n.* **edge, rim, lip, border, top**   1. *center, interior*
Please don't fill my cup to the brim.
2. *v.* **overflow, spill**
Her eyes brimmed with tears when she
heard the bad news.

bring
1. *v.* **carry, convey, bear, transport**   1. *send, remove*
Bring your lunch with you.
2. *v.* **draw, sell for, command, fetch, earn, produce, yield**
Fruits bring high prices in the winter.

brink
n. **edge, verge, limit**
The mountain climber clung precariously
to the brink of the cliff.

brisk
1. *adj.* **quick, lively, energetic, stimulating**   1. *slow, sluggish, lethargic, listless, stagnant*
The athlete has a brisk workout each day.
adv. The sailboat moved briskly.
2. *adj.* **sharp, keen**   2. *gentle, soft*
The sails caught the brisk wind.

brittle
adj. **fragile, delicate, breakable, frail, weak**   *durable, strong, tough*
Thin glass such as crystal is brittle.

broad
1. *adj.* **wide, large, expansive**   1. *narrow*
The horse jumped across a broad ditch.
2. *adj.* **widespread, extensive**   2. *limited, restricted, confined*
Television reaches a broad audience.
3. *adj.* **general, non-specific**   3. *specific, focused*
Just give us a broad outline of your plan.

broken
1. *adj.* **defective, damaged, faulty, inoperable**   1. *operable, usable, in working order*
Sam took the broken clock in for repair.
2. *adj.* **shattered, destroyed, split, smashed**   2. *whole, intact, sound*
Amy's broken leg is healing slowly.

browse
1. *v.* **search, explore, surf**
I browsed various websites for data.
n. My browser is a search engine for the
Internet.
2. *v.* **skim, scan, leaf through, glance at**   2. *study, pore over, ponder*
I browsed through some magazines.

brutal
adj. **cruel, savage, harsh, merciless, ruthless**   *kind, considerate, humane, gentle, civilized*
Many soldiers were killed in the brutal
battle.
n. Many acts of brutality occur in wars.

buddy
n. **chum, friend, playmate, comrade, pal**   *rival, enemy, alien, adversary, foe, stranger*
Tzen and Roger have been buddies for a
long time.

bug
1. *n.* **insect**
Our picnic lunch attracted ants and
several other kinds of bugs.

	2.	*n.*	**defect, flaw, shortcoming** My computer keeps crashing because of a bug in an application.	**2.** *improvement*
	3.	*v.*	**irritate, bother, annoy** My brother's whining bugged me.	**3.** *soothe, calm*
build		*v.*	**erect, construct, raise, make, create, assemble, manufacture, put up** The Smiths built a new house by the sea.	*destroy, demolish, wreck, pull down, ruin, dismantle*
bulk		*n.*	**majority, preponderance, biggest share** Which candidate got the bulk of the votes?	*minority, bit, portion, fraction, section*
burden		*v.*	**weigh down, hinder, hamper, oppress** Don't burden her with more work. *n.* The financial burden was too much for them to bear.	*lighten, unload, relieve, lessen*
burly		*adj.*	**strong, sturdy, husky** The bullies took off when they saw the burly guard approaching.	*puny, feeble, weak*
burn		*v.*	**set on fire, ignite, incinerate, cremate** Where can we burn the garbage?	*put out, stifle, extinguish, smother*
burst		*v.*	**explode, blow up, erupt, rupture** The car veered when the tire burst.	
business	**1.**	*n.*	**trade, commerce** Stores do good business at Christmas.	
	2.	*n.*	**work, career, profession, vocation** What line of business are you in?	**2.** *hobby, leisure*
	3.	*n.*	**affair, concern, interest** My private life is my business.	
bustle	**1.**	*n.*	**hustle, hurry, fuss, flurry, activity** Before the party there was a great bustle in the kitchen.	**1.** *inactivity, quiet*
	2.	*v.*	**hustle, hurry, scurry** The performers bustled about the dressing room before the play began.	**2.** *linger, dawdle*
busy		*adj.*	**occupied, active, working, engaged** The busy doctor had no time for lunch. *v.* The students busied themselves at the computers. *adv.* They worked busily all day long.	*resting, relaxed, unoccupied, idle, unemployed, inactive*
buy		*v.*	**purchase, get, acquire, obtain** Ann bought a bracelet at the jewelers. *n.* It proved to be a good buy.	*sell, market, auction, dispose of, vend*

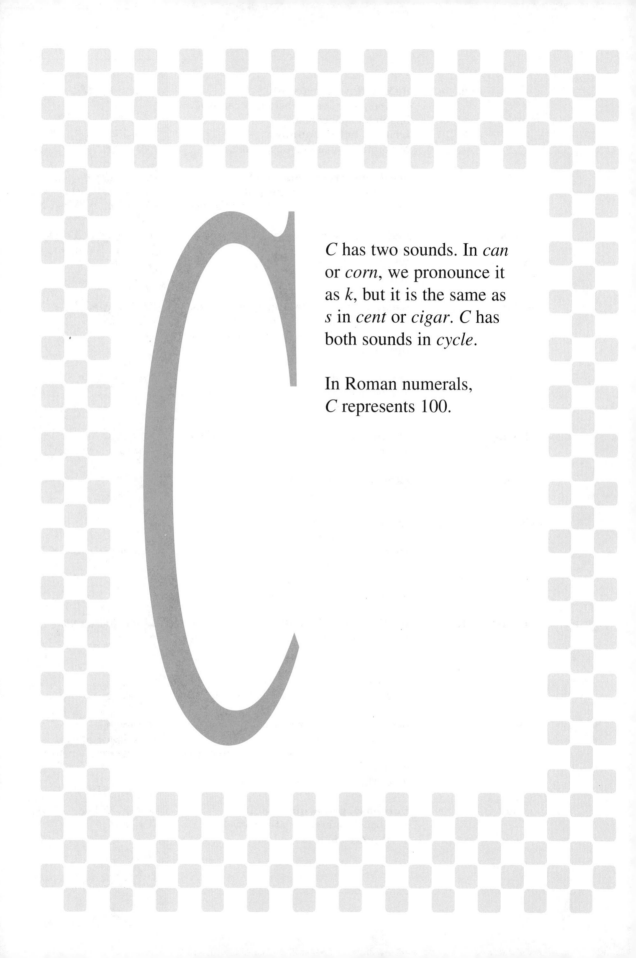

C has two sounds. In *can* or *corn*, we pronounce it as *k*, but it is the same as *s* in *cent* or *cigar*. *C* has both sounds in *cycle*.

In Roman numerals, *C* represents 100.

cable
1. *n.* **wire**
Cables transmit Internet and television signals.
2. *n.* **cord, heavy chain, rope**
The anchor was attached to a cable.
3. *n.* **cablegram, telegram, wire**
The soldier sent a cable to inform his family that he had been injured.
v. He cabled that he was coming home.

cage
1. *n.* **coop, box, crate**
Canaries are kept in cages in pet shops.
2. *v.* **enclose, confine, keep in**
The zookeeper caged the angry lion.
adj. The caged lion roared ferociously.
    2. liberate, release, set free

cake
1. *n.* **lump, mass, slab, loaf, bar, brick**
Please put a cake of soap on the sink.
2. *v.* **harden, stiffen, set, congeal, solidify**
Mud cakes in the sun.
    2. soften, dissolve

calamity
n. **disaster, catastrophe, tragedy, misfortune**
The destruction caused by the flood was a calamity for the town.
    blessing, benefit, good fortune, comfort, boon

calculate
v. **compute, count, appraise, figure**
We calculated that we had just enough money for lunch.
n. Our calculation was accurate.
    guess, estimate

call
1. *n.* **shout, cry, whoop, yell**
The call for help awoke the family.
v. He called for help at the top of his voice.
    1. whisper, murmur, silence
2. *n.* **visit, stop**
Rani made a call at the hospital to see her friend.
v. She called on her friend on her way home from school.
3. *v.* **telephone, phone**
Yen called for an ambulance when she saw the accident.
4. *v.* **collect, convene, assemble, summon**
The organizers called the members to a meeting.
    4. scatter, send away, break up, dismiss
5. *v.* **name, designate, term**
They called their baby Virgil.
    5. misname, misterm

callous
1. *adj.* **tough, hardened**
Skin on the feet can become callous from ill-fitting shoes.
    1. soft, supple, pliant, tender, flexible
2. *adj.* **insensitive, unfeeling, indifferent, unconcerned**
The callous person ignored the child's cries for help.
    2. sensitive, caring, compassionate, concerned

calm
1. *n.* **tranquility, peace, serenity, quiet**
A siren shattered the calm of the night.
    1. disturbance, agitation, turbulence

	2.	*v.*	**ease, relax, soothe, pacify, allay, tranquilize** Quiet music calms the nerves.	**2.** *agitate, excite, arouse, upset, disturb*
	3.	*adj.*	**quiet, peaceful, composed, placid, tranquil, serene** The boat glided over the calm waters.	**3.** *violent, rough, turbulent, frantic, excited, agitated*
camouflage		*v.*	**disguise, mask, conceal, screen, cover** The hunters wore green to camouflage themselves in the woods. *n.* The polar bear's white coat acts as a camouflage in the snow.	*expose, reveal, display, uncover*
cancel	1.	*v.*	**cross out, delete, remove, eliminate** She canceled Al's name from her guest list.	**1.** *maintain, keep*
	2.	*v.*	**eradicate, nullify, abandon, withdraw, void, rescind** I canceled my subscription to the magazine. *n.* I sent a notice of cancelation.	**2.** *renew, restore, sustain, continue, keep*
candid		*adj.*	**frank, honest, open, straightforward, blunt** Ed is so honest you can always count on him for a candid opinion. *adv.* He candidly told Lin her essay was a disappointment.	*crafty, wily, deceitful, cunning, insincere*
cantankerous		*adj.*	**grouchy, grumpy, cranky, irritable, ill-tempered, peevish, disagreeable** The cantankerous child was sent to bed.	*pleasant, friendly, good-natured, calm, agreeable, serene*
capable	1.	*adj.*	**competent, talented, proficient, able, skillful** The three most capable students received scholarships.	**1.** *incompetent, incapable*
	2.	*adj.*	**able to do, has potential for** Although she is young, Laila is capable of good work.	**2.** *incapable, unable to do*
capital	1.	*n.*	**cash, assets, money** The owner invested $25,000 in capital in the business.	
	2.	*adj.*	**chief, main, principal, leading, primary, foremost, dominant** A country's seat of government is found in its capital city.	**2.** *subordinate, minor, lesser, least important*
	3.	*adj.*	**splendid, excellent, choice, delightful** We had a capital time at the party.	**3.** *unpleasant, poor, inferior*
capsize		*v.*	**upset, overturn, tip, invert** The small boat capsized in the rough seas.	*set upright*
capsule	1.	*n.*	**container, can, receptacle** The food was packed in an air-tight capsule.	

	2.	*n.*	**tablet, pill** The doctor prescribed antibiotic capsules for my infection.	
captain		*n.*	**leader, chief, head, commander** The captain explained the game plan to the team.	*follower, subordinate*
captivate		*v.*	**charm, delight, enthrall, fascinate, entrance, enrapture, dazzle** The singer captivated the audience with her performance.	*disgust, repel, horrify, disenchant*
captive	1.	*n.*	**prisoner, convict, hostage** The captives were taken to the jail.	**1.** *free person*
	2.	*adj.*	**enslaved, imprisoned, restrained, jailed, incarcerated** The captive men were treated roughly.	**2.** *free, released, acquitted*
captivity		*n.*	**confinement, incarceration, restraint, imprisonment, detention** Wild animals often die in captivity.	*liberty, freedom, independence*
capture	1.	*v.*	**catch, seize, trap, arrest, apprehend, nab** The police captured the robbers after a short chase. *n.* The capture of the robbers was reported in the news. *adj.* The captured robbers were taken to jail.	**1.** *release, discharge, set free*
	2.	*v.*	**conquer, overwhelm, occupy** The army captured the village after a fierce battle.	**2.** *surrender*
	3.	*v.*	**attract, draw** The unusual painting captured everyone's attention.	**3.** *repel, repulse*
car		*n.*	**automobile, auto, motor vehicle** Alex bought a car as soon as he got his driver's license.	
care	1.	*n.*	**worry, anxiety, bother, concern** Few people are free from cares.	**1.** *unconcern*
	2.	*n.*	**heed, caution, precaution** "Take care when you cross the road," reminded Mom.	**2.** *neglect, carelessness, negligence*
	3.	*n.*	**attention, supervision** The twins were placed in the care of their aunt while their parents were away. *v.* Their aunt cared for them.	**3.** *disregard, neglect*
careful	1.	*adj.*	**thoughtful, considerate** The doctor's careful words eased the patient's worries.	**1.** *inconsiderate, neglectful*
	2.	*adj.*	**exacting, thorough, precise, meticulous** Dad did a careful check of the contract.	**2.** *imprecise, inaccurate*

3. *adj.* **cautious, vigilant, alert, watchful, mindful, wary**
The students were careful when experimenting in the laboratory.
adv. They handled things carefully.

3. *heedless, haphazard, careless*

careless **1.** *adj.* **thoughtless, rash**
Andy failed the mathematics test because of careless mistakes.
n. He regretted his carelessness.

1. *cautious, careful, mindful, alert*

2. *adj.* **slipshod, messy, disorganized**
His careless work was rejected.

2. *neat, orderly*

cargo *n.* **load, freight, goods, shipment**
The cargo was unloaded from the container ship.

carry **1.** *v.* **bear, move, take, convey, haul, transport, transfer**
Rico carried the baby on his back.

1. *drop, let go, release, put down*

2. *v.* **conduct, relay, transmit, transfer**
Copper wiring carries electric current.

2. *repel, resist, repulse*

3. *v.* **bear, sustain, support, shoulder, prop**
Pillars carry the weight of the roof.

3. *let fall, drop*

case **1.** *n.* **box, container, carton, crate**
The cases of fruit were shipped in refrigerated freight cars.

2. *n.* **example, instance, event, situation, occurrence, circumstance**
In this particular case, the dentist decided to extract the tooth.

cash *n.* **money, coins, bills, funds, currency**
The sign said, "Only cash accepted."

cast **1.** *n.* **mold, form, shape**
His broken leg was put in a cast.

2. *n.* **players, actors, actresses, troupe, performers**
The play's cast included a famous actress.

2. *audience*

3. *n.* **look, appearance, complexion**
The man's face has a pallid cast.

4. *v.* **heave, fling, throw, hurl, pitch, project, propel**
The children cast stones into the lake.

4. *catch, hold, seize, trap, grip*

casual **1.** *adj.* **accidental, chance, unplanned, unintentional, inadvertent**
We had a casual meeting at the reception.

1. *planned, contrived, intentional*

2. *adj.* **infrequent, random, occasional, irregular**
Farms hire casual workers in the summer.

2. *frequent, regular, constant, certain*

3. *adj.* **indifferent, unconcerned, blasé, apathetic, nonchalant**
He was warned about his casual attitude toward his work.

3. *concerned, enthusiastic, ardent*

adv. He casually told the boss he didn't care if he was fired.

4.	*adj.*	**informal, relaxed**	**4.** *formal, rigid, stern*

The party will be a casual affair, so come in casual clothes.

catastrophe   *n.*   **calamity, devastation, disaster, debacle**   *blessing, advantage, boon, good fortune, comfort, help*

The forest fire was a catastrophe.

catch

1. *n.*   **buckle, clasp, hook, fastener, clamp**
I couldn't fasten the catch on my necklace.

2. *n.*   **condition, requirement**
The jeans were on sale for half price, but the catch was you had to buy two pairs.

3. *v.*   **snatch, grab, snare, seize, grasp**   **3.** *let go, free, miss, drop, fumble*
The drowning child caught the rope.

4. *v.*   **apprehend, capture, snare, arrest, trap, seize, corner, nab**   **4.** *free, liberate, release*
The police officer caught the burglar.

5. *v.*   **overtake, pass**   **5.** *lag behind, falter, give up*
The runner caught the leader at the end of the race.

category   *n.*   **classification, section, level, division, class, rank, type, sort**

The books were divided into two categories — fiction and non-fiction.

cause

1. *n.*   **creator, reason, source, inducement**   **1.** *effect, result, outcome*
A cigarette was the cause of the fire.

2. *n.*   **reason, goal, purpose**
They raised money for a good cause.

3. *v.*   **make, compel, provoke**   **3.** *prevent, stop, prohibit*
Her stress caused her to fall ill.

caution

1. *n.*   **care, heed, notice, discretion, attention**   **1.** *rashness, recklessness, foolhardiness*
Use caution when crossing the streets.

2. *v.*   **warn, advise**
Dad cautioned me to drive carefully.

cautious   *adj.*   **careful, wary, watchful**   *rash, careless, thoughtless, unthinking*

The cautious cyclist avoided the busy street.
adv. She rode cautiously along the side of the road.

cavity

1. *n.*   **hole, opening, gap**   **1.** *filling*
The dentist found a cavity in my tooth.

2. *n.*   **cavern, basin, excavation, depression, hole, hollow**   **2.** *hill, elevation*
The heavy rains caused a cavity to develop under the road.

cease   *v.*   **stop, halt, terminate, end**   *begin, initiate, start, commence*

When the teacher walked in, the noise in the classroom ceased.

cede	*v.*	**yield, grant, surrender, relinquish** The defeated nation ceded territory to the conqueror.	*hold, occupy, retain, keep, save, maintain*
celebrate	*v.*	**commemorate, observe, keep** We celebrated her birthday with a party.	*disregard, overlook*
celebrated	*adj.*	**famous, distinguished, illustrious, noted** Crowds lined up to listen to the celebrated scientist speak.	*unknown*
celebration	1. *n.*	**observance, party, fete, jubilee, commemoration** The July 4th celebrations usually include fireworks.	**1.** *dirge, lament*
	2. *n.*	**gaiety, merrymaking** There will be a big celebration if we win.	**2.** *sadness, sorrow, grief, mourning*
celebrity	*n.*	**well-known person, famous person** The celebrity was mobbed by admirers.	*unknown, nobody*
celestial	1. *adj.*	**heavenly, stellar, cosmic** The stars are celestial bodies.	**1.** *earthly, terrestrial*
	2. *adj.*	**divine, ethereal, holy, angelic** The congregation was inspired by the celestial music from the organ.	**2.** *mundane, worldly, mortal, human*
cell	1. *n.*	**enclosure, cubicle** The prisoner was confined in a cell.	
	2. *n.*	**small unit, division, portion** All living things are composed of cells.	
cement	1. *n.*	**concrete** The sidewalk was paved with cement.	
	2. *v.*	**join, bind, fasten, connect, unite** They cemented the agreement with a handshake.	**2.** *separate, undo, disconnect*
center	1. *n.*	**midpoint, middle, heart, core, nucleus** My office is in the center of the city. *adj.* Central locations are most desired and therefore expensive.	**1.** *outside, exterior, rim, circumference, perimeter, edge*
	2. *v.*	**concentrate, focus, converge on** The discussion centered on the elections. *n.* The film star was the center of everyone's attention.	**2.** *decentralize, spread out, branch out*
central	*adj.*	**main, chief, leading, principal, prime** Jane is the central character in the novel.	*subsidiary, auxiliary, secondary, peripheral*
ceremony	*n.*	**ritual, rite, performance, custom, observance** The Wongs had a traditional Chinese wedding ceremony. *adj.* They wore ceremonial dress for the occasion.	

certain				
	1.	*adj.*	**confident, sure, assured, definite, positive** Liz was certain that she would win the first prize.	1. *doubtful, uncertain, indefinite, dubious*
	2.	*adj.*	**destined, sure, inevitable, predestined, unavoidable** That book will have certain success!	2. *doubtful, dubious*
	3.	*adj.*	**some, a few, specific** Certain people enjoy spicy foods.	3. *many, most, all*
chain	1.	*n.*	**series, succession, progression** The marriage was the first in a chain of happy events.	
	2.	*v.*	**tie, moor, tether, attach, connect, fasten, secure** Ken chained his bicycle to the tree.	2. *untie, loosen, release, set free, untether*
challenge	1.	*n.*	**dare, provocation** Sven accepted Jim's challenge to a race. *v.* Rick challenged Jo to a match.	
	2.	*n.*	**effort** Learning the new dance was a real challenge for me.	2. *snap, easy task*
	3.	*v.*	**defy, question, doubt, dispute** Tom challenged the referee's decision.	3. *accept, agree with, concur*
champion	1.	*n.*	**winner, victor, conqueror** It takes years of training to become an Olympic champion.	1. *loser*
	2.	*n.*	**supporter, defender, ally, protector, guardian** Mother Teresa was a champion of the sick and needy. *v.* She championed the cause of the needy.	2. *enemy, foe, rival, adversary*
	3.	*adj.*	**unbeaten, best, superior** Who is the champion speller?	3. *worst, poorest*
chance	1.	*n.*	**luck, fortune, accident** Lin and Tom met by chance at the rodeo.	1. *purpose, design, plan, aim*
	2.	*n.*	**opportunity, occasion, possibility** I have a chance to make more money on this new job.	
	3.	*v.*	**venture, gamble, risk, wager, bet** They were warned not to chance their money on the project.	
change	1.	*n.*	**coins, silver** Sam dumped the change out of his pockets.	
	2.	*n.*	**adjustment, variation, shift, alteration, substitution, deviation** There will be a change of plans if it rains.	2. *continuance, constancy*
	3.	*n.*	**switch, swap, replacement, exchange** The actors made a quick change of costumes between acts.	
	4.	*v.*	**adjust, shift, vary, alter** After some thought, she changed her mind about buying the new car.	4. *continue, keep, hold, remain, retain*

changeable	*adj.*	**variable, unsettled, unstable, fluctuating** Spring weather is changeable.	*reliable, steady, dependable, constant*
chaos	*n.*	**confusion, disorder, turmoil, tumult, anarchy, discord, disarray, shambles** The riots left the town in utter chaos. *adj.* The town was a chaotic sight.	*order*
character	1. *n.*	**personality, disposition, nature, temperament** He is feared for his surly character.	
	2. *n.*	**figure, symbol, letter, sign, mark** We learned to write Chinese characters in school.	
characteristic	1. *n.*	**quality, trait, peculiarity, attribute** A curly tail is a characteristic of pigs.	
	2. *adj.*	**distinctive, typical, peculiar** Each fruit has its own characteristic taste.	*2. aberrant, irregular*
charade	*n.*	**deception, fake, trick, sham, pretense** The smile was a charade to conceal her disappointment.	*fact, reality*
charge	1. *n.*	**cost, price, amount, expense** The show was poorly attended as the charge was too high.	
	2. *v.*	**command, bid, instruct, tell, demand, order, direct** The judge charged the jury to state its verdict.	*2. request, ask, desire, invite*
	3. *v.*	**attack, rush, stampede, assail** The bull charged at the matador.	*3. retreat, recoil, withdraw, fall back*
charm	1. *n.*	**magic, spell, enchantment, sorcery** In the Irish legend, the leprechaun cast a charm on the village.	
	2. *n.*	**good-luck piece, amulet, talisman** Many people believe charms can protect them or bring them luck.	*2. curse*
	3. *n.*	**grace, attractiveness** The actor turned on his charm for us.	*3. awkwardness, clumsiness*
	4. *v.*	**enchant, delight, entice, captivate, beguile, enrapture, enthrall** He charmed everyone with his warmth. *adj.* He told charming tales of long ago.	*4. tire, bore, weary, repel, disgust, annoy, displease, irritate, disturb, repulse*
chart	*n.*	**map, graph, plan, draft, plot, diagram, outline** The flow chart showed the steps we had to take to complete the assignment. *v.* We charted our course of action before beginning.	
chase	*v.*	**pursue, hunt, trail, track, follow** The hounds chased the foxes.	*avoid, flee, evade, shun, dodge*

chat	*v.*	**talk, converse, chatter** They chatted about their old school. *n.* The friends had an interesting chat.	*be quiet, be silent, listen*
chatter	*v.*	**jabber, prattle, babble, gabble** The monkeys chattered endlessly. *n.* The chatter annoyed the zookeeper.	*be quiet, be silent, listen*
cheap	*adj.*	**low-priced, inexpensive, cut-rate, thrifty, economical** They went to the flea market to look for cheap furniture.	*expensive, costly, dear, high-priced, pricey, valuable, deluxe*
cheat	*v.*	**swindle, deceive, trick, defraud, mislead, dupe, hoodwink** A con artist cheated Sam of his savings. *n.* Police are looking for the cheat.	*be trustworthy, be reliable*
check	1. *n.*	**examination, investigation, analysis, inquiry** The police ran a check on the fingerprints through the computer.	
	2. *n.*	**rein, control, restraint, curb, bridle** A dog should be kept in check in a park.	**2.** *at liberty*
	3. *v.*	**examine, inspect, verify** Lara checked the dictionary for the meaning of the word.	**3.** *ignore*
	4. *v.*	**retard, slow, reduce, lessen, decrease, lower, minimize** Yetta checked the car's speed on the wet pavement.	**4.** *hasten, increase, accelerate, speed up, advance, quicken*
	5. *v.*	**control, moderate, curb, restrain** Dad told Kim to check his tongue. *n.* Kim has to keep a check on his temper.	**5.** *free, liberate*
cheer	1. *n.*	**yell, shout, cry, hurrah, applause** The crowd's cheers encouraged the team. *v.* The crowd cheered the team to victory. *adj.* Who led the cheering section?	**1.** *jeer, ridicule, boo*
	2. *n.*	**happiness, joy, mirth, festivity, celebration, gladness** Birthdays are a time of cheer.	**2.** *sorrow, grief, sadness, gloom, melancholy*
	3. *v.*	**brighten, console, support, help, encourage, comfort** Visitors cheer patients in a hospital.	**3.** *depress, discourage, dishearten*
cheerful	1. *adj.*	**bright, glad, happy, joyful, merry, sunny, joyous, sprightly** She greeted everyone with a cheerful smile. *adv.* She cheerfully welcomed her guests.	**1.** *sad, unhappy, gloomy, glum, depressed, sullen*
	2. *adj.*	**bright, sunny, sparkling, comfortable, pleasant, appealing** The children were delighted with their cheerful classroom.	**2.** *dull, drab, unpleasant, gloomy, dreary*
cherish	1. *v.*	**treasure, prize, value, love, idolize, protect, revere, worship** Animals cherish their young.	**1.** *abandon, give up, desert, forsake, reject*

2. *v.* **cling to, keep in mind**
For many years, the patient cherished the hope of being cured.

2. *discard, reject, dispense with*

chest **1.** *n.* **case, box, cabinet, bin, container**
The medicine chest was kept out of the children's reach.
2. *n.* **bosom, breast**
The baby nestled on his mother's chest.

chew *v.* **gnaw, crunch, grind, munch, masticate**
Nan was told to chew her food carefully.

chic *adj.* **stylish, smart, elegant, fashionable**
Erin's chic hairdo drew admiring looks.

dowdy, unstylish, unfashionable

chief **1.** *n.* **head, boss, leader, director, manager**
Who is the chief of the fire department?
2. *adj.* **main, foremost, leading, first, prime, principal, capital**
Oil is the chief export of Iran.

1. *subordinate, attendant, servant*
2. *last, least, slightest, minor*

child *n.* **infant, baby, tot, youngster, minor**
Who's minding the children while their parents are away?

adult, grown-up

childish **1.** *adj.* **childlike, infantile, juvenile, young, babyish, immature**
We laughed at the baby's childish babble.
2. *adj.* **silly, stupid, foolish, absurd**
We were annoyed with Ian's childish behavior.

1. *adult, grown, mature, old*

2. *wise, clever, sensible, sagacious, profound*

chill **1.** *n.* **coolness, crispness, coldness**
Ed shivered in the chill of the night.
adj. The chilly breeze made us shiver.
2. *v.* **cool, refrigerate, frost, make cold**
Mike chilled the pop before the party.

1. *warmth, coziness*

2. *heat, warm*

chip **1.** *n.* **piece, part, bit, fragment, wedge, flake**
The floor of the carpenter's workshop was covered with wood chips.
2. *v.* **break, crack, splinter, whittle, chisel**
Glenn chipped a hole in the ice to catch the fish.

1. *whole, entirety*

2. *join, mend, repair*

chirp *v.* **sing, call, warble, trill**
The birds chirped happily at daybreak.

choice **1.** *n.* **selection, option, preference, election**
Simi is my choice for a writing partner.
2. *n.* **variety, quantity, diversity, medley, assortment, mixture**
There is a wide choice of dishes on the menu.

2. *limitation, restriction*

choke	1.	*v.*	**strangle, stifle, suffocate, smother, asphyxiate, throttle** The tight collar almost choked the pup.	
	2.	*v.*	**suppress, hold back, control** The angry customer choked back a rude reply.	**2.** *release, let out, let go*
choose		*v.*	**pick, select, decide on, elect, prefer** The judges took a long time to choose a winner.	*discard, reject, refuse, dismiss, decline, leave*
chop		*v.*	**cut, cleave, lop, hew, fell, hack, slash** The soldiers chopped their way through the undergrowth of the jungle.	
chore		*n.*	**job, task, duty** Al finished his chores before watching TV.	*pleasure, relaxation*
chronic		*adj.*	**persistent, continuing, constant, continual** He suffers from chronic back pain.	*temporary, fleeting, passing*
chubby		*adj.*	**fat, plump, pudgy, hefty, chunky, stout, portly** No more candies for the chubby child.	*slim, slight, thin, skinny, lean, slender*
chuckle		*v.*	**giggle, laugh, snicker, snigger** The audience chuckled when Dad snored in the middle of the concert.	*cry, weep, sob, wail*
chum		*n.*	**pal, friend, companion, buddy, comrade, mate, ally, playmate** The chums do many things together.	*enemy, foe, opponent, rival, antagonist, stranger, adversary*
civil		*adj.*	**polite, courteous, refined, cultured** The salesperson treated the angry customer in a civil manner.	*impolite, rude, discourteous*
claim	1.	*n.*	**title, right** State your claim to the property.	**1.** *disclaimer*
	2.	*v.*	**insist, assert, declare, contend** The suspect claimed he was innocent.	**2.** *disclaim, reject, renounce, disown*
	3.	*v.*	**take, exact** The accident claimed many lives.	**3.** *give, restore, return*
clamor	1.	*n.*	**commotion, outcry, uproar, racket** The no-smoking rule caused a clamor at the party.	**1.** *quiet, calm, peace*
	2.	*v.*	**shout, demand** The starving refugees clamored for food.	
clamp	1.	*n.*	**lock, fastener, catch, snap, brace, vise** The test tube was held in place by a clamp.	
	2.	*n.*	**restriction, control** There's a clamp on drinking and driving. *v.* Police are clamping down on drunk drivers.	**2.** *freedom*

clap
1. *n.* **crash, bang, burst**
The clap of thunder frightened the baby.
2. *v.* **applaud, cheer, acclaim, praise** — 2. *boo, jeer*
The audience clapped thunderously as the actor took his bow.

clarify
1. *v.* **make clear, explain, elucidate, define** — 1. *confuse, muddle, mislead, perplex*
Please clarify the rules of the game.
2. *v.* **purify, refine, filter, cleanse, clean** — 2. *pollute, dirty, soil, contaminate*
Filtration plants clarified the water so it would be safe to drink.

clash
1. *n.* **quarrel, disagreement, conflict, fight, dispute, argument** — 1. *agreement, accord, harmony, understanding*
There was a violent clash between the gangs.
2. *v.* **disagree, differ, conflict** — 2. *agree, concur, coincide, harmonize*
His political views clashed with mine.

clasp
1. *n.* **hook, catch, buckle, clamp, fastener**
The clasp on the bracelet is loose.
2. *v.* **grip, grasp, clutch, hold, embrace** — 2. *release, let go, drop, relinquish*
Mom clasped the baby to her breast.

class
1. *n.* **grade, rank, quality, type, degree**
The company president flies first class.
2. *v.* **rank, grade, identify, mark, classify**
The laboratory classed the virus as lethal.

classic
adj. **excellent, enduring, immortal** — *inferior, minor*
Kit had a collection of classic books.

classify
v. **sort, grade, arrange, categorize**
A government agency classifies meat according to its quality.
n. The classification is strictly done.

clatter
n. **noise, racket, rattle, clash** — *silence, quiet*
Try not to make a clatter when stacking the dishes.
v. The dishes clattered to the floor.

claw
v. **tear, scratch, rip open, rip apart**
The hungry bears clawed at the sacks of food.

clean
1. *v.* **scour, wash down, scrub, cleanse** — 1. *dirty, soil*
The housekeeper cleaned the apartment.
2. *v.* **sterilize, purify, disinfect, cleanse** — 2. *pollute, infect, poison, contaminate*
The dentist cleaned his instruments with disinfectant.
3. *adj.* **spotless, stainless, untarnished** — 3. *stained, soiled, tarnished, dirty*
The clean silverware sparkled.
4. *adj.* **sanitary, pure, uncontaminated** — 4. *unsanitary, impure, contaminated*
Fish from clean lakes are safe to eat.
5. *adj.* **clear-cut, distinct, sharp, precise** — 5. *indistinct, cluttered*
The skyscrapers cut a clean silhouette against the sky.

clear	1.	*v.*	**clean, cleanse, purify** She opened all the windows to clear the air in the smoky room.	**1.** *pollute, contaminate*
	2.	*v.*	**remove, rid, empty** We cleared the junk out of the basement.	**2.** *fill, occupy*
	3.	*v.*	**clarify, explain** Her explanation cleared up the mystery.	**3.** *confuse, muddle, puzzle, confound*
	4.	*v.*	**acquit, release, excuse, absolve, exonerate** The jury believed the suspect was innocent and cleared him of all charges.	**4.** *implicate, accuse, charge*
	5.	*v.*	**receive, get, make, realize, earn** We cleared a handsome profit on the sale of the house.	**5.** *lose, miss out on, suffer a loss*
	6.	*adj.*	**transparent** We could see the bottom of the lake through the crystal clear water.	**6.** *opaque, muddy*
	7.	*adj.*	**sunny, cloudless, bright, fair** It was a clear day, with not a cloud in the sky.	**7.** *dark, dismal, cloudy, dreary*
	8.	*adj.*	**distinct, audible** Announcers need to have clear voices.	**8.** *indistinct, inaudible, garbled*
	9.	*adj.*	**distinct, precise, definite, explicit** Mervyn has a clear understanding of the problem.	**9.** *obstructed, blocked, indistinct, obscured*
	10.	*adv.*	**totally, fully, completely, entirely** The laser beam cut clear through the metal.	**10.** *somewhat, partially, partly*
clever	1.	*adj.*	**intelligent, bright, talented, skillful, expert, smart, adroit, accomplished, proficient, capable** The clever student won a scholarship.	**1.** *dull, unintelligent, inept, stupid, foolish*
	2.	*adj.*	**witty, keen** The play's success rested on its clever dialogue.	**2.** *dull, boring, silly*
client		*n.*	**customer, patron, buyer, purchaser** The new lawyer advertised for clients.	*seller, dealer, vendor, retailer, merchant*
cliff		*n.*	**bluff, precipice, steep hill** The house was perched on the edge of the cliff.	*plain*
climax		*n.*	**peak, culmination, apex, highlight** The climax of the play was when the identity of the killer was revealed.	*anticlimax, lowest point, nadir*
climb		*v.*	**ascend, go up, scale, rise** Pat climbed to the top of the ladder. *n.* Dave made a fast climb to the presidency of the company.	*go down, descend, come down, fall*
cling	1.	*v.*	**stick, adhere, attach** The plastic wrap clings to the plate.	**1.** *loosen, detach*
	2.	*v.*	**grasp, hold tightly, clutch, grip, clench** The boy clung to the overturned canoe.	**2.** *let go, drop, release*

clip
1. *n.* **fastener, holder**
Chloe put a clip in her unruly hair.
2. *v.* **snip, crop, cut**
I clipped the article from the newspaper.

cloak
1. *n.* **cape, wrap, mantle**
Rachel wore a long cloak to protect herself from the rain.
2. *v.* **hide, disguise, cover, mask, conceal** — *2. reveal, disclose, uncover, exhibit*
The spy's true identity is cloaked in secrecy.

close
1. *n.* **conclusion, end, finish, completion, termination** — *1. beginning, start, commencement, opening*
The audience stayed until the close of the show.
2. *v.* **conclude, finish, end, terminate** — *2. begin, open, start, commence*
When did the exhibition close?
3. *v.* **block, shut off, seal, bar** — *3. open, unseal*
The police closed the highway because of a bad accident.
4. *v.* **shut, fasten** — *4. open, unlock*
He closed the door to keep out the flies.
5. *adj.* **sticky, stuffy, unventilated, heavy, stale, oppressive** — *5. fresh, brisk, refreshing, exhilarating*
The air in the room became close after all the windows were shut.
6. *adj.* **intimate, dear, familiar** — *6. estranged, unfamiliar, distant*
They have been close friends for years.
7. *adj.* **stingy, cheap, miserly** — *7. generous, liberal*
Miserly people are close with their money.
8. *adj.* **confined, cramped, restricted, tight, narrow, compact** — *8. spacious, roomy, large*
Some people feel claustrophobic in close quarters.
9. *adv.* **near, nearby, adjacent** — *9. at a distance, removed, afar, afield*
We live close to the shopping center.

clothes
n. **apparel, attire, clothing, garments**
The children packed their old clothes for camp.
v. They were warmly clothed for skiing.

clothing
n. **clothes, attire, apparel, garb, garments**
She wore sturdy clothing for the hike.

cloudy
1. *adj.* **overcast, misty, murky, hazy** — *1. clear, fair*
Cloudy skies prevented the viewing of the eclipse.
2. *adj.* **opaque, murky, thick, filmy** — *2. clear, transparent, translucent*
We couldn't see the bottom of the pool through the cloudy water.

club
1. *n.* **organization, group, association**
The tennis club was recruiting members.
2. *n.* **weapon, stick, bat, mallet**
The hunters used clubs to kill their prey.

	3.	*v.*	**hit, strike, whack, pound, beat, batter** The robber clubbed his victim on the head.	**3.** *caress, fondle, pet*
clue		*n.*	**hint, sign, guide** The police searched for clues to help them identify the kidnapper.	*proof, evidence*
clump	1.	*n.*	**cluster, group, batch, bundle** The hunter hid behind a clump of bushes.	
	2.	*n.*	**thump, bump, thud** The clump of heavy footsteps woke her. *v.* The men clumped up the stairs in their boots.	
clumsy		*adj.*	**awkward, ungainly, bungling, bumbling, cumbersome** The clumsy waiter bumped into the table and dropped the plates. *adv.* The skater fell clumsily on the ice.	*coordinated, graceful, dexterous*
clutch		*v.*	**grab, grasp, grip, seize, hold, clench, clasp, squeeze** Luke clutched my hand as we crossed the road.	*relinquish, let go, release, drop*
coach	1.	*n.*	**trainer, instructor, tutor** The coach of the soccer team was well known for discipline.	**1.** *learner, player*
	2.	*v.*	**train, drill, instruct** The quarterback of the football squad coached the junior team.	
coarse	1.	*adj.*	**rough, ragged, harsh** The coarse wool scarf irritated my skin.	**1.** *smooth, fine, polished*
	2.	*adj.*	**crude, vulgar, unrefined** We found his coarse jokes offensive.	**2.** *refined*
coast	1.	*n.*	**shore, seaboard** There are beautiful beaches on the coast of Jamaica.	
	2.	*v.*	**glide, float, drift** The toboggans coasted downhill.	**2.** *steer, direct*
coat	1.	*n.*	**topcoat, overcoat, jacket, cloak** The heavy winter coat kept her warm.	
	2.	*v.*	**cover, wrap, envelop** Oil from the leaking tanker coated the entire beach. *n.* A thick coat of oil covered the beach.	
coax		*v.*	**persuade, urge, cajole** She coaxed her shy friend into coming to the party.	*discourage, dissuade*
coerce		*v.*	**compel, force, make, oblige, drive** Who coerced the suspect into confessing?	

coil		*v.*	**wind, twine, twist, twirl, spiral, curl**	*uncoil, unwind, ravel, loosen, untangle*

coil   *v.*   **wind, twine, twist, twirl, spiral, curl**   *uncoil, unwind, ravel, loosen, untangle*
The vine coiled around the tree.
n. Electric coils heated the garage.

cold   1. *adj.*   **cool, frosty, freezing, chilly**   1. *warm, hot, heated*
It was too cold to go outside.
   2. *adj.*   **reserved, indifferent, unfriendly, aloof, callous**   2. *friendly, amiable, outgoing, extroverted*
Leo had difficulty making friends because of his cold personality.

collapse   *v.*   **topple, cave in, fall down, give way, deflate, buckle, disintegrate**   *rise, lift, build, erect, construct*
The houses collapsed in the hurricane.
n. The collapse of the business left many people without jobs.

colleague   *n.*   **partner, collaborator, co-worker, associate**   *enemy, competitor, antagonist, foe*
They are colleagues at a law firm.

collect   1. *v.*   **assemble, amass, gather, congregate**   1. *disperse, scatter*
Fans collected outside the stage door after the show.
   2. *v.*   **raise, solicit, obtain, secure, glean**   2. *dispense, dispose*
The students collected money for the heart fund.
   3. *v.*   **accumulate, gather, compile, save**   3. *throw away, give away, get rid of*
Do you collect stamps?
n. Colin is an avid stamp collector.
n. He has a fine stamp collection.

collide   1. *v.*   **hit, smash, strike, crash, bump**
Two oil tankers collided in the heavy fog.
n. Slippery conditions caused the collision of cars on the highway.
   2. *v.*   **clash, disagree, oppose, differ**   2. *agree, parallel, resemble*
During the panel discussion, the two politicians collided in their views.
n. Such a heated collision was expected.

colloquial   *adj.*   **informal, popular, everyday**   *formal, conventional*
The teacher told students not to use colloquial expressions in their essays.

color   1. *n.*   **brilliance, brightness, vividness**   1. *dullness, plainness*
Costumes of the various ethnic groups added to the color of the pageant.
adj. Her colorful clothes made her stand out in the crowd.
   2. *n.*   **tint, stain, tone, shade, dye**
The red color of the dye came out in the wash.
v. Victor colored his hair dark brown.
   3. *v.*   **distort, warp, twist, bend, misrepresent, mislead**   3. *state verbatim*
The journalist colored the report with her own prejudices.

colossal		*adj.*	**giant, mammoth, enormous, huge, vast, immense, gigantic, immense** Dinosaurs were colossal creatures.	*minute, tiny, miniature, small*
combat	1.	*n.*	**battle, conflict, struggle, fight, fray, warfare** The troops were engaged in heavy combat.	**1.** *peace, concord, amity*
	2.	*v.*	**battle, fight, struggle, oppose, resist** Medical science combats disease.	**2.** *give up, give in, submit, surrender*
combination		*n.*	**mixture, mix, blend, union** Purple is a combination of red and blue.	*separation, division*
combine		*v.*	**consolidate, merge, unite, join, amalgamate** The scientists combined their efforts in researching a cure for cancer.	*separate, divide, sever*
come	1.	*v.*	**arrive, reach, appear** Our friends came home from Italy today.	**1.** *leave, go, depart*
	2.	*v.*	**approach, draw near, advance** "Come this way," ordered the usher.	**2.** *go, leave, depart, wait, stay*
	3.	*v.*	**reach, stretch, expand to, extend** Her hair comes to her waist.	**3.** *contract, shrink*
	4.	*v.*	**develop, mature, evolve, progress** We hope peace will come out of the talks between the warring nations.	**4.** *regress, remain, stay, continue*
comfort	1.	*v.*	**console, cheer, gladden, reassure** Friends comforted the grieving family. *n.* The friends were a great comfort in their time of sorrow.	**1.** *disturb, depress, dishearten*
	2.	*v.*	**ease, soothe, alleviate, relieve** The doctor prescribed drugs to comfort the patient's pain. *n.* The drugs helped him to sleep in comfort.	**2.** *worsen, intensify*
comfortable	1.	*adj.*	**contented, relaxed, satisfied** Ariel was comfortable sitting by the fire. *adv.* She snuggled comfortably into the big armchair.	**1.** *uneasy, disturbed, ill-at-ease*
	2.	*adj.*	**sufficient, ample, suitable, enough, adequate** The students were given a comfortable period of time to complete their project.	**2.** *insufficient, inadequate, meager*
command	1.	*n.*	**demand, order, direction** Soldiers have to obey the captain's commands.	
	2.	*n.*	**power, control, authority** The general has command over the army.	
	3.	*v.*	**order, charge, direct, instruct, demand** The officer commanded the troops to fire on the enemy.	

commence		*v.*	**begin, start**	end, finish, stop, conclude, complete

commence   *v.*   **begin, start**
The wedding ceremony will commence at two o'clock.
n. Graduation is also called commencement.
end, finish, stop, conclude, complete

comment   *n.*   **remark, opinion, statement**
The critic's mean comments upset the singer.
v. Everyone commented about his bad behavior.

commerce   *n.*   **business, trade, marketing**
New York City is an important center of commerce.
adj. The project is a commercial success.

commit
1. *v.* **perform, do, perpetrate**
A gang committed the chain of robberies.
2. *v.* **entrust, assign, put in safekeeping**   *2. dismiss, discharge, relieve of*
The doctor committed the drug addict to a rehabilitation center.

common
1. *adj.* **ordinary, everyday, commonplace, customary, typical, usual**   *1. unique, rare, novel*
Computers are common in homes today.
2. *adj.* **frequent, usual, familiar, habitual, constant, regular**   *2. irregular, rare, infrequent, occasional*
Floods are common in this town.
3. *adj.* **general, prevalent, well-known, open, accepted, widespread, public**   *3. obscure, limited, restricted*
It is common knowledge that Batman's sidekick is Robin.
4. *adj.* **communal, shared, mutual, joint**   *4. private, personal, individual*
The estate is the common property of the family members.

commotion   *n.*   **uproar, disturbance, confusion, stir**   *order, quiet, calm*
The bat caused a commotion when it flew into the tent.

communicate
1. *v.* **inform, advise, tell, reveal, divulge, disclose, notify, declare**   *1. keep secret, censor, conceal*
The media communicated news of the disaster.
2. *v.* **correspond with, confer, contact, share information**   *2. be out of reach, be removed from, be incommunicado*
They communicate by e-mail daily.
n. They keep in close communication.

community
1. *n.* **likeness, unity, similarity, uniformity**   *1. diversity, difference*
Community of interest helps people to work together.
2. *adj.* **public, joint, cooperative, group**   *2. private, individual*
The arena was built to support community activities.
n. The community worked together to build the arena.

compact	1.	*n.*	**case, container, box**	
			Face powder is carried in a compact.	
	2.	*n.*	**agreement, contract, promise, pact**	
			The two countries signed a defense compact.	
	3.	*adj.*	**close, thick, full, dense, compressed**	**3.** *wide-open, loose*
			Cabbage leaves form a compact head.	
	4.	*adj.*	**small**	**4.** *big, large, roomy*
			A compact car is easy to handle.	
companion		*n.*	**friend, chum, comrade, buddy, pal**	*enemy, foe, stranger, adversary*
			The childhood companions shared memories at their reunion.	
company	1.	*n.*	**business, firm, corporation**	
			She is the president of the company.	
	2.	*n.*	**visitors, guests, callers**	
			We're having company for dinner tonight.	
compare		*v.*	**match, correlate, analyze, examine**	*distinguish, contrast*
			She compared the two brands to see which was the better buy.	
			n. We did a comparison of prices before we made our choice.	
compartment		*n.*	**section, part, portion**	
			We traveled in the first-class compartment of the train.	
compassion		*n.*	**pity, sympathy, consideration, tenderness, understanding, kindness**	*cruelty, indifference, hard-heartedness*
			The plight of the refugees aroused our compassion.	
			adj. The refugees were grateful to their compassionate benefactors.	
compatible		*adj.*	**agreeable, harmonious, amicable**	*incompatible, hostile, adverse, discordant*
			Jeff was glad to find a compatible roommate at college.	
compel		*v.*	**force, coerce, impel, make, urge**	
			Poor weather compelled the travelers to stay for the night.	
compete		*v.*	**contest, vie**	*cooperate, assist, aid*
			The skiers competed for the trophy.	
			n. It was a tough competition.	
			n. The competitors performed well.	
			adj. Everyone was fiercely competitive.	
competent		*adj.*	**capable, able, efficient, skilled**	*incompetent, unable, inefficient, unskilled*
			Jamie is a competent skater.	
compile		*v.*	**gather, collect, accumulate, assemble**	*scatter, disperse*
			Daphne compiled a list of books to read during the holidays.	

complacent	*adj.*	**contented, smug, self-satisfied** Chandra was told to get rid of her complacent attitude and to work hard.	*discontented, dissatisfied, anxious*
complain	*v.*	**grumble, protest, disapprove, grouse, criticize, lament** Customers complained of poor service in the restaurant. *n.* Their complaints resulted in some improvements.	*approve, praise, recommend*
complete	1. *v.*	**finish, conclude, end** Charles completed his homework before dinner.	**1.** *start, begin, commence*
	2. *adj.*	**entire, whole, total, full** There is a complete set of the encyclopedia in the library.	**2.** *partial, deficient, incomplete*
completely	*adv.*	**entirely, fully, totally, utterly, wholly, absolutely, perfectly** We were completely satisfied with the home entertainment center.	*somewhat, partly, partially*
complex	1. *adj.*	**multiple, mixed, composite, compound** The human body needs complex vitamins to remain healthy.	**1.** *single, homogeneous*
	2. *adj.*	**complicated, intricate, involved, confusing** The case proved too complex for the local police.	**2.** *apparent, clear, obvious, simple*
complicated	*adj.*	**intricate, complex, involved, difficult** We had trouble understanding the long, complicated story.	*simple, easy, uncomplicated, uninvolved*
compliment	1. *n.*	**praise, acclaim, approval, congratulations** The producer received many compliments on the excellent movie.	**1.** *abuse, reproof, disapproval, criticism*
	2. *v.*	**praise, commend, congratulate** We complimented Karen on her superb cooking. *adj.* She received many complimentary remarks.	**2.** *disapprove, criticize*
comply	*v.*	**meet, conform, submit, acquiesce** Students have to comply with the school's rules and regulations.	*differ, disagree, disobey, object*
component	1. *n.*	**part, piece, segment, ingredient, section** Television sets are made of many essential components.	**1.** *whole, total, aggregate*
	2. *adj.*	**basic, primary, fundamental, integral, central, main, necessary** The battery is a component part of a flashlight.	**2.** *incidental, superficial, insignificant, unessential*

compose	1.	*v.*	**score, create, originate, form, write, design, invent, fashion, conceive** Kelly composed a song for the school's centennial celebrations. *n.* The composer was congratulated for his fine musical composition.	
	2.	*v.*	**constitute, comprise, blend, make up** Grandma composed a concoction of herbs for my sore throat.	
comprehend		*v.*	**understand, grasp, perceive, discern** We couldn't comprehend the speech. *n.* The speech was beyond anyone's comprehension.	*misunderstand, misinterpret, misconstrue*
compute		*v.*	**calculate, measure, count, reckon** He computed the cost of the supplies.	*guess, speculate*
comrade		*n.*	**chum, friend, companion, associate** Mark and Dan are long time comrades.	*enemy, foe, stranger*
conceal		*v.*	**hide, cover, screen, mask, disguise, camouflage** The loser concealed his disappointment behind a smile.	*reveal, expose, uncover*
concede		*v.*	**yield, grant, admit, allow, acknowledge** They conceded that the best team won the championship.	*deny, refuse*
conceit		*n.*	**vanity, self-admiration, egotism** Ann was full of conceit after winning first prize.	*modesty, humility*
conceited		*adj.*	**arrogant, egotistic, vain** No one likes the conceited actor.	*humble, modest*
concentrate	1.	*v.*	**pay attention, think, focus** Sam was told to concentrate on his work. *n.* He listened to the lecture with deep concentration.	1. *ignore, be inattentive*
	2.	*v.*	**gather, assemble, amass, congregate, accumulate** Protesters concentrated on the campus.	2. *disperse, spread, scatter, separate, disband*
concept		*n.*	**idea, theory, notion** A democratic country believes in the concept of equality for its citizens.	
concerned	1.	*adj.*	**interested, involved, affected** Concerned citizens protested against the proposed dumpsite.	1. *disinterested, unconcerned, indifferent*
	2.	*adj.*	**bothered, upset, distressed, anxious, troubled, worried, agitated, disturbed** We were concerned when the skiers did not return by nightfall.	2. *calm, at ease, unconcerned, undisturbed, placid, unperturbed*

concert	1.	*n.*	**recital, musical performance, show** Min performed at a charity concert.	
	2.	*n.*	**agreement, harmony, concord, accord, unity, union** The nations signed the treaty in concert.	**2.** *disagreement, discord, strife, dispute*
concise		*adj.*	**brief, short, condensed, succinct, terse** He gave a concise report of the meeting.	*long, lengthy, extended, expanded*
conclude	1.	*v.*	**finish, stop, end, terminate, cease** We were glad when the argument concluded peacefully.	**1.** *begin, start, commence*
	2.	*v.*	**arrange, settle, sign** Canada and the United States concluded a trade agreement.	**2.** *discontinue, cease, end, break off*
	3.	*v.*	**reason, deduce, infer, assume, judge** Based on the tests, the doctor concluded that Jan was suffering from lung cancer.	**3.** *doubt, question, wonder*
conclusion	1.	*n.*	**end, finish, completion, termination** At the conclusion of the play, the mystery was still unsolved.	**1.** *beginning, start, introduction, prelude*
	2.	*n.*	**decision, judgment, resolution** After examining the patient, the surgeon reached the conclusion that surgery was not necessary.	
concrete	1.	*n.*	**cement** The sidewalk was paved in concrete.	
	2.	*adj.*	**definite, particular, precise, exact, solid, real, detailed, specific** The witness provided concrete evidence against the accused.	**2.** *inaccurate, obscure, inexact, ambiguous, indecisive*
concur		*v.*	**agree, approve, assent, consent** The judges concurred in their choice of a winner.	*disagree, dispute, disapprove, object*
condemn	1.	*v.*	**find guilty, convict** After studying the evidence, the jury condemned him as a spy.	**1.** *acquit, excuse, pardon, exonerate, forgive*
	2.	*v.*	**doom, sentence** The murderers were condemned to death.	
	3.	*v.*	**denounce, criticize** The media condemned the government for turning away refugees. *n.* A letter of condemnation was sent to the chemical plant for polluting the water.	**3.** *praise, hail, laud, extol*
condense		*v.*	**abridge, abbreviate, summarize, consolidate, compress** Phil condensed his novel for publication in a magazine.	*lengthen, extend, expand, stretch*
condition	1.	*n.*	**shape, state** The old car is in excellent condition.	

2. *n.* **requirement, stipulation, specification**
The main condition for the sale is that the buyer must pay cash.

3. *v.* **accustom, train**
Astronauts are conditioned for weightlessness in space.

conduct

1. *n.* **behavior, actions, demeanor**
He was thrown out of the concert for disorderly conduct.

2. *v.* **behave, act**
She conducted herself with dignity throughout the ordeal.

3. *v.* **direct, guide, lead, manage**
Sylvia conducted the visitors on a tour of the city.
n. She works as a tour conductor.

3. *follow*

4. *v.* **carry, send, transmit, convey, transfer, disseminate**
Those pipes conduct heat throughout the building.

confess

v. **admit, concede, acknowledge, own up, disclose, divulge**
He confessed that he had cheated in the examination.
n. He made his confession to his teacher.

withhold, hide, conceal

confide

v. **reveal, tell, admit, disclose, divulge**
She confided her problems to her parents.

conceal, keep secret, hide

confidence

1. *n.* **trust, faith**
I have full confidence in my doctor.

1. *distrust*

2. *n.* **assurance, security**
The captain's air of confidence inspires his teammates.

2. *fear, nervousness, insecurity*

confident

1. *adj.* **positive, sure, certain, convinced**
I am confident I will succeed.

1. *doubtful, uncertain*

2. *adj.* **self-assured, assertive, fearless, bold**
The two most confident students were selected for the debating team.
adv. They argued confidently and won the debate.

2. *insecure, timid, unsure*

confidential

adj. **secret, private, classified, privy, personal**
The teacher wrote a confidential report on the graduating students.

public, open

configuration

n. **pattern, shape, outline, form, contour**
Astronomers study the different configurations of stars in the universe.

confine

1. *v.* **hold back, restrain, limit**
Let's confine this meeting to urgent matters only.

1. *release, let out, let loose*

	2.	*v.*	**imprison, cage, shut up, incarcerate** The sheriff confined the robber in a cell.	**2.** *release, set free, liberate*
confirm		*v.*	**approve, endorse, ratify, affirm, sanction, validate** The airline confirmed our reservation on the flight to Washington. *n.* Martine phoned for a confirmation of her appointment.	*cancel, veto, refuse, revoke, rescind*
confiscate		*v.*	**impound, usurp, seize, appropriate, secure, take, commandeer** The customs officer confiscated the illegal merchandise.	*return, restore, compensate*
conflict	**1.**	*n.*	**fight, struggle, strife, battle, encounter, clash, contest** We hope that the conflict will not develop into a major war.	**1.** *peace, concord, collaboration*
	2.	*n.*	**hostility, dispute, disagreement, dissension, antagonism** Their differing ideas created conflict between the two friends. *v.* His ideas conflicted with Kay's.	**2.** *concurrence, agreement, cooperation*
conflicting		*adj.*	**contrary, opposing, contradictory, clashing** The leaders held conflicting views about trade regulations.	*like, compatible, similar, parallel*
conform		*v.*	**comply, adapt, follow, obey** Citizens must conform to the laws of the country. *n.* Conformity to the law is expected of citizens. *n.* A person who follows the rules is a conformist.	*conflict, disagree, differ*
confound		*v.*	**confuse, bewilder, perplex, puzzle** The maze confounded the children, and they couldn't find their way out.	*simplify, clarify, explain, clear, untangle, enlighten*
confront		*v.*	**face, resist, oppose** The neighbors confronted each other over the fence. *n.* It was a nasty confrontation.	*comply, agree, evade*
confuse	**1.**	*v.*	**muddle, bewilder, puzzle, fluster, jumble, unsettle, agitate, confound** We were confused by the conflicting reports of the witnesses.	**1.** *clarify, untangle, simplify, enlighten, explain*
	2.	*v.*	**mistake, mix up** People often confuse Michelle with her twin sister Lisa.	**2.** *distinguish, tell apart, discriminate*
confusion	**1.**	*n.*	**disorder, disarray** It took months to sort out the confusion at our new home.	**1.** *order*

	2.	*n.*	**bewilderment, commotion, agitation** The crowd was thrown into confusion when the fire alarm sounded.	**2.** *quiet, calm, order*
congenial		*adj.*	**agreeable, compatible, sympathetic, pleasant, harmonious** Congenial classmates help make school enjoyable.	*disagreeable, incompatible, unsympathetic, unpleasant*
congratulate		*v.*	**compliment, rejoice with, wish well** The mayor congratulated the winner. *n.* Congratulations poured in from all over the world.	*rebuke, criticize*
congregate		*v.*	**convene, meet, converge, gather, collect, assemble** Fans congregated outside the hotel waiting for the star to appear.	*disperse, disband, separate, scatter, break up*
connect	**1.**	*v.*	**unite, attach, join, combine, link, fasten** The electrician connected the wires. *n.* The telephone connection was so poor that I could hardly hear.	**1.** *disconnect, unfasten, untie*
	2.	*v.*	**associate, relate, link** Marriage connects the two families. *n.* His connection with the Smith family helped him get the job.	**2.** *disassociate, shun*
conquer	**1.**	*v.*	**subdue, defeat, vanquish, crush, win, triumph, prevail** Alexander the Great conquered many parts of the world. *n.* He was a remarkable conqueror. *n.* His conquests are recorded in all the history books.	**1.** *lose, retreat, yield*
	2.	*v.*	**overcome, master** Mary conquered her fear of water and learned to swim.	**2.** *yield, give in to, submit*
conscious	**1.**	*adj.*	**awake, alert** Carolyn was conscious soon after the operation. *n.* She regained consciousness quickly.	**1.** *unconscious, insensible*
	2.	*adj.*	**informed, aware, discerning, cognizant** Derek made a conscious decision to return to school.	**2.** *uninformed, unaware*
consensus		*n.*	**agreement, accord, consent** The decision was reached by a consensus of the board of governors.	*disagreement, discord*
consent	**1.**	*n.*	**assent, approval, permission, agreement** We had to get our parents' consent to go on the school trip.	**1.** *refusal, dissent, disagreement, denial*

	2.	*v.*	**allow, approve, agree, concur, comply, accede, permit** The judge consented to the accused person's request for bail.	**2.** *reject, deny, decline, negate, refuse, disagree, disapprove*
consequence	**1.**	*n.*	**outcome, end, result, product, effect** People are responsible for the consequences of their actions.	**1.** *cause, origin, beginning, source*
	2.	*n.*	**importance, significance** Stem cell research is of great consequence to humanity.	**2.** *insignificance, triviality, paltriness, unimportance*
conservation		*n.*	**protection, preservation, maintenance** We are concerned with the conservation of the nation's natural resources.	*destruction, waste, misuse, consumption, dissolution*
conservative		*adj.*	**moderate, careful, cautious** She is a conservative investor who does not take risks.	*changing, risky, radical*
conserve		*v.*	**store, save up, reserve, accumulate** During the drought the people were told to conserve water.	*waste, use, use up, empty, squander, spend, consume*
consider		*v.*	**think about, ponder, contemplate, deliberate, reflect on, examine** Have you considered which university you're going to? *n.* He gave the issue a lot of consideration.	*ignore, reject, disregard, deny, refuse*
considerable	**1.**	*adj.*	**important, noteworthy, significant** The mayor has considerable influence on the council's decision.	**1.** *insignificant*
	2.	*adj.*	**ample, bountiful, much, abundant, plentiful, substantial** The United States is blessed with considerable natural resources.	**2.** *small, scant, insufficient, meager, insubstantial*
	3.	*adj.*	**huge, great, big** The university received a considerable donation from an alumni.	**3.** *puny, small, trivial*
considerate		*adj.*	**thoughtful, kind, solicitous, caring** Carlo is always considerate of his parents.	*inconsiderate, neglectful, indifferent*
consist		*v.*	**comprise, include** The human body consists of millions of cells.	*exclude*
consistent	**1.**	*adj.*	**uniform, regular, constant** Will has been a consistent part of her life for the last ten years. *adv.* They have been seeing each other consistently for ten years.	**1.** *inconsistent, divergent*
	2.	*adj.*	**compatible, matching, conforming, congruous** His recovery is consistent with the doctor's expectations.	**2.** *incongruous, discrepant, incompatible*

console		*v.*	**comfort, solace, encourage**	*trouble, hurt, distress*

console   *v.*   **comfort, solace, encourage**   *trouble, hurt, distress*
Claude consoled his sister after her cat disappeared.
n. She was beyond consolation when her cat was lost.

consolidate
1. *v.* **combine, unite, condense, compress**   1. *scatter, cut, sever, separate, divide*
The two small publishing houses consolidated into one.
n. The consolidation resulted in a large, profitable organization.
2. *v.* **fortify, strengthen, build up, increase**   2. *weaken, cripple, tear down*
The merger of the companies consolidated their financial position.

conspicuous
1. *adj.* **notable, prominent, eminent, obvious, renowned, outstanding, illustrious**   1. *unimportant, unknown*
She played a conspicuous role in the country's fight for independence.
2. *adj.* **noticeable, visible, evident, obvious**   2. *hidden, inconspicuous, invisible*
The movie star's shimmering gold outfit was conspicuous at the reception.

conspire   *v.*   **plot, scheme, contrive**
The army conspired to overthrow the government.
n. It was a well-planned conspiracy.

constant
1. *adj.* **steady, uniform, continual, non-stop, perpetual, incessant, lasting**   1. *interrupted, intermittent, periodic, occasional, sporadic*
Planets move around the sun in a constant motion.
adv. Planets rotate constantly around the sun.
2. *adj.* **faithful, devoted, loyal, steadfast, firm, staunch, abiding, dependable**   2. *unreliable, inconsistent, uncertain*
Swee and Subash have been constant companions for years.

constraint
1. *n.* **force, pressure, compulsion, coercion**   1. *free will*
The accused confessed under constraint.
2. *n.* **reserve, bashfulness, timidity, restraint**   2. *bravado*
The winner smiled with constraint when she received the award.
3. *n.* **captivity, detention, confinement**   3. *freedom, liberty*
The men held the thief in constraint till the police arrived.

construct   *v.*   **build, erect, make, compose**   *dismantle, tear down, take apart*
They constructed a bridge over the river.
n. The construction of the bridge took a whole year.

consume
1. *v.* **destroy, exhaust, waste, demolish**   1. *preserve, save, protect*
The building was consumed by fire.

	2.	*v.*	**use up, utilize, spend** Dad's big old car consumes a lot of gas. *n.* The car's gas consumption is high.	**2.** *hoard, collect, gather, accumulate*
	3.	*v.*	**eat, drink, swallow, devour** The children consumed all the cake.	**3.** *fast*
	4.	*v.*	**take up, wrap up, engross** Golf consumes all her spare time. *adj.* She has a consuming passion for golf.	**4.** *waste*
consumer		*n.*	**user, buyer, customer, purchaser** North Americans are big consumers of processed foods.	*salesperson, vendor, dealer*
contact	1.	*n.*	**touch, connection, meeting, junction** Electric wires must be in contact to complete a circuit.	**1.** *distance, separation*
	2.	*v.*	**communicate, talk to, reach** Mission Control contacted the astronauts in the spacecraft. *n.* They have had no contact with their former neighbors for years.	
contagious		*adj.*	**infectious, transferable, catching, transmissible, communicable** Measles is a contagious disease, hence patients are usually kept in isolation.	*non-communicable, non-contagious*
contain	1.	*v.*	**hold, include, comprise, consist of** The parcel contained food for the poor. *n.* A vase is a container for flowers.	**1.** *exclude, preclude, be void of*
	2.	*v.*	**restrain, restrict, hold, keep back, stop, check** Don couldn't contain his excitement when he heard the news.	**2.** *release, let go, relinquish*
contaminate		*v.*	**pollute, infect, dirty, soil, sully** Factory wastes can contaminate lakes and rivers. *n.* Bacteria can cause contamination of the water supply. *adj.* The villagers fell ill after drinking contaminated water.	*purify, cleanse, clean, clarify, refine, filter*
contemporary	1.	*n.*	**peer, counterpart, equal** Winston Churchill and Franklin Roosevelt were contemporaries.	
	2.	*adj.*	**current, present, modern** Chico bought contemporary furniture for his new apartment.	**2.** *old-fashioned, dated, obsolete, antiquated*
	3.	*adj.*	**simultaneous, co-existent** Pollution and nuclear warfare are contemporary social issues.	
contempt	1.	*n.*	**scorn, disdain, derision, malice** He was charged with contempt of the law.	**1.** *respect, esteem, honor, admiration*
	2.	*n.*	**shame, dishonor, disgrace** The people showed their contempt for the traitor.	**2.** *praise, honor*

content	*adj.*	**satisfied, pleased, happy, gratified** Manny is content with his new home. *v.* He contented himself with a small house. *n.* He lives a life of contentment.	*discontented, unhappy, displeased, dissatisfied*
content	*n.*	**ingredient, part, substance, element, component, constituent** Ice cream has a high content of fat.	
contest	1. *n.*	**competition, match, challenge** Rick took part in a writing contest.	
	2. *n.*	**battle, fight, feud, dispute, conflict** There was a nasty legal contest for the custody of the children. *n.* They were both tough contestants.	
	3. *v.*	**argue, debate, question, oppose** They contested their grandmother's will in court.	**3.** *defend, uphold, agree with, accept*
context	*n.*	**text, meaning, substance** There was a misunderstanding because he was quoted out of context.	
continual	1. *adj.*	**constant, uninterrupted, unbroken, regular, unremitting** Because of an infection, Jo heard a continual ringing in her ears.	**1.** *interrupted, broken, irregular, sporadic*
	2. *adj.*	**ceaseless, lasting, unending, eternal, perpetual, endless, permanent** John F. Kennedy's grave is marked with a continual flame. *adv.* The flame burns continually.	**2.** *fleeting, brief, short, transitory, passing, momentary, temporary*
continue	1. *v.*	**stay, linger, remain** The show continued all week.	**1.** *leave, go, depart*
	2. *v.*	**resume, recommence, renew** After lunch, the students continued their discussion.	**2.** *discontinue, postpone, stop, halt*
	3. *v.*	**persist, persevere, keep on, progress, press onward** Terry Fox continued on his run despite the pain he suffered.	**3.** *end, give up, cease*
contract	1. *n.*	**agreement, pact** The bride and groom signed the marriage contract.	
	2. *v.*	**shrink, decrease, constrict, reduce** Metal contracts in the cold.	**2.** *stretch, expand, enlarge*
contradict	1. *v.*	**refute, deny, disclaim** The defendant contradicted the charge made against him.	**1.** *admit, accept, affirm*
	2. *v.*	**oppose, confront, defy** The witnesses contradicted each other. *n.* One witness's story was a complete contradiction of the other's.	**2.** *back up, side with*

contribute	*v.*	**give, subscribe, donate, bestow** They contribute time and money to charity. *n.* They made a generous contribution to the hospital fund.	*receive, accept*
contrite	*adj.*	**repentant, regretful, sorry** The contrite boy promised never to steal again.	*unrepentant*
controversial	*adj.*	**debatable, contentious, disputable, questionable** Capital punishment is a controversial issue.	*incontestable, indisputable*
controversy	*n.*	**dispute, debate, argument, dissension, altercation** The controversy over capital punishment is widely debated.	*agreement, accord*
convene	*v.*	**assemble, meet, gather, collect, congregate, convoke** The council convened at eight o'clock. *n.* Delegates voted at the convention.	*disperse, scatter, break up, dissolve*
convenient	1. *adj.*	**advantageous, ready, useful, timesaving, labor-saving, available** Frozen dinners are convenient for those who work. *n.* They are a real convenience.	1. *unserviceable, disadvantageous*
	2. *adj.*	**near, handy, easy to reach, accessible** Neighborhood stores are convenient places to shop.	2. *far, distant, inaccessible*
conventional	1. *adj.*	**customary, regular, standard, typical, usual, prevailing, common** The bride wore a conventional white gown.	1. *unusual, unpopular, atypical*
	2. *adj.*	**correct, right, established, sanctioned** The conventional curtsy was given to the queen.	2. *unconventional, unorthodox*
converse	*v.*	**talk, chat, speak, discuss** Laurie conversed in French with the storekeeper. *n.* They had a long conversation.	
convert	*v.*	**change, alter, transform, revise** They converted the house into an office. *n.* The conversion took two years to complete.	
convey	1. *v.*	**transport, send, carry, move, dispatch** Trucks conveyed the new cars to the port.	1. *keep, preserve, retain*
	2. *v.*	**transmit, conduct, communicate** Please convey my regards to your Dad.	
convict	1. *n.*	**prisoner, captive, criminal, felon** The convict was captured in the swamp.	1. *free person*

	2.	*v.*	**find guilty, sentence** The jury convicted the defendant. *n.* The conviction will be appealed.	*2. acquit, liberate, find not guilty, clear, exonerate*

conviction		*n.*	**belief, view, persuasion** She had strong convictions on the issue of cloning.	*doubt, uncertainty, misgiving*
convince		*v.*	**persuade, assure, prove to** The suspect convinced the police that she had been wrongfully arrested. *adj.* She had convincing evidence of her innocence.	*dissuade*
cool	1.	*v.*	**get cold, lose heat** Jim let the soup cool before eating it.	*1. heat, thaw, warm*
	2.	*adj.*	**chilly, nippy** Cool breezes caused the group to go indoors.	*2. warm, hot, tepid, heated*
	3.	*adj.*	**unruffled, calm, composed, deliberate** Astronauts are trained to remain cool under stress.	*3. ruffled, anxious, rash, excitable, wild*
	4.	*adj.*	**fashionable, sensational** Kerry bought a cool outfit for the dance.	
cooperate		*v.*	**collaborate, work together** Schools cooperate with businesses to train students for the workplace. *n.* They work in cooperation. *adj.* This cooperative venture benefits everyone.	*act independently, oppose, rival, thwart, counteract*
cope		*v.*	**endure, contend, tolerate, face, put up with, live through, suffer** He had to cope with a series of tragedies.	*avoid, resist, elude, evade*
copy	1.	*n.*	**facsimile, simulation, replica, duplicate, reproduction** Give Ali a copy of this letter.	*1. original*
	2.	*v.*	**duplicate, reproduce, reprint, transcribe, scan, photostat** She copied my notes on the photocopier.	*2. originate, invent, introduce, print*
	3.	*v.*	**imitate, match, mirror, repeat, follow, emulate, mimic, ape** Children often copy the behavior of adults.	*3. originate, create, invent*
cord		*n.*	**string, rope, twine** The package was tied with cord.	
cordial		*adj.*	**warm, friendly, genial, affable, amicable** The speaker received a cordial welcome.	*cold, distant, aloof, discourteous*
core		*n.*	**essence, heart, kernel, nucleus, hub, gist, focus, center** Acid rain is at the core of the pollution problem.	*edge, exterior, periphery*

correct 1. *v.* **repair, improve, rectify, amend**
Sheena had to correct the mistakes she had made in the test.
n. She had to make many corrections.

2. *adj.* **true, accurate, right, exact, precise, perfect**
The first response given was correct.

3. *adj.* **fitting, proper, appropriate, suitable**
Is there a correct way to address the head of state?

1. *err, mistake*

2. *inaccurate, wrong, incorrect, imprecise, false*

3. *inappropriate, unsuitable, improper*

correspond 1. *v.* **match, harmonize, resemble**
The driver's account of the accident corresponds with that of a witness.

2. *v.* **communicate with, write to, exchange letters**
She corresponded regularly with her pen pal.
n. Their correspondence lasted many years.

1. *vary, differ, clash*

corrode *v.* **destroy, erode, deteriorate, decay, degenerate, eat away, consume**
Acid corrodes metal.
n. How can such corrosion be prevented?

build, construct, establish

corrupt 1. *v.* **taint, make immoral**
Bad company corrupts many people.

2. *adj.* **evil, wicked, immoral, dishonest**
The corrupt dictator was finally overthrown.
n. The overthrow of the dictator ended years of corruption in the country.

1. *improve, ennoble, purify*

2. *good, moral, honest, upright*

cosmetic *adj.* **restorative, corrective, beautifying**
He required cosmetic surgery to remove the scars caused by the fire.

cost 1. *n.* **price, charge, worth, expense, value**
The cost of houses is too high for many people.

2. *n.* **damage, hurt, detriment**
The nation won the battle at a great cost in lives.

costly *adj.* **expensive, dear, high-priced, valuable, precious**
Diamonds are costly gems.

cheap, inexpensive, low-priced, worthless, reasonable

costume *n.* **suit, outfit, dress, apparel, clothes, garb**
The guests wore national costumes for the event.

council *n.* **assembly, gathering, bureau, cabinet, committee, board**
Who will be the head of the students' council?
n. Sean is one of the student councillors.

counsel

1. *n.* **advice, suggestion, recommendation, guidance**
Lawyers provide counsel.
2. *v.* **advise, guide, suggest**
The guidance teacher counseled the students.
n. Teachers often act as counselors for the students.

count

1. *v.* **figure, calculate, tally, score, compute, add up, total, enumerate**
The cashier counted the change.
n. What was the final count?
2. *v.* **depend, rely, trust**
Aisha counted on her family for help.

1. *estimate, guess*

counterfeit

adj. **artificial, false, forged, bogus, fraudulent, invalid, fictitious**
They were arrested for trying to shop with counterfeit money.

real, genuine, authentic, valid

countless

adj. **incalculable, innumerable, myriad, uncountable, limitless**
Countless mosquitoes attacked us.

few, several, some

couple

1. *n.* **pair, twosome, set**
Matt and Min make a handsome couple.
2. *v.* **tie, join, link, unite, pair, connect**
A hitch coupled the trailer to the van.

1. *single, one, individual, separate*
2. *separate, detach, untie, disconnect*

courage

n. **bravery, spirit, nerve, valor, mettle, fearlessness, audacity, gallantry**
She was awarded a medal for her courage in rescuing the child.
adj. The courageous woman plunged into the river to save the child.

fear, cowardice, timidity

course

n. **route, path, circuit, direction**
They charted a course of action for the campaign.

courtesy

n. **politeness, respect, manners**
Senior citizens should be accorded courtesy.
adj. The courteous boy gave up his seat to the elderly man.

rudeness, disrespect

cover

1. *n.* **lid, top, covering, cap, seal**
Put the cover on the paint pot to prevent the paint from hardening.
2. *v.* **conceal, hide, screen, mask, disguise, camouflage**
The bird covered its nest with leaves.
3. *v.* **wrap, enclose, encase, envelop**
Cover the turkey with foil before roasting it.

2. *reveal, open, uncover, disclose*
3. *unwrap, uncover*

4. *v.* **cross, travel, journey, traverse**
The runner covered the distance in record time.

5. *v.* **report upon, recount, broadcast**
Megan was assigned by the newspaper to cover the Olympic Games.

cowardly *adj.* **fearful, timid, cowering**
The cowardly person ignored the victim's cries for help.
adv. He shut his ears and slunk away cowardly.

courageous, brave, bold, fearless

cozy *adj.* **snug, comfortable, warm**
Amy snuggled into her cozy bed.

uncomfortable, unpleasant

crack 1. *n.* **opening, slit, break, chink, cut**
The earthquake caused cracks to appear in many buildings.

2. *n.* **snap, crackle, stroke**
Circus lions respond to the crack of the trainer's whip.

3. *v.* **split, open, splinter, burst, break, snap, cleave**
The stone cracked the car's windshield.
adj. The cracked windshield had to be replaced.

3. join, attach, connect, link, tie, bind, mend

crafty *adj.* **wily, foxy, sly, cunning, tricky, astute, shrewd**
The crafty fox waited in the bushes for the lamb.

direct, honest, straightforward

cram 1. *v.* **stuff, jam, pack, fill**
I crammed my suitcase with clothes.

1. empty, remove

2. *v.* **gorge, satiate**
The children crammed themselves with ice cream and cake at the party.

2. disgorge

3. *v.* **study hurriedly**
Glenn crammed for the test all night.

cramp *n.* **spasm, kink, stitch, crick**
The swimmer got a cramp in his leg and had to get out of the pool.

cramped *adj.* **confined, restricted, tight**
We work in a cramped office.

cranky *adj.* **cross, disagreeable, irritable, peevish, grouchy, cantankerous, grumpy**
Some folks get cranky when they are tired.

good-natured, pleasant, calm, agreeable

crash 1. *n.* **clatter, clash, din, noise**
We were awakened by the loud crash.

2. *n.* **collision, impact, smash**
Plane crashes are more common in bad weather.
v. The cars crashed on the slippery road.

	3.	*v.*	**fail, break** I lost the file I was working on when my computer crashed.	
crave		*v.*	**need, want, desire, covet, long for, yearn, hanker** The lonely child craved attention.	*loathe, be revolted by*
crawl	1.	*v.*	**creep, wriggle, worm** The spider crawled up the wall.	
	2.	*v.*	**plod, drag, creep** The traffic crawled along in rush hour. *n.* Traffic was reduced to a crawl in rush hour.	**2.** *progress, advance*
craze		*n.*	**fad, rage, trend, novelty** What is the latest teenage craze?	
crazy	1.	*adj.*	**mad, insane, demented, lunatic** The crazy man was institutionalized.	**1.** *sane*
	2.	*adj.*	**ridiculous, senseless, foolish** You will lose money if you invest in that crazy scheme.	**2.** *sensible*
create	1.	*v.*	**make, originate, invent, design, devise, conceive, formulate, compose, produce** Michelangelo created great works of art. *n.* The Statue of Liberty is an inspiring creation. *adj.* Artists are creative individuals.	**1.** *end, destroy, finish, wipe out, exterminate, nullify, demolish, dismantle*
	2.	*v.*	**cause, produce** The scientists created a stir with the announcement of their discovery.	**2.** *prevent, impede*
credit	1.	*n.*	**belief, faith, credence, confidence** The teacher gave little credit to Jon's excuse for not completing his homework.	**1.** *disbelief, doubt, suspicion*
	2.	*n.*	**hire purchase, installment buying** She couldn't afford the television, so she bought it on credit.	**2.** *cash*
	3.	*n.*	**recognition, honor, praise** The credit for the success of the team belongs to the coach. *v.* The press credited the coach for his excellent training.	**3.** *blame, dishonor, criticism*
	4.	*v.*	**believe, rely on, trust, acknowledge** It was difficult to credit the journalist's story as there was a lack of evidence.	**4.** *doubt, deny, suspect*
credulous		*adj.*	**gullible, naive, trusting, innocent, unsophisticated, simple** The credulous man paid $500 for a stone with "magic powers!"	*experienced, sophisticated, suspicious*
crest	1.	*n.*	**top, crown, pinnacle, summit, peak** We climbed to the crest of the hill.	**1.** *bottom, base, foot*

2. *n.* **emblem, coat of arms**
The school's crest is sewn on the blazer pocket.

crevice *n.* **chasm, cleft, gap, fissure**
The mountaineer slipped and plunged into the crevice.

crew *n.* **team, squad, group, company**
The crew underwent rigorous training before the flight.

crime *n.* **felony, offense, misdemeanor, wrongdoing, misdeed, illegality**   *legality*
The accused was found guilty of committing the crime of kidnapping.
adj. The crime rate has risen alarmingly in the city.

criminal 1. *n.* **lawbreaker, felon, culprit, offender**
Criminals often serve time in prison.
2. *adj.* **unlawful, illegal, felonious**   2. *lawful, legal*
Robbery is a criminal offense.

cripple *v.* **hurt, injure, disable, enfeeble, incapacitate**   *strengthen, energize, invigorate, stimulate*
A power failure crippled the town.
adj. The Red Cross sent aid to the people in the crippled town.

crisp 1. *adj.* **firm, fresh, stiff**   1. *limp, soft, pliant*
Crisp lettuce is needed in salads.
2. *adj.* **brisk, bracing, invigorating, fresh**   2. *dull, boring, tedious*
stimulating, refreshing, exhilarating
The crisp morning air refreshed us.
3. *adj.* **terse, abrupt, short, brief**   3. *verbose, lengthy, loquacious*
The government issued a crisp statement about the crisis.

critical 1. *adj.* **disapproving, fault-finding, negative**   1. *endorsing, supportive, positive*
Elle received a highly critical report of her work from her boss.
2. *adj.* **crucial, life-threatening, dangerous**   2. *stable*
The patient was in a critical condition after the operation.
3. *adj.* **vital, crucial, important**   3. *unimportant, irrelevant*
Your support has been critical to the success of this project.

criticize 1. *v.* **reprove, censure, reprimand, reproach, find fault with**   1. *praise, approve, endorse, support*
Neighbors criticized the teenagers for their rowdy behavior.
n. Most people do not like criticism.
2. *v.* **analyze, review, evaluate, study, probe, scrutinize, examine**
The newspaper reviewer criticized the new ballet.

n. The critics were full of praise for the new play.

crooked	1.	*adj.*	**winding, curved, bent, askew, zigzag** Let's take the crooked path into the park.	1. *straight, direct*
	2.	*adj.*	**dishonest, criminal, corrupt, illegal, unlawful** The public must be protected from crooked dealers.	2. *honest, legal, straightforward, trustworthy*
crop	1.	*n.*	**harvest, yield, product** Excellent weather results in large farm crops.	
	2.	*v.*	**cut, trim, shorten** The photographer cropped the border of the photo.	2. *enlarge, extend, increase*
cross	1.	*n.*	**hybrid, mixture, crossbreed** The puppy is a cross between a spaniel and a terrier.	1. *purebred, pedigree, thoroughbred*
	2.	*n.*	**affliction, obstacle, misfortune, trial, hardship** That disease is an awful cross to bear!	2. *blessing, benefit, advantage*
	3.	*v.*	**sail, navigate, travel, traverse** Vikings crossed the Atlantic Ocean.	
	4.	*v.*	**intersect** The town is situated where two major roads cross.	4. *parallel*
	5.	*adj.*	**annoyed, angry** Lian was cross with Bill for being late.	5. *even-tempered, pleasant, calm*
crouch	1.	*v.*	**squat, bend, stoop** The runners crouched at the starting line of the race.	1. *stretch, stand up*
	2.	*v.*	**cower, cringe, grovel** The prisoners crouched in terror.	2. *spurn, scorn, disdain*
crowd	1.	*n.*	**mob, throng, swarm, mass, multitude, horde** Police were called to control the crowd outside the stadium.	1. *solitary person, no one*
	2.	*v.*	**shove, push, cram, squeeze, stuff, jam** During rush hour, people crowded into the subway car.	
crown	1.	*n.*	**coronet, tiara, diadem** The queen wore a magnificent crown during her coronation.	
	2.	*n.*	**top, crest, apex, pinnacle, summit** The hikers reached the crown of the hill.	2. *bottom, base, foot*
	3.	*v.*	**adorn, make complete, make perfect** The baker crowned the wedding cake with roses.	
crowning		*adj.*	**supreme, highest, ultimate, chief, paramount, principal, main, best** Beautiful hair is her crowning glory.	*secondary, worst, poorest, lowest*

crucial		*adj.*	**critical, significant, urgent, important** Choosing the right university is a crucial decision for most young people.	*insignificant, unimportant, inconsequential*
crude	1.	*adj.*	**rough, rudimentary** The campers built a crude shelter with twigs and blankets.	**1.** *sophisticated, refined*
	2.	*adj.*	**raw, natural, unprocessed** Crude oil is processed in refineries.	**2.** *manufactured, processed*
	3.	*adj.*	**uncouth, vulgar, coarse, rude** We were offended by his crude manners.	**3.** *polite, refined*
	4.	*adj.*	**clumsy, ungainly, awkward** The boxer's crude footwork cost him the match.	**4.** *smooth, graceful, dexterous*
cruel	1.	*adj.*	**brutal, painful, distressing** He lost his fortune by a cruel twist of fate.	**1.** *pleasing, beneficial*
	2.	*adj.*	**pitiless, callous, merciless, ruthless** The enemy attacked with cruel determination.	**2.** *merciful, compassionate, humane, forgiving*
cruise		*n.*	**voyage, sail, trip** A cruise is a relaxing way to spend a vacation. *v.* The family cruised in the Caribbean last winter.	
crumble		*v.*	**break up, disintegrate, decay** Buildings crumbled during the earthquake.	*build, put together, unite, combine*
crunch		*v.*	**bite, chew, munch, gnaw** The children crunched happily on the candy. *adj.* They enjoy crunchy peanuts.	
crush	1.	*v.*	**squash, smash, pulverize** The machine crushed the stones into gravel.	
	2.	*v.*	**defeat, beat, overwhelm, annihilate** The army crushed the rebellion.	**2.** *yield, give up, concede, relinquish*
crust		*n.*	**shell, casing, surface, coating** Everyone loves Dan's crispy pie crusts.	*interior, center, inside*
cry	1.	*n.*	**shout, call, yell** We were alarmed when we heard a cry in the dark. *v.* The accident victim cried for help.	**1.** *whisper, murmur, silence*
	2.	*v.*	**mourn, weep, sob** The movie was so sad that everyone in the audience cried.	**2.** *laugh, rejoice, exult, innocent*
culprit		*n.*	**offender, felon, criminal, wrongdoer** The police identified the culprit responsible for the thefts.	

cultivate	1.	*v.*	**dig, plow, make grow, garden, till, farm, plant, sow** Homesteaders cultivated the land.	*1. reap, destroy, neglect, abandon*
	2.	*v.*	**encourage, promote, assist, advance, further, help, bolster, foster, support** Mom cultivated our interest in music by taking us to many concerts.	*2. discourage, stifle, impede, retard, weaken, hinder*
cunning		*adj.*	**clever, sly, crafty, wily, shrewd** Todd was not taken in by the cunning salesperson.	*stupid, foolish, simple, direct, straightforward*
curb	1.	*n.*	**guard, protection, restraint, barrier, check** Leashes act as curbs on pets.	
	2.	*n.*	**edge, border, rim, ledge** People sat on the curbs of the sidewalks to watch the parade.	*2. interior, center*
	3.	*v.*	**restrain, hold, check, restrict, retard, impede, subdue** She has learned to curb her hot temper.	*3. release, let go, free, liberate, express*
cure	1.	*n.*	**remedy, correction, medicine** Scientists are still trying to find a cure for cancer.	*1. cause, origin, reason, source*
	2.	*v.*	**restore, heal, make healthy** The new drug cured his illness.	*2. infect, contaminate*
	3.	*v.*	**preserve, salt, pickle** People cured meat and fish before the refrigerator was invented.	
curious	1.	*adj.*	**inquiring, eager, searching, inquisitive, interested** Curious children ask many questions. *n.* Children have a natural curiosity about everything.	*1. indifferent, uninterested*
	2.	*adj.*	**strange, odd, queer, unique, unusual, rare, exceptional** It is curious that no one has heard from Ben in a year.	*2. normal, common, usual*
curl		*v.*	**twist, bend, coil, roll up, curve, crimp, wave** Tracie curled her hair into ringlets.	*straighten*
current		*adj.*	**contemporary, prevailing, up-to-date** Moshe writes a current affairs column for the newspaper.	*out-of-date, dated, obsolete, antiquated*
currently		*adv.*	**presently, now** This recording is currently at the top of the list.	*yesterday, before, previously*
curt		*adj.*	**brief, short, concise, terse, abrupt** Paul returned her wave with a curt nod of the head.	*lengthy, wordy, verbose, detailed*

curtail	v.	shorten, lessen, cramp, decrease, clip, abbreviate, reduce, abridge Harry had to curtail his spending in order to save for college.	lengthen, increase, extend, add, expand
custom	n.	fashion, practice, manner, habit, routine It is our custom to sing the national anthem at the start of an event.	irregularity, oddity
customary	adj.	conventional, usual, routine, habitual, common, regular It is customary in North America to shake hands when you meet.	irregular, unusual, uncommon, rare, odd
customer	n.	purchaser, buyer, client, consumer, patron, shopper Many stores believe in the policy that the customer is always right.	seller, dealer, retailer, vendor, merchant, marketer
cut	1. n.	gash, groove, slit, slash, puncture, incision, gouge, opening, penetration Jay got a nasty cut on his head when he fell off his bicycle. v. He cut himself badly in the fall.	1. closure
	2. n.	piece, slice, chunk Sirloin steak is an expensive cut of beef.	
	3. n.	segment, slice, portion, part, section That cut from the movie is a classic.	3. whole, entirety
	4. n.	shape, form, construction Designer gowns are known for their excellent cut.	
	5. n.	reduction, decrease The government announced a cut in taxes just before the election. v. The company closed two branches to cut costs.	5. increase, inflation, expansion
	6. n.	insult, indignity, abuse, offense His thoughtless remark was a cut to me! v. His remarks cut me to the quick.	6. tribute, praise, courtesy
	7. v.	clip, snip, trim Francesco cuts my hair. n. He always gives me a good haircut.	7. grow
	8. v.	record, tape The singer recently cut a compact disc.	
cynical	adj.	disbelieving, sneering, scornful His cynical friends did not think he could win first prize. n. It was discouraging to have such cynics for friends.	idealistic, believing, optimistic, genial

D

The Phoenician picture-word for door was *daleth*. From it came our letter *D* which looked like a doorway, lying on its side.

The Greeks called this letter *delta* and drew it as a triangle.

The Romans made it stand up more gracefully as *D*. We still print it in Roman style.

In Roman numerals, *D* represents 500.

daily	*adv.*	**every day, each day** We should exercise daily. *adj.* Mom's daily drive to work takes twenty minutes.	*rarely, irregularly, never, seldom*
dainty	*adj.*	**delicate, refined, exquisite, elegant** The bride wore a dainty lace veil. *adv.* The flower girl walked daintily down the aisle.	*coarse, inelegant, harsh*
dam	1. *n.* 2. *v.*	**embankment, dike, barrier, wall** A dam controls the flow of the river. **clog, choke, hinder, obstruct, block** The beaver dammed the creek and flooded the roadway.	 **2.** *clear, open*
damage	1. *n.* 2. *v.*	**destruction, injury, harm, hurt, loss** The earthquake caused widespread damage. **injure, hurt, harm, spoil, break** He damaged the radio when he accidentally dropped it. *adj.* Damaged goods are often sold at reduced prices.	**1.** *improvement, benefit, advantage* **2.** *repair, mend, fix, improve*
damages	*n.*	**reparations, compensation, reimbursement** The court awarded damages of $5,000 to the victims.	
damp	*adj.*	**soggy, moist, wet, clammy, humid** The jogger's shirt was damp with perspiration. *adj.* The shirt was damp with sweat. *v.* Tom dampened the cloth before wiping the table.	*dry, parched, arid*
danger	*n.*	**peril, hazard, risk, menace** The children were warned of the danger of playing with fire.	*safety, security, preservation, protection, certainty*
dangerous	*adj.*	**risky, unsafe, perilous, hazardous** The icy roads made driving dangerous.	*safe, secure, sure, protected*
dare	1. *v.* 2. *v.*	**challenge, defy, confront** Liz dared me to ski down the steep slope. *n.* I accepted her dare. **venture, attempt, take a chance, risk** I didn't dare skip class.	 **2.** *fear, avoid*
daring	*adj.*	**bold, brave, courageous, fearless** The daring firefighter dashed into the burning house to save the child.	*timid, cowardly, afraid, frightened*
dark	*adj.*	**dim, gloomy, murky, shady** He groped his way down the dark hall. *n.* She got lost in the dark.	*bright, clear, light, brilliant, vivid*

n. When the power went out we were left in complete darkness.

v. Darken the room so we can show some movies.

dart
1. *n.* **arrow, missile**
   Jen aimed the dart at the bull's eye.
2. *v.* **rush, dash, run, race, hurry** — *2. dally, linger, loiter, dawdle*
   She darted home for a quick meal.

dash
1. *n.* **pinch, trace, touch, sprinkling** — *1. large amount, a lot*
   This soup needs just a dash of salt.
2. *n.* **race, run, sprint**
   Which runner won the fifty-yard dash?
3. *v.* **race, rush, run, hurry, dart** — *3. amble, loiter, dawdle*
   Lim dashed into the classroom just before the bell rang.
4. *v.* **disappoint, frustrate, spoil, shatter** — *4. encourage, increase, raise*
   The storm dashed our hopes for a picnic.

data
n. **information, facts, evidence, results, statistics**
Sam input the data into the computer.

date
1. *n.* **time, day, span, period**
   We remember important dates in history.
2. *n.* **appointment, rendezvous, engagement**
   Jo and I made a date to go to a movie.
3. *v.* **mark, register, record, chronicle**
   Always date important documents.
4. *v.* **escort, go out with, associate with**
   Ray has been dating Chris for some time.

dated
adj. **old-fashioned, out-of-date, antiquated, obsolete** — *contemporary, fresh, modern, current*
We rejected his dated information.

dawdle
v. **dally, linger, loiter, loaf, idle** — *hurry, speed, race, dart, hustle*
Greg dawdled on his way home and was late for supper.

dawn
1. *n.* **origin, beginning, birth** — *1. end*
   The invention of the computer was the dawn of the Information Age.
2. *n.* **daybreak, sunrise** — *2. evening, sunset, dusk*
   The newspapers are delivered at dawn.
3. *v.* **become understood, become clear**
   After failing her tests, it finally dawned on her that she should work harder.

daydream
n. **fancy, reverie, fantasy**
In her daydream Lena imagined that she was rich and famous.
v. "Stop daydreaming," she was told.

daze
v. **stun, bewilder, mix up, shock, perplex**
The blow to his head dazed the boxer.

n. The accident victim stumbled around in a daze.

dazzle *v.* **blind, confuse, daze, overpower, astonish, amaze**
The sudden glare of the car's headlights dazzled the cyclist.
adj. The dazzling lights blinded the cyclist.

dead *adj.* **deceased, extinct**
The accident victim was dead when the ambulance arrived.
alive, live, living, animated

deaden *v.* **muffle, smother, cushion, blunt, dull**
The thick carpet deadened the sound of our footsteps.
increase, amplify

deadly *adj.* **fatal, destructive, harmful, lethal**
The cobra produces a deadly venom.
strengthening, health-giving, vital

deal
1. *n.* **arrangement, contract, agreement, compromise**
Juan and Susie made a deal to help each other with their homework.
2. *v.* **do business, trade, bargain**
I deal with this store because it has the best prices.
3. *v.* **give out, hand out, distribute**
Life deals some people many hard knocks.
3. collect, gather, assemble
4. *v.* **handle, treat, attend to**
The guidance counselor will deal with the student's problems.
4. avoid, ignore, disregard

dealer *n.* **trader, merchant, distributor, retailer**
My uncle is a used car dealer.
buyer, customer, purchaser

dear
1. *adj.* **loved, cherished, close, favorite**
I was sad when my dear friend moved.
1. disliked, despised, unimportant
2. *adj.* **expensive, costly, high-priced**
That bike is too dear for my budget.
2. low-priced, cheap, inexpensive, worthless

debate
1. *n.* **discussion, contest, war of words**
They held a heated debate on the pros and cons of the plan.
2. *v.* **argue, discuss, dispute, question**
The lawyers hotly debated the issue of child custody.
adj. Who will win is debatable.
2. agree, concede

debris *n.* **remains, rubble, wreckage, ruins, trash**
The town was reduced to a pile of debris after the earthquake.

debt *n.* **dues, obligation, bill, liability**
I will settle my debts when I get my pay.
n. A debtor is someone who owes money.
credit, asset

decay	*v.*	**rot, decompose, spoil, putrefy** Meat decays rapidly in the heat. *n.* Eating too much sugar can cause tooth decay.	*bloom, grow, flourish, refresh*
deceive	*v.*	**cheat, bluff, fool, trick, mislead, dupe, swindle** The salesperson deceived me into buying a faulty car. *n.* Consumers must be aware of deceit by disreputable businesses.	*be honest, advise, counsel, help*
decent	1. *adj.*	**respectable, proper, appropriate, ethical, nice** It was very decent of you to help me. *n.* Please have the decency not to say anything rude to them.	1. *indecent, improper*
	2. *adj.*	**fair, suitable, adequate, satisfactory** We paid a decent price for the car.	2. *unfair, inadequate*
decide	*v.*	**determine, rule, conclude, settle** We decided on Hawaii for our vacation.	*hesitate, waver, vacillate*
decipher	*v.*	**solve, unravel, read, explain, interpret, translate, decode** The agent deciphered the code. *adj.* The code is decipherable.	*misconstrue, misunderstand, encode*
decision	*n.*	**verdict, conclusion, ruling, decree, resolution** We made the right decision.	
decisive	1. *adj.*	**determined, firm** A decisive person makes a good leader.	1. *indecisive, uncertain, unsure*
	2. *adj.*	**convincing, crucial, definite, absolute** Lord Nelson won a decisive victory at the Battle of Waterloo.	2. *uncertain, unimportant*
deck	1. *n.*	**floor, surface, platform** They sunbathed on the deck of the ship.	
	2. *v.*	**adorn, decorate, beautify** Deck the room with flowers.	2. *deface, mar, spoil*
declare	*v.*	**proclaim, announce, reveal, assert** The judge declared us the winners. *n.* The people applauded the declaration.	*conceal, hide, withhold*
decline	1. *v.*	**refuse, say no, reject** I declined her invitation because I had another engagement.	1. *accept, say yes, consent*
	2. *v.*	**lose value, cheapen, drop, fall, lower, decrease, weaken** Car sales declined last year. *n.* The decline in sales meant the store had to close down.	2. *increase, improve, gain, rise*
decompose	*v.*	**decay, rot, spoil, disintegrate, putrefy** The garbage decomposed in the heat.	*flourish, refresh, grow, bloom, compose*

decorate	*v.*	**beautify, adorn, array, trim** We decorated the gym with streamers for the dance. *n.* The party decorations are beautiful.	*deface, mar, spoil*
decrease	*v.*	**reduce, lessen, lower, deflate, shrink, weaken, diminish** The driver decreased his speed as he approached the sharp curve. *n.* There is a decrease in the demand for ice cream in the winter.	*increase, enlarge, swell, expand*
decrepit	*adj.*	**broken-down, worn-out, dilapidated** The decrepit car was towed to the junkyard.	*well-kept, new, in good shape*
deed	*n.*	**act, feat, effort, accomplishment** Lou is remembered for his kind deeds.	
deep	1. *adj.*	**yawning, fathomless** Brian fell into a deep pit in the ground. *adv.* The workers dug deep in the ground to make a well.	1. *shallow, on the surface*
	2. *adj.*	**intense, profound, acute** Jay was in deep despair over the loss of his dog.	2. *light*
deface	*v.*	**injure, mar, disfigure, deform, scar, mark, mutilate, vandalize** Vandals defaced the wall with graffiti.	*beautify, adorn, decorate*
defeat	1. *n.*	**failure, loss, setback** Our team suffered a crushing defeat in the volleyball tournament.	1. *success, victory, triumph, conquest, win*
	2. *v.*	**beat, trounce, vanquish, subdue, conquer, overcome** Nelson defeated Napoleon at the Battle of Waterloo.	2. *surrender, yield, submit*
defect	1. *n.*	**flaw, fault, imperfection, blemish** A defect in the brakes caused the accident. *adj.* Defective brakes can cause accidents.	1. *improvement, advantage*
	2. *v.*	**run away, forsake, abandon, leave** He defected from his homeland because of the harsh government.	2. *stay, remain*
defend	*v.*	**protect, guard, support, shield, secure** The bear defended her cub against the hunter. *n.* Mary spoke in defense of animal rights. *adj.* The activist is defensive of her right to take a stand.	*desert, abandon, leave, resign*
defer	1. *v.*	**put off, delay, postpone, suspend** The school deferred the examination because of the storm.	1. *expedite, hasten, quicken, advance*

2. *v.*   **yield, surrender, give in**
He deferred to his parents' wishes in his choice of a school.

defiance   *n.*   **opposition, disobedience, challenge, rebellion**
The soldier was punished for his defiance of orders.

support, obedience

defiant   *adj.*   **rebellious, disobedient, insubordinate, uncooperative**
The defiant student was suspended for breaking school rules.

obedient, supportive, cooperative

deficient   *adj.*   **inadequate, defective, insufficient**
Water rationing was imposed because of deficient rainfall.
n. A deficiency of vitamins in your diet can make you ill.

excessive, sufficient, ample, satisfactory

define   *v.*   **describe, state, explain**
She defined her goals in a speech.
n. He looked up the definition of the word in the dictionary.

confuse, distort, mix up

definite   *adj.*   **sure, decided, distinct, clear**
They have set a definite date for their wedding.

indefinite, indistinct, undecided, uncertain

deflate   *v.*   **reduce, flatten**
We deflated the air mattress before packing it away.

inflate, expand, raise

deform   *v.*   **twist, warp, injure, mutilate, distort, disfigure**
His legs were deformed by polio.

enhance, make better

deformed   *adj.*   **misshapen, disfigured, maimed**
The puppy was born with a deformed leg.
n. The deformity of his leg made it difficult for him to walk.

perfect, whole

defraud   *v.*   **cheat, swindle, deceive, rob**
Con artists defrauded them of their savings.

reward, assist, help

defy   **1.** *v.*   **mock, oppose, resist, disobey**
He defied his curfew and was punished.
2. *v.*   **challenge, dare**
We defied Tina to run the marathon.

1. obey, conform to, agree

degree   *n.*   **measure, amount, extent, rate, grade, mark, range**
She has a large degree of support on this issue.

dehydrate   *v.*   **dry up, dry, parch, drain**
The sun dehydrated the athletes.

moisten, wet, hydrate

dejected		*adj.*	**unhappy, downcast, discouraged, sad** She was dejected after she failed the test.	*happy, cheerful, merry*
delay	1.	*n.*	**setback, hesitation, reprieve, deferment** Rain caused a delay in the start of the ball game.	**1.** *progress, speed, advance*
	2.	*v.*	**hinder, retard, postpone, defer** A traffic jam delayed the arrival of the bus.	**2.** *advance, hurry, hasten*
delegate	1.	*n.*	**ambassador, representative, envoy, commissioner, emissary** Every country sent a delegate to the conference.	
	2.	*v.*	**authorize, entrust, appoint, assign, nominate** The committee delegated Bev to decorate the gym. *n.* The committee agreed on the delegation of duties to all members.	
delete		*v.*	**erase, remove, take out, cancel, omit** The editor deleted two paragraphs to shorten the story. *n.* The author protested against the deletion of the two paragraphs.	*insert, add*
deliberate	1.	*v.*	**consider, examine, think over, ponder, contemplate, discuss** We deliberated on a new plan to raise funds. *n.* After much deliberation we decided to adopt the new policy.	**1.** *pass over, reject, discard*
	2.	*adj.*	**intentional, conscious, calculated, careful** The basketball player took deliberate aim at the basket and scored. *adv.* She deliberately said something that would hurt him.	**2.** *unintentional, careless*
delicate		*adj.*	**fragile, frail, fine, tender, dainty** Kim needs special care because of her delicate health.	*rough, coarse*
delicious		*adj.*	**enjoyable, sweet, tasteful, pleasing, appetizing, palatable** Can I get the recipe for those delicious cookies?	*unpalatable, unsavory, distasteful*
delight	1.	*n.*	**joy, pleasure, happiness** It was a delight to see all my old friends.	**1.** *sorrow, pain, distress*
	2.	*v.*	**please, charm, make happy, enchant, entertain** She delighted us with her stories.	**2.** *disappoint, sadden, displease*
deliver	1.	*v.*	**hand over, transfer, bring, dispense, give out** The messenger delivered the parcel. *n.* She put the delivery in the mailbox.	**1.** *hold, keep, retain*

2. *v.*   **rescue, save, liberate, free, release**   **2.** *hold, keep, retain*
The police delivered the child from his
kidnappers.

delude   *v.*   **trick, deceive, fool, mislead, dupe**
He deluded everyone into believing that
he was a doctor.

deluxe   *adj.*   **grand, fine, expensive, elegant,**   *ordinary, regular,*
choice, splendid, super, prime,   *mundane, everyday,*
sumptuous   *mediocre, cheap*
We stayed in a deluxe hotel on our holiday.

demand   **1.** *n.*   **need, requirement, want**
There is a great demand for computer
programmers.
   2. *v.*   **claim, ask, urge, require**   **2.** *give, offer, present*
The striking workers demanded better
pay.

demolish   *v.*   **wreck, destroy, ruin, level, smash,**   *construct, build,*
raze   *make, restore*
Wrecking crews demolished the house.
n. The demolition of the building was
done with explosives.

demonstrate   *v.*   **show, illustrate, explain, exhibit,**   *hide, conceal, cover*
display
Pablo will demonstrate how his invention
works.
n. The gymnast gave a demonstration on
the bar.

demonstration   *n.*   **protest, rally, march, parade**
The animal rights activists held a
demonstration outside the research center.

denote   *v.*   **mark, indicate, mean**
That arrow sign denotes right turns only.

dense   *adj.*   **compact, solid, close, thick**   *thin, scanty, sparse*
He cleared a path through the dense forest.

dent   *n.*   **nick, indentation, hollow**
She put a dent in the fender when she
backed into the gatepost.
v. She dented the car fender in an
accident.

depart   *v.*   **go away, leave, withdraw, exit, go**   *remain, stay, wait,*
The bus departs from the station at noon.   *arrive*
n. The plane's departure was delayed by
heavy fog.

depend   *v.*   **trust, rely on, count on**   *distrust*
You can always depend on Sam to do a
good job.

dependable	*adj.*	**reliable, trustworthy, steady, loyal** Rashid is a dependable babysitter.	*undependable, unreliable*
depict	*v.*	**describe, portray, represent, draw** The author depicted the pioneers as strong people.	
deplete	*v.*	**use up, reduce, decrease, drain, lessen** The costly gift depleted our funds.	*increase, strengthen, fill*
deplore	*v.*	**mourn, grieve, regret, lament** The activists deplored the use of animals for scientific experiments. *adj.* They denounced the deplorable act.	*rejoice, cheer, delight in, revel*
deport	*v.*	**banish, exile, cast out** The Immigration Department deported the spy.	*import, bring in*
deposit	1. *n.*	**partial payment, installment** They put down a deposit on their new house.	**1.** *withdrawal*
	2. *v.*	**place, put in, drop** Deposit waste paper in the basket.	**2.** *withdraw, take out, remove*
deprive	*v.*	**take from, strip, rob, divest** The judge deprived the abusive man of all rights to see his children.	*give, add, assist*
deprived	*adj.*	**underprivileged, needy, poor** We raised money for deprived children.	*privileged, rich*
depths	*n.*	**abyss, bottom, base** The diver explored the ocean depths for sunken treasure.	*surface, top*
derelict	*adj.*	**abandoned, broken, deserted, neglected** The roof of the derelict house leaked.	*cared for, lived in*
derive	*v.*	**obtain, gain, receive, acquire** The students derived much satisfaction from their success.	*forfeit, lose, divest*
descend	*v.*	**go down, drop, slip, slide, settle, sink** The elevator descended swiftly.	*ascend, go up, climb*
descent	1. *n.*	**sinking, coming down, drop, decline** Our ears popped as the plane made its descent.	**1.** *rise, growth*
	2. *n.*	**slope, fall, slant** The descent of the hill is quite steep here.	**2.** *ascent, climb, rise*
describe	*v.*	**explain, outline, express, illustrate** The newspaper described the actor as being "tall, dark, and handsome." *n.* He did not fit the description.	

desert	*n.*	**wasteland, barren plains** Few vegetation can grow in a desert.	*rain forest, wetlands, oasis*
desert	*v.*	**abandon, forsake, leave, quit, defect** He deserted his family and moved to the city.	*remain, stay, continue*
deserve	*v.*	**be worthy of, merit, earn** Jan deserved the award for her brilliant work.	*be unworthy of*
design	1. *n.*	**pattern, decoration** The wallpaper design is too busy for this small room.	
	2. *n.*	**blueprint, outline, sketch, plan** Ann created a design for a new car.	
	3. *v.*	**create, plan, prepare, fashion** Alma designed a new computer program.	
desirable	*adj.*	**good, acceptable, valuable, attractive** We bought the house because it is in a desirable neighborhood.	*undesirable, bad, harmful*
desire	1. *n.*	**longing, wish, craving, yearning** Aikiko has a strong desire to succeed in his new job.	*1. hatred, dislike, disgust, aversion, indifference*
	2. *v.*	**want, require, crave, long for** The weary traveler desired food and rest.	*2. be revolted by*
desolate	*adj.*	**lonely, forlorn, miserable, bleak, wretched, barren, abandoned** Antarctica is a desolate continent.	*pleasant, lovely, enjoyable, inhabited*
despair	1. *n.*	**hopelessness, gloom, depression** The workers were in despair when the plant closed down.	*1. hope, courage*
	2. *v.*	**lose hope, give up** After a long search, he despaired of ever finding his lost dog.	*2. hope, expect, anticipate*
desperate	1. *adj.*	**reckless, careless, wild, rash** The desperate man robbed the bank in broad daylight.	*1. calm, careful, collected*
	2. *adj.*	**drastic, daring, bold** A desperate attempt was made to save the trapped miners.	
	3. *adj.*	**despairing, hopeless, despondent** I am desperate for a job. *n.* Out of desperation, the hungry children begged for food on the streets.	*3. confident, contented, satisfied*
despicable	*adj.*	**mean, base, disgraceful** Child abuse is a despicable act.	*kind, worthy*
despise	*v.*	**scorn, hate, abhor, detest, loathe** The athletes despise those who use illegal drugs.	*love, cherish, admire, exalt, respect, esteem*

destiny	*n.*	**fate, fortune, lot** The fortune teller said it was my destiny to be rich and famous.	*choice, option, selection*
destitute	*adj.*	**poor, needy, impoverished** Many people were left destitute after the stock market crashed.	*rich, affluent, well-to-do, wealthy*
destroy	*v.*	**ruin, wreck, smash, demolish** The art collection was destroyed by fire.	*create, construct, save, build, renew, repair*
destruction	*n.*	**ruin, waste, devastation, demolition** The flood caused destruction of the crops.	*restoration, preservation*
detach	*v.*	**separate, unfasten, disconnect, sever** Dad detached the trailer from the car.	*unite, join, connect, attach, fasten*
detail	*n.*	**feature, item, fact, aspect, portion** She took care of every detail of the party.	*whole, total, sum*
detain	*v.*	**delay, hold, retard, hinder, keep** Police detained the suspect for a day.	*free, let go, deliver*
detect	*v.*	**notice, see, discover, observe, determine** I detected from his red eyes that he had been crying. *n.* Careful research led to the detection of the problem. *adj.* Although she tried to hide it, her fear was detectable.	*miss, omit, pass by*
detective	*n.*	**investigator, sleuth, private eye** The detective studied the clues to solve the mystery.	
detention	*n.*	**restraint, confinement, imprisonment** The suspect was kept in detention.	*freedom, release*
deter	*v.*	**dissuade, caution, discourage, hinder** The unfavorable reviews of the movie deterred me from seeing it.	*encourage, persuade, urge, promote*
deteriorate	*v.*	**decline, degenerate, decrease** His health deteriorated rapidly. *n.* Acid rain has led to the deterioration of our lakes.	*improve, get better*
determination	*n.*	**persistence, resolution, conviction, stubbornness, obstinacy** It takes a great deal of determination to overcome a failure. *adj.* The determined salesperson wouldn't take no for an answer.	*indecision, unsteadiness*
determine	**1.** *v.*	**settle, decide, fix upon, resolve** The examination results will determine my future.	**1.** *confuse, muddle, unsettle*

	2.	*v.*	**find out, learn, discover** Have the police determined the cause of the accident?	**2.** *conceal, suppress, ignore*
detest		*v.*	**hate, loathe, despise, abhor** She detests him because he is a bully.	*like, prefer, love, admire, respect*
develop	**1.**	*v.*	**expand, enlarge, extend, build up** Develop your outline into a story. *n.* Exercise is essential for the development of muscles.	**1.** *reduce, condense, shorten, abbreviate*
	2.	*v.*	**contract, acquire, cultivate, form** She developed an interest in science at an early age.	**2.** *lose*
	3.	*v.*	**grow up, mature, evolve, advance** The tadpole developed into a frog.	**3.** *deteriorate, regress, recede*
device	**1.**	*n.*	**apparatus, invention, contrivance, contraption, gadget, mechanism** The garlic press is a handy little device.	
	2.	*n.*	**scheme, trick, design, ruse, plan** What device did the swindler use to get you to give him the money?	
devise		*v.*	**invent, design, construct, plan, create** The teenagers devised a new video game.	
devote		*v.*	**dedicate, apply, set apart, give** Yun devotes many hours to her violin.	*waste, squander, abuse*
devotion		*n.*	**attachment, commitment, dedication** The teacher won an award for her devotion to duty.	*indifference, neglect, carelessness*
devour		*v.*	**swallow, eat, gobble, consume, take in** He devoured the hamburger in two bites.	
dexterity		*n.*	**proficiency, skill, ability** Conchita demonstrated her dexterity on the trampoline. *adj.* She is a dexterous gymnast.	*awkwardness, ineptitude*
diagnose		*v.*	**identify, conclude, analyze** The doctor diagnosed June's symptoms as chicken pox. *n.* Her diagnosis proved correct.	
diagram		*n.*	**plan, illustration, sketch, layout** The diagram explained how to set up the equipment.	
dialogue		*n.*	**talk, conversation, discussion, debate** The dialogue between the two leaders led to a trade agreement.	
dictate	**1.**	*v.*	**order, command, direct, instruct** The organizer dictated where everything should be sent.	**1.** *beg, ask, plead*

	2. *v.*	**tell, speak, deliver** The teacher dictated a paragraph in French for the students to record. *n.* The students wrote the teacher's dictation in their notebooks.	**2.** *listen, answer*
dictator	*n.*	**tyrant, despot, oppressor, autocrat** The ruthless dictator was overthrown in a coup.	
die	**1.** *v.*	**expire, perish, pass away, succumb** Many people die from heart attacks.	**1.** *live, exist, survive*
	2. *v.*	**decline, wither, fade, weaken** The applause died down as the musician started to play.	**2.** *flourish, grow, increase, continue*
differ	**1.** *v.*	**clash, disagree, object, dispute** They differed on the issue of capital punishment.	**1.** *agree, concede*
	2. *v.*	**vary, contrast, diverge** The identical twins look alike, but differ in their personalities. *n.* There is not much difference between the copy and the original.	**2.** *resemble, match*
different	*adj.*	**unlike, distinct, diverse, separate** We have different opinions about this. *adv.* We think differently.	*similar, alike, same*
difficult	**1.** *adj.*	**arduous, tough, grueling, challenging** It was a difficult climb up the steep hill.	**1.** *easy, manageable*
	2. *adj.*	**hard, complicated, complex, advanced** I struggled with the difficult math problem.	**2.** *simple, elementary, straightforward*
	3. *adj.*	**bothersome, troublesome, demanding, uncooperative** She is such a difficult person no one would work with her.	**3.** *pleasant, undemanding, cooperative*
difficulty	**1.** *n.*	**hardship, burden, barrier, obstacle, hindrance, complication** Despite her illness and other difficulties, she finished the project.	**1.** *aid, assistance, help*
	2. *n.*	**mess, muddle, trouble, crisis** The gambler is in financial difficulty.	**2.** *ease, comfort*
digest	**1.** *v.*	**summarize, condense** Digest your project into a one-page essay.	**1.** *expand, enlarge*
	2. *v.*	**dissolve, assimilate, convert, absorb** Chewing food makes it easier to digest.	
dignity	*n.*	**grandeur, nobility, stateliness, self-respect, importance, honor** Everyone admires the queen's dignity. *adj.* His dignified behavior in the debate won him respect.	*servility*

dilapidated		*adj.*	**neglected, ruined, decrepit** The dilapidated building was pulled down because it was an eyesore.	*in good repair, cared for, attended, preserved*
dilate		*v.*	**enlarge, swell, expand, widen** The pupil dilates in the dark to let more light into the eye.	*shrink, narrow, contract*
dilemma		*n.*	**predicament, scrape, fix, quandary** He was in a dilemma as to which car to buy.	*solution*
diligent		*adj.*	**hard-working, industrious, attentive** The diligent student stands at the top of her class. *adv.* She worked diligently on her project.	*lazy, careless, indifferent, inattentive*
dilute		*v.*	**weaken, thin out, reduce** We diluted the soup by adding water.	*thicken, condense*
dim		*adj.*	**obscure, faint, indistinct, hazy, dull** We couldn't read in the dim light.	*bright, clear, distinct, brilliant*
diminish		*v.*	**decrease, lessen, reduce, shrink, dwindle** We waited until the snowfall diminished before setting off.	*increase, expand*
din		*n.*	**clamor, roar, noise, racket, pandemonium** Our neighbors complained about the din of our party.	*silence, quiet, calm, stillness*
dingy		*adj.*	**dirty, grimy, faded, shabby** We cleaned and painted the dingy apartment before moving in.	*clean, spotless, bright*
dip	1.	*v.*	**slope, decline, bend, tilt, plunge, drop** The plane dipped so suddenly that we were afraid something was wrong.	1. *ascend, increase, rise*
	2.	*v.*	**submerge, immerse, dunk, rinse** Fred dipped his doughnut in his coffee. *n.* Kim took a dip in the lake to cool off.	2. *lift, raise*
direct	1.	*v.*	**manage, control, conduct, supervise** Hannah directed the class play. *n.* She did a good job as the director.	1. *serve, follow*
	2.	*v.*	**aim, conduct, lead, guide, point** The tour guide directed us to a good restaurant.	2. *follow*
	3.	*adj.*	**straight, shortest** I always take the direct route to school.	3. *indirect, crooked, roundabout*
	4.	*adj.*	**candid, frank, blunt, straightforward** She is a straightforward person and always gives a direct answer.	4. *deceptive, misleading, indirect*
direction	1.	*n.*	**course, aim, route, path, way** If you go in that direction you will be heading north.	

2. *n.* **recipe, instruction, order, plan**
Follow the directions on the box to build the model airplane.

directly *adv.* **immediately, at once, instantly** *later*
Come directly home after the movie.

dirt **1.** *n.* **filth, grime**
The floor was covered with dirt.
2. *n.* **earth, loam, soil**
The gardener spread a load of dirt over the flowerbeds.

dirty *adj.* **soiled, filthy, polluted, grubby, messy** *clean, decent,*
We washed all the dirty dishes. *unspoiled, neat,*
v. The dog dirtied the rug with its muddy *sanitary*
paws.

disability *n.* **weakness, inability, defect, handicap** *fitness, ability, power,*
He has a hearing disability. *strength*

disable *v.* **cripple, maim, impair, incapacitate** *heal, mend*
The burglar disabled the security system.
adj. The disabled man limped to his seat.

disagree *v.* **differ, argue, dispute, vary** *agree, concur, accept*
I disagree with your opinion because it is based on incorrect information.
n. They settled their disagreement after long negotiations.

disagreeable *adj.* **nasty, unpleasant, bad-tempered,** *pleasant, agreeable*
grouchy, bothersome
The disagreeable boy had no friends.

disappear *v.* **leave, depart, fade, vanish** *appear, arrive, come*
The moon disappeared behind dark clouds.
n. Al's sudden disappearance puzzled us.

disapprove *v.* **condemn, object to, dislike** *like, approve*
We disapprove of smoking in our house.
n. I showed my disapproval with a frown.

disaster *n.* **calamity, misfortune, mishap,** *good fortune,*
catastrophe, tragedy *blessing, benefit,*
The earthquake was a terrible disaster. *advantage*
adj. It was a disastrous event.

discard *v.* **throw away, dump, reject** *keep, preserve, save,*
The librarian discarded all the torn books. *retain*

discern *v.* **see, observe, notice, detect, perceive** *disregard, overlook*
We discerned from her frown that she was unhappy.

discharge **1.** *v.* **release, unload, project, emit, eject** **1.** *load*
The factory discharged its chemical waste into the lake.

n. The discharge of the cannon made a loud boom.

2. *v.* **let go, dismiss, sack, fire**
The dishonest cashier was discharged.

3. *v.* **release, set free, acquit**
The judge discharged the accused because of lack of evidence.

2. employ, hire, keep, hold

3. charge

discipline
1. *n.* **self-control, order, restraint, regulation**
Show some discipline and work hard.

2. *v.* **chastise, reprimand, punish, correct**
The coached disciplined some team members for their unruly behavior.

1. chaos, disorder, confusion

2. reward, praise, encourage

disclose
v. **tell, make known, reveal**
He disclosed his secret to me.
n. His disclosure of the secret upset me.

hide, conceal

discount
n. **reduction, markdown, deduction**
Will you give me a discount on this toy since it's damaged?
v. The store discounted the price of all clothing by fifty percent.

increase, markup

discover
v. **find, locate, find out, detect, invent**
We discovered a wonderful picnic spot.
n. We were given a reward for our discovery of the missing money.

miss, overlook

discreet
adj. **careful, polite, cautious, reserved, sensible, guarded**
The detective made discreet inquiries.
n. She is easily offended so use discretion when you deal with her.

foolish, reckless, indiscreet, rash, impetuous

discrepancy
n. **difference, disagreement, inconsistency, variance, disparity**
Discrepancies between his story and everyone else's showed that he was lying.

accord, agreement

discriminate
1. *v.* **distinguish, differentiate, separate**
Can you discriminate between the real and the fake diamonds?

2. *v.* **show prejudice**
The firm discriminated against female workers by paying them less than men.

discrimination
n. **prejudice, bigotry, racism, sexism, ageism**
Martin Luther King fought to end racial discrimination.

tolerance

discuss
v. **talk over, debate, consider, confer**
She discussed her plans with her parents.
n. They had an in-depth discussion on her choice of college.

disdain	1.	*n.*	**scorn, contempt** Our offer was rejected with disdain.	1. *regard, respect, admiration, esteem*
	2.	*v.*	**snub, spurn, despise, scorn** The salesperson disdained the price we offered for the car.	2. *like, admire*
disease		*n.*	**infection, illness, malady, ailment** Chicken pox is a common childhood disease.	*health, vigor*
disgrace	1.	*n.*	**shame, disfavor, reproach, dishonor** He was in disgrace after his arrest for drunk driving.	1. *favor, honor, respect*
	2.	*v.*	**degrade, defame, shame** They disgraced themselves with their terrible behavior. *adj.* Their rude behavior was disgraceful.	2. *glorify, honor*
disguise	1.	*n.*	**mask, veil, costume, camouflage** No one could guess the identity of the person behind the disguise.	
	2.	*v.*	**conceal, camouflage, hide, mask** The celebrity disguised herself with a wig and sunglasses.	2. *reveal, uncover*
disgust	1.	*n.*	**dislike, distaste, aversion, loathing** Their cruel actions filled me with disgust.	1. *approval, liking, admiration*
	2.	*v.*	**repel, sicken, offend, revolt** It disgusts me when people chew with their mouth open. *adj.* Cockroaches are disgusting insects.	2. *attract, appeal*
dishonest		*adj.*	**crooked, deceitful, false, sneaky** The dishonest students cheated in the examinations. *n.* They were punished for their dishonesty.	*honest, true, lawful, honorable*
dismal		*adj.*	**dreary, dingy, gloomy, somber** Everything seems dismal on a grey day.	*bright, joyful, happy, cheerful*
dismay	1.	*n.*	**alarm, concern, anxiety, distress, fright, dread, horror** The traveler was filled with dismay when he lost his passport.	1. *confidence, relief, joy, happiness*
	2.	*v.*	**frighten, scare, alarm, distress, dishearten** The news of the accident dismayed them.	2. *relieve, cheer, encourage*
dismiss	1.	*v.*	**let out, discharge, send off** The principal dismissed school because of the snowstorm. *n.* The students rushed home after their dismissal.	1. *retain, keep, hold*
	2.	*v.*	**reject, discard, spurn** She dismissed the idea because it was impractical.	2. *retain, consider*

disorder	1.	*n.*	**illness, sickness, malady, ailment** Fred missed school because of a stomach disorder.	**1.** *health*
	2.	*n.*	**disturbance, uprising, rumpus, commotion, riot** The country was plunged into disorder when the President was assassinated. *adj.* The police arrested the mob for disorderly conduct.	**2.** *order, peace, tranquility*
	3.	*n.*	**clutter, muddle, mess, confusion** They left their room in total disorder.	**3.** *order, arrangement*
dispatch	1.	*n.*	**speed, efficiency, haste** Kay does all her work with great dispatch.	**1.** *inefficiency*
	2.	*v.*	**send, transmit, forward** The hospital dispatched an ambulance to the accident scene.	**2.** *receive, get, obtain*
dispel		*v.*	**remove, scatter, dismiss, drive away, disperse** The smooth flight dispelled our fear of flying.	*reinforce, recall*
dispense		*v.*	**distribute, give out, assign** A pharmacist dispenses drugs.	*keep, retain*
disperse		*v.*	**scatter, break up, disband, dispel** The police dispersed the rowdy spectators after the game.	*gather, collect, assemble*
displace		*v.*	**dislocate, dislodge, move, transfer, disarrange, shift** The war displaced many people.	*arrange, place, put in order*
display	1.	*n.*	**exhibition, presentation, show, demonstration** We admired the art display in school.	
	2.	*v.*	**exhibit, arrange, show, present** We displayed our artwork at the fair.	**2.** *hide, conceal, cover*
disposable	1.	*adj.*	**extra, available, usable** The young lawyer has disposable income.	
	2.	*adj.*	**replaceable, throwaway** We used disposable cups at the party.	
dispose		*v.*	**throw away, get rid of, dump** The city disposes of garbage at the dump. *n.* Our school has special bins for the disposal of recyclable materials.	*retain, keep, save, hoard*
dispute	1.	*n.*	**disagreement, argument, quarrel, debate** The children had a dispute over whose turn it was to ride the horse.	**1.** *agreement, harmony*
	2.	*v.*	**contradict, debate, argue, quarrel** She disputed his claim that the eldest child should go first.	**2.** *agree, harmonize, concur*

disrupt		*v.*	**interrupt, upset, disturb**
			Hecklers disrupted the principal's speech.
			n. The fire alarm caused a disruption in the play.

dissect   *v.*   **cut, slice, section, analyze, dismember**
The biology students dissected a frog so that they could study it.

dissolve   *v.*   **melt, thaw, disintegrate**   *solidify, harden*
Molly dissolved the crystals in water.

distance
1. *n.* **length, space, interval, span**
What is the distance from San Diego to Toronto?
2. *n.* **background, horizon**   *2. foreground, neighborhood, environs*
I could see the ships in the distance through my binoculars.

distant
1. *adj.* **faraway**   *1. neighboring, close, nearby, near*
Our new neighbors moved here from a distant country.
2. *adj.* **remote, far-off**   *2. near, immediate*
Sue likes to speculate on what life will be like in the distant future.
3. *adj.* **aloof, cold, indifferent, reserved, reticent**   *3. warm, excited, welcoming*
Our new teacher is distant in manner.

distinct
1. *adj.* **lucid, plain, obvious, clear, definite**   *1. blurred, indefinite, obscure*
The object has a distinct shape.
2. *adj.* **separate, discrete**   *2. identical, similar, alike*
Keep your notes from both experiments in distinct files.
3. *adj.* **clear, sharp, audible, enunciated**   *3. muffled, distorted, inaudible*
We heard the distinct sound of crying.
adv. We distinctly heard the cries above the din.

distinguish
1. *v.* **differentiate, separate, identify**   *1. confuse*
I can't distinguish between the copy and the original.
2. *v.* **detect, discover, see, discern**   *2. miss, overlook*
We could barely distinguish the cars through the thick fog.
3. *v.* **bring honor on, become acknowledged, become famous**
She distinguished herself as the fastest runner in the school.

distinguished   *adj.*   **famous, celebrated, notable, prominent**   *unknown, obscure, mediocre*
Everyone wanted the distinguished writer's autograph.

distort   *v.*   **twist, misrepresent, slant**
The reporter distorted the news story to make it sensational.
n. The distortion of news is unethical.

distract	*v.*	**divert, confuse, draw away** The crook distracted me while his accomplice stole my wallet. *n.* The phone call was a welcome distraction from my chores.	*focus, concentrate*
distress	*n.*	**discomfort, pain, concern, unhappiness, worry, trouble** Lim's illness caused us great distress. *v.* The bad news distressed us.	*pleasure, joy, mirth, satisfaction, happiness*
distribute	*v.*	**give out, deal, hand out, share, dispense** The soldiers distributed the supplies to the refugees. *n.* We stood in line for the distribution of the books.	*hoard, keep, collect*
disturb	*v.*	**annoy, bother, irritate, unsettle, interrupt, upset** Sirens disturbed the peace of the night. *n.* They were thrown out of the theater for causing a disturbance.	*soothe, pacify, calm, appease, compose*
dive	*v.*	**plunge, dart, rush into, leap into** The lifeguard dived into the pool to save the drowning child. *n.* The plane took a nose dive into the bushes.	
diverse	*adj.*	**different, unlike, varied** Our school has students from diverse cultural backgrounds.	*same, identical*
diversion	1. *n.* 2. *n.*	**hobby, pastime, amusement, enjoyment** Dad's favorite diversion is golf. **change, deflection, detour** Floods caused a diversion in the route.	1. *work, job, toil, occupation, drudgery*
divert	*v.*	**sidetrack, turn aside, change** Police diverted traffic towards the detour.	
divide	*v.*	**part, separate, share, distribute** Jan divided the cake among the guests. *n.* A fence marked the division of the two backyards. *adj.* A number is even if it is divisible by two.	*join, unite, attach, connect*
divulge	*v.*	**tell, reveal, disclose** Don't divulge my secret to anyone.	*hide, keep secret, conceal*
dizzy	*adj.*	**giddy, silly, confused, shaky** Great heights can make people feel dizzy.	*clear-headed, steady, calm*

do		*v.*	**perform, act, accomplish, achieve, make, bring about** How will you do your project?	
docile		*adj.*	**orderly, quiet, meek, humble, obedient** The docile dog trotted behind its owner.	*determined, stubborn, disobedient, fierce*
dock	1.	*n.*	**wharf, pier, landing, quay** Several boats were tied to the dock.	
	2.	*v.*	**join, hook up, link** The shuttle docked at the space station.	*2. leave, separate, blast off*
dodge		*v.*	**lurch, duck, sidestep, avoid, evade** He dodged out of the bike's path just in time.	*meet, approach, face*
dole	1.	*n.*	**welfare, handout, charity** The jobless person lived on the dole.	
	2.	*v.*	**give, distribute, hand out, deal** The parents doled out the children's allowances.	*2. keep, hoard, collect*
doleful		*adj.*	**sad, unhappy, dismal, gloomy, dejected** May was doleful when she broke her toy.	*cheerful, joyous, merry, happy*
domain		*n.*	**territory, land, estate, kingdom, area** The ruler's domain stretched from sea to sea.	
domestic	1.	*adj.*	**tame, settled** Most dogs are domestic animals, but there are still some wild ones.	*1. wild, untamed, feral, unruly*
	2.	*adj.*	**homegrown, indigenous, homemade, native** Domestic products are often cheaper.	*2. foreign, imported*
dominant	1.	*adj.*	**prevailing, most powerful, chief** Serena and Venus Williams are dominant tennis players. *n.* Their dominance is evident.	*1. weakest, least powerful*
	2.	*adj.*	**assertive, bossy** Kiow has a dominant personality.	*2. humble, retiring*
dominate		*v.*	**control, rule, direct, command** He dominated the meeting by not letting anyone else speak.	
donate		*v.*	**give, contribute, grant** Milly donates blood regularly to the Red Cross. *n.* The charity was asking for donations of food and clothes.	*keep, retain*
dormant		*adj.*	**sleeping, hibernating, asleep, inactive** Many animals are dormant during the winter season.	*awake, moving, active*

dot *n.* **speck, spot, fleck, mark, point**
Mark a dot to show where to put the nail.
v. She carefully dotted all of her i's.

double 1. *n.* **twin, mate, duplicate** **1.** *opposite*
Make doubles of the photographs so that
we'll have an extra set.

2. *v.* **multiply, make twice as much**
He doubled his sales and made twice as
much money.

3. *v.* **replace, substitute for, stand in for**
Sean doubled for the star in the movie.

4. *adj.* **twofold, dual** **4.** *single*
She does the work of two people but she is
not paid double wages.
adv. Our employer pays us double to
work on holidays.

doubt 1. *n.* **suspicion, disbelief, distrust** **1.** *belief, certainty,*
Her suspicious behavior cast doubts on *trust, faith*
her intentions.

2. *v.* **suspect, be uncertain, distrust,** **2.** *believe, trust,*
question *be convinced*
His stories are so wild that I doubt if they
are true.

doubtful *adj.* **uncertain, undecided, hesitant** *sure, certain, definite,*
We are doubtful about his chances for *positive*
success.

dowdy *adj.* **shabby, sloppy, unattractive, frumpy** *neat, chic, smart, tidy*
She was wearing a dowdy old dress.
adv. She was dowdily dressed.

downcast *adj.* **sad, discouraged, depressed, unhappy** *happy, glad, thrilled,*
The players were downcast when they lost *encouraged*
the game.

downpour *n.* **rainstorm, shower, cloudburst, deluge**
We were caught without umbrellas in a
downpour.

drab *adj.* **dull, monotonous, faded, dingy, dreary** *exciting, bright,*
The drab room was brightened with new *colorful*
wallpaper.

draft 1. *n.* **sketch, outline, plan, blueprint**
He is revising the first draft of his essay.
v. She drafted a plan for the trip.

2. *n.* **recruitment, selection, conscription**
The football coach is conducting a draft
for new players.
v. The government drafted civilians to
fight in the war.

3. *n.* **breeze, current of air, wind**
There is a draft coming in that window.
adj. A drafty room is uncomfortable.

4. *n.* **money order, cashier's check**
Suli's grandmother sent her a draft for fifty dollars for her birthday.

drag

1. *v.* **tug, tow, pull, draw, lug**
Toni dragged her sled up the hill.
   1. *push, shove*

2. *v.* **dawdle, lag, go slowly**
Time seemed to drag while we waited for the recess bell to ring.
   2. *progress, rush*

drain

1. *n.* **pipe, trench, outlet, duct**
Pour the water down the drain in the sink.

2. *v.* **filter, flow**
Three rivers drain into this valley.

3. *v.* **empty, draw out, exhaust, weaken**
Her illness drained her energy.
   3. *revive, refresh, replenish*

drama

1. *n.* **the stage, acting, theater**
Craig studied drama for several years to become an actor.

2. *n.* **play, piece, work, show, production**
My class is putting on a historical drama.

dramatic

adj. **exciting, striking, moving**
We watched the dramatic events of the riots on television.
dull, ordinary, bland

drastic

adj. **extreme, radical, desperate, severe**
Putting a lock on the refrigerator is a drastic way to diet.
moderate, cautious

draw

1. *v.* **pull, haul, drag, attract, bring**
The tow truck drew the car to the garage.
   1. *push, shove, repel*

2. *v.* **attract, bring in**
The big stars draw people to the movies.
   2. *repel, turn away*

3. *v.* **extract, take out, bring out**
Keri drew money from her savings account to pay for the trip.
   3. *put in, deposit, put away*

4. *v.* **approach, move**
The stores got busier as the holidays drew near.

5. *v.* **sketch, design, depict**
Manuel drew a picture of the scene.
n. He displayed the drawing on the wall.

drawn

adj. **haggard, pinched, wrinkled, strained**
Her drawn face told us something was wrong.
smooth, unwrinkled, relaxed

dread

1. *n.* **fear, anxiety, horror, terror, fright**
The strange sounds filled me with dread.
   1. *hope, courage, calm, confidence*

2. *v.* **be afraid of, fear**
She dreaded writing the test because she hadn't studied for it.
   2. *look forward to*

dreadful

adj. **awful, terrible, alarming, frightful**
We were horrified by the dreadful news about the space shuttle Columbia.
harmless, pleasing, lovely, assuring

dream	1.	*n.*	**vision, nightmare, trance, fantasy** My dream was that I won the lottery.	*1. reality*
	2.	*v.*	**imagine, fancy, visualize, fantasize** I dream of being a famous writer someday.	
dreary		*adj.*	**dismal, dingy, gloomy, cheerless** I work in a dreary office with no windows.	*bright, joyful, cheerful*
drench		*v.*	**douse, soak, saturate, wet** A sudden downpour drenched us.	*dry, parch*
dress	1.	*n.*	**clothing, clothes, garments, attire** Casual dress will be fine for the barbecue.	
	2.	*v.*	**change, clothe, robe, outfit** I have to dress for the party.	*2. strip, disrobe, undress*
drift	1.	*n.*	**heap, mass, pile, bank** The children jumped into the huge drifts of snow.	
	2.	*n.*	**trend, flow, direction, course** I knew what he was leading up to from the drift of the conversation.	
	3.	*v.*	**sail, float, be carried along** Clouds drifted slowly across the blue sky.	*3. be motionless*
drill	1.	*v.*	**bore, punch, puncture, pierce** Pat drilled a hole in the wall.	
	2.	*v.*	**exercise, train, practice, rehearse** He drilled the dancers in their routine. *n.* A fire drill teaches you what to do in a real fire.	
drip		*v.*	**trickle, dribble, drop** My wet clothes dripped water on the floor. *adj.* We were dripping wet after being caught in the rain.	
drive	1.	*n.*	**energy, impulse, force** Ali has the drive and ambition to be very successful.	
	2.	*v.*	**compel, make, prod, urge** His parents drive him to try harder.	*2. discourage, hinder, restrain*
	3.	*v.*	**steer, navigate, direct** I am learning how to drive a car. *n.* We went for a drive in the new car.	
droop		*v.*	**hang down, sag, sink, lower** The flowers drooped in the intense heat.	*rise, revive, perk up*
drop	1.	*n.*	**drip, globule, bead, trickle, speck** Dew drops glistened on the roses.	
	2.	*v.*	**fall, slide, lower, topple** The temperature dropped suddenly. *n.* The lake froze when there was a drop in temperature.	*2. lift, raise, go up*

3. *v.* **let go, release, omit, exclude**
The team dropped Jim after he missed several practices.

3. include, add to, pick up

drown **1.** *v.* **swamp, overwhelm, engulf, submerge**
The audience drowned out the speaker with loud boos.

2. *v.* **suffocate, extinguish**
The mouse drowned in a large puddle.

2. resuscitate, revive, revitalize

drowsy *adj.* **sleepy, lazy, tired, slow**
The drowsy child was put to bed.

alert, lively

dry **1.** *adj.* **arid, parched, dehydrated**
Few plants can survive in the dry desert.

1. wet, soggy, damp, moist, humid, juicy

2. *adj.* **dull, boring, tedious, uninteresting**
I fell asleep during his dry speech.

2. interesting, witty, stimulating

dual *adj.* **twofold, double**
Two people can play this video game because it has dual controls.

single

dubious **1.** *adj.* **uncertain, doubtful, hesitant, undecided**
I am dubious about my chance for success in that difficult exam.

1. certain, sure, positive, definite

2. *adj.* **questionable, suspicious**
Ugly rumors are circulating about his dubious past.

due **1.** *adj.* **unpaid, owing, payable, outstanding**
Jim paid the amount due on his account.

1. settled, paid

2. *adj.* **scheduled, expected**
The train is due at four-thirty.

3. *adj.* **proper, suitable, deserved**
We treat our elders with due respect.

3. improper, unsuitable

dull **1.** *adj.* **boring, dry, uninteresting, tedious**
He slept through the dull movie.

1. interesting, stimulating

2. *adj.* **gloomy, dismal, murky, dim**
It was a dull, rainy day.

2. bright, cheerful, merry

3. *adj.* **stupid, slow**
He does poorly in school not because he is dull, but because he is lazy.

3. clever, intelligent, smart, witty, bright, keen

4. *adj.* **blunt, unsharpened**
Please sharpen this dull knife.

4. sharp

5. *adj.* **faint, soft, low**
I barely heard the dull knock on the door.

5. distinct, loud

dumb *adj.* **mute, silent, unable to speak**
We were struck dumb with surprise when we heard the news.

able to speak, vocal

dump **1.** *n.* **junkyard, garbage disposal, rubbish heap**
Garbage trucks take garbage to the dump.

	2.	*v.*	**empty, unload** The trucks dumped the gravel at the construction site.	**2.** *fill, load, pack*
dupe		*v.*	**trick, fool, deceive** He duped me into buying a broken bike.	*guide, assist*
duplicate	1.	*n.*	**imitation, replica, copy, facsimile** I sent a duplicate of my certificate and kept the original.	**1.** *original*
	2.	*v.*	**copy, reproduce** She duplicated her notes for me.	**2.** *originate*
durable		*adj.*	**lasting, sound, strong, sturdy** We chose durable furniture for the children's room.	*weak, fragile, flimsy*
duration		*n.*	**period, term, extent, span** I was sick for the duration of the trip.	
duty	1.	*n.*	**obligation, responsibility** We should place duty before pleasure.	**1.** *irresponsibility*
	2.	*n.*	**job, task, work** Your duties include market research.	**2.** *entertainment, diversion, sport*
	3.	*n.*	**customs, tax, tariff** We had to pay duty to bring our purchases across the border.	
dwell	1.	*v.*	**inhabit, live, occupy, reside, stay** The blue heron dwells in swampy regions. *n.* I visited the struggling actor in his humble dwelling.	**1.** *move, leave*
	2.	*v.*	**ponder, brood, think or speak about, harp on** Don't dwell on your past; look ahead to the future.	**2.** *forget, dismiss, overlook*
dwindle		*v.*	**shrink, decline, fade, lessen** Hopes of finding the lost children dwindled with each passing day.	*increase, grow, multiply, expand*
dye		*v.*	**stain, color, tint** I dyed my white shirt a deep blue. *n.* We used yellow and blue dye to turn the fabric green.	*bleach*
dynamic		*adj.*	**active, powerful, vigorous, forceful, energetic** The business is thriving under the new owner's dynamic leadership.	*slow, dull, passive, listless, inert*

E is used more often than any other letter in our alphabet. Not only does it represent two vowel sounds by itself (*pen*, *seen*), but it may also change the sounds of other vowels when it ends a word (*hop*, *hope*).

The Romans used *E* to represent 250.

eager		*adj.*	**keen, enthusiastic, anxious, zealous, fervent, ardent** The eager students completed their project in a day. *adv.* Fans waited eagerly for the arrival of their favorite rock star.	*indifferent, apathetic, unconcerned, disinterested*
eagerness		*n.*	**zest, enthusiasm, anticipation, desire, excitement, readiness** We were touched by their eagerness to help.	*reluctance, aversion, opposition*
early	1.	*adj.*	**long ago, ancient** Early peoples lived in caves.	1. *contemporary, modern, recent*
	2.	*adv.*	**in advance, ahead of time, beforehand, prematurely** She arrived early for the party. *adj.* We had an early dinner because we were so hungry.	2. *late, slow, tardily, behind time*
earn	1.	*v.*	**deserve, merit, rate, win, gain, attain** After years of hard work and training, the skaters have earned their gold medals.	1. *usurp, fail, forfeit*
	2.	*v.*	**get, obtain, acquire, profit, gain** He earns good wages as a cook. *n.* Most people are wage earners.	2. *spend, consume, exhaust*
earnest		*adj.*	**zealous, ardent, sincere, serious, fervent** Earnest efforts are being made to reduce pollution. *adv.* Activists are working earnestly to help save our environment.	*indifferent, uninterested, insincere, flippant*
earnings		*n.*	**pay, payment, income, salary, wages, receipts, returns** People spend most of their earnings on housing and food.	*expenses, outlay*
ease	1.	*n.*	**rest, respite, repose, calmness, comfort** The patient was put at ease before the surgery.	1. *pain, unrest, discomfort, irritation*
	2.	*n.*	**facility, skill, dexterity, adroitness** Ian jumped over the fence with ease.	2. *difficulty, trouble, clumsiness, ineptitude*
	3.	*n.*	**leisure, pleasure, contentment, comfort** Everyone envies Peter's life of ease.	3. *adversity, hardship, discomfort*
	4.	*v.*	**relieve, reduce, soothe, lessen** Take a pill to ease your headache.	4. *increase, irritate, aggravate*
easy	1.	*adj.*	**simple, effortless, uninvolved, uncomplicated** We were relieved that it was an easy test.	1. *difficult, complex, involved, complicated*
	2.	*adj.*	**calm, peaceful, mild, serene, gentle, affable** Our host's easy manners helped us relax.	2. *raucous, harsh, irritating, strident*

eat	1.	*v.*	**devour, dine, digest, consume, sup** The hungry child ate all the food. *n.* Eating is a pleasure for some.	**1.** *fast, starve*
	2.	*v.*	**corrode, erode, wear away** Rust eats into the metal on cars.	**2.** *build, increase, improve, swell*
ebb		*v.*	**recede, fall back, decline, decrease, subside, withdraw, wane, regress** The ocean tide rises and ebbs daily. *n.* Beaches become wider with the ebb of the tide.	*rise, increase, advance, enlarge, grow, intensify*
eccentric		*adj.*	**unusual, odd, strange, bizarre, non-conformist, singular, unconventional** People avoid her because of her eccentric behavior. *n.* She is known as an eccentric.	*usual, common, ordinary, conventional, conformist*
eclipse		*v.*	**overshadow, darken, dim, conceal, cover** Jay's career eclipsed his brother's. *n.* Will there be a total or partial eclipse of the moon?	*disclose, expose*
economize		*v.*	**save, be thrifty, conserve, scrimp** Naomi economized on food when she was unemployed. *adj.* She had economical meals. *adv.* She lived economically. *n.* Her economy helped her survive.	*waste, spend, splurge*
ecstasy		*n.*	**joy, delight, rapture, bliss, happiness, pleasure** They were in ecstasy when they won an Olympic gold medal. *adj.* They were ecstatic about their victory.	*sadness, discontent, dejection, depression*
edge	1.	*n.*	**brink, verge, brim, periphery, border, outside, rim** Zinnias were planted along the edge of the lawn. *v.* Flowers edged the lawn.	**1.** *center, inside, interior*
	2.	*n.*	**blade** The razor's edge is sharp.	
	3.	*n.*	**head start, advantage, handicap** That extra player gave the hockey team the edge.	**3.** *disadvantage*
educate		*v.*	**teach, instruct, tutor, train, enlighten, develop** Teachers educate their pupils. *n.* In many countries, education is compulsory until the age of sixteen.	*misinform*
eerie		*adj.*	**strange, peculiar, weird, ghostly, frightful, ominous, mysterious** The eerie scream made my hair stand.	*usual, ordinary, common*

effect	1.	n.	result, consequence, conclusion, outgrowth, aftermath	1. cause, reason, rationale
			The effect of hours of hard training was an impressive victory for the team.	
	2.	n.	impression, influence	
			Her inspirational words had a lasting effect on us.	
	3.	v.	accomplish, achieve, cause, bring about, realize	3. prevent
			It is difficult to effect change.	
effective		adj.	productive, efficient, competent, capable, useful	ineffective, unproductive
			This new drug is effective in curing headaches.	
		adv.	It effectively gets rid of headaches.	
efficient	1.	adj.	capable, adept, effective, proficient, productive, competent, skillful	1. inefficient, unskilled, incompetent, ineffective, incapable
			The efficient cashier will be promoted.	
		n.	His efficiency is much admired.	
		adv.	He worked efficiently on the project.	
	2.	adj.	economical, suitable, serviceable	2. uneconomical, wasteful, unsuitable
			Gas is an efficient way to heat the house.	
effort	1.	n.	work, toil, labor, exertion	1. inactivity, rest, idleness, ease
			Their success came after years of effort.	
	2.	n.	attempt, undertaking, venture	
			Their fundraising effort was a success.	
eject		v.	oust, exclude, expel, dismiss, remove, evict	admit, let in, receive, allow, welcome, include
			The conductor ejected the rowdy person from the bus.	
elaborate	1.	adj.	ornate, decorated, ornamented, adorned	1. plain, simple, unadorned, ordinary
			Many cathedrals have elaborate interiors.	
	2.	adj.	detailed, complicated, complex, intricate, involved, thorough	2. simple, plain, uncomplicated
			They drew up elaborate plans for a plaza.	
		adv.	The plaza is designed elaborately.	
	3.	v.	expand, extend, embellish, enlarge	3. condense, abridge, reduce, lessen
			The author elaborated on his ideas in his new book.	
elapse		v.	slip away, pass, go by, transpire	
			How much time elapsed before help came?	
elasticity		n.	spring, resilience, flexibility	hardness, brittleness, rigidity
			Human muscles have elasticity.	
		adj.	Rubber bands are elastic.	
elated		adj.	overjoyed, happy, delighted, ecstatic	depressed, gloomy, disappointed
			The runner was elated with his victory.	
elder		adj.	senior, older	younger, junior
			Mary asked her elder sister for advice.	

elect		*v.*	**choose, select, vote for** The students elected a class president. *n.* The election was a close one.	*cast out, reject, vote out*

elect   *v.*   **choose, select, vote for**   *cast out, reject, vote out*
The students elected a class president.
n. The election was a close one.

elegant
1. *adj.*   **tasteful, classic, fancy**   **1.** *crude, plain, ordinary*
We dined in an elegant restaurant.
adv. It was elegantly decorated.
2. *adj.*   **cultured, dignified, refined, aristocratic**   **2.** *crude, unrefined, uncouth*
The elegant woman was most charming.
n. There was an air of elegance about her.

elementary
1. *adj.*   **rudimentary, introductory, simple**   **1.** *advanced, difficult, complicated, complex*
Kim learned elementary arithmetic in grade one.
2. *adj.*   **fundamental, basic, essential**   **2.** *advanced, secondary*
An elementary education is required in North America.

elevate
1. *v.*   **raise, lift, heighten, hoist**   **1.** *lower, depress*
The stage crew elevated the platform to allow the performers to be seen.
n. A hill is an elevation.
n. Elevators move people from one floor to another.
2. *v.*   **promote, advance, improve, upgrade**   **2.** *demote, downgrade*
The officer was elevated to the rank of colonel.

elicit   *v.*   **extract, obtain, draw out**   *instill, put in*
The FBI elicited useful information from witnesses.

eligible   *adj.*   **qualified, suitable, fit**   *ineligible, unfit, unqualified*
There are many eligible candidates for the job.

eliminate   *v.*   **remove, eject, discard, expel**   *include, accept*
The champions eliminated our team in the playoffs.
n. We were unhappy with our elimination.

elude   *v.*   **avoid, evade, dodge, avert, escape**   *face, meet, encounter, seek*
The escaped convict eluded arrest.

emaciated   *adj.*   **thin, scrawny, gaunt, skeletal**   *fat, obese, plump, well-fed, corpulent*
The emaciated person suffered from an eating disorder.

emancipate   *v.*   **liberate, free, release, deliver**   *restrain, confine, imprison, enslave*
President Lincoln emancipated the slaves in 1863.
n. The emancipation of slaves came after years of struggle.

embark
1. *v.*   **board, load**   **1.** *disembark*
The ship's passengers embarked at Miami.
n. Miami was the port of embarkation.

2. *v.* **set out, begin, start**
He embarked on his new job with both
fear and eagerness.

2. *conclude, end*

embarrass *v.* **disconcert, distress, vex, bother,
upset, humiliate**
His rudeness embarrassed his parents.
adj. What an embarrassing moment!
n. They blushed in embarrassment.

*encourage, help,
assist, assure,
reassure*

emerge **1.** *v.* **appear, come out**
A large crowd emerged from the stadium
at the end of the game.

1. *disappear, hide,
go in*

2. *v.* **become known**
The truth finally emerged after hours of
investigation.

2. *stay hidden*

emergency *n.* **crisis, dilemma, distress**
Nurses are trained to stay calm during
emergencies.

routine, normalcy

eminent **1.** *adj.* **famous, noted, renowned, exalted,
important, celebrated, prominent**
The eminent scientists were applauded
for their latest discovery.

1. *unknown, obscure,
unheard of,
unimportant*

2. *adj.* **high, elevated, raised, lofty**
The church on the hill is in an eminent
position.

2. *low, depressed*

emit *v.* **give off, radiate, beam, discharge**
Cars emit carbon monoxide.
n. Such emissions pollute the air.

*absorb, take in,
consume, ingest,
receive*

emotion *n.* **feeling, sentiment, passion**
Humans experience many different
emotions.

*unemotional,
apathetic*

emotional *adj.* **stirring, moving**
Watching our team receive their gold
medal was an emotional moment for us.

emphasize *v.* **stress, accent, accentuate, highlight**
Advertisements emphasize the qualities
of the products that are for sale.
n. The main emphasis of any
advertisement is the product.

negate

employ **1.** *v.* **hire, engage, contract**
The factory employs hundreds of workers.
n. Many people are seeking employment.
n. The factory owner is the employer.
n. The workers are the employees.

1. *dismiss, let go, fire*

2. *v.* **use, apply, utilize**
Surgeons employed the latest techniques
and equipment to save her life.

empty	1.	*v.*	**flow out, drain, discharge** The St. Lawrence River empties into the Atlantic Ocean.	**1.** *flow in, absorb*
	2.	*v.*	**clear out, pour out, clean out** Please empty your desks before you leave.	**2.** *fill, pack, stuff, cram*
	3.	*adj.*	**bare, vacant, unoccupied, blank, void** The empty lot will be turned into a park.	**3.** *full, filled, occupied*
	4.	*adj.*	**meaningless, senseless, vacuous, pointless, insincere** The speech contained empty promises.	**4.** *meaningful, purposeful*
enable		*v.*	**allow, let, permit, empower** Computers enable us to do many jobs much faster.	*prohibit, prevent, obstruct, impede*
enchant		*v.*	**delight, please, charm, thrill, bewitch, captivate, fascinate** The singer enchanted the audience. *adj.* It was an enchanting performance.	*disgust, repel, offend, displease*
enclose	1.	*v.*	**encompass, surround, encircle, circle, contain, ring** Hedges enclosed the gardens. *n.* Horses are kept in enclosures.	
	2.	*v.*	**insert, put in, include** Enclose the invoice with the check.	**2.** *exclude, take out, remove*
encompass	1.	*v.*	**enclose, circle, encircle, ring, surround, contain** The army encompassed the town so that no one could escape.	
	2.	*v.*	**include, contain, consist of** The entire farm encompassed four acres.	**2.** *exclude, lack*
encounter	1.	*n.*	**meeting, appointment, rendezvous** Brief encounters with friends are pleasant.	
	2.	*n.*	**conflict, fight, battle, confrontation, struggle, skirmish, engagement** Fierce border encounters between the nations led to war.	**2.** *withdrawal, retreat*
	3.	*v.*	**meet, come or stumble across, find** Will scientists encounter life on other planets?	**3.** *leave, part*
encourage	1.	*v.*	**cheer, hearten, inspire, comfort, reassure** The doctor's news encouraged the patient to fight the disease. *adj.* The encouraging news cheered us. *n.* Patients need all the encouragement they can get.	**1.** *discourage, dishearten, depress*
	2.	*v.*	**stimulate, spur, bolster, boost** The company offered free gifts to encourage sales.	**2.** *discourage, hinder, deter, obstruct*
encroach		*v.*	**trespass, infringe, invade, violate** His question encroached upon our privacy.	

end	1.	*n.*	**tip, point, edge, tail, extremity** The emergency exit is at the end of the corridor.	**1.** *center, middle, start*
	2.	*n.*	**conclusion, close, finish, finale** Did you watch the end of the movie?	**2.** *beginning, start, opening, outset*
	3.	*n.*	**aim, purpose, intention, goal, object** There is no obvious end to the argument.	
	4.	*n.*	**demise, death** President Kennedy met his end in Dallas.	**4.** *origin, birth, beginning*
	5.	*v.*	**finish, stop, halt, cease, terminate, discontinue, conclude** Please end this meaningless argument.	**5.** *begin, start, commence, initiate*
endanger		*v.*	**imperil, jeopardize** Hunting has endangered many species of animals.	*save, preserve, shield, protect, defend*
endeavor		*v.*	**try, attempt, aim, struggle, strive** Captain Scott endeavored to reach the South Pole. *n.* He made an honest endeavor to reach his goal.	*quit, give up*
endless	1.	*adj.*	**limitless, unbounded, measureless, uninterrupted, continuous** Outer space is endless.	**1.** *fixed, bounded, finite*
	2.	*adj.*	**perpetual, eternal, everlasting, ceaseless** Without an education, many people live in an endless cycle of poverty.	**2.** *temporary, fleeting, brief, periodic*
endorse		*v.*	**approve, sanction, support, speak for** Famous people often endorse products in advertisements. *n.* They earn large sums of money from the endorsements.	*censure, condemn, denounce*
endow		*v.*	**bequeath, bestow, give** She endowed her paintings to the gallery. *n.* The art gallery appreciated the endowment.	*receive, acquire, obtain*
endure	1.	*v.*	**last, continue, remain, persist, stay, linger** Her contribution to society will endure forever. *adj.* She made an enduring contribution to society.	**1.** *cease, end, stop*
	2.	*v.*	**suffer, tolerate, bear, undergo** The arthritic patient endured great pain. *n.* Such pain is beyond endurance.	**2.** *avoid, resist*
enemy		*n.*	**foe, adversary, antagonist, opponent, attacker** The politician has made many enemies.	*friend, ally, helper, supporter*
energetic		*adj.*	**lively, active, vigorous, vital** The energetic child refused to go to bed.	*lazy, inactive, sluggish*

energy	1.	*n.*	**force, power, strength, vigor, vitality, drive** Proper diet and exercise is essential for physical energy.	
	2.	*n.*	**power, force** Home appliances use electrical energy.	
enforce		*v.*	**execute, compel, oblige, impose** The police enforce law and order. *n.* Law enforcement is necessary for stability in a country.	*abandon, evade, negate*
engage	1.	*v.*	**employ, hire, contract, retain** Who engaged that plumber for the job?	**1.** *dismiss, fire, discharge, release*
	2.	*v.*	**involve, occupy, absorb** The guest engaged us in conversation.	
	3.	*v.*	**commit, promise, pledge** We engaged ourselves to the cause.	
engaged	1.	*adj.*	**betrothed, plighted, pledged** Pierre and Lu are engaged to be married. *n.* The engagement has been announced.	**1.** *free, unattached*
	2.	*adj.*	**busy, involved, occupied, employed** The class was engaged in a science experiment.	**2.** *uninvolved, idle, unoccupied*
	3.	*adj.*	**in use, taken, filled, assigned** All the telephone lines were engaged during the crisis.	**3.** *not in use, free, clear, open, available*
engulf		*v.*	**swallow up, inundate, submerge, immerse, flood, swamp** The tidal wave engulfed the coastal town.	*emerge, rise, come up*
enhance		*v.*	**magnify, intensify, heighten, increase, advance, augment** Winning the award will enhance the dancer's career.	*lessen, decrease, diminish, reduce, shorten*
enigma		*n.*	**puzzle, riddle, mystery, secret, bafflement, conundrum** The cause of the illness is an enigma. *adj.* It is an enigmatic problem.	
enjoy		*v.*	**delight in, like, be fond of** Misha enjoys singing. *adj.* Do you find singing enjoyable?	*dislike, hate, deplore*
enjoyment		*n.*	**pleasure, delight, happiness, joy** TV gives most people hours of enjoyment.	*unhappiness, sorrow, sadness, grief, misery*
enlarge		*v.*	**expand, increase, extend, augment** We enlarged our house by adding a room. *n.* I made an enlargement of the photo.	*decrease, reduce, shrink, make smaller*
enormous		*adj.*	**huge, immense, tremendous, vast, colossal, monstrous** Enormous amounts of money are spent on space research.	*tiny, minute, little, small, petite, puny, diminutive, undersized*

enough	*adj.*	**ample, sufficient, adequate** We didn't have enough time to complete the test. *adv.* He earned enough to pay the bills.	*insufficient, scant, inadequate, deficient*
enrich	*v.*	**improve, better, enhance** Cereal companies enrich their products with vitamins. *n.* We go for enrichment classes in math.	*destroy, deteriorate*
enter	1. *v.*	**come into, go in, set foot in** Please knock before you enter.	1. *leave, exit, depart*
	2. *v.*	**register, record, inscribe, list, file, post** Guests entered their names in the book.	2. *erase, remove*
	3. *v.*	**join, enroll** Has Jon entered the race?	3. *quit, leave, withdraw*
	4. *v.*	**begin, start, take up** Sam entered college at fifty years of age.	4. *end, give up*
eternal	*v.*	**endless, everlasting, infinite** An eternal flame was lit at the site of the World Trade Center in New York City.	
enterprise	*n.*	**project, task, adventure, venture, scheme, undertaking, endeavor, pursuit** The moon landing was a bold enterprise.	
enterprising	*adj.*	**bold, adventurous, daring** The enterprising students started a business selling caps.	*cautious, careful, hesitant, timid*
entertain	1. *v.*	**amuse, delight, beguile, charm** A clown entertained the children. *n.* Rock stars are popular entertainers.	1. *bore, tire, weary*
	2. *v.*	**host, welcome, receive** The President entertained the royal visitors at a gala dinner.	2. *neglect, exclude, ignore, shun*
enthusiasm	*n.*	**eagerness, zeal, fervor, zest, energy** The speaker aroused enthusiasm for his cause. *adj.* The enthusiastic listeners gave the speaker a standing ovation.	*indifference, ennui, apathy, boredom*
entice	*v.*	**lure, attract, draw, charm, tempt** In the early 1900s, the government enticed settlers with free land. *adj.* Money is often an enticement that is hard to resist.	*repel, repulse*
entire	*adj.*	**complete, whole, total** The entire room is painted yellow. *adv.* The room is entirely yellow.	*incomplete, partial*
entrance	1. *n.*	**doorway, access, entry, approach** We greeted the guests at the entrance.	1. *exit, outlet*

	2.	*n.*	**arrival, entry** The movie star made a dramatic entrance at the party.	**2.** *departure, exit*
entreat		*v.*	**beg, urge, implore, beseech** The sick child entreated the nurse to stay.	*command, demand*
enumerate		*v.*	**count, compute, number, reckon, calculate** Census takers enumerated the population of the country. *n.* How accurate is the enumeration?	*miscount*
environment		*n.*	**surroundings, habitat** Acid rain harms the natural environment.	
envy	**1.**	*n.*	**jealousy** The loser's envy was obvious. *adj.* Her envious classmates ignored her.	**1.** *good will*
	2.	*v.*	**desire, covet** Many people envy her confidence.	**2.** *share*
epidemic		*n.*	**pestilence, scourge, blight, plague** A flu epidemic spread across the country.	
episode	**1.**	*n.*	**installment, part** There are three episodes in this TV series.	**1.** *whole, entirety*
	2.	*n.*	**occurrence, happening, occasion, event** The Vietnam War will be remembered as a dreadful episode in history.	
equal	**1.**	*n.*	**match, counterpart, peer** These tennis players are ranked as equals.	
	2.	*v.*	**correspond to, parallel, match** Jo and Reg equaled each other in ability.	**2.** *differ, vary, deviate from*
	3.	*adj.*	**identical, matching, same, even, like** Use equal amounts of water and sugar.	**3.** *unequal, different, varying, disparate*
equip		*v.*	**furnish, supply, outfit, provide** The owner equipped the car with a phone and a stereo. *n.* The car had all the latest equipment.	*strip, remove*
equitable		*adj.*	**fair, just, impartial, proportionate** There should be equitable opportunities for everyone. *adv.* The money will be shared equitably.	*unfair, unjust, disproportionate*
equivalent		*adj.*	**equal, interchangeable, synonymous, commensurate, correspondent** The fractions ²/₄ and ¹/₂ are equivalent.	*unequal, uneven, disproportionate*
era		*n.*	**period, epoch, generation, age, time** Dinosaurs lived in the prehistoric era.	
eradicate		*v.*	**abolish, eliminate, erase** The government eradicated slavery.	*save, protect, preserve, defend*

erase	1.	*v.*	**blot out, remove, scratch out, rub out** Lu erased the mistakes in her letter. *n.* Pencil erasers are made of rubber.	1. *retain, keep, enter*
	2.	*v.*	**obliterate, wipe out, eliminate, eradicate** Nuclear war could erase all forms of life on Earth.	2. *protect, preserve*
erect	1.	*v.*	**build, construct, raise** The council voted to erect a new city hall.	1. *demolish, remove, tear down*
	2.	*v.*	**assemble, put together, set up, fit together** Sonja erected a model spaceship from the parts in the kit.	2. *take apart, dismantle, disassemble, undo*
	3.	*v.*	**establish, found, form, institute, organize, create** The town erected a fund to fight cancer.	3. *demolish*
	4.	*adj.*	**upright, vertical, perpendicular** The soldier stood erect at his post.	4. *horizontal, flat, prone, level*
erode		*v.*	**disintegrate, break down, wear down** Wind erodes topsoil. *n.* Soil erosion is a serious problem for farmers.	*preserve, protect*
err		*v.*	**be mistaken, blunder, fail, misjudge** Sam erred in his decision to skip class.	*be correct, be right*
errand		*n.*	**task, mission** We hired a student to run errands for us.	
erratic		*adj.*	**variable, unpredictable, inconsistent, irregular, changeable** His erratic behavior caused us concern.	*consistent, reliable, steady, constant*
error		*n.*	**mistake, blunder, fault, faux pas** The student made an error in her test. *adj.* Her smile gave us the erroneous impression that all was well.	*correction, accuracy*
erupt		*v.*	**explode, emit, eject, discharge** Molten lava erupted from the volcano. *n.* The volcanic eruption was a spectacular sight.	*lie dormant*
escape	1.	*n.*	**flight, retreat, withdrawal** The criminal's escape terrified the town.	1. *retention, capture, imprisonment*
	2.	*v.*	**flee, evade, avoid, elude** Everyone in the building escaped the fire.	2. *stay, remain, confront, incur*
escort		*v.*	**accompany, go with, attend** Bodyguards escorted the sports star through the crowd. *n.* Bodyguards are his constant escorts.	
espionage		*n.*	**spying, reconnaissance** Industrial espionage sometimes occurs in highly competitive industries.	

essential		*adj.*	**necessary, vital, important, indispensable, fundamental** The formula listed the essential ingredients in the potion.	*unnecessary, trivial, unimportant, redundant*
establish	1.	*v.*	**set up, build, install, found, erect** Explorers established settlements in North America.	*1. break up, dismantle*
	2.	*v.*	**prove, verify, confirm, authenticate, validate** A driver's license establishes the identity of the driver.	*2. disprove, refute, deny*
esteem		*n.*	**respect, honor, regard, admiration** Our principal is held in great esteem.	*disrespect, dishonor, disregard*
estimate		*v.*	**evaluate, assess, gauge, guess, appraise** Estimate the size of this room. *n.* How accurate was your estimate?	
eternal		*adj.*	**everlasting, unending, endless, perpetual, permanent, ceaseless** Earth is in an eternal orbit of the sun. *adv.* We will be eternally grateful for your help.	*temporary, brief, fleeting, transient*
ethics		*n.*	**morality, conduct, code of morals** Lawyers and medical doctors have a code of ethics to guide them. *adj.* He is an ethical man and can be trusted totally.	
evacuate		*v.*	**empty, clear, vacate, abandon, leave** People evacuated the coastal towns before the hurricane struck. *n.* The evacuation of the towns saved many lives.	*stay, remain*
evade		*v.*	**avoid, elude, get away from, escape** The witness evaded the lawyer's question.	*confront, meet, face*
evaluate		*v.*	**appraise, judge, assess, estimate** Insurance adjusters evaluated the cost of damages from the accident.	
evaporate	1.	*v.*	**dissolve, vanish, disappear, fade** Our hopes of victory evaporated in the final round.	*1. appear, emerge, materialize*
	2.	*v.*	**vaporize** Water evaporates when boiled.	*2. liquefy, solidify*
even	1.	*adj.*	**smooth, level, flat, regular** The floor has an even surface.	*1. uneven, rough, irregular*
	2.	*adj.*	**same, identical, equal, tied** The score at the end of the game was even.	*2. uneven, unequal*

event	1.	*n.*	**happening, incident, occurrence, experience, occasion**
			Our holidays were full of exciting events.
	2.	*n.*	**chance, case, possibility**
			The picnic will be canceled in the event of rain.

eventually   *adv.*   **ultimately, in the end, finally**   *never*
Eventually there will be a cure for cancer.

every   *adj.*   **each, all**
Every citizen has a responsibility to vote.

evict   *v.*   **oust, remove, put out, eject, dismiss**   *admit, let in, welcome, receive*
The tenants were evicted from their homes for not paying their rent.
n. The tenants pleaded with the landlord to delay the eviction.

evident   *adj.*   **apparent, clear, obvious, visible, plain, unmistakable**   *concealed, hidden, obscure*
It was evident that the marathon runner was tiring.
adv. The runner is evidently tired.

evil	1.	*n.*	**wrong, wickedness, corruption**	**1.** *virtue, good, goodness*
			No evil exists in Utopia.	
	2.	*adj.*	**wicked, bad, corrupt, sinful**	**2.** *kind, virtuous, good*
			In the fairy tale, the evil stepmother was punished.	

exact	1.	*adj.*	**precise, accurate, correct, perfect**	**1.** *incorrect, inaccurate*
			The storekeeper had the exact change.	
			adv. She cut the cake exactly into eighths.	
	2.	*adj.*	**sharp, distinct, clear-cut, lucid, definite, obvious, clear**	**2.** *blurred, unclear, indistinct, obscure, indiscernible*
			Exact silhouettes are easy to identify.	
	3.	*adj.*	**strict, demanding, rigorous, severe, stringent, rigid, exacting**	**3.** *flexible, lax, undemanding*
			Commanding officers issue exact orders.	

exaggerate   *v.*   **magnify, enlarge, expand, stretch, overstate**   *minimize, lessen, understate*
The reporters exaggerated the seriousness of the incident.
adj. The exaggerated account of the incident alarmed many people.
n. The reporters were reprimanded for their exaggeration of the truth.

examination   *n.*   **test, assessment**
I am studying for my final examination.

examine   *v.*   **check, inspect, observe, investigate, survey, probe, search, scrutinize**   *neglect, ignore, disregard*
Scientists carefully examined the fossils.
n. The prehistoric remains will undergo thorough examinations.

example	1.	*n.*	**model, ideal, paragon, prototype** Lena is an example of a good student.	
	2.	*n.*	**representation, sample, specimen** Show me an example of your work.	
exasperate		*v.*	**irritate, annoy, peeve, aggravate** The students exasperated the teacher with their lack of attention. *n.* Ed left in exasperation when we wouldn't play with him.	*please, soothe, satisfy,* *calm, comfort, console*
excavate		*v.*	**dig, shovel, hollow out, scoop out** Archaeologists excavate historical sites.	*fill in, fill, bury, close*
exceed		*v.*	**surpass, excel, outpace, outdo,** **outstrip, pass, go beyond** Her success exceeded all expectations.	*fall behind, lag,* *fall short of*
excel		*v.*	**beat others, surpass others,** **be superior, do better than** Yoko excels in mathematics.	*be inferior to, fail*
excellent		*adj.*	**superior, superb, admirable,** **outstanding, wonderful, great** The prize-winning stories are excellent. *adv.* The authors wrote excellently.	*poor, inferior,* *imperfect*
except		*prep.*	**excluding, omitting, saving, without,** **but, aside from, other than** The whole family went except for Ian.	*including, inclusive* *of, together with,* *as well as*
exceptional		*adj.*	**unusual, rare, special, extraordinary** Pavarotti is an exceptional opera singer. *adv.* He sings exceptionally well.	*usual, common,* *ordinary, regular,* *normal*
excess		*n.*	**abundance, surplus, oversupply** There is an excess of wheat this year. *adj.* The excess wheat will be exported.	*scarcity, lack,* *deficiency, dearth,* *shortage*
excessive		*adj.*	**superfluous, exorbitant, extravagant,** **extreme, profuse** Excessive rainfall can ruin crops.	*scant, lean, poor,* *insufficient, meager,* *inadequate*
exchange		*n.*	**interchange, transaction, swap** There was an exchange of gifts at school. *v.* We exchanged gifts on Christmas Day.	
excite		*v.*	**arouse, stir, stimulate, agitate,** **provoke, animate, thrill** The roller coaster ride excited everyone. *adj.* An excited group of spectators waited for the arrival of the movie star. *n.* The movie star caused excitement.	*calm, soothe, quiet,* *pacify, relax, subdue*
exclaim		*v.*	**shout, call out, say loudly, cry out, yell** "Watch out!" exclaimed the waiter when I almost bumped into him. *n.* His exclamation startled me.	*murmur, mutter,* *whisper, mumble*

exclude	*v.*	**bar, ban, shut out, reject, prohibit, keep out** The referee excluded the feisty player from the game. *n.* The fans applauded the exclusion.	*allow, admit, welcome, include*
excrete	*v.*	**shed, emit, discharge, eliminate** The body excretes sweat through the pores in the skin.	*soak up, absorb, retain*
excursion	*n.*	**trip, jaunt, journey, outing, expedition** Bus excursions to Orlando are popular.	
excuse	**1.** *n.* **2.** *v.*	**reason, explanation, defense** Is there an excuse for your lateness? **pardon, forgive, overlook** Please excuse me for being late.	 **2.** *accuse, blame*
execute	**1.** *v.* **2.** *v.*	**kill, put to death, slay** The rebels executed the dictator. *n.* Executions were frequent during the French Revolution. **perform, do, complete, finish, achieve, accomplish** The skater executed a triple spin.	**1.** *rescue, save, protect, preserve*
exempt	*adj.*	**free, clear, excused, absolved** Antiques are exempt from customs duty.	*responsible, liable, subject to*
exertion	*n.*	**effort, struggle, work, action** Physical exertion keeps one healthy.	*rest, repose, relaxation*
exhaust	**1.** *v.* **2.** *v.*	**use up, consume, deplete** The stranded survivors exhausted their food supply. **tire, weary, fatigue, debilitate** The long climb up the mountain exhausted everyone. *n.* Marathon runners can collapse from exhaustion.	**1.** *preserve, save, store, keep, restore, replenish* **2.** *strengthen, invigorate*
exhibit	**1.** *n.* **2.** *v.*	**show, display, presentation** Handicrafts were on exhibit at the fair. **expose, reveal, display, show, present** The latest software will be exhibited at the computer fair.	 **2.** *conceal, hide, cover*
exhilarate	*v.*	**enliven, excite, stimulate, invigorate, gladden, refresh** The good news exhilarated all of us.	*depress*
exile	**1.** *n.*	**banishment, expulsion, deportation, expatriation** Napoleon spent his exile on the island of Elba. *n.* Napoleon was an exile on Elba.	**1.** *repatriation*

	2.	v.	**cast out, banish, expel, deport** The government exiled the traitor.	**2.** *repatriate*

exist		v.	**live, survive, be, endure** Dinosaurs existed a long time ago. *n.* The refugees led a miserable existence in the camps.	*die, pass away, expire*
exit	1.	n.	**way out, outlet** Fire exits in public buildings are mandatory by law.	**1.** *entrance, way in*
	2.	n.	**departure, withdrawal** The leading character made a dramatic exit from the stage.	**2.** *arrival, entrance*
	3.	v.	**leave, depart, go out** Exit by the main door.	**3.** *enter, go in, arrive*
exotic		adj.	**foreign, unusual, fascinating, alien, different** Travel posters often show pictures of exotic places.	*local, common, ordinary, mundane*
expand		v.	**grow, extend, dilate, amplify, swell, stretch, inflate** Mercury expands and contracts with changes in temperature. *n.* The expansion of the company resulted in the hiring of more people.	*contract, shrink, reduce, decrease, deflate*
expanse		n.	**extent, area, space, stretch** We drove across the vast expanse of the prairies.	
expedition		n.	**excursion, voyage, journey, trip, quest** Captain Cook's expedition circumnavigated the world.	
expel		v.	**eject, oust, dismiss, exclude, discharge, evict, suspend, remove** Our school expels students who drink or take drugs. *n.* Students face expulsion if they drink or take drugs.	*admit, include, welcome, let in, receive*
expense		n.	**cost, amount, charge, outlay, price** Enormous expenses were incurred in the search for the *Titanic*.	*profit, income, return, gain, saving*
expensive		adj.	**costly, high-priced, dear** Emeralds are expensive jewels.	*inexpensive, cheap, low-priced*
experience	1.	n.	**training, background, practice** The job applicant had no previous experience with computer programming. *adj.* The company hired an experienced computer programmer.	**1.** *inexperience*

2. *v.* **encounter, undergo, endure**
The refugees experienced many hardships in their flight to safety.
n. They hope to forget their bad experiences.

2. *avoid, escape*

experiment *n.* **investigation, trial, test, examination, research**
Scientists conduct experiments to prove their hypotheses.
v. Scientists experimented with the new source of energy.

expert **1.** *n.* **authority, specialist, master**
Art experts evaluated the painting.

1. *novice, beginner, tyro*

2. *adj.* **accomplished, skillful, adept, able, proficient, practiced**
Expert divers are needed to retrieve the sunken treasure.
adv. The diver expertly recovered the sunken treasure.

2. *inept, inexperienced*

explain *v.* **clarify, describe, make clear, clear up**
Explain the meaning of the word.
n. The teacher's explanation helped Ann understand the problem.

puzzle, confuse, confound, perplex, mystify, baffle

explicit *adj.* **detailed, clear, definite, precise**
The witness gave an explicit description of the accident.

confused, vague, sketchy, obscure

explode *v.* **burst, blow up, detonate**
Bombs exploded in the battle zone.
n. The loud explosions frightened us.
n. Explosives must be handled with caution.
adj. Explosive devices are dangerous.

exploit **1.** *n.* **deed, feat, achievement, venture, escapade**
The first space flight was a daring exploit.

2. *v.* **use, take advantage of**
The gambler exploited the other player's weaknesses.

2. *help, aid, assist*

explore *v.* **search, examine, investigate, probe**
Astronauts are exploring space.
n. Henry Hudson was an explorer.

export *v.* **ship, send out, sell abroad**
The United States exports fruits.
n. Japan's exports include cars.

import, bring in

expose **1.** *v.* **uncover, bare, reveal, show**
She exposed her wound to help it dry.

1. *cover, conceal, hide*

2. *v.* **disclose, reveal, show, uncover**
The FBI exposed him as a spy after months of investigation.

2. *conceal, hide*

express	1.	*v.*	**tell, voice, state, utter, speak, declare, reveal, communicate** Please express your ideas clearly.	*1. keep silent, remain silent, withhold*
	2.	*v.*	**ship, dispatch, forward, send, deliver** Export companies express goods around the world. *n.* Certain items are sent by express.	
expressive		*adj.*	**eloquent, dramatic, stirring, emphatic, strong, spirited, meaningful, stimulating** The expressive speaker held the audience's attention. *adv.* He spoke expressively.	*indifferent, boring, dull, uninspiring, inarticulate*
exquisite		*adj.*	**delicate, choice, fine, precise, exact, dainty** Everyone admired the exquisite details on the cameo ring. *adv.* The ring was designed exquisitely.	*ordinary, common, coarse, mediocre, average*
extend	1.	*v.*	**offer, give, impart** We extend our best wishes to you.	*1. get, receive*
	2.	*v.*	**expand, enlarge, increase, lengthen, stretch** We extended our holiday by a week. *n.* The extension to our house will be completed soon.	*2. decrease, reduce, compress, condense, consolidate, contract, limit, shorten*
extent		*n.*	**size, amount, scope, magnitude, range, limit, degree** We have not assessed the extent of the damage caused by the flood.	
exterior	1.	*n.*	**outside, surface, skin** The exterior of the building was covered in ivy.	*1. inside, interior*
	2.	*adj.*	**external, outside, outer** Exterior walls need to be painted often.	*2. interior, internal*
exterminate		*v.*	**destroy, kill, abolish, stamp out, wipe out, annihilate, eradicate** Chemical sprays were used to exterminate the cockroaches. *n.* Cockroaches are controlled by extermination.	*preserve, keep, save, protect, maintain*
external	1.	*adj.*	**exterior, outward, outer, outside** Some cars have thermometers that indicate the external temperature.	*1. internal, interior, inward, inner, inside*
	2.	*adj.*	**foreign** Who is responsible for external affairs in our government?	*2. native, home, national*
extinct		*adj.*	**obsolete, defunct, dead, annihilated** Dinosaurs are extinct. *n.* No one is sure what caused the extinction of the dinosaurs.	*existent, existing, current, alive, living*

extinguish	*v.*	**put out, quench, choke, smother, douse, suffocate, stifle, wipe out** Kevin extinguished the blaze with the fire extinguisher.	*fan, instigate, set, promote, initiate, incite, cause*
extort	*v.*	**extract, force, wrench, steal, exact** Blackmailers use threats to extort money from their victims. *n.* The blackmailer was charged with extortion.	*restore, give back, return*
extra	*adj.*	**additional, added, further, more, excess** Extra supplies were shipped to the famine victims.	*less, limited, insufficient, deficient*
extract	1. *n.* 2. *v.*	**quotation, selection, excerpt, passage** Read your favorite extract from the book. **take out, remove, draw out** The dentist extracted the loose tooth.	1. *entirety, whole* 2. *insert, add, put in*
extraordinary	*adj.*	**remarkable, amazing, unusual, rare** Helen Keller was an extraordinary woman.	*usual, normal, ordinary, common*
extraterrestrial	*adj.*	**unearthly, alien, inhuman** No one knows if extraterrestrial beings exist.	*earthly, worldly, terrestrial*
extravagance	*n.*	**waste, excess, lavishness, indulgence** The couple's extravagances led to their bankruptcy. *adj.* Their extravagant lifestyle was the talk of the town.	*economy, thrift, frugality*
extreme	1. *n.* 2. *adj.* 3. *adj.* 4. *adj.*	**height, limit, apex, end, climax, top** The music brought the audience to the extreme of pleasure. **maximum, drastic, intense, acute** Tim suffered extreme pain when he was injured in the accident. **farthest, most remote, outermost** Navigation is difficult in the extreme areas of the Arctic. **radical, fanatical, excessive, immoderate** Some people have extreme political views.	 2. *minimum* 3. *nearest, closest* 4. *moderate, cautious, restrained*
extricate	*v.*	**free, liberate, loosen, dislodge, disengage, release, disentangle** The rescuers extricated the driver from the badly wrecked car.	*restrain, keep, hold, capture, seize, entangle*
eye	*v.*	**watch, view, observe, scrutinize, inspect, look at, examine, regard** Maggie eyed the ice cream longingly.	*ignore, neglect, overlook, disregard*

F

The English language took this letter from the Romans, who borrowed it from an early Greek alphabet.

The Irish monks, who copied the Gospels in "manuscript" writing, created the small *f* and other small letters, when they began to use quills for writing.

The capital *F* was used as a symbol for *francs* in French money before the introduction of the Euro dollar.

fabric		*n.*	**cloth, textile, material** Synthetic fabrics require easy care.	
fabulous	1.	*adj.*	**incredible, astonishing, amazing, astounding, marvelous, wonderful** A trip to Tibet would be a fabulous adventure.	**1.** *simple, usual, normal, routine*
	2.	*adj.*	**mythical, legendary, fictitious** The unicorn is a fabulous animal.	**2.** *historical, real, authentic, genuine*
facade	1.	*n.*	**front, outside, exterior, face** Many old buildings have ornate facades.	**1.** *interior, inside, back, rear*
	2.	*n.*	**appearance, expression, face** Even though she lost the match, Joy put on a brave facade and smiled.	
face	1.	*n.*	**countenance, visage** Chris protected her face from the sun with a big hat.	
	2.	*n.*	**outside, front, surface, exterior, facade** The face of the building was covered with marble from Italy.	**2.** *interior, inside, rear, back*
	3.	*v.*	**front, be opposite to, look out on, be turned toward** All the windows face the lake.	
	4.	*v.*	**brave, defy, meet, confront, encounter** Firefighters face many dangers on the job.	**4.** *avoid, withdraw, evade, elude*
facet		*n.*	**aspect, face, side** Well-cut diamonds have many facets.	
facility	1.	*n.*	**dexterity, adroitness, ease, skill, ability, capability** The gymnast shows great facility on the parallel bars.	**1.** *awkwardness, difficulty, inability*
	2.	*n.*	**equipment, tools, buildings** The school has excellent sports facilities.	
	3.	*n.*	**agency, bureau, company, amenity** In case of an emergency call the nearest medical facility.	
fact		*n.*	**certainty, truth, reality, actuality** Aging is a fact of life.	*lie, falsehood, fantasy, fiction*
factor		*n.*	**part, portion, component, determinant, element, condition** Many factors contribute to the success of a business.	*whole*
facts		*n.*	**events, details, actions, data, statistics, circumstances, evidence** During the trial many facts were revealed to the jury.	
factual		*adj.*	**exact, precise, accurate, true** A witness gave a factual report of the accident.	*inaccurate, untrue, contrived, fictitious*

faculty	1.	*n.*	**ability, skill, talent, gift, capacity, flair** Yoko has a faculty for mathematics.	1. *inability, weakness, failing*
	2.	*n.*	**teaching staff, teachers, department** Dr. Ho is a member of the Dental Faculty of the university.	
fad		*n.*	**craze, rage, whim** Skateboards were a fad last summer.	*tradition, custom, habit*
fade	1.	*v.*	**droop, wither, lose color** The flowers faded in the intense heat.	1. *flourish, revive, endure, last*
	2.	*v.*	**grow faint, die away** The picture faded from the TV screen.	2. *become clear, become sharp*
fail	1.	*v.*	**be unsuccessful, miss, flunk** Many pupils failed the test. *n.* The high failure rate was upsetting.	1. *pass, succeed, excel, win, triumph*
	2.	*v.*	**decline, deteriorate, weaken** Grandma's health failed after her fall.	2. *improve, strengthen*
faint	1.	*v.*	**collapse, black out, swoon** During the rock concert, many fans fainted in the crowded stadium. *n.* Sue crumpled in a faint when she heard the bad news about the accident.	
	2.	*adj.*	**indistinct, vague, unclear, faded, dim** The faint outline of a ship could be seen on the horizon.	2. *sharp, clear, distinct, prominent*
	3.	*adj.*	**weak, feeble, faltering, languid, frail** The survivor spoke in a faint whisper.	3. *strong, hearty, energetic, vigorous*
fair	1.	*adj.*	**beautiful, attractive, pretty, lovely** Helen of Troy was said to be the fairest woman in Greece.	1. *unattractive, ugly, displeasing*
	2.	*adj.*	**clear, sunny, dry, pleasant, fine** We had a fair day for the hike.	2. *wet, cloudy, dark, stormy*
	3.	*adj.*	**just, impartial, honest, proper** The judge made a fair decision.	3. *unfair, dishonest, partial*
	4.	*adj.*	**passable, tolerable, reasonable** Your writing is fair but can be improved with practice.	
faith		*n.*	**belief, trust, confidence, reliance** I have faith in your ability to do well.	*doubt, disbelief, distrust, suspicion*
faithful		*adj.*	**true, loyal, dependable, constant, honest, sure, devoted, reliable** A faithful employee is a great asset to a company.	*fickle, unreliable, disloyal, false, unfaithful*
fake	1.	*n.*	**fraud, phony, imitation, counterfeit** The famous painting proved to be a fake.	1. *original*
	2.	*v.*	**counterfeit, falsify, forge, simulate** The spy faked his passport.	
	3.	*adj.*	**phony, counterfeit, bogus, false** The fake money confiscated by the police will be destroyed.	3. *authentic, real, genuine*

fall	1.	*n.*	**tumble, spill, collapse** Lee suffered a bad fall while skiing. *v.* Ian slipped and fell on the icy road.	**1.** *rise, get up*
	2.	*v.*	**decline, drop, go down, sink, plunge** Stock prices fell when war broke out. *n.* We were happy to hear about the fall in the price of airline tickets.	**2.** *climb, ascend, rise, increase*
	3.	*v.*	**happen, occur, take place** My birthday falls on a Saturday this year.	
fallacy		*n.*	**error, untruth, blunder, misconception** There are many fallacies in that book.	*truth, verity, fact*
false	1.	*adj.*	**incorrect, erroneous, mistaken, wrong** They had a false notion of the cause of the accident.	**1.** *right, true, correct, accurate, exact*
	2.	*adj.*	**bogus, counterfeit, fake, imitation** A con artist substituted a false diamond for the real one.	**2.** *authentic, real, genuine, natural*
	3.	*adj.*	**disloyal, unfaithful, faithless** Suyi's false friends deserted her when she lost all her money.	**3.** *loyal, faithful, true, sincere*
falter	1.	*v.*	**totter, waver, stagger, stumble** The boxer's punch caused his opponent to falter and fall to the floor.	
	2.	*v.*	**stutter, stammer, hesitate** The shy child faltered as she tried to ask for help.	
fame		*n.*	**renown, notoriety, glory, repute, distinction, prestige** Marie Curie achieved fame as the discoverer of radium.	*anonymity, obscurity*
familiar	1.	*adj.*	**well-known, customary, usual** It was nice to see my friend's familiar face again when I returned.	**1.** *unfamiliar, new, strange, unknown*
	2.	*adj.*	**friendly, informal, close** The group members became familiar after working together on the project.	**2.** *formal, aloof, reserved*
famished		*adj.*	**starving, hungry** The lost child was famished after three days without food.	*well-fed, filled, satisfied, sated*
famous		*adj.*	**well-known, renowned, celebrated, distinguished** Robert Frost was a famous poet.	*unknown, obscure, anonymous*
fan	1.	*n.*	**follower, supporter, devotee, admirer, enthusiast** Fans cheered at the team's victory parade.	**1.** *non-supporter, opponent*
	2.	*v.*	**stir up, incite, arouse** The union leader's speech fanned the workers' anger.	**2.** *douse, dampen, discourage, kill*

fanatic		*n.*	**zealot, devotee, enthusiast** Fanatics can speak with intense emotion about their beliefs. *adj.* Their fanatical beliefs make many people uncomfortable.	
fancy	1.	*n.*	**fantasy, imagination, illusion** Are Martians objects of fancy?	**1.** *reality, fact*
	2.	*n.*	**liking, fondness, preference** Nan took a fancy to my white poodle.	**2.** *dislike, distaste, aversion*
	3.	*v.*	**imagine, picture** Fancy that! What a story!	
	4.	*adj.*	**decorated, fussy, ornamental, elaborate** Sue Ling wore a fancy dress to the party.	**4.** *plain, unadorned, simple, ordinary*
fantastic	1.	*adj.*	**fanciful, weird, strange, queer, great, imaginary, peculiar, whimsical** I wonder what fantastic creatures live on other planets?	**1.** *common, ordinary, regular, routine*
	2.	*adj.*	**extraordinary, great, terrific, amazing, excellent, wonderful** The children had a fantastic time at Disneyland.	**2.** *bad, miserable*
fantasy		*n.*	**imagination, illusion, fiction, reverie, dreams** Megan has a fantasy about traveling back in time.	*reality, actuality*
far		*adj.*	**distant, remote** Our new home is very far from town.	*near, close, handy*
farewell	1.	*n.*	**goodbye, adieu** The astronaut waved farewell before boarding the spacecraft.	**1.** *hello*
	2.	*adj.*	**parting, last** The actor's farewell performance was well attended.	**2.** *initial, first, opening, debut*
fascinate		*v.*	**charm, enchant, delight, enthrall** The magician's tricks fascinated the audience. *adj.* We had a fascinating time watching the whales.	*disgust, repel, displease, bore*
fashion	1.	*n.*	**manner, way** Mario told the same story in a different fashion.	
	2.	*n.*	**style, trend** Movie stars dress in the latest fashions. *adj.* They wear fashionable clothes. *adv.* They dress fashionably.	
	3.	*v.*	**shape, make, mold, form, create** The artist fashioned the statue out of clay.	
fast	1.	*adj.*	**quick, rapid, fleet, swift, speedy** Jesse Owens was a fast runner.	**1.** *slow, sluggish*

	2.	*adv.*	**securely, tightly, firmly** Be sure the boat is tied fast to the dock. *adj.* The police had a fast hold of the suspect.	**2.** *loosely, insecurely*
	3.	*adv.*	**thoroughly, soundly, completely, fully** Dad was fast asleep in front of the TV.	**3.** *hardly, barely, just*
fasten		*v.*	**tie, connect, link, attach, hook, bind, clasp, clamp** Stuart fastened the yacht to its mooring.	*untie, disconnect, loosen, release*
fat		*adj.*	**stout, plump, portly, obese, fleshy** The fat pigs were shipped to the market.	*skinny, lean, thin, slim, slight, slender*
fatal		*adj.*	**deadly, mortal, lethal** A drunk driver caused the fatal accident. *n.* With care and courtesy, many traffic fatalities could be prevented.	*harmless, slight, non-lethal*
fate		*n.*	**destiny, lot, chance, fortune, doom** It was his fate to die at war.	
fated		*adj.*	**destined, doomed, sure, certain** She was fated to win the lottery.	
fatigue	**1.**	*n.*	**weariness, exhaustion** The mountain climber was suffering from fatigue and lack of oxygen.	**1.** *vim, vigor, energy*
	2.	*v.*	**tire, exhaust, weary** The long walk in heavy snow fatigued us.	**2.** *revive, renew, strengthen*
fault	**1.**	*n.*	**mistake, error, slip, blunder** Several faults in the skater's performance cost her the medal.	
	2.	*n.*	**failing, weakness, flaw, defect** Bill's one fault is that he's always late.	**2.** *strength, virtue*
faultless		*adj.*	**perfect, ideal, correct, accurate, flawless** Glenn wrote a faultless mathematics test.	*imperfect, faulty, defective*
faulty		*adj.*	**imperfect, unsatisfactory, defective, flawed, blemished** Faulty brakes in the car caused the accident.	*satisfactory, correct, perfect, faultless*
favor	**1.**	*n.*	**kindness, service, courtesy** Can you please do me a favor and drive me to school tomorrow?	**1.** *rebuff, unkindness, discourtesy*
	2.	*v.*	**prefer, like, approve, sanction, back, lean toward, be partial to, promote** Which candidate do you favor?	**2.** *dislike*
favorable	**1.**	*adj.*	**approving, positive** The principal speaks of you in a favorable way. *adv.* Our proposal was favorably received by the committee.	**1.** *disapproving, negative*

	2.	*adj.*	**helpful, useful, beneficial** Favorable winds shortened our voyage.
	3.	*adj.*	**promising, hopeful** The weather looks favorable for the picnic tomorrow.

2. harmful, unfavorable
3. threatening

favorite
1. *n.*   **choice, pet, preferred one, best-liked one**
The smallest puppy was my favorite.

1. least-liked one

2. *adj.*   **choice, special, best-liked, preferred**
Min's favorite dessert is chocolate cake.

2. least-liked, unwanted, unwelcome

fear   *n.*   **fright, dread, terror, horror, anxiety**
We tried to overcome his fear of the dark.
adj.   Sam is fearful of the dark.
v.   Children often fear the dark.

bravery, boldness, courage

fearless   *adj.*   **bold, brave, courageous, daring, gallant, heroic**
The crowd cheered their fearless leader.
adv.   The leader told the people to face the enemy fearlessly.

timid, scared, cowardly, fearful, afraid, frightened

feast
1. *n.*   **banquet, meal, festival**
There was a grand feast to celebrate the team's victory.

1. famine, fast

2. *v.*   **dine, gorge**
We feasted on the restaurant's fine food.

2. starve, fast

feat   *n.*   **achievement, deed, act, exploit, accomplishment, attainment**
It was quite a feat for Marilyn Bell to swim across Lake Ontario.

feature
1. *n.*   **highlight, attraction, main item, prominent part**
What is the feature at the sports show?
v.   The concert featured a young soloist.

2. *n.*   **characteristic, point, trait, attribute**
Fiery red hair is his most distinctive feature.

fee   *n.*   **remuneration, pay, salary, charge, compensation**
How much is the lawyer's fee?

donation, gift, endowment

feeble   *adj.*   **weak, puny, frail, ailing**
The refugees were feeble from hunger.
adv.   The trapped boy cried feebly for help.

healthy, strong, firm, hearty, robust

feel
1. *n.*   **touch, sensation, texture**
I like the feel of soft materials like silk.

2. *v.*   **touch, handle**
The doctor gently felt my twisted ankle.

3. *v.*   **grope, make one's way**
Di felt her way in the darkness to find the light switch.

4. *v.* **seem, appear**
The crocuses make it feel like spring has arrived.

5. *v.* **sense, be aware of, experience**
I feel cold with the window open.

5. *be unaware of, be insensitive to*

6. *v.* **think, believe, consider**
How do you feel about the new book?

feeling

1. *n.* **sensation**
I get a funny feeling in my stomach when I fly.

2. *n.* **emotion, reaction**
Cindy hurt Andy's feelings with her harsh remarks.

3. *n.* **opinion, belief, thought**
What are your feelings about freedom of the press?

feign *v.* **pretend, invent, simulate, fabricate, sham, falsify, affect, imitate, assume**
The student feigned illness to avoid the examination.

fence *n.* **barrier, railing, wall**
The robber climbed over the fence.

ferocious *adj.* **fierce, savage, wild, ruthless, brutal, barbarous, violent**
The tiger is a ferocious beast.
n. Its ferocity is terrifying.
adv. The tiger charged ferociously at the hunter.

mild, meek, gentle, tame, delicate

fertile

1. *adj.* **fruitful, productive, rich, arable**
Land along the Nile River is fertile.
v. The farmer fertilized the land to produce better crops.

1. *barren, useless, unproductive, poor*

2. *adj.* **inventive, resourceful, imaginative**
The author of the Harry Potter books has a fertile mind.

2. *infertile, unimaginative*

fervent *adj.* **eager, ardent, zealous, devoted, passionate**
Fervent prayers were offered to end the war.
adv. The people prayed fervently for help.

indifferent, apathetic, dispassionate

festival *n.* **holiday, fete, celebration**
Religious festivals are celebrated worldwide.

festive *adj.* **merry, happy, joyful, jolly**
Everyone was in a festive mood on New Year's Eve.

sad, mournful, tragic

fetch *v.* **bring, get, obtain, carry**
Fetch the book from the library, please.

send, throw, toss, dispatch

feud		*n.*	**quarrel, row, dispute, strife** The feud between the families lasted for generations. *v.* The two families feuded for years.	*peace, harmony*
few		*adj.*	**not many, scarcely any** Few people attended the meeting.	*many, numerous, innumerable*
fib	1.	*n.*	**lie, falsehood, untruth, fiction** Don't believe those fibs about how much money he makes.	**1.** *truth*
	2.	*v.*	**lie, bluff, mislead** They fibbed about not being involved in the prank.	**2.** *tell the truth*
fidget		*v.*	**squirm, wriggle, twitch** The applicant fidgeted nervously during the interview.	*relax, sit still*
fidgety		*adj.*	**restless, uneasy, jittery, nervous** The thunderstorm has made the class fidgety.	*calm, quiet, relaxed, at ease*
fierce	1.	*adj.*	**wild, savage, cruel, furious, ferocious, brutal** The gangs fought a fierce battle for the territory. *adv.* They fought fiercely for weeks.	**1.** *tame, gentle, mild, calm, peaceful, docile, submissive*
	2.	*adj.*	**strong, powerful, intense, extreme** The fierce storm caused a power failure.	**2.** *weak, faint, moderate, calm*
fiery	1.	*adj.*	**fierce, ardent, passionate, impetuous, unrestrained** A fiery debate took place between the two candidates running for mayor.	**1.** *indifferent, mild, apathetic, phlegmatic*
	2.	*adj.*	**hot, blazing, glowing** No one escaped from the fiery inferno.	**2.** *quenched, extinguished*
fight		*n.*	**struggle, battle, combat, contest, conflict, quarrel, brawl** Which boxer won the fight? *v.* The soldiers fought bravely till the end.	*peace, harmony*
figure	1.	*n.*	**outline, shape, form, design, pattern** The skater traced the figure 8 on the ice.	
	2.	*n.*	**cost, amount, value, sum** The dealer named an impossibly large figure for the painting.	
	3.	*v.*	**compute, calculate, solve** Can you figure out the answer to the math problem?	
file	1.	*n.*	**list, dossier, record, catalog, inventory** Keep the information in the files.	
	2.	*n.*	**row, queue, string, line** The soldiers marched in single file.	

	3.	*v.*	**classify, index, arrange, store, list, categorize** The clerk filed the documents by date.
	4.	*v.*	**scrape, pulverize, grind, smooth** Manicurists file nails with emery boards.
fill	1.	*v.*	**pack, stuff, pour in, put in** Rena filled the jug with juice.
	2.	*v.*	**occupy, serve** Wendy filled the position of treasurer for the club.
filter	1.	*v.*	**seep, penetrate, ooze, trickle, leak, permeate, soak through, drain** Water from the spring run-off filtered through the rocks.
	2.	*v.*	**clean, purify, strain, sieve, filtrate** We filter water to make it safe for drinking.
filth		*n.*	**dirt, impurity, contamination, garbage, pollution** We were disgusted with the filth in the cabin. *adj.* We cleaned up the filthy mess.
final		*adj.*	**last, concluding, ultimate** The final game of the basketball season will be played tomorrow.
finance	1.	*n.*	**money matters, banking, investment** Lim is trained in finance. *adj.* She handles the financial matters of the company.
	2.	*v.*	**fund, pay for, provide funds for, underwrite, subsidize, endow** Michelle financed her college tuition by working on the weekends.
find	1.	*n.*	**discovery** Tutankhamen's tomb was an exciting find for archaeologists.
	2.	*v.*	**discover, detect, recover** Molly found her lost ring in her glove.
fine	1.	*n.*	**penalty, forfeit** The driver received a fine for speeding. *v.* He was fined fifty dollars.
	2.	*adj.*	**delicate, detailed, refined** Aunt Sue does fine embroidery.
	3.	*adj.*	**very good, excellent, superior** Ken has proved to be a fine pupil.
	4.	*adj.*	**clear, bright, sunny, pleasant** They had a fine day for their wedding.
	5.	*adj.*	**attractive, handsome** Isn't this a fine looking car?
	6.	*adj.*	**tiny, minute, powdery, pulverized** The beach has fine white sand.

Antonyms column:

3. *disorder, disarrange, disorganize*

1. *empty, drain*

2. *leave, vacate*

2. *pollute, putrefy, contaminate*

cleanliness, purity, spotlessness

first, initial, opening

2. *lose, mislay, misplace*

1. *reward, award*

2. *coarse, crude*

3. *poor, inferior*

4. *dull, dreary, dark, cloudy*

5. *unattractive, ugly*

6. *coarse*

finish	**1.**	*n.*	**end, completion, close, conclusion** He fought gamely to the finish of the match.	**1.** *beginning, start, commencement*
	2.	*n.*	**surface, exterior, coating, veneer** This stain gives furniture a shiny finish.	
	3.	*v.*	**end, complete, conclude** Haven't you finished the essay yet?	**3.** *start, begin, commence*
fire	**1.**	*n.*	**flame, blaze, conflagration, holocaust** Forest fires endanger wildlife.	
	2.	*n.*	**verve, dash, sparkle, vim, enthusiasm** The new leader was advised to show more fire in his speech.	**2.** *dullness, boredom, weariness, tedium*
	3.	*v.*	**kindle, ignite, inflame, light** The President's speech fired everyone's enthusiasm for the cause.	**3.** *extinguish, quench, smother*
	4.	*v.*	**shoot** The police recruits fired at the target.	**4.** *hold fire*
firm	**1.**	*n.*	**business, establishment, company, organization, enterprise** Martine works for a publishing firm.	
	2.	*adj.*	**solid, sturdy, hard, tight** The opponents shook hands with a firm grip.	**2.** *weak, shaky, soft, flabby*
	3.	*adj.*	**immovable, secure, rigid, steady, fixed** Make sure the tent poles are firm. *adv.* We hammered them in firmly.	**3.** *wobbly, unstable, unsteady*
	4.	*adv.*	**determined, decided, resolved, fearless, adamant** Anton stood firm in his resolve not to reveal the secret.	**4.** *undecided, fearful*
first	**1.**	*adj.*	**initial, original, earliest, opening, introductory, inaugural** Marconi received the first transatlantic wireless message from St. John's, Newfoundland.	**1.** *last, final, ultimate*
	2.	*adj.*	**foremost, chief, prime, principal, highest, leading, primary** Personal safety is our first concern on this expedition.	**2.** *secondary, lesser*
fishy		*adj.*	**suspicious, doubtful, strange, misleading, peculiar** The scheme to invest in that gold mine seems fishy.	*trustworthy, honest, aboveboard*
fit	**1.**	*n.*	**size, shape** "Your suit is a good fit," she remarked.	
	2.	*v.*	**agree, match, coincide** The views of the partners fitted well.	**2.** *disagree*
	3.	*adj.*	**suitable, appropriate, apt, proper, right** This movie has too much violence in it and is not fit for children.	**3.** *inappropriate, improper, unfit*
	4.	*adj.*	**healthy, strong** It took Matt a long time to become fit after the accident.	**4.** *unhealthy, unfit, weak*

fitness		*n.*	**health, vigor, strength** Fitness is important to Dad so he jogs daily.	*weakness, poor health, sickness*
fix	1.	*v.*	**adjust, repair, correct, mend** Jan fixed the faulty wiring on her lamp.	**1.** *damage, spoil, ruin*
	2.	*v.*	**settle on, decide, determine, establish** Let's fix the date for the next meeting.	**2.** *vacillate, waver*
	3.	*v.*	**connect, fasten, secure, attach** Mom fixed the light to the ceiling.	**3.** *detach, loosen, disconnect*
flabbergasted		*adj.*	**astonished, amazed, dumbfounded, confounded** We were flabbergasted when we saw our test results. *v.* The excellent results flabbergasted us.	*unmoved, stoic*
flamboyant		*adj.*	**showy, flashy, ornate, gaudy** The dancers wore flamboyant costumes at the Mardi Gras parade.	*drab, dull, somber, bland, conservative*
flame	1.	*n.*	**blaze, fire, flare** Flames shot out from the burning house.	
	2.	*v.*	**burn, blaze, flare** The logs flamed brightly in the fireplace.	**2.** *smolder*
flare	1.	*n.*	**flash, spark, flame** Flares warned oncoming motorists of the accident.	
	2.	*v.*	**flash, blaze, burn, glow** Warning lights flared in the dark.	
	3.	*v.*	**erupt, explode, go off, burst, blow up, break out** Fighting flared up suddenly at the border.	**3.** *remain dormant, stay quiet, fizzle*
flash		*v.*	**glitter, twinkle, sparkle, glow, shimmer** The meteor flashed across the sky. *n.* A sudden flash of lightning startled us. *adj.* The flashing lights on the police car warned us of the detour.	
flashy	1.	*adj.*	**showy, gaudy, loud, garish** The actor always wears flashy clothes. *adv.* He dresses flashily.	**1.** *simple, quiet, plain, conservative*
	2.	*adj.*	**glittering, shiny, dazzling** The fireworks exploded in flashy streaks across the sky.	
flat	1.	*adj.*	**level, even, horizontal** The prairies are flat stretches of land.	**1.** *uneven, hilly, mountainous, rolling*
	2.	*adj.*	**tasteless, dull, unpleasant, stale** The food in the hospital was flat.	**2.** *sharp, bubbling, tasty, sparkling*
flaunt		*v.*	**display, boast, parade** Some people flaunt their wealth in a vulgar way.	*conceal, hide, be modest*

flavor	1.	*n.*	**taste, savor, tang, relish, seasoning** Barbecued meat has a unique flavor. *v.* Ping flavored the meat with spices.	
	2.	*n.*	**character, mark, quality, feeling, characteristic, trait, feature, attribute, distinction, identity** His stories all have the flavor of the Orient.	**2.** *generality*
flaw		*n.*	**defect, imperfection, fault, blemish** Some pieces of pottery are on sale because they have flaws. *adj.* The flawed pieces have been reduced in price.	*perfection*
flawless		*adj.*	**perfect, sound, faultless** The skater gave a flawless performance to win the medal.	*imperfect, damaged, defective, flawed*
flee		*v.*	**run away, take flight, desert** The wanted man fled from the police.	*remain, stay, stand firm*
fleece	1.	*n.*	**hair, wool** Fleece from sheep is turned into wool.	
	2.	*v.*	**strip, rob, swindle, steal, deceive** Swindlers fleece innocent people of their money.	**2.** *reimburse, repay, pay, pay back*
flex		*v.*	**bend, tighten, contract** Trevor flexed his muscles before he lifted the weights.	*relax*
flexible	1.	*adj.*	**pliable, supple, limber, springy** The flexible gymnast impressed us with her performance on the bars.	**1.** *rigid, unbending, inflexible, stiff*
	2.	*adj.*	**adaptable, variable, adjustable** We keep flexible working hours. *n.* There is a certain amount of flexibility in the training program.	**2.** *inflexible, rigid, constrained*
flicker		*v.*	**waver, shimmer, quiver, fluctuate** The candle flickered and went out. *adj.* The flickering light cast eerie shadows in the room.	*remain steady*
flimsy	1.	*adj.*	**sheer, thin, gauzy, fragile** My flimsy chiffon dress was ruined in the wash.	**1.** *thick, heavy, substantial, sturdy*
	2.	*adj.*	**poor, weak, feeble** That's a flimsy excuse for not helping your friend.	**2.** *real, good, sound*
fling		*v.*	**throw, heave, toss, pitch, hurl, sling** The pitcher flung the ball to third base.	*catch, receive*
flip	1.	*n.*	**flick, toss, tap, throw, snap** He removed the crumb from his jacket with a flip of his finger.	

2. *v.*   **thumb, turn over, turn, leaf, skim**
She flipped through the book to find her favorite story.

                                                   2. peruse, study, ponder

flippant   *adj.*   **impudent, rude, smart, saucy, pert, bold, forward, impertinent**
Pam was told to stop disrupting the class with her flippant remarks.

polite, courteous, shy, well-mannered

float   *v.*   **drift, hover, glide, sail**
The canoe floated on the calm lake.

sink, settle

flock   **1.** *n.*   **group, herd, brood, pack, swarm, set, collection, company, throng**
A flock of sheep grazed peacefully on the hillside.

         2. *v.*   **troop, congregate, crowd**
People flock to the beach on hot days.

flop   *v.*   **tumble, slump, drop, fall, topple**
The exhausted runner flopped to the ground.

rise, ascend, climb

flounder   **1.** *v.*   **struggle, toss, wallow, grope, fumble, stumble, stagger**
The child floundered in the water before being rescued.

1. rise, emerge

         2. *v.*   **struggle, falter, blunder**
Her new business floundered for the first six months before taking off.

2. flourish

flourish   **1.** *v.*   **thrive, prosper, succeed**
His business flourishes in the summer.

1. lessen, decline, wither, fade, fail

         2. *v.*   **wave, twirl, brandish, flaunt**
The drum major flourished her baton before marching on.

flout   *v.*   **mock, ridicule, deride, scorn, taunt**
He flouted the school rules and was suspended.

respect, revere, honor, venerate

flow   **1.** *n.*   **stream, course**
There is a constant flow of water into the pond.

         2. *v.*   **glide, stream, gush, move, run, pass**
The Mississippi River flows into the Gulf of Mexico.

2. stagnate, stop

fluid   **1.** *n.*   **liquid, solution**
Water is a fluid.

1. solid

         2. *adj.*   **changeable, flexible**
Our plans are still fluid at this stage.

2. firm, fixed

flurry   **1.** *n.*   **gust, light snowfall, squall**
The flurry of snow didn't last long.

         2. *n.*   **fluster, disturbance, agitation, panic**
There was a flurry of activity in the school before the science fair.

2. quiet, calm

fluster	1.	*n.*	**turmoil, flurry, confusion, ferment** What a fluster when the band did not arrive for the party.	**1.** *quiet, calm*
	2.	*v.*	**confuse, agitate, excite, upset, bother, disturb, startle** The arrival of unexpected guests flustered the host. *adj.* Sharon became flustered during the interview.	**2.** *calm, quiet*
fly	1.	*v.*	**soar, wing, glide, travel** Birds fly south every fall.	
	2.	*v.*	**flutter, flap, float, wave** The flag flew above the Pentagon.	
focus	1.	*n.*	**center, focal point, core, heart, nucleus, hub, middle** The new baby was the focus of everyone's attention.	**1.** *periphery, border, outside, perimeter*
	2.	*v.*	**direct, center, aim, fix, concentrate** The photographer focused the camera on the leader of the parade.	
foe		*n.*	**enemy, rival, adversary, opponent** He made peace with his foes.	*friend, companion, ally, comrade*
foggy	1.	*adj.*	**misty, murky, hazy, clouded** The coastline often gets foggy weather.	**1.** *fine, bright, clear, sunny*
	2.	*adj.*	**confused, puzzled, unclear, vague, obscure, blurred** Pedro has only a foggy idea of how to get to the beach.	**2.** *clear, lucid, thorough, accurate*
foil		*v.*	**frustrate, circumvent, hinder, thwart, check** Anti-missile devices foiled the enemy attack.	*aid, assist, help, oblige, expedite*
folk	1.	*n.*	**people, persons, individuals** It is good for older folk to keep active.	
	2.	*n.*	**relatives, kin, family** Karl's folks are coming to the wedding.	
follow	1.	*v.*	**go after, chase, pursue, track** The sheriff followed the cattle rustlers into the hills.	**1.** *lead, direct, guide*
	2.	*v.*	**come after, go behind** "H" follows "G" in our alphabet.	**2.** *precede, come before*
	3.	*v.*	**obey, adhere to, observe** We have to follow the rules of the school.	**3.** *ignore, disregard, neglect, disobey*
	4.	*v.*	**imitate, copy, mimic** The children followed the dance instructor's steps.	**4.** *disregard, ignore*
	5.	*v.*	**understand, grasp** I cannot follow what you're saying.	**5.** *misunderstand*
	6.	*v.*	**trace, observe, track** The scientists followed the orbit of the space shuttle on their computer screens.	**6.** *lose track of*

follower		*n.*	**disciple, supporter, admirer** Mahatma Gandhi had many followers.	*leader, opponent*
folly		*n.*	**silliness, madness, absurdity, rashness, foolishness** It is sheer folly to go canoeing during a violent storm.	*wisdom, good sense, good judgment, prudence*
fond		*adj.*	**attached to, loving, affectionate, sentimental** Pat was very fond of her cousin Pierre. *adv.* She thought of him fondly.	*distant, cold, disinterested, unconcerned*
fondness		*n.*	**affection, concern, liking, tenderness, preference** Pat had a fondness for Pierre.	*dislike, aversion*
food		*n.*	**provisions, rations, fare, edibles, nourishment** Food is kept fresh in the refrigerator.	
fool	1.	*n.*	**dunce, idiot, simpleton, nitwit, ninny** Hugo made a fool of himself at the party.	1. *wise person, genius, sage*
	2.	*v.*	**play, joke, clown** Two boys were fooling around in the library.	2. *be serious*
	3.	*v.*	**trick, deceive, dupe, outwit** You didn't fool me with that disguise!	3. *be truthful, be straightforward*
foolhardy		*adj.*	**reckless, thoughtless, careless, rash, foolish** Jumping from the top of the tower was a foolhardy stunt.	*cautious, careful, thoughtful, wary, prudent*
foolish		*adj.*	**silly, crazy, absurd, ridiculous, daft** It is foolish to pay so much for those boots. *n.* You might regret your foolishness.	*wise, thoughtful, intelligent, clever*
forbid		*v.*	**prohibit, prevent, refuse** Airlines forbid smoking during flight.	*allow, approve, permit, let, encourage*
force	1.	*n.*	**power, strength, might, energy** The force of the blow knocked the man down.	1. *weakness, feebleness*
	2.	*n.*	**troops, body, group, unit** This company has a workforce of one hundred.	
	3.	*v.*	**require, make, compel, drive, oblige** Bad weather forced us to postpone the game.	3. *allow, permit*
forecast	1.	*n.*	**prediction, prophecy, outlook** The weather forecast was accurate.	
	2.	*v.*	**predict, foretell, anticipate** The company forecasts great sales for next year.	
foreign		*adj.*	**strange, unfamiliar, unknown, alien** Would you enjoy a trip to a foreign land?	*native, known, domestic, aboriginal*

foreigner		*n.*	**stranger, alien, outsider** The children held a party to welcome the visiting foreigners.	*native, aboriginal*

foreigner   *n.*   **stranger, alien, outsider**   *native, aboriginal*
The children held a party to welcome the visiting foreigners.

forever
1. *adv.* **permanently, eternally, endlessly, forevermore, perpetually, always**   *1. temporarily, now, at present, for a time*
Atlantis is a city said to be lost forever.
2. *adv.* **continuously, ceaselessly, regularly, constantly**   *2. sporadically, erratically, irregularly*
This child is forever whining for attention.

forfeit   *v.*   **give up, hand over, give over, lose, relinquish, abandon**   *maintain, keep, preserve*
The team forfeited the game because they were late.
n. What a forfeit to pay for tardiness!

forget   *v.*   **overlook, disregard**   *remember, recall, recollect*
Nan was sad when everyone forgot her birthday.

forgive   *v.*   **pardon, excuse, overlook**   *accuse, blame, condemn, resent, retaliate*
"Please forgive me, I won't cheat again," he said.
adj. The forgiving teacher let him off with just a detention.
n. She showed him forgiveness.

forlorn   *adj.*   **dejected, woebegone, sad, neglected, lonely, downcast, forsaken, deserted, unhappy, miserable, wretched**   *merry, happy, content, satisfied, cheerful*
We felt sorry for the forlorn child weeping in the corner.

form
1. *n.* **shape, figure, outline**
A strange form showed against the lighted window.
2. *v.* **make, shape, mold, design, construct**   *2. destroy, ruin, wreck, dismember*
The class formed many interesting objects with clay.

formal
1. *adj.* **ceremonial, dignified, proper, solemn**   *1. casual, easy, regular, informal*
The wedding will be a formal affair.
n. After the formality of the wedding ceremony there will be a merry party.
2. *adj.* **ceremonial, black tie, white tie, evening clothes, full dress**   *2. casual*
Formal dress is required for the ball.
adv. We will be dressed formally.

format   *n.*   **arrangement, mold, make-up, form, construction, pattern**
Most television talk shows have a similar format.

former   *adj.*   **previous, preceding, prior, earlier**   *succeeding, following, ensuing, coming*
Who was your former teacher?

formula		*n.*	**rule, principle, recipe, prescription** The formula for the new vaccine is still a secret.	
formulate		*v.*	**devise, concoct, frame, make, produce, express, form, prepare** Scientists formulated plans for the peaceful uses of nuclear energy.	*destroy, blot out, erase*
forsaken	1.	*v.*	**abandon, desert, leave, disown, renounce, abdicate, give up** Soldiers cannot forsake their duty.	1. *keep, cling to, maintain*
	2.	*adj.*	**abandoned, forlorn, deserted, neglected, desolate** The children found the forsaken puppies.	2. *remembered, cared for, cherished*
fortunate		*adj.*	**lucky, blessed, timely** It was fortunate they were away when their house exploded. *adv.* Fortunately no one was killed or injured in the explosion.	*unlucky, unfortunate*
fortune	1.	*n.*	**wealth, riches, prosperity** She lost a fortune on the stock market.	1. *poverty, penury*
	2.	*n.*	**luck, chance, lot, fate** Her success was the result of skill and good fortune.	2. *misfortune, bad luck*
foul	1.	*adj.*	**dirty, filthy, unclean, nasty, polluted, impure** Foul air can lead to acid rain. *v.* The oil spill fouled the water.	1. *clean, sweet, pure*
	2.	*adj.*	**unfair, illegal** Foul play is not encouraged in sports.	2. *fair, legal*
	3.	*adj.*	**unfavorable, stormy** The foul weather delayed the flight for several hours.	3. *fair, good, favorable*
found	1.	*v.*	**set up, establish, organize, originate, institute, produce** Who founded Harvard University? *n.* Was the founder a missionary?	1. *end, uproot*
	2.	*adj.*	**discovered, unearthed, detected** Found items are placed in the "lost and found" box.	2. *lost, missing, irretrievable*
foundation	1.	*n.*	**organization, institution, endowment, establishment** They set up a charitable foundation to help poor students.	
	2.	*n.*	**base, cornerstone, groundwork, basis, support** The foundation for the new stadium was laid last month.	2. *top, roof, covering, superstructure*
fraction		*n.*	**part, section, piece, bit, portion, division, segment** A quarter is a fraction of a dollar.	*whole, total*

fracture		*n.*	**break, split, crack** Lynda suffered a fracture of her shoulder after falling off a horse. *v.* Jim fractured his arm in a hockey mishap.	
fragile		*adj.*	**frail, delicate, weak, brittle, breakable** This crystal is too fragile to put in the dishwasher.	*strong, tough, sturdy, durable*
fragment		*n.*	**piece, part, fraction, scrap, chip, bit, shred, section** Fragments of ancient pottery were found in the tomb.	*whole, total*
fragrance		*n.*	**aroma, scent, sweet smell, perfume** This perfume has a light fragrance.	
fragrant		*adj.*	**sweet smelling, perfumed, scented** Lilacs are fragrant after the rain.	*stinking, foul, scentless*
frail	1.	*adj.*	**fragile, delicate, brittle, breakable** Fine crystal is frail and should be handled carefully.	**1.** *strong, sturdy, unbreakable*
	2.	*adj.*	**weak, infirm, delicate, feeble** Grandpa was frail from his long illness.	**2.** *strong, sturdy, powerful, tough*
frank		*adj.*	**candid, open, sincere, direct, honest, forthright, straightforward, blunt** The people demanded frank answers from the government about the new tax.	*deceitful, secretive, insincere, dishonest, reserved*
frantic		*adj.*	**frenzied, excited, agitated, crazy** The travelers were frantic when they lost their airline tickets.	*calm, composed, docile, cool*
fraud	1.	*n.*	**deceit, trickery, deception, swindle, duplicity, guile** The bank teller was charged with fraud after a large sum of money disappeared.	**1.** *fairness, openness, honesty*
	2.	*n.*	**imposter, quack, pretender, cheat, charlatan** The new doctor proved to be a fraud who had never attended medical school.	
free	1.	*v.*	**release, let go, discharge, liberate** President Lincoln freed all slaves after the Civil War.	**1.** *imprison, confine, incarcerate, seize*
	2.	*adj.*	**unhindered, unfettered, unrestrained** The judge ruled that the suspect was free to leave.	**2.** *restrained, fettered, hindered, confined*
	3.	*adj.*	**without cost, without fee, gratis, complimentary** The restaurant gave the children a free meal on its opening day.	
	4.	*adj.*	**generous, liberal, lavish** The wealthy man is free with his money.	**4.** *miserly, stingy*

	5.	*adj.*	**unfastened, loose** The drowning man grabbed the free end of the rope.

5. bound, fastened, tied

freedom   *n.*   **liberty, independence**
Freedom of the press is guaranteed in a democratic society.

slavery, subjection, bondage

freeze   1. *v.*   **turn to ice, congeal, harden, solidify**
Water freezes at 32 degrees Fahrenheit.

1. liquefy, melt, thaw, turn to liquid

     2. *v.*   **stop, halt, become motionless**
Wendy froze in fear when she heard a creak in the dark.

2. proceed

frequent   *adj.*   **many, numerous, repeated, regular**
Mom makes frequent business trips.

rare, infrequent, few, occasional

frequently   *adv.*   **often, regularly, usually, repeatedly**
Susan goes swimming frequently.

rarely, seldom, infrequently

fresh   1. *adj.*   **new, novel, recent, modern, innovative**
The family emigrated to Australia and made a fresh start in life.

1. old, former, previous

     2. *adj.*   **impudent, saucy, bold, rude**
The child was scolded for her fresh reply.

2. polite, courteous, mannerly

     3. *adj.*   **unspoiled, newly grown**
The market sells fresh fruits and vegetables.

3. stale, spoiled, putrid

     4. *adj.*   **young, vigorous, healthy, glowing, wholesome, spry**
Most children have fresh complexions.

4. tired, worn out, exhausted

     5. *adj.*   **bracing, pure, refreshing, brisk, invigorating**
We love the fresh air in the countryside.

5. polluted, stale, contaminated

     6. *adj.*   **potable, safe, drinkable, clean, pure**
Fresh water is required to sustain life.

6. dirty, brackish, unsafe, contaminated

fret   1. *v.*   **fuss, complain, fume, whine**
The children fretted because of the heat.
adj. The fever made the baby fretful.

1. relax

     2. *v.*   **worry, grieve, agonize, be concerned**
Why fret over something that cannot be changed?

2. be content, be resigned

friction   1. *n.*   **abrasion, grinding, resistance, counteraction, rubbing**
Friction in the car's brake drum caused the wheel to overheat.

1. lubrication

     2. *n.*   **animosity, discontent, trouble, disagreement**
Friction between the neighboring countries eventually led to war.

2. friendliness, compatibility, cooperation, harmony

friend   *n.*   **chum, pal, buddy, companion, crony, comrade, ally**
Shen, Matt, and Brian are good friends.
n. They value each other's friendship.

enemy, foe, rival, opponent, adversary

friendly		*adj.*	**kind, helpful, neighborly, agreeable** Friendly neighbors welcomed us when we moved into our new home.	*unfriendly, hostile, aloof, distant*
fright		*n.*	**scare, shock, terror** We had a fright when the burglar alarm went off.	
frighten		*v.*	**scare, terrify, intimidate, alarm, shock, startle** Thunder frightens most children.	*comfort, calm, soothe*
frightened		*adj.*	**scared, fearful, alarmed, terrified, startled** The frightened deer bounded away.	*brave, daring, courageous, heroic*
frightful		*adj.*	**dreadful, terrible, shocking, fearful, ghastly, horrible, horrid** The sinking of the *Titanic* was a frightful event.	*pleasing, inviting, appealing*
frigid	1.	*adj.*	**very cold, freezing, glacial** Antarctica has a frigid climate.	**1.** *hot, sizzling, torrid*
	2.	*adj.*	**unfriendly, cool** The girl gave him a frigid stare when he bumped into her.	**2.** *friendly, warm, cordial*
fringe	1.	*n.*	**edge, border, outskirts, boundary** They live on the fringe of the city. *v.* Tall trees fringed the garden.	**1.** *center, heart, core*
	2.	*n.*	**edging, border, hem, trimming** The bride's gown had an elaborately embroidered fringe.	
frivolous		*adj.*	**trivial, trifling, petty, superficial, silly, unimportant** Pupils cannot skip classes for frivolous reasons.	*serious, grave, important, earnest*
frolic		*v.*	**sport, romp, frisk, play, gambol** The children frolicked in the water. *n.* They enjoyed their frolic in the pool.	*sulk, pout*
front	1.	*n.*	**forward part, facade** The bus waited at the front of the school.	**1.** *back, rear*
	2.	*v.*	**cover, pretense** The hostel was a front for hiding illegal immigrants.	
frown		*n.*	**scowl, glare** Her frown told us that she was displeased. *v.* Tom frowned at the rude waiter.	*smile, grin*
frugal		*adj.*	**thrifty, prudent, careful, economical, parsimonious** The frugal woman saved a lot of money. *adv.* They lived frugally while they saved for a house.	*wasteful, lavish, extravagant, self-indulgent, generous*

fruitful	1.	*adj.*	**productive, rich, abundant** The orchard had a fruitful harvest.	**1.** *poor, sparse, meager*
	2.	*adj.*	**successful, profitable, productive** Many good ideas were generated at the fruitful meeting.	**2.** *fruitless, useless, unproductive*
frustrate		*v.*	**foil, balk, disappoint, defeat, prevent, thwart, hinder, deter, discourage** Bitter weather frustrated the mountain climbers. *n.* They canceled the expedition in frustration.	*aid, help, encourage, assist, support, promote*
fuel	1.	*n.*	**combustible material** Gas, oil, and coal are fuels.	
	2.	*v.*	**take on fuel, feed, fill up, stoke** The family fueled the fire upon entering the cold cottage.	
fugitive		*n.*	**deserter, runaway, escapee** The police caught the fugitives after a wild chase.	*pursuer*
fulfill		*v.*	**accomplish, complete, achieve, realize** I fulfilled my ambition when I graduated with honors.	*fail, give up, neglect, overlook*
full	1.	*adj.*	**filled, brimming with, packed, stuffed** I drank a full bottle of water.	**1.** *empty, void*
	2.	*adj.*	**complete, whole, entire** The full orchestra will perform tonight. *adv.* The carton is fully packed.	**2.** *partial*
	3.	*adj.*	**filled, reserved, in use, assigned, taken, occupied, busy, engaged** Are all the seats on the plane full?	**3.** *empty, available, open, unassigned, unreserved*
fumble	1.	*v.*	**mishandle, bungle, botch, mismanage** The quarterback fumbled the ball. *n.* It was a costly fumble.	**1.** *handle, manage, control*
	2.	*v.*	**grope, search** Lu fumbled in her purse for her keys.	
fun		*n.*	**amusement, entertainment, merriment, enjoyment** We had fun at the beach party.	*drudgery, toil*
function	1.	*n.*	**duty, role, part, use, capacity** What is the function of the Supreme Court?	
	2.	*n.*	**meeting, party, reception, celebration, get-together, social gathering** Many functions are held at hotels.	
	3.	*v.*	**perform, run, work, operate, serve, act** Some people function best under stress.	**3.** *be inoperative, be inactive*

fundamental		*adj.*	**rudimentary, basic, elementary, essential, underlying, primary, important, indispensable, cardinal, necessary** Freedom is a fundamental right in any democracy.	*secondary, nonessential, unimportant, incidental, superficial*
funny	1.	*adj.*	**comical, amusing, droll, humorous, laughable, diverting** I enjoy funny movies.	*1. sad, sober, grave, serious, mournful*
	2.	*adj.*	**strange, peculiar, odd, unusual, uncommon** I have a funny feeling in my stomach.	*2. regular, usual, normal, common*
furious	1.	*adj.*	**angry, mad, infuriated, irate, enraged** Dad was furious when I was fined for speeding.	*1. calm, serene*
	2.	*adj.*	**violent, fierce, raging, ferocious, wild** The ocean liner survived the furious storm. *adv.* The wind blew furiously for days.	*2. gentle, smooth, placid, calm*
furnish	1.	*v.*	**provide, give, supply** My friend furnished me with the answer.	*1. keep, withhold, retain*
	2.	*v.*	**equip, outfit, stock** We furnished our house with modern furniture.	*2. dismantle*
furtive		*adj.*	**sly, stealthy, secretive, deceitful, shifty** The man's furtive look roused the suspicion of the security guard. *adv.* The robber crept furtively upstairs at midnight.	*open, aboveboard, straightforward*
fury	1.	*n.*	**anger, frenzy, wrath, rage, furor** Sulin was in a fury when she caught the boy kicking a puppy.	*1. calmness*
	2.	*n.*	**violence, force, might** The coastal towns felt the full fury of the hurricane.	*2. feebleness, weakness*
fuse		*v.*	**merge, unite, combine, blend, amalgamate** The choir and the orchestra fused in unison at the finale.	*divide, separate, part*
fusion		*n.*	**union, coalition, blending** The reaction caused by nuclear fusion produces great energy.	
fuss	1.	*n.*	**trouble, bother, disturbance, complaint** The tenants raised a fuss when the landlord raised their rent.	*1. peace*
	2.	*n.*	**ado, stir, bustle, confusion, agitation, hubbub, flurry, bustle** There was a big fuss in the house on the day of the wedding.	*2. tranquility, quiet, peace, calm*

3. *v.* **fret, fidget, worry, complain, whine, whimper, object**
The passengers fussed about the delay in the flight.

3. *be content, approve, favor, sanction*

fussy

1. *adj.* **exacting, critical, particular, demanding, hard to please**
Our family is fussy about buying only fresh vegetables.

1. *easygoing, nonchalant, unconcerned*

2. *adj.* **ornate, elaborate, cluttered, showy**
That fussy dress would not be suitable for this affair.

2. *plain, simple, unadorned*

futile

adj. **useless, worthless, ineffective, fruitless, vain, unsuccessful**
The efforts to save the wrecked trawler proved futile.

successful, effective, fruitful, worthy

future

1. *n.* **tomorrow, hereafter, time to come**
She has a bright future ahead of her.

1. *past*

2. *adj.* **eventual, projected, coming, later, following, anticipated**
Karl's future plans include a trip to Austria.

2. *past, former, previous*

fuzzy

1. *adj.* **downy, woolly, furry, hairy**
Peaches have a fuzzy skin.
n. I don't enjoy eating the fuzz.

1. *smooth, silken, rough, bald*

2. *adj.* **hazy, blurred, unclear, out of focus**
Unless you focus the camera properly, the picture will be fuzzy.

2. *clear, sharp, definite, defined*

G

This ancient Greek and Roman letter was once the same as *C*. When combined with *h* in English, it once represented the same sounds as *ch* in *loch*. Nowadays, the sound may be the same as *f* in *laugh*, or it may remain silent, as in *night*.

In our slang, *G* represents "grand," or one thousand dollars; it is sometimes contracted to "G" as in "ten G's."

gabby	*adj.*	talkative, chatty, garrulous, loquacious Cellphones are a boon for gabby people. *n.* Yang has the gift of the gab. *v.* He gabs on the phone for hours.	*quiet, laconic, taciturn*
gag	1. *v.*	silence, muffle, repress, stifle The kidnappers gagged their victim so he was unable to call for help.	
	2. *v.*	choke, retch, be nauseated Domo ate too fast and gagged on his food.	
gain	1. *n.*	profit, dividend, earnings We made a gain on the sale of our house.	1. *loss, decrease*
	2. *v.*	profit, earn The company gained $1 million on the deal.	2. *lose*
	3. *v.*	increase, grow, expand, enlarge The baby gained weight rapidly.	3. *decrease, shrink, lessen, diminish*
	4. *v.*	advance, overtake, progress The challenger is gaining on the leader in the race.	4. *move backward, retreat, halt, stop*
	5. *v.*	achieve, get, obtain, realize, attain Thomas Edison gained world recognition for his inventions.	5. *lose, forfeit*
gallant	*adj.*	brave, bold, courageous, valiant, daring, heroic, fearless Dave enjoys reading tales of gallant knights of old. *n.* King Arthur is known for his gallantry.	*cowardly, timid, fearful*
game	1. *n.*	amusement, entertainment, fun, play, recreation, diversion The children played games at the party.	1. *work, labor, toil*
	2. *n.*	match, tournament, contest We watched a baseball game on TV.	
	3. *n.*	wild fowl, fish, wild animals, quarry, prey Hunting for game is not allowed on a nature reserve.	3. *domestic animals, farm animals*
	4. *adj.*	sporting, plucky, spirited, brave, resolute, determined Terry Fox was admired for his game spirit.	4. *uncertain, hesitant, irresolute, indecisive*
	5. *adj.*	lame, crippled The horse with the game leg was put to sleep.	5. *sound, fit*
gang	*n.*	group, clan, band, mob, horde The entire gang went to the beach.	*individual*
gangster	*n.*	mobster, criminal, ruffian, thug, crook Gangsters are a menace to society.	*law-abiding person*
garbage	*n.*	waste, refuse, trash, rubbish, scraps We are running out of space to dump garbage.	

gather	1.	*v.*	**infer, conclude, deduce, assume** I gather from your remarks that you approve of our plans.	1. *doubt, question, wonder*
	2.	*v.*	**pick up, collect, take in** After the class, the monitors gathered up the books.	2. *scatter, spread, distribute*
	3.	*v.*	**collect, assemble, group, congregate, converge, convene, meet** The children gathered around the teacher for a story. *n.* We have a family gathering at Thanksgiving.	3. *scatter, disperse, part, break up, disband*
gaudy		*adj.*	**flashy, showy, garish, glaring, ornate** Students are not allowed to wear gaudy jewelry to school.	*dull, drab, simple, plain, subtle*
gauge	1.	*n.*	**measure, mark, scale, standard** The gas gauge registered the tank as full.	
	2.	*v.*	**weigh, measure, estimate, judge** Joe gauged the distance from the house to the lake to be two miles.	
gaunt		*adj.*	**lean, skinny, bony, thin, underfed, emaciated, haggard** Mei-ling looked gaunt after her illness.	*well-fed, fleshy, plump, fat, overweight*
gaze		*v.*	**stare, watch, gape, look, observe** Astronomers gaze at the stars through telescopes. *n.* Astronomers are star-gazers.	*glance, peek, glimpse*
general	1.	*adj.*	**common, usual, customary, normal, prevailing** The general opinion is that smoking should be banned. *adv.* Do you generally do your homework before watching television?	1. *rare, unusual*
	2.	*adj.*	**public, extensive, widespread, universal** The unions organized a general strike of workers across the nation.	2. *confined, restricted, limited*
	3.	*adj.*	**broad, approximate, loose** Give me a general outline of the story.	3. *detailed, specific, precise, explicit*
generate		*v.*	**create, form, make, produce, supply, furnish, originate** We hope the publicity will generate interest in the play.	*destroy, squash, squelch, dismantle, tear down*
generous	1.	*adj.*	**benevolent, magnanimous, philanthropic, public-spirited** She made a generous donation to the hospital.	1. *close, stingy, mean, miserly, petty, tightfisted*
	2.	*adj.*	**ample, plentiful, abundant, large, bountiful, overflowing** Dad heaped a generous helping of dessert on my plate.	2. *small, meager, insufficient*

genial		*adj.*	**pleasant, warm, friendly, cordial, cheerful, kind, affable, sociable, courteous, congenial, approachable** The genial TV talk show host soon put everyone at ease.	*unfriendly, hostile, antagonistic, discourteous, unapproachable*
gentle	1.	*adj.*	**soft, balmy, light, calm, pleasant, mild** Leaves fluttered in the gentle breezes.	*1. rough, fierce, violent, strong*
	2.	*adj.*	**tender, kind, delicate, careful, soft** Jake gave the kitten a gentle pat. *adv.* Marie gently picked up the injured bird.	*2. harsh, cruel, unkind, rough*
	3.	*adj.*	**tamed, broken, docile, domesticated** The riding instructor put the beginner rider on a gentle horse.	*3. wild, untamed, savage*
	4.	*adj.*	**gradual, moderate, slight** We rolled down the gentle slope on our bicycles.	*4. steep*
genuine	1.	*adj.*	**real, true, honest, valid, actual, sincere** Most people have a genuine concern for the environment.	*1. insincere, hypocritical, simulated, affected*
	2.	*adj.*	**authentic, real, true** The vase proved to be a genuine antique.	*2. bogus, fake, counterfeit, sham*
get		*v.*	**obtain, acquire, receive, earn, attain, secure, procure, win, achieve, gain** Which candidate got the most votes in the last election?	*lose, surrender, forgo, forfeit, abandon*
ghastly	1.	*adj.*	**awful, terrible, horrible, dreadful** The accident scene was a ghastly sight.	*1. pleasing, attractive*
	2.	*adj.*	**pale, wan, ashen, pallid, deathlike, macabre, ghostlike, frightful** The ghastly faces of the earthquake survivors touched everyone.	*2. rosy, ruddy, comely*
ghost		*n.*	**spirit, vision, apparition, phantom, specter** Do you believe in ghosts? *adj.* The storyteller told tales of ghostly figures in the night.	
giant		*adj.*	**huge, enormous, immense, gigantic, stupendous, jumbo, massive, colossal** The giant dinosaurs are extinct.	*tiny, petite, little, miniature, wee, minute*
giddy	1.	*adj.*	**dizzy, unsteady, faint, lightheaded** A person can get a giddy feeling from spinning in a merry-go-round.	*1. stable, steady, stationary*
	2.	*adj.*	**silly, flighty, frivolous, capricious** Lou was told to forget his giddy ideas and concentrate on his studies.	*2. serious, earnest, thoughtful*
gift	1.	*n.*	**present, offering, donation** Did you receive many gifts on your birthday?	*1. loan, purchase*

	2.	*n.*	**talent, skill, aptitude, ability** The teacher recognized Min's musical gift. *adj.* The gifted violinist appeared on nationwide television.	*2. hindrance, disadvantage, obstacle*
gigantic		*adj.*	**huge, immense, enormous, massive, stupendous, colossal, great, giant** During the hurricane, the coast was battered by gigantic waves.	*tiny, petite, little, small, wee, miniature, minute, dwarf, diminutive*
gist		*n.*	**essence, point, kernel, core, meaning, substance** Just tell me the gist of your proposal.	
give	1.	*v.*	**provide, furnish, supply, grant** The principal gave the students permission to hold a science fair.	*1. deny, refuse, take away, remove*
	2.	*v.*	**bestow, present, endow, award, donate, dole out, bequeath** They are giving the money raised at the fair to charity.	*2. maintain, keep, withhold*
glad		*adj.*	**happy, pleased, delighted, joyous** Jeya is glad to be in America. *adv.* The Rajah family gladly moved to America.	*sad, gloomy, unhappy, sorrowful*
glamour		*n.*	**charm, allure, attraction, appeal, magnetism, romance** Large cities have a glamour all their own. *adj.* Fans flocked to see the glamorous movie star.	
glare	1.	*n.*	**shine, shimmer, bright light** I shielded my eyes from the glare of the oncoming headlights.	*1. dullness*
	2.	*v.*	**scowl, frown, glower** The opponents glared at each other before the match.	*2. smile, laugh*
glaring	1.	*adj.*	**brilliant, dazzling, bright, glowing, blinding, blazing** Wear sunglasses to protect your eyes from the glaring sun.	*1. dull, dim*
	2.	*adj.*	**obvious, conspicuous, evident** Ken lost marks for the glaring spelling errors in his essay.	*2. inconspicuous, obscure, hidden, concealed*
gleam	1.	*n.*	**glimmer, ray, beam, glow, flash** The searchers saw a gleam of light between the trees.	
	2.	*n.*	**measure, small amount, iota** There's not a gleam of truth in his story.	*2. abundance, wealth, surplus*
	3.	*v.*	**shine, sparkle, glimmer, glitter** Nadia's eyes gleamed with pleasure when she heard the good news. *adj.* She flashed a gleaming smile at the crowds.	

glee	*n.*	**joy, cheer, fun, gaiety, mirth, delight** The children laughed in glee at the clown's jokes. *adj.* The gleeful audience shouted for an encore.	*dejection, grief, unhappiness, sorrow*
glimpse	*n.*	**flash, sight, flicker, glance, peek** They caught a glimpse of the deer before it bounded off. *v.* Hong glimpsed at her notes just before the test.	
glitter	*n.*	**sparkle, glisten, shine, twinkle** We saw the glitter of the city lights from the plane. *v.* A diamond tiara glittered on her head.	
global	*adj.*	**worldwide, universal** We watch global news on television every night.	*local, individual, neighborhood*
gloomy	1. *adj.*	**downhearted, depressed, unhappy, sad, dejected, glum, miserable, melancholy** Yun is gloomy because her friend Tanya is moving away.	**1.** *happy, cheerful, pleasant, jolly, content, pleased*
	2. *adj.*	**dark, dismal, depressing, dim, cloudy** Rooms with a northern exposure can be gloomy.	**2.** *bright, pleasant, cheerful, sunny*
glorious	1. *adj.*	**marvelous, splendid, magnificent, grand, dazzling, spectacular** The choir gave a glorious performance at the Christmas concert. *adv.* The choir sang gloriously.	**1.** *average, mediocre, uneventful, ordinary*
	2. *adj.*	**distinguished, triumphant, famous, renowned** Alexander the Great was a glorious conqueror.	**2.** *unimportant, insignificant*
glory	*n.*	**honor, fame, renown, praise** The athletes returned in glory from the Olympic Games.	*disgrace, shame, ignominy*
glossy	*adj.*	**shiny, lustrous, polished, smooth** Print the photograph on glossy paper. *n.* Jenny put some gloss on her lips.	*dull, unpolished*
glow	*n.*	**gleam, shine, sheen, radiance** Northern lights cause a glow in the sky. *v.* The campfire glowed in the dark.	*blackness, darkness*
glum	*adj.*	**morose, moody, gloomy, sullen, sad** The loser left with a glum face.	*happy, cheerful, sunny, jaunty*
glut	*n.*	**excess, oversupply, overload, profusion, abundance, surplus** The oil glut caused prices to fall.	*scarcity, lack, deficiency*

goal		*n.*	**aim, ambition, object, purpose, intention** Jose's goal is to become a lawyer.

good	1.	*n.*	**benefit, advantage, interest, welfare** Laws are designed for the good of all.	**1.** *harm, handicap, impediment*
	2.	*adj.*	**excellent, first-rate, great, wonderful** The book was so good that I couldn't put it down till the end.	**2.** *bad, terrible, poor*
	3.	*adj.*	**honest, true, just, kind, worthy** That person has a good reputation.	**3.** *dishonest, bad, sneaky, fraudulent*
	4.	*adj.*	**skillful, expert, able, qualified** Eugene is a good skier.	**4.** *poor, inept, inexperienced*
	5.	*adj.*	**reliable, safe, dependable, sound, stable, healthy** Be sure the used car is in good condition before you buy it.	**5.** *bad, defective, unsafe, unreliable, unhealthy*

goods	1.	*n.*	**materials, merchandise, commodities, wares** Some imported goods are taxed.	
	2.	*n.*	**property, belongings, possessions** Personal goods can be insured.	

gorge	1.	*n.*	**chasm, abyss, ravine, gully** The lamb fell into the gorge.	
	2.	*v.*	**stuff, fill, cram, overeat, satiate** Sam gorged on candy and became sick.	**2.** *empty, void, disgorge*

gorgeous	*adj.*	**splendid, magnificent, beautiful, superb, breathtaking, stunning** We photographed the gorgeous view.	*unimpressive, unattractive, ugly*

gory	*adj.*	**bloody, blood-soaked, bloodstained, grisly, revolting** Bullfights can be gory events.	*pleasant, agreeable, likeable*

govern	*v.*	**rule, control, direct, manage, lead, administer** A board of directors governs the school.	*obey, follow, submit, comply*

grab	*v.*	**snatch, seize, clutch, take** The thug grabbed the woman's purse and ran off.	*return, give back, restore, reimburse*

grace	1.	*n.*	**dexterity, agility, nimbleness** The ballerinas danced with grace. *adv.* They danced gracefully.	**1.** *awkwardness, stiffness, clumsiness*
	2.	*n.*	**blessing, prayer, thanksgiving** We say grace before meals.	**2.** *curse*
	3.	*n.*	**charm, allure, elegance** She is much admired for her grace.	**3.** *coarseness, awkwardness*
	4.	*n.*	**favor, goodwill** Shane was in the teacher's good graces for helping the new students.	**4.** *disfavor*
	5.	*v.*	**honor, favor** The mayor graced the graduation ceremony with her presence.	**5.** *discredit*

gracious	1.	*adj.*	**courteous, charming, friendly** The governor's gracious greeting put everyone at ease.	1. *rude, vulgar, crude*
	2.	*adj.*	**elegant, refined, tasteful** The guests were full of admiration for the governor's gracious mansion.	2. *crude, coarse, austere*
grade	1.	*n.*	**rank, classification, level, rating** Rob's school grades have improved.	
	2.	*v.*	**rank, rate, measure, classify** The teacher graded her students' essays.	
gradual		*adj.*	**slow, continuous, steady, gentle** It is a gradual climb to the top of the hill. *adv.* Our old car gradually made it to the top of the hill.	*sudden, abrupt, steep*
graft	1.	*n.*	**corruption, swindle, theft, fraud** The manager was found guilty of graft and fired from his job.	1. *purity, goodness*
	2.	*v.*	**join, splice, unite, fuse** Surgeons grafted new skin over the burn patient's wound. *n.* The skin grafts healed.	2. *sever, separate, sunder*
grand	1.	*adj.*	**splendid, superb, elegant, gorgeous, impressive, stately, fine, magnificent, majestic, imposing, sumptuous** The ceremony was held in a grand ballroom.	1. *plain, ordinary, commonplace, unimposing*
	2.	*adj.*	**lofty, stately, dignified, elevated, high, noble, great, illustrious** Royalty occupies a grand position in some societies.	2. *low, mediocre, ordinary, modest, unassuming, common*
	3.	*adj.*	**good, first-class, excellent** That job is a grand opportunity for one so young.	3. *poor, inferior, imperfect*
grant	1.	*n.*	**award, gift, donation, present, endowment, bequest** The museum received a substantial grant from the millionaire.	1. *deduction, deprivation, loss*
	2.	*v.*	**allow, permit, give, confer** Air traffic controllers granted the pilot permission for takeoff.	2. *refuse, prohibit, reject, decline*
graphic	1.	*adj.*	**pictorial, visual, illustrated** Computers can produce incredible graphic designs. *n.* Chris used the computer application to place several graphics in his report.	1. *textual, written*
	2.	*adj.*	**explicit, striking, clear, precise, exact, concrete, realistic, lucid, definite, vivid** The veteran's graphic descriptions of his war experiences horrified everyone.	2. *obscure, abstract, ambiguous, hazy*

grasp

1. *n.* **reach, hold, clutch, grip**
The mountain climber lost her grasp and plunged into the ravine.
v. The rescuers grasped her arms and hauled her up.

2. *v.* **comprehend, understand, follow**
Did you grasp what the teacher was saying?
n. He has a good grasp of astronomy.

    2. misunderstand, ignore, be ignorant of, have no idea of

grate

1. *v.* **scrape, grind, scratch, rub**
Grate the cheese for the pizza.

2. *v.* **annoy, irritate, irk, bother**
Doug's loud voice grates on my nerves.

    2. please, enchant

grateful

adj. **thankful, appreciative, obliged**
The grateful refugees thanked us for our donations.
adv. Our donations were gratefully received.

    thankless, ungrateful

grave

1. *adj.* **somber, sober, solemn, serious**
We were concerned when we saw the doctor's grave face.

    1. joyous, merry, happy, cheerful

2. *adj.* **important, momentous, weighty**
Grave decisions are made in Congress.

    2. trivial, frivolous, insignificant

3. *adj.* **hazardous, precarious, dangerous, critical, serious, ominous, threatening**
That accident victim is in grave condition.

    3. good, excellent, secure

gravitate

v. **be attracted to, incline toward, drift toward**
Most metals gravitate to magnets.

    be repulsed by, drift away

graze

1. *v.* **browse, skim, flip through, search, surf, glance at**
Justin grazed websites to find a good deal.

    1. study, peruse, select, choose

2. *v.* **touch lightly, scrape, brush**
The police officer was only slightly injured when the bullet grazed her arm.

great

1. *adj.* **immense, gigantic, majestic, huge, vast, large, big, huge**
The Great Wall of China is an awesome sight.

    1. small, little, puny, diminutive

2. *adj.* **eminent, noted, renowned, prominent, celebrated, famous, well-known, important, remarkable**
Sir Winston Churchill was a great leader.

    2. unknown, obscure, anonymous

3. *adj.* **good, excellent, wonderful, terrific**
Everyone had a great time at the party.

    3. terrible, bad, awful

greedy

1. *adj.* **gluttonous, piggish, ravenous**
The greedy girl ate up the whole cake.

2. *adj.* **grasping, avaricious, selfish, miserly, stingy, covetous, mercenary**
The greedy landlord raised the rent again.

    2. generous, giving, unselfish, charitable

grief	n.	**sorrow, woe, sadness, mourning, pain, misery, anguish, heartache, distress** Survivors of the hurricane saw grief and destruction everywhere. *n.* They grieved over the loss of their loved ones.	*happiness, joy, gladness, exultation*
grim	1. *adj.*	**severe, harsh, hard, stern, forbidding, austere** There were many grim faces when the bad news was announced.	**1.** *smiling, happy, cheerful, pleasant*
	2. *adj.*	**awful, horrible, ghastly, grisly, hideous, gruesome** The grim stories about war depressed us.	**2.** *funny, pleasant, humorous, lighthearted*
grind	1. *n.*	**hard work, drudgery, toil, labor, tedium** The grind of college life wore him out. *v.* Jeff grinds away at his books all day.	**1.** *pleasure, recreation, leisure*
	2. *v.*	**grate, crush, pulverize** He ground the coffee beans in the grinder.	**2.** *solidify, mold*
grip	*v.*	**seize, hold, clasp, clutch, grasp, grab** The child gripped his father's hand. *n.* The police officer held the suspect in a firm grip.	*release, drop, let go, relinquish*
groan	*n.*	**moan, cry, sob, lament, whimper** There were groans of agony from the injured. *v.* The injured person groaned in pain.	*laugh, chuckle, giggle*
groom	1. *v.*	**tend, rub down** Chico groomed the horse before the race.	
	2. *v.*	**make attractive, ready, prepare, preen** Sam groomed himself for the interview. *n.* Good grooming is important always.	
grope	*v.*	**feel, fumble, hunt, search** They groped their way in the dark room.	
gross	1. *adj.*	**whole, entire, total** What is your gross annual income?	**1.** *net, remaining*
	2. *adj.*	**coarse, bad, vulgar, offensive** The student was expelled from school for gross misconduct.	**2.** *refined, elegant, inoffensive*
grotesque	*adj.*	**malformed, ugly, deformed, distorted, twisted, misshapen** Grotesque masks are often seen on Halloween.	*beautiful, lovely, appealing, handsome, well-formed*
grouchy	*adj.*	**ill-tempered, crusty, surly, irritable, sullen, rude** Everyone avoids the grouchy salesclerk. *n.* Tim is a grouch in the mornings.	*pleasant, affable, friendly*

ground	1.	*n.*	**earth, soil, land, terra firma, dirt** Fertile ground is needed for farming.	1. *water, air, space*
	2.	*n.*	**reason, basis** He filed for divorce on the grounds of desertion.	
groundless		*n.*	**false, unfounded, unreasonable** His allegations proved to be groundless.	*justifiable, reasonable*
group	1.	*n.*	**set, association, collection, assembly, company, cluster, bunch** The children huddled in a group at recess.	1. *individual*
	2.	*v.*	**classify, file, arrange, sort, collect, gather, cluster, combine** We grouped the children by age.	
grow	1.	*v.*	**develop, swell, enlarge, expand, increase, spread, amplify, flourish** Plants need water to grow. *n.* Water is needed for plant growth.	1. *dwindle, shrink, lessen, decrease, get smaller, wither*
	2.	*n.*	**cultivate, plant, raise, tend, produce** Farmers grow crops annually.	2. *harm, impede, restrict, neglect*
growl		*n.*	**snarl, groan** The dog's growl frightened off the intruder. *v.* The dog growled at the postal worker.	
grudge		*adj.*	**spite, rancor, animosity, resentment, ill feeling, grievance** He holds no grudge against you for his loss.	*goodwill, kindness, benevolence*
gruesome		*adj.*	**ghastly, horrible, hideous, grisly, grim, frightening, ugly, revolting** There were some gruesome sights in the disaster area.	*likeable, pleasant, agreeable, attractive, appealing*
gruff	1.	*adj.*	**abrupt, brusque, blunt, impolite, rude, unfriendly, cross, surly, harsh** We were not frightened by the guard's gruff manner. *adv.* The guard gruffly told us to leave.	1. *polite, courteous, civil, gracious, refined, affable*
	2.	*v.*	**hoarse, rough, grating, rasping, husky, jarring, harsh, guttural** I dislike the announcer's gruff voice.	2. *mild, sweet, smooth, harmonious, resonant*
grumble		*n.*	**complain, protest, fuss, whine, fret, object, criticize, mutter, carp, find fault** Customers grumbled about the high prices at the store.	*approve, accept, sanction, praise*
guard	1.	*n.*	**protector, sentry, sentinel, defender** The guards stood erect at the entrance to the palace.	1. *attacker, intruder, trespasser*

2. *v.* **covering, cover, protection, shield**
She carefully removed the skate-guards and stepped onto the ice.

3. *v.* **defend, protect, watch, shield**
Soldiers guard the borders.

3. *neglect, disregard, forsake*

guess *n.* **suppose, imagine, estimate, conjecture**
Pam correctly guessed the number of beans in the jar.
n. What a lucky guess!

deduce, prove, establish, know

guide 1. *n.* **leader, pilot, conductor, pathfinder**
Sherpa guides led the mountain climbers to the summit of Mt. Everest.

1. *follower, imitator*

2. *n.* **manual, chart, handbook, guidebook, instructions, map**
Each new car owner is given a guide about the vehicle.

3. *v.* **model, example, pattern, design**
Dressmakers use a guide to cut out the material.

4. *v.* **lead, escort, conduct, pilot, steer**
Who guided the tourists through the White House?
adj. Planes follow guiding beams.

4. *follow, pursue, come after, accompany*

5. *v.* **direct, supervise, oversee, manage**
The counselor guided the students with their choice of university.
n. They appreciated his guidance.

5. *mislead, obey, take orders, follow*

guilty 1. *adj.* **at fault, in error, culpable**
The suspect was found guilty of shoplifting.

1. *innocent, blameless*

2. *adj.* **embarrassed, shamefaced, contrite**
His guilty face told us he had done something wrong.

2. *guiltless*

gullible *adj.* **naive, innocent, credulous, trusting, unsuspecting**
Cheats prey on gullible people.

incredulous, skeptical, suspicious, dubious, doubtful

gush *v.* **burst, stream, pour out, flow out, flow, spout, rush, surge, spew**
Blood gushed from the wound.

drip, trickle, drop, dribble, ooze, drain

guttural *adj.* **hoarse, throaty, gruff, deep, low**
Certain languages have guttural sounds.

high-pitched, shrill, nasal, clear, ringing

gyp *v.* **cheat, swindle, defraud, dupe, bamboozle, trick, deceive, mislead**
The used-car salesman gypped him.

deal honorably, be fair

gyrate *v.* **spin, rotate, whirl, revolve, turn, spiral, twirl, pirouette**
The blades of the helicopter gyrated rapidly.

H

Many words originate from Phoenician and Greek picture-words. *H* was first known as *cheth* which meant *fence*. The letter in its earliest form resembled a fence with two or three bars.

Sometimes *H* is silent, as in words like *heir*, *hour*, and *honor*. In some English dialects, the *h* is dropped when speaking to make *houses* sound like *'ouses* and horses, *'orses*.

habit

1. *n.* **custom, practice, rule, routine**
The Japanese have a traditional habit of bowing to each other when they meet.
2. *n.* **quirk, tendency, compulsion**
Todd is trying to stop his habit of biting his nails.

habitual

1. *adj.* **regular, usual, customary, normal, routine, standard**
Rose takes a habitual walk each morning.
adv. She habitually rises early to exercise.

1. unusual, abnormal

2. *adj.* **compulsive, addictive, dependent**
He lost his job because of his habitual gambling.

2. rare, infrequent, occasional, sporadic

hack

1. *n.* **cut, slash, gash, wound**
The woodcutter made hacks in the tree with his axe.
2. *v.* **rip, tear, cut, gash, chop, slash, break, mangle, split, mutilate, chip, lacerate**
The marines hacked at the thick jungle vines.

haggard

adj. **gaunt, worried, weary, exhausted, worn-out, careworn**
Marie looks haggard after her long illness.

hearty, lively, fresh, vigorous

hail

1. *v.* **call, signal to, signal for, summon**
The doorman hailed a taxi with a loud whistle.
2. *v.* **salute, cheer, applaud, acclaim**
The citizens hailed their new leader.

2. ignore, disregard, boo

hair-raising

adj. **terrifying, frightening, shocking, fearful, dreadful, awful, terrible**
Mario frightened us with a hair-raising ghost story.

comforting, relaxing, soothing

hale

adj. **vigorous, healthy, hearty, strong, well, robust, sound**
At eighty, Grandpa is still hale and hearty.

weak, ailing, frail

halt

1. *n.* **stop, recess, pause, break**
The traffic ground to a halt because of an accident.
v. The bus halted to pick up passengers.

1. start, beginning, continuation

2. *v.* **end, check, suspend, arrest**
Is it possible to halt air pollution?

2. proceed, advance, continue

hammer

v. **drive, hit, pound, beat, strike, bang**
The carpenter hammered the nails into the boards.
n. Carpenters use a hammer to drive in nails.

yank, pull, extract

hamper

1. *n.* **basket**
The patient received several hampers of fruit from his friends.

	2.	*v.*	**hinder, obstruct, impede, hold back** A sore toe hampered the runner.	**2.** *aid, help, assist, hasten*
hand	1.	*n.*	**palm and fingers, fist, paw** Tim cut his hand on the window.	
	2.	*n.*	**support, help, assistance, aid** Ross gave us a hand when we moved.	**2.** *hindrance*
	3.	*v.*	**pass, give, deliver** The clerk handed me the parcel.	
handicap	1.	*n.*	**difficulty, hindrance, burden, drawback, disadvantage, limitation** Lack of formal education can be a handicap in job hunting.	**1.** *assistance, asset, advantage, help*
	2.	*v.*	**limit, hinder, impede** Bad weather handicapped the golfers.	**2.** *assist, help, aid, benefit, promote*
handle	1.	*n.*	**knob, pull, hold** The door handle is quite loose.	
	2.	*v.*	**touch, feel, finger, stroke, hold** They handled the china carefully.	
	3.	*v.*	**manipulate, operate, manage** She handles her job very efficiently.	
handsome	1.	*adj.*	**good-looking, beautiful, attractive** In fairy tales, the princess usually marries the handsome prince.	**1.** *ugly, revolting, unattractive, repulsive, unsightly*
	2.	*adj.*	**generous, large, considerable** Hans made a handsome donation to the school's building fund.	**2.** *small, puny, insignificant*
handy	1.	*adj.*	**useful, convenient, helpful** A microwave oven is a handy appliance.	**1.** *useless, inconvenient*
	2.	*adj.*	**clever, skilled, resourceful, adept** Sam is handy at making garden furniture.	**2.** *awkward, clumsy, unskilled*
	3.	*adv.*	**available, nearby, within reach, near** Always keep the first aid kit handy.	**3.** *far away, out of reach*
hang		*v.*	**suspend, dangle, drape, fasten** Hang your coat in the closet.	*let fall, drop*
haphazard		*adj.*	**offhand, slipshod, careless, casual, random, unintentional** Plans proceeded in a haphazard way. *adv.* The organizers met haphazardly.	*careful, studied, planned, organized, deliberate*
happen		*v.*	**occur, take place, come to pass** A terrible accident happened on the expressway this morning.	
happily	1.	*adv.*	**fortunately, luckily** Happily, no one was killed in the fire.	**1.** *unfortunately, unluckily*
	2.	*adv.*	**contentedly, joyfully** They lived happily in their new home.	**2.** *unhappily, discontentedly*
happiness		*n.*	**joy, delight, gladness, pleasure** Carla was filled with happiness at the thought of winning the scholarship.	*sorrow, misery, gloom, grief, sadness, unhappiness*

happy	*adj.*	**joyful, merry, glad, delighted, cheerful, jolly, jovial, sunny, cheery, pleased** Judy is happy because she won first prize.	*sad, sorrowful, dejected, moody, miserable, forlorn*
harass	*v.*	**disturb, annoy, bother, plague, vex, distress, torment** Creditors harassed the merchant. *n.* He closed his store to avoid the harassment.	*leave alone, ignore*
harbor	1. *n.*	**dock, port, quay, inlet** Many freighters sail into the harbor at New York.	
	2. *v.*	**shield, conceal, protect, shelter, house** The family harbored the escaped prisoner.	**2.** *turn in*
hard	1. *adj.*	**firm, solid, rigid, stiff** The new concrete is hard now.	**1.** *soft, yielding, pliable*
	2. *adj.*	**difficult, exacting** "That was a hard test," moaned Salim.	**2.** *easy, simple*
	3. *adj.*	**stern, severe, pitiless, strict, harsh** The judge issued a hard sentence on the drunk driver.	**3.** *gentle, kind, tender-hearted*
	4. *adj.*	**willing, eager, diligent, industrious** The new employee is a hard worker. *adv.* He works hard every day.	**4.** *lazy, unwilling*
hardhearted	*adj.*	**cruel, unfeeling, heartless** The hardhearted owner evicted the tenants for not paying the rent.	*sympathetic, considerate, kind, warm-hearted*
hardship	*n.*	**burden, trial, misfortune** People lived through terrible hardships during the war.	*pleasure, advantage, happiness*
hardy	*adj.*	**strong, vigorous, robust, fit, sturdy** Mountain climbers are hardy people.	*weak, delicate, feeble, frail*
harm	1. *n.*	**hardship, injury, wrong, hurt, damage** Humans have done much harm to the environment.	**1.** *good, benefit, improvement, aid, assistance*
	2. *v.*	**hurt, damage, injure** The early frost harmed the crops. *adj.* Many pesticides are harmful to human beings.	**2.** *help, benefit, improve, assist, aid*
harmless	*adj.*	**safe, inoffensive** Only harmless pesticides should be used.	*harmful, injurious, dangerous, poisonous*
harmony	*n.*	**cooperation, understanding, agreement, accord, friendship** These two groups work in complete harmony. *adj.* They have a harmonious relationship.	*conflict, discord*

harness	1.	*n.*	**lines, reins, traces, halter, bridle** Let's put the harness on the horse.	
	2.	*v.*	**utilize, make useful** The new dam will harness great energy from the falls.	
harsh	1.	*adj.*	**rough, grating, sharp, jarring, piercing** We shut the door to avoid his harsh yells.	**1.** *pleasing, mild, agreeable, gentle*
	2.	*adj.*	**arduous, tough, severe, demanding** The army made a harsh trek across the desert.	**2.** *easy, pleasant*
	3.	*adj.*	**mean, stern, cruel, severe, unkind** The children were terrified of their harsh guardian. *adv.* He treated them harshly.	**3.** *kind, merciful, gentle, considerate, loving*
harvest	1.	*n.*	**reaping, crop gathering** The farmers were busy with the harvest.	**1.** *sowing, planting, seeding*
	2.	*n.*	**yield, crop** The grape harvest this year was plentiful.	
	3.	*v.*	**reap, gather, cut, mow, pick, collect** The farmer harvested the crop before the frost came.	**3.** *seed, plant, sow*
hassle		*n.*	**struggle, argument, quarrel, squabble, conflict, trouble** There was a hassle over who should cut the grass.	*agreement, accord*
haste		*n.*	**speed, swiftness, rush** The doctor went in haste to help the patient. *v.* Yen hastened to answer the phone. *adv.* He walked hastily.	*slowness, tardiness, delay*
hasty	1.	*adj.*	**swift, rushed, hurried, quick, fast, speedy** We had a hasty lunch between classes.	**1.** *slow, leisurely*
	2.	*adj.*	**rash, thoughtless, reckless** Don't make a hasty decision when you buy a house or a car.	**2.** *careful, cautious, thoughtful*
hate		*v.*	**dislike, detest, despise, abhor** The baby hated the taste of the medicine. *n.* She was filled with hate.	*like, regard, respect, love*
hateful		*adj.*	**obnoxious, distasteful, nasty, revolting, sickening, nauseating** Many people think that hunting is a hateful pastime.	*enjoyable, pleasant*
hatred		*n.*	**ill will, dislike, aversion, hostility** Hatred sometimes leads to violence.	*love, kindness, fondness, affection*
haughty		*adj.*	**proud, arrogant, stuck-up, snobbish** The haughty girl refused to make friends with the new students.	*unassuming, unpretentious, humble, modest*

adv. She haughtily stomped off when we approached her for help.
n. There is no need for haughtiness.

haul
1. *n.* **amount, catch, take**
The fishing crew pulled in a good haul of cod.
2. *v.* **pull, drag, carry, draw, transport, lug**   2. *shove, push*
Lumberjacks hauled logs from the bush all winter.

have
1. *v.* **own, possess, hold**
Do you have a car?
2. *v.* **take, get, obtain**   2. *give up, forfeit, relinquish*
Please have a seat.
3. *v.* **allow, permit**   3. *disallow, forbid, refuse*
My parents won't have a dog in the house.
4. *v.* **must, be compelled, be obliged**
I have to do my homework tonight.

haven
n. **refuge, shelter, retreat, harbor**
The travelers tried to find a haven from the storm.

havoc
n. **destruction, disaster, calamity, ruin, damage**
The hurricane wreaked havoc over a wide area.

hazard
1. *n.* **threat, risk, danger, peril**   1. *safeguard, protection, security, assurance*
The travelers faced many hazards on the icy highways.
adj. The ice storm created hazardous driving conditions.
2. *v.* **risk, venture, take a chance on**
Hazard a guess about my age.

haze
n. **fog, smoke, vapor, mist**
Forest fires created a haze over the valley.

hazy
1. *adj.* **cloudy, foggy, misty, murky, smoky**   1. *clear, bright, sunny, cloudless*
On humid days the atmosphere can become quite hazy.
2. *adj.* **uncertain, obscure, vague, confused**   2. *clear, certain, clear-cut, positive, definite, sure*
She has only a hazy idea of how the accident happened.

head
1. *n.* **leader, boss, chief, ruler**   1. *follower, worker, servant*
His aunt is head of the company.
v. She has headed the company for years.
2. *n.* **mind, brain, intellect, intelligence**
Rita has a good head for mathematics.
3. *v.* **guide, direct, steer, proceed**
Everyone headed home after the party.

headfirst
adv. **headlong**   *feet-first*
Shawn toppled headfirst into the river.

headlong	1.	*adv.*	**headfirst** Tom fell headlong down the stairs.	*1. feet-first*
	2.	*adv.*	**thoughtlessly, recklessly, rashly** Sue ran headlong into the path of the car.	*2. carefully, cautiously, warily*
headstrong		*adj.*	**stubborn, bullheaded, rash, reckless, hotheaded, obstinate** The headstrong hockey player was penalized for fighting.	*obliging, obedient, careful*
headway	1.	*n.*	**headroom, space** We had to crouch to enter the cave as there was not enough headway.	
	2.	*n.*	**progress, advancement** Scientists have made some headway in their search for a cure for AIDS.	*2. setback, relapse*
heal		*v.*	**cure, repair, remedy, mend, fix** Time is said to heal all wounds.	*injure, damage, make ill, infect*
healthy		*adj.*	**well, vigorous, robust, sound, fit** Fiona gave birth to a healthy girl. *n.* The baby is in good health.	*ill, sickly, unhealthy, ailing, frail, delicate*
heap	1.	*n.*	**pile, load, mass, stack, accumulation** There were heaps of gravel in the yard.	*1. bit, handful*
	2.	*v.*	**pile, collect, gather, stack** We heaped the fallen leaves in piles.	*2. scatter, spread, strew*
hearsay		*n.*	**rumor, gossip, idle talk** It is only hearsay that the company is in trouble.	*fact, truth*
heartless		*adj.*	**hardhearted, cruel, pitiless, merciless** It is heartless not to help the needy.	*gentle, kind, merciful, humane*
hearty	1.	*adj.*	**warm, sincere, cheerful, enthusiastic** We received a hearty welcome from our friends.	*1. insincere, cold, unenthusiastic*
	2.	*adj.*	**strong, well, hardy, vigorous, robust** My grandmother is hale and hearty.	*2. sickly, weak, ill, ailing, frail, delicate*
heat	1.	*n.*	**warmth, high temperature** The heat in the desert is unbearable.	*1. cold*
	2.	*n.*	**passion, ardor, fervor, excitement** He slammed the table in the heat of the argument. *adj.* It was a heated argument.	*2. calm, composure, reflection, indifference*
	3.	*v.*	**make hot, bring to a boil, cook** Heat the leftovers in the microwave. *adj.* I burnt my hand on the heated pot.	*3. cool, let cool*
heave	1.	*v.*	**hoist, raise, lift, elevate, toss, fling** The workers heaved the bales of cotton onto the truck.	
	2.	*v.*	**rise and fall, undulate** The patient's chest heaved as he struggled to breathe.	

heavy	1.	*adj.*	**weighty, burdensome, massive** That parcel is too heavy to carry.	1. *light*
	2.	*adj.*	**sad, gloomy, sorrowful** With a heavy heart, he told them the sad news.	2. *happy, cheerful, joyful*
	3.	*adj.*	**dense, thick, intense** We could not drive in the heavy fog.	3. *light, thin*
heckle		*v.*	**pester, badger, taunt, harass, boo** The crowd heckled the speaker at the rally. *n.* The hecklers were ordered to leave.	*applaud, agree with, appreciate*
hectic		*adj.*	**wild, frantic, busy** The opening day of school can be hectic.	*calm, restful, serene, peaceful, relaxing*
hedge	1.	*n.*	**row of bushes, border, barrier** A thick hedge surrounds the garden.	
	2.	*v.*	**surround, edge, fence, border, enclose** Evergreens hedged the yard.	
heed	1.	*n.*	**attention, notice, care, regard** The patient paid heed to the doctor's advice and stayed in bed.	1. *inattention, neglect*
	2.	*v.*	**observe, pay attention to, follow** They heeded their parents' advice.	2. *ignore, neglect, disobey*
help	1.	*n.*	**aid, assistance, support** Thank you for your help.	1. *hindrance, obstruction*
	2.	*v.*	**aid, assist, befriend, support** We helped all those in need.	2. *hamper, hinder, obstruct*
hermit		*n.*	**recluse, solitary, loner** Many religious hermits live in the deserts of the Middle East.	
heroic		*adj.*	**valiant, brave, fearless, bold, gallant, courageous, daring** She is remembered for her heroic deeds. *n.* People admire heroism.	*cowardly, timid, fearful*
hesitate		*v.*	**falter, pause, waver, delay** The student hesitated before entering the principal's office. *n.* She agreed to help without any hesitation.	*advance, hurry, hasten*
hide	1.	*n.*	**skin, pelt** People tan the hides of some animals.	
	2.	*v.*	**conceal, cover** The boy hid the frog in his pocket. *adj.* The hidden frog began to croak.	2. *uncover, expose, exhibit, reveal, show*
hideous		*adj.*	**horrible, ugly, revolting, ghastly, frightful, terrible, awful** The actor wore a hideous mask.	*beautiful, lovely, handsome, pleasing, attractive*
high	1.	*adj.*	**tall, lofty, towering** The high mountains are snow-capped.	1. *low, short, stunted*

	2.	*adj.*	**leading, exalted, senior, important** Dad has a high position in the company.	**2.** *unimportant, inferior, secondary*
	3.	*adj.*	**great, extreme** The police are working to reduce the high crime rate.	**3.** *low, average*
highlight	**1.**	*n.*	**peak, climax, high point** The highlight of our trip was our visit to the White House.	**1.** *low point, disappointment*
	2.	*v.*	**stress, emphasize, underline, accent** The minister's speech highlighted the need to conserve energy.	**2.** *neglect, overlook, slight*
hike		*n.*	**march, walk, tramp, trek** After the long hike, everyone was tired and hungry. *v.* The girl guides hiked three miles.	
hilarious		*adj.*	**funny, comical, merry, lively, laughable** We all laughed at Peng's hilarious stories.	*sad, miserable, unhappy, gloomy, woebegone*
hinder		*v.*	**obstruct, delay, block, hamper, curb, thwart** Lack of funds hindered the research.	*help, aid, assist, support*
hindrance		*n.*	**obstruction, obstacle, handicap** The thick smoke was a hindrance to the firefighters' rescue efforts. *v.* Smoke hindered their efforts.	*aid, support, help*
hint	**1.**	*n.*	**suggestion, inkling, clue, idea** There was not a hint of cloud in the sky.	
	2.	*v.*	**imply, suggest, intimate** Mom hinted that I might receive a gift.	**2.** *conceal, keep quiet, cover, hide*
hire	**1.**	*v.*	**employ, appoint, engage** The new factory will hire fifty people.	**1.** *dismiss, fire, let go, discharge*
	2.	*v.*	**lease, rent, charter, engage** Frida hired a car for the trip.	
historic		*adj.*	**memorable, important, significant** Neil Armstrong's historic moon landing took place in 1969.	*unimportant, insignificant, mundane*
hit	**1.**	*n.*	**blow, bump, knock, strike** He suffered a direct hit to his head.	
	2.	*n.*	**success, winner, bestseller** The play was a big hit.	**2.** *failure, flop*
	3.	*v.*	**strike, rap, beat, slap, punch** The batter hit a home run.	**3.** *miss*
hitch	**1.**	*n.*	**problem, delay, mishap, mistake, difficulty, hindrance** The ceremony went off without a hitch.	**1.** *aid, support, help*
	2.	*v.*	**couple, attach, fasten, connect, secure** We hitched the trailer to the van. *n.* A hitch was used to pull the trailer.	**2.** *unfasten, untie, unhook, disconnect, loosen*

hoard	*v.*	**collect, stockpile, save, accumulate, store** Squirrels hoard nuts for the winter. *n.* There was a hoard of acorns in a hollow tree.	*spend, distribute*
hoarse	*adj.*	**husky, rough, harsh, cracked** His cold gave him a hoarse voice.	*sweet, mellow, pleasant, musical*
hoax	*n.*	**trick, deception, fraud, fake, spoof** The story of the flying saucer was a hoax.	*truth, fact, reality*
hobo	*n.*	**drifter, tramp, vagabond, bum, vagrant** The dogs barked at the scruffy hobo.	
hoist	1. *n.*	**lift, elevator** A hoist was used to lift the grand piano onto the stage.	
	2. *v.*	**raise, lift, heave, elevate, take up** The movers hoisted the piano to the third floor.	2. *lower, take down*
hold	1. *n.*	**grasp, clutch, grip** The police officer kept a firm hold on the suspect.	
	2. *v.*	**keep, guard, reserve, set aside** The airline will hold the tickets until Thursday.	2. *give up, cancel, put on the market*
	3. *v.*	**contain, enclose, accommodate** That suitcase holds a lot of clothes.	
	4. *v.*	**clutch, grip, grasp, clasp** The child held his mother's hand.	4. *drop, let go, release*
	5. *v.*	**bind, stick, cling, adhere** Will the glue hold a hook to the wall?	5. *loosen, come undone*
	6. *v.*	**have, conduct, execute** The committee held a meeting today.	6. *cancel, postpone*
	7. *v.*	**restrain, keep, restrict, detain** Police held the suspect until bail was posted.	7. *release, free, let go*
	8. *v.*	**keep, have, possess, occupy** President Bill Clinton held office for two terms.	8. *give up, leave*
hole	*n.*	**cavity, opening, gap, pit, cave, shaft, excavation, hollow** The gardener dug a hole to plant the bush.	
holler	*v.*	**shout, call, yell, scream, bellow** The letter carrier hollered when the dog attacked him.	*whisper*
hollow	*adj.*	**empty, vacant, unfilled** The chocolate egg is hollow.	*solid, filled, full*
holy	*adj.*	**religious, godly, devout, sacred, blessed, divine** A church is a holy place.	*sacrilegious, evil, wicked*

homeland	*n.*	**birthplace, native land** The refugees longed to return to their homeland.	*adopted land*
homely	*adj.*	**plain, ordinary, simple** He has a homely face but a wonderful personality.	*beautiful, attractive, lovely*
honest	*adj.*	**reliable, sincere, trustworthy, fair, honorable, aboveboard** The honest man turned in the wallet that he found.	*dishonest, deceitful, devious, unreliable, insincere*
honesty	*n.*	**fairness, truthfulness, openness** Honesty is to be admired.	*dishonesty, deceit, deception*
honor	*n.*	**respect, esteem, glory, fame, renown, tribute** A scholarship was established in honor of Terry Fox. *v.* They honored his memory by erecting a statue of him.	*dishonor, disgrace, disrepute*
hope	**1.** *n.* **2.** *v.*	**anticipation, expectation** May all your hopes come true. **wish, desire, trust** We hoped that you would win.	**1.** *despair, fear* **2.** *dread, fear, doubt*
horrible	*adj.*	**dreadful, awful, horrid, terrible, frightful, repulsive, loathsome** Smallpox is a horrible disease.	*pleasant, attractive, good, pleasing, delightful*
horrid	*adj.*	**terrible, dreadful, awful, frightful, horrible, repulsive** This medicine has a horrid taste.	*pleasant, pleasing, appealing*
horror	*n.*	**fear, panic, dismay, terror, dread, alarm** The strange face at the window filled me with horror.	*bravery, hope, courage, comfort, delight*
hospitable	*adv.*	**friendly, sociable, kind, neighborly** The Yuens are hospitable hosts. *n.* Their friends always enjoy their hospitality.	*hostile, unfriendly, unkind, unsociable*
hostile	*adj.*	**unfriendly, antagonistic** The police had to control the hostile demonstrators.	*friendly, devoted, loyal, hospitable*
hot	*adj.*	**fiery, flaming, blazing, glowing, heated, burning, torrid** The campers cooked potatoes over the hot coals.	*cold, frigid, freezing, chilly, frosty*
hotheaded	*adj.*	**headstrong, rash, bad-tempered** It is difficult to work with hotheaded people.	*easygoing, even-tempered*

house

1. *n.* **residence, home, abode, dwelling**
   They expect to move into their new house in June.
2. *n.* **line, royal family, clan, dynasty**
   Queen Elizabeth II is of the House of Windsor.
3. *n.* **store, shop, cafe, business**
   There is a pancake house on Main Street.
4. *v.* **shelter, accommodate, lodge**   *4. evict, expel*
   We housed the visitors overnight.

howl

n. **cry, yelp, whine, wail**
The dog's howls kept us awake.
v. The dog howled all night long.

hug

v. **cuddle, squeeze, embrace, hold**
Jane hugged her sister when they met.

huge

adj. **immense, great, gigantic, vast, enormous, monstrous, giant**   *tiny, wee, miniature, little, small*
The family laughed at Tang's story of the huge fish that got away.

humane

adj. **gentle, kind, merciful, compassionate**   *cruel, brutal, pitiless, inhumane*
Treat animals in a humane way.

humble

1. *adj.* **modest, unassuming, shy, meek**   *1. haughty, vain, boastful, arrogant, proud, conceited*
   The humble woman shyly acknowledged the applause.
2. *adj.* **plain, lowly, not grand**   *2. grand, elegant, pretentious*
   The shepherd lives in a humble hut.

humid

adj. **damp, moist, muggy, clammy, sticky**   *dry, arid, parched*
We perspired profusely on the humid day.
n. The humidity was unbearable.

humiliate

v. **shame, embarrass, disgrace, humble**   *please, honor, elate*
The bad publicity humiliated the athletes.
n. Their humiliation was complete.

hunch

n. **idea, premonition, feeling, suspicion**
I've got a hunch that it will rain today.

hunger

1. *n.* **famine, starvation, lack of food**   *1. fullness, satiety*
   Hunger is a continuing problem in Africa.
2. *v.* **desire, wish, want, yearn for**   *2. dread*
   The sailors hungered for the sight of land.

hungry

adj. **famished, starved, ravenous**   *well-fed, satisfied, full, fed*
Growing children are always hungry.

hunt

1. *n.* **search, pursuit, chase, quest**   *1. capture, discovery*
   The hunt is on for the escaped convict.
2. *v.* **seek, pursue, chase, search, follow, track, trace**   *2. find*
   The ranch hands hunted for the lost cattle.

hurl		*v.*	**throw, pitch, cast, toss, fling**	*catch, grasp*
			Manuel hurled the discus sixty yards.	
hurry	1.	*n.*	**rush, scramble**	
			I'm in a hurry to catch my bus.	
	2.	*v.*	**rush, speed, hasten, scurry, dash**	**2.** *slow down, dawdle*
			We hurried home for dinner.	
hurt	1.	*n.*	**injury, wound**	
			The doctor treated the boy's hurt in the hospital.	
	2.	*v.*	**harm, damage, wound, injure**	**2.** *cure, heal, benefit, help, assist*
			Kim hurt her knees while skiing.	
	3.	*v.*	**ache, sting, pain**	
			Her knees still hurt from the injury.	
husky	1.	*adj.*	**hoarse, rough, harsh, cracked**	**1.** *smooth, musical, soft, sweet, mellow*
			A cold may cause a husky voice.	
	2.	*adj.*	**strong, hefty, solid, well-built, powerful**	**2.** *weak, frail, puny, sickly*
			The husky boy had no trouble carrying the heavy box.	
hustle	1.	*n.*	**scramble, hurry, scurry, rush, jostle**	**1.** *delay*
			What a hustle to get to school on time!	
			v. We hustled all the way down the street.	
	2.	*n.*	**stir, fuss, excitement, bustle**	**2.** *peace, quiet, calm*
			We escaped from the hustle of the city to our cottage in the country.	
hyperactive		*adj.*	**overactive, over-animated**	*sluggish, dull, slow*
			The hyperactive child had trouble concentrating in class.	
hypocrite		*n.*	**insincere person, two-faced person, deceitful person**	*sincere person, genuine person, honest person*
			I would be a hypocrite if I said I liked that outfit.	
			adj. It would be hypocritical of me to say that I like it when I don't.	
hypothesis		*n.*	**theory, proposal, thesis, assumption**	*fact, certainty, proof*
			The scientists stated their hypothesis before the experiment.	
			v. The detective hypothesized about the motive for the crime.	
hypothetical		*adj.*	**supposed, imaginary, possible**	*real, actual, true, proven, demonstrated*
			The lawyer spoke of a hypothetical situation.	
hysteria		*n.*	**frenzy, panic, delirium**	
			The passengers were close to hysteria when the plane was hijacked.	
			adj. The plane's crew calmed the hysterical passengers.	

I

I, the third of the five English vowels, is also a word: the first person singular. When used as a word, it is always capitalized. A speaker or writer uses *I* when referring to himself or herself.

I represented a single thing in Roman numerals.

icy	1.	*adj.*	**frozen, glazed, frosted, iced, slippery** Drive carefully on icy streets.	**1.** *thawed*
	2.	*adj.*	**cold, frigid, frosty, polar, freezing** Many people drowned in the icy waters when the *Titanic* sank.	**2.** *hot, torrid, warm*
	3.	*adj.*	**unfriendly, hostile, cold** The rowdy students were silenced with an icy stare from their teacher.	**3.** *friendly, warm, welcoming*
idea		*n.*	**thought, notion, opinion, concept** Christopher Columbus had the brilliant idea that the world was round.	
ideal	1.	*n.*	**goal, aim** She has set herself lofty ideals in life.	
	2.	*adj.*	**perfect, supreme, exemplary, classic** She is the ideal size for a gymnast. *n.* With her skill and her dedication, she is every coach's ideal.	**2.** *imperfect, faulty*
	3.	*adj.*	**unattainable, utopian, fanciful, imaginary, unreal, abstract** Many people think world peace is an ideal goal.	**3.** *practical, down-to-earth, attainable*
identical		*adj.*	**alike, twin, same, indistinguishable** Even close friends could not tell the identical twins apart.	*different, unlike, distinct, separate, divergent, opposite*
identify		*v.*	**recognize, label, classify, name, catalog, analyze, describe** The witness identified the robber from the pictures in the police files. *n.* The process of identification took a long time.	
idle	1.	*adj.*	**inactive, unused, unemployed** The printing presses stood idle during the strike.	**1.** *active, busy, used, engaged, employed*
	2.	*adj.*	**lazy, indolent, shiftless** The idle worker soon lost his job.	**2.** *industrious, diligent, busy*
ignite		*v.*	**set on fire, burn, incinerate, light** The scout leader ignited the campfire with a torch.	*extinguish, quench, put out*
ignorant	1.	*adj.*	**uneducated, illiterate** The ignorant villagers were conned by the slick salesperson.	**1.** *educated, literate, learned, wise*
	2.	*adj.*	**unaware, uninformed, clueless** Many people are ignorant of the benefits of a healthy diet. *n.* Ignorance of the law is not excused by the courts.	**2.** *aware, informed, cognizant*
ignore		*v.*	**disregard, pass over, overlook, scorn** The skater got in trouble because he ignored the sign warning of thin ice.	*heed, pay attention to, obey, follow*

ill	1.	*adj.*	**sick, unwell, ailing, indisposed, infirm** The school was closed because many students were ill with influenza. *n.* The students' illness caused concern.	**1.** *well, healthy, hale*
	2.	*adj.*	**unfortunate, bad, evil, unfavorable** The project was plagued with ill luck from the beginning. *adv.* You shouldn't speak ill of others.	**2.** *good, favorable, fortunate*
	3.	*adv.*	**barely, scarcely, hardly** Anton bought a car even though he could ill afford it.	**3.** *amply, well, comfortably*
illegal		*adj.*	**unlawful, illicit, illegitimate, banned, forbidden, unauthorized, prohibited** The driver was fined for making an illegal turn. *adv.* He was fined for turning illegally.	*lawful, legitimate, permissible, legal, authorized, sanctioned*
illegible		*adj.*	**obscure, unintelligible, indistinct, unreadable, indecipherable** The teacher refused to read the essay because the writing was illegible.	*legible, distinct, clear, intelligible, easy to read*
illuminate	1.	*v.*	**brighten, lighten** Streetlights illuminate the roads.	**1.** *darken, obscure*
	2.	*v.*	**explain, clarify, interpret, elucidate** Illuminate your answer with a diagram.	**2.** *confuse, puzzle, confound*
illusion	1.	*n.*	**mirage, fancy, fantasy, vision, hallucination, apparition** Many magic tricks are merely optical illusions.	**1.** *form, reality, body, substance*
	2.	*n.*	**misconception, mistake, delusion, misunderstanding, false notion** The dictator was under the illusion that he would rule forever.	**2.** *fact, knowledge, understanding*
illustration	1.	*n.*	**example, sample, model, specimen** That statue is an illustration of the sculptor's style.	
	2.	*n.*	**picture, photograph, drawing, cartoon** The illustrations in the book were done by a famous artist.	
illustrious		*adj.*	**renowned, famous, eminent, famed, important, distinguished, celebrated** Yo-Yo Ma is an illustrious cellist.	*unknown, obscure, hidden*
imaginary		*adj.*	**hypothetical, theoretical, fancied, fanciful, whimsical, unreal, illusory** The Equator is an imaginary line around the center of the Earth.	*real, factual, actual, existing*
imagination		*n.*	**fantasy, fancy, creativity** Writers of science fiction stories have vivid imaginations. *adj.* Imaginative plots appeal to readers.	*reality, actuality*

imagine	*v.*	**visualize, picture, conceive, fancy** Can you imagine living on the moon?	
imitate	1. *v.*	**emulate, follow, model** People often imitate those whom they admire. *n.* Imitation is the sincerest form of flattery.	1. *initiate*
	2. *v.*	**copy, mimic, duplicate, echo, simulate, ape, match** The parrot imitated its owner's voice. *n.* Parrots are good imitators. *n.* The pearl necklace turned out to be a cheap imitation.	
immaculate	1. *adj.*	**spotless, clean, pristine** The house is in immaculate condition.	1. *dirty, soiled, filthy, stained*
	2. *adj.*	**sinless, pure, innocent, undefiled** Saints lead immaculate lives.	2. *sinful, defiled*
immature	*adj.*	**youthful, naive, childish, young, green, inexperienced, callow** Her immature attitude got her into trouble at work. *n.* His immaturity showed when he threw a tantrum after losing the game.	*mature, adult, experienced, sophisticated*
immediately	*adv.*	**instantly, right away, directly, at once, now, quickly, promptly, rapidly** Come over here immediately! *adj.* There was an immediate reply to our request for help.	*later, in a while, in the future, sometime*
immense	1. *adj.*	**huge, great, big, large, vast, enormous, gigantic, mighty, colossal, tremendous** She inherited an immense fortune from her aunt.	1. *small, tiny, miniature, wee, puny, insignificant*
	2. *adj.*	**boundless, eternal, limitless, infinite** Outer space is immense.	2. *finite, limited, restricted*
immerse	1. *v.*	**submerge, dip, douse, plunge, soak, drench, dunk** The pilgrims immersed themselves in the holy river.	
	2. *v.*	**engross, engage, involve, absorb** The students immersed themselves in their discussion. *adj.* They were so immersed in their work they didn't hear the bell ring.	
imminent	*adj.*	**impending, near, at hand, destined, approaching, expected** The sailors returned to shore when they heard that a storm was imminent.	*remote, distant, future, afar, possible*
immortal	*adj.*	**undying, permanent, everlasting, perpetual, endless, abiding, enduring** Shakespeare's plays have immortal appeal.	*temporary, fleeting, mortal, perishable, transitory*

immovable		*adj.*	**fixed, firm, immobile, stationary, stable, fastened** The Sphinx is immovable.	*portable, mobile, movable, loose, free, removable*
immune	1.	*adj.*	**unaffected by, protected against, safe, impervious, resistant** They are immune to the disease as they have been immunized against it. *n.* Babies have a natural immunity to certain diseases.	1. *affected by*
	2.	*adj.*	**not liable, exempt, unaffected** No one is immune from the law.	2. *liable, answerable, bound by*
impact	1.	*n.*	**collision, contact, clash, slam, bump** The driver got the full force of the impact when he hit the tree.	
	2.	*n.*	**influence, effect, force** The computer has had a tremendous impact on our lives.	
impair	1.	*v.*	**spoil, hurt, damage, injure** Smoking impairs health to a large degree.	1. *improve, repair, enhance*
	2.	*v.*	**weaken, lessen, diminish, handicap** Alcohol impairs a person's concentration powers. *adj.* The drunk driver was charged with impaired driving.	2. *augment, enhance, strengthen, facilitate*
impart		*v.*	**give, inform, tell, convey, disclose, divulge, reveal** Teachers impart knowledge to their students.	*conceal, hide, suppress, withhold*
impartial		*adj.*	**unbiased, fair, just, unprejudiced, non-partisan, neutral, objective** Umpires should make impartial decisions in a game.	*partial, biased, partisan*
impassable		*adj.*	**closed, blocked, obstructed, impenetrable** The highway was made impassable by a multi-car accident.	*open, unobstructed, passable*
impatient	1.	*adj.*	**restless, anxious, eager, keen** The children were impatient to set off on their holidays. *n.* They were restless from their impatience. *adv.* They called impatiently to their parents to hurry up.	1. *patient, calm*
	2.	*adj.*	**fretful, irritable, bothered, intolerant** The impatient man tooted his horn at the car in front of him.	2. *patient, relaxed, content*
impeccable		*adj.*	**perfect, faultless, immaculate, flawless** Impeccable grooming is a must for television news anchors. *adv.* They must be impeccably groomed.	*imperfect, deficient, defective*

impede	*v.*	thwart, block, hinder, deter, obstruct, hamper The strong current impeded the swimmer's progress.	*help, assist, aid, expedite*
impediment	*n.*	hindrance, obstruction, obstacle, restriction, encumbrance, restraint Heavy luggage is an impediment to a traveler.	*assistance, aid, benefit, advantage, help*
impel	1. *v.*	urge, drive, excite, induce Curiosity impelled the explorers to continue with their quest.	1. *inhibit, repress*
	2. *v.*	move, push, prod, propel, shove, drive The crash impelled the passengers into the windshield.	2. *restrain, hold back*
imperative	1. *adj.*	urgent, necessary, essential, crucial, compulsory It is imperative that everyone be vaccinated at once.	1. *optional, unnecessary*
	2. *adj.*	authoritative, masterful, commanding The children quieted when they heard the principal's imperative tones.	2. *unauthoritative, supplicatory, mild, conciliatory*
imperfection	*n.*	fault, flaw, stain, blemish, defect, weakness Imperfections in jewels lower their value.	*perfection*
impertinent	1. *adj.*	irrelevant, pointless, inappropriate, inapplicable The paper contained impertinent data.	1. *pertinent, applicable, appropriate, relevant*
	2. *adj.*	impudent, rude, saucy, bold, insolent, brazen, impolite Ken was kept in for recess for his impertinent behavior. *n.* Such impertinence cannot be tolerated.	2. *respectful, polite, courteous*
impetuous	*adj.*	rash, hasty, headstrong, impulsive Mei's impetuous temper often gets her into trouble.	*thoughtful, careful, cautious*
implant	*v.*	insert, root, stick in, embed The surgical team implanted a donor's heart in the patient. *n.* She needed a dental implant after losing her tooth in an accident.	*remove, take out*
implement	1. *n.*	utensil, device, tool, instrument, apparatus Hardware stores sell garden implements.	
	2. *v.*	enforce, carry out The schools implemented the new rules.	2. *abandon, give up, ignore*
implicate	*v.*	accuse, associate, entangle, involve, incriminate The witness implicated a neighbor in the crime.	*state, declare, acquit, extricate, dissociate*

imply		*v.*	**suggest, infer, hint, intimate** The students' frowns implied they were having trouble with the test.	*declare, state, express*
impolite		*adj.*	**rude, discourteous, impertinent, saucy, bold, forward, disrespectful** It is impolite to interrupt when someone is speaking.	*courteous, polite, respectful*
import		*v.*	**bring in, buy abroad** Canada imports many goods from the United States.	*export, sell abroad, send away*
important	1.	*adj.*	**significant, essential, pressing** Important decisions are made by the government. *n.* The doctor stressed the importance of eating a balanced diet.	*1. trivial, minor, inconsequential, unimportant, petty*
	2.	*adj.*	**well-known, illustrious, prominent, notable, eminent** The Prime Minister is an important person.	*2. obscure, unknown, unrecognized*
impose		*v.*	**force upon, inflict, place on** The government imposed a curfew after the riots.	*remove, lift*
imposing		*adj.*	**impressive, striking, stirring, exciting, grand, majestic** The Eiffel Tower in Paris is an imposing structure.	*unimpressive, commonplace, uninteresting*
impossible		*adj.*	**unattainable, unworkable, futile, hopeless, unachievable** It is impossible to live on the sun.	*possible, attainable*
impostor		*n.*	**pretender, charlatan, quack** The impostor carried fake documents.	
impractical		*adj.*	**unrealistic, unworkable, illogical** A space colony was considered impractical a decade ago.	*practical, logical, reasonable, viable*
impressive	1.	*adj.*	**striking, moving, exciting, thrilling, stirring, notable, effective** The actor gave an impressive performance. *v.* His performance impressed the audience.	*1. dull, common, uninspiring*
	2.	*adj.*	**grand, noble, stately, majestic** The Taj Mahal is an impressive structure.	*2. simple, ordinary, unassuming, modest*
impromptu		*adj.*	**unprepared, spontaneous, unrehearsed** It is difficult to make an impromptu speech.	*prepared, studied, premeditated, rehearsed*
improper	1.	*adj.*	**unsuitable, unbecoming, incorrect, inappropriate** It is improper to wear pajamas to work.	*1. proper, correct, fitting, suitable, appropriate*

2. *adj.* **wrong, indecent, immoral, shameful, wicked, vulgar**
It used to be considered improper for women to expose their ankles in public.

2. *decent, proper, right, moral*

impudent *adj.* **forward, brazen, rude, impertinent, brash, insolent, bold, sassy**
The impudent girl was told to mind her manners.
n. She apologized for her impudence.

shy, polite, courteous, respectful, well-mannered

impulsive **1.** *adj.* **rash, hasty, thoughtless, impetuous**
Vani regretted his impulsive remarks as soon as he said them.

1. *cautious, wary, careful*

2. *adj.* **spontaneous, automatic, involuntary, instinctive**
Ann gave an impulsive cheer when she heard the good news.
n. Have you acted on impulse?
adv. The crowd cheered impulsively.

2. *premeditated, prepared, rehearsed*

impure *adj.* **dirty, contaminated, polluted, tainted**
We shouldn't drink impure water.
n. Impurities in drinking water can be harmful to our health.

clean, pure, uncontaminated

inadequate *adj.* **insufficient, not enough, deficient, too little**
Inadequate ventilation made the workers drowsy.

enough, adequate, sufficient, abundant, too much, ample

inappropriate *adj.* **unsuitable, improper, out of place, unbecoming, incorrect**
Slang is considered inappropriate language in formal reports.

suitable, fitting, appropriate, proper

inaugurate *v.* **begin, originate, introduce, initiate, start, install in office**
The president-elect was inaugurated in a moving ceremony.
adj. President Kennedy's inaugural address touched many people.

end, terminate, conclude, finish

incense *v.* **anger, enrage, cross, infuriate, annoy, provoke**
The umpire's call incensed the baseball fans.

calm down, soothe, pacify

incentive *n.* **stimulus, inducement, impetus, enticement, spur**
The salespeople were offered a bonus as an incentive for more sales.

restraint, curb, constraint, check, deterrent, limitation

incessant *adj.* **ceaseless, endless, continuous, constant, continual, uninterrupted, perpetual**
The dog's incessant barking annoyed the neighbors.

occasional, rare, periodic, random, sporadic, infrequent, irregular adv. The dog barked incessantly all through the night.

incident   *n.*   **event, occasion, episode, affair, happening, occurrence**
The nasty incident took place yesterday.

incidental   *adj.*   **minor, casual, secondary, subordinate**   *major, significant, principal, essential, main, fundamental*
Winning is incidental to the thrill of participation.

incite   *v.*   **rouse, excite, stimulate, provoke, induce, prompt, inspire, foment**   *calm, discourage, check, restrain, allay, soothe, abate, pacify*
The leader's speech incited the people to rebel.

inclement   *adj.*   **harsh, bitter, cruel, severe, raw, foul**   *calm, mild, benign, pleasant*
The game was postponed because of inclement weather.

incline
1. *n.*   **slope, grade, inclination, hill**   1. *plain, flat*
The incline was used as a toboggan run in the winter.
2. *v.*   **lean, bend, bow, turn, slope, slant, tilt, veer**   2. *straighten*
Plants incline towards the sun.
3. *v.*   **prefer, favor, dispose**   3. *disincline*
Based on the evidence, I am inclined toward a guilty verdict.
n. Do you have the inclination to travel?

include
1. *v.*   **contain, embrace, consist of, cover, incorporate, be composed of, be comprised of**   1. *exclude, omit*
The package price includes air travel and hotel.
2. *v.*   **enter, incorporate, insert, combine, add, append**   2. *discard, reject, exclude*
Please include this report in the file.

incompetent   *adj.*   **incapable, unfit, inefficient, inexpert, unable, bungling, ineffectual**   *able, fit, capable, qualified, expert, competent, proficient*
The incompetent worker was fired.

inconvenient   *adj.*   **bothersome, disturbing, awkward, troublesome, inopportune, unsuitable**   *convenient, timely, suitable, opportune*
Would it be inconvenient for you to drive me home?
n. It is a great inconvenience to drive you home as you live so far away.

incorporate   *v.*   **include, combine, consolidate, unite, join, embody, merge**   *exclude, eliminate*
The plan incorporated the students' suggestions.

incorrect	*adj.*	**false, mistaken, inaccurate, unreliable, wrong, imprecise, erroneous, fallacious** I got lost because I was given incorrect directions to the house. *adv.* The patient was incorrectly given the wrong medicine.	*true, accurate, reliable, correct, precise*
increase	1. *n.*	**growth, development, extension, enlargement, escalation, expansion** The increase in the cost of gas is causing concern.	**1.** *reduction, decrease, decline*
	2. *n.*	**addition, gain, increment, boost** An increase in salary is always appreciated.	**2.** *decrease, cut, reduction, loss*
	3. *v.*	**extend, enlarge, expand, magnify, improve, strengthen, grow, swell** The company's profits increased by thirty percent last year.	**3.** *decrease, lessen, reduce, shrink*
incredible	*adj.*	**unbelievable, improbable, extraordinary, remarkable** Sean showed incredible bravery when he risked his life to save the drowning man. *adv.* It was incredibly brave of him.	*credible, believable, ordinary, common, unremarkable*
incur	*v.*	**obtain, get, acquire, bring on, meet with** The company incurred heavy losses during the strike.	
indecent	*adj.*	**improper, wrong, immoral, wicked, shameful** Swearing is considered by many to be indecent language. *n.* The book was banned because of its gross indecency.	*proper, decent, right, moral*
indefinite	1. *adj.*	**vague, uncertain, unsure, blurred, unspecified, unclear, ambiguous** Our plans for the trip are still indefinite.	**1.** *certain, clear, definite, specified, defined, precise*
	2. *adj.*	**unlimited, infinite** Outer space has indefinite dimensions.	**2.** *limited, finite*
independent	1. *adj.*	**autonomous, self-governing** Canada is an independent nation. *n.* The U.S.A. was formed after the War of Independence.	**1.** *subordinate, dependent*
	2. *adj.*	**self-reliant, self-sufficient** She is an independent thinker and cannot be easily swayed.	**2.** *dependent*
indicate	*v.*	**show, designate, denote, register, signify, reveal** Their smiles indicate that they were successful in the competition. *n.* A person's facial expression is a good indicator of his or her mood.	

n. We took her yawn as an indication that she was bored.

indifference	*n.*	**unconcern, disinterest, disregard, apathy, detachment, nonchalance** The team's indifference led to its defeat. *adj.* The indifferent players were defeated.	*concern, interest, regard, attention*
indigenous	*adj.*	**native, natural** Penguins are indigenous to the Antarctic region.	*alien, foreign*
indignant	*adj.*	**angry, piqued, upset, displeased, irritated, offended, resentful** The indignant customer stomped out of the store.	*pleased, content, flattered, satisfied*
indirect	1. *adj.*	**roundabout, circuitous, oblique, zigzag, crooked, twisting, rambling** The indirect route to the hotel was the more scenic one.	1. *direct, straight, straightforward, immediate*
	2. *adj.*	**ambiguous, evasive** We were suspicious when he gave us an indirect answer.	2. *clear, direct, straightforward*
indispensable	*adj.*	**essential, vital, necessary, required, needed** Oxygen is indispensable to human life.	*dispensable, useless, unnecessary, unimportant*
indistinct	*adj.*	**vague, indefinite, obscure, blurred, dim, faint, inaudible** Her voice was indistinct as the telephone connection was very bad.	*clear, distinct, definite, sharp*
individual	1. *n.*	**person, human being** Most individuals enjoy holidays.	
	2. *adj.*	**singular, peculiar, unique, special, distinctive** Each student has an individual approach to research.	2. *ordinary, commonplace, everyday, general*
	3. *adj.*	**separate, single, sole, solitary** Each candy bar had an individual wrapper. *adv.* Each candy bar was wrapped individually.	3. *collective, public, common, multiple*
induce	1. *v.*	**urge, convince, persuade, prompt, influence** Advertisers induce consumers to buy their products.	1. *dissuade, discourage, deter, restrain*
	2. *v.*	**cause, bring about, effect, produce** The medicine induced sleep.	2. *restrain, cancel, nullify*
indulge	*v.*	**revel, gratify, pamper** Holiday resorts encourage people to indulge their whims. *n.* Indulgence should not be carried too far.	*thwart, deny, be severe*

industrious		*adj.*	**diligent, busy, active, hard-working** The industrious students completed their project ahead of time.	*idle, inactive, unoccupied*
ineffective		*adj.*	**useless, weak, worthless, inadequate** The medicine proved ineffective as a painkiller.	*effective, useful, potent*
inefficient	1.	*adj.*	**wasteful, extravagant** High horsepower engines are inefficient.	*1. economical*
	2.	*adj.*	**incompetent, incapable, ineffective** Inefficient planning caused the project to fail. *n.* The workers were fired for their inefficiency.	*2. competent, fit, able, capable, adept, expert, effective*
inevitable		*adj.*	**unavoidable, sure, certain, destined, inescapable, unpreventible, assured** When our two star players were hurt, it was inevitable that our team would lose.	*doubtful, contingent, avoidable, escapable, preventable*
inexpensive		*adj.*	**cheap, thrifty, low-priced, modest, economical** On their budget they can only afford an inexpensive car.	*costly, expensive, high-priced, uneconomical*
infallible		*adj.*	**unerring, exact, unquestionable, perfect, true, authoritative, right, reliable, certain, dependable** There is no guarantee that the research findings would be infallible.	*erroneous, false, questionable, doubtful, dubious, contestable*
infer	1.	*v.*	**conclude, deduce, reason, gather, understand, guess, assume** I inferred from her frown that I was not welcome.	
	2.	*v.*	**imply, insinuate, suggest, hint** The letter inferred that I was lazy. *n.* The inference was not a fair one.	
inferior	1.	*adj.*	**secondary, minor, subordinate, junior, lesser, lower** In the army, all ranks are inferior to that of a General.	*1. superior, senior, higher*
	2.	*adj.*	**second-rate, mediocre, poor** I was warned to avoid that store because it sells inferior products. *n.* The inferiority of the products is obvious.	*2. first-rate, top, superior*
infiltrate	1.	*v.*	**seep, trickle, permeate, filter, penetrate** Shafts of sunlight infiltrated the thick forest.	*1. flood, flow, ooze, stream*
	2.	*v.*	**enter, penetrate** Spies infiltrated the company and stole valuable information.	

infinite	1.	*adj.*	**unlimited, boundless, incalculable, measureless, untold, immeasurable** The universe is infinite.	*1. limited, restricted, definite*
	2.	*adj.*	**endless, eternal, perpetual, incessant, constant** The nurse has infinite patience.	*2. fleeting, short, temporary*
inflate	1.	*v.*	**blow up, pump up, expand, swell, fill** Bob inflated the balloons for the party.	*1. deflate, empty*
	2.	*v.*	**exaggerate, magnify, enlarge, amplify** The media inflated the news event beyond the facts.	*2. minimize, reduce, underestimate*
influence		*n.*	**control, power, sway, effect** The media has a strong influence on how people think. *v.* The media influences people's opinions.	*impotence*
inform		*v.*	**instruct, tell, notify, relate, mention** He informed us that he was moving.	*conceal, withhold*
information		*n.*	**facts, data, knowledge, news** A computer is able to store and process a great deal of information.	
infrequent		*adj.*	**rare, occasional, sparse, scarce, few** Healthy people make infrequent visits to the doctor.	*frequent, usual, regular, customary, habitual*
infuriate		*v.*	**provoke, enrage, aggravate, vex, anger, arouse, incense** The matador infuriated the bull.	*calm, soothe, quiet, placate*
ingenious		*adj.*	**creative, imaginative, inventive, resourceful, clever, crafty, astute** He escaped punishment with an ingenious excuse.	*dull, unimaginative, inept, uninventive*
ingredient		*n.*	**component, element, constituent, part** This recipe calls for many ingredients.	
inhabit		*v.*	**occupy, stay, live in, dwell, reside, lodge** Polar bears inhabit the North Pole. *n.* The inhabitants of the village were shocked by the earthquake.	*vacate, desert, abandon*
initial		*adj.*	**first, primary, introductory, beginning** "A" is the initial letter of the English alphabet.	*last, terminal, final, concluding*
initially		*adv.*	**at first, in the beginning, originally** Initially, the world was thought to be flat.	*finally, in the end, at the end,*
initiate		*v.*	**open, start, begin, commence, inaugurate, introduce** The two countries initiated trade discussions recently.	*close, end, finish, complete, conclude*

injure	*v.*	**hurt, harm, wound, damage, impair**	*heal, repair*
		Shen injured his knee in a rugby game.	
	n.	His injuries were severe.	

injurious	*adj.*	**harmful, damaging, bad, detrimental, dangerous**	*beneficial, helpful, advantageous*
		Smoking is injurious to health.	

injustice	*n.*	**prejudice, bias, partiality, inequity, inequality**	*justice, justness, fairness, equity, equality*
		Laws are made to prevent injustice.	

innocent	1. *adj.*	**guiltless, blameless, upright, faultless**	**1.** *guilty, culpable*
		Laws are made to protect innocent citizens.	
	2. *adj.*	**inexperienced, raw, naive, callow**	**2.** *experienced, worldly*
		Innocent youths can be easily influenced.	
	n.	Many people exploit the innocence of youth.	
	3. *adj.*	**harmless, safe, inoffensive, innocuous**	**3.** *dangerous, harmful*
		The teenagers had a day of innocent fun at the beach.	

innovation	*n.*	**change, alteration, variation, reform, transformation**	
		Henry Ford made innovations in the automobile industry.	
	n.	Bill Gates was an innovator in the software industry.	
	adj.	He was an innovative man.	

input	1. *n.*	**data, information, knowledge, facts, statistics, findings**	
		Once Brad gives us his input, our report will be complete.	
	2. *v.*	**enter, type, put in**	**2.** *delete*
		We input our data into the computer.	

inquire	1. *v.*	**ask, question**	**1.** *answer, reply, respond*
		We inquired if the dogs were for sale.	
	n.	The answer to our inquiry was yes!	
	2. *v.*	**investigate, probe, study, examine, analyze, look into, inspect, review**	**2.** *ignore, overlook*
		The detective inquired into the matter of the missing children.	

inquisitive	*adj.*	**curious, inquiring, questioning, searching, prying**	*indifferent, apathetic, unconcerned, disinterested*
		Young children are naturally inquisitive.	

insane	1. *adj.*	**unbalanced, deranged, mad**	**1.** *sane, rational*
		The accused was declared insane and not fit to stand trial.	
	n.	The accused was found not guilty because of insanity.	
	2. *adj.*	**foolish, idiotic, daft, stupid, ridiculous**	**2.** *sensible, thoughtful, reasonable*
		Everyone scoffed at the insane plan.	

insert	1.	*n.*	**addition, inclusion** The entry form is an insert in the magazine.	
	2.	*v.*	**put in, embed, inject, include, implant** Jane inserted the key into the lock.	**2.** *take out, extract, remove, exclude*
inside	1.	*adj.*	**inner, inward, innermost** It is an advantage to run on the inside track in a race.	**1.** *outer, peripheral, outermost*
	2.	*adv.*	**indoors, within** We dashed inside when it rained.	**2.** *outside, in the open, outdoors*
	3.	*prep.*	**within, surrounded by, bounded by** The pupils are inside the schoolyard.	**3.** *beyond, outside of*
insight		*n.*	**understanding, discernment, intuition, awareness** Anne Frank's diary provided deep insights into her life in hiding.	*misunderstanding, ignorance*
insignificant		*adj.*	**trivial, petty, unimportant, irrelevant, trifling** Why argue over such an insignificant matter?	*important, meaningful, significant*
insipid	1.	*adj.*	**tasteless, flat, flavorless, bland** The soup was so dilute it was insipid.	**1.** *piquant, zesty, flavorful, tasty*
	2.	*adj.*	**weak, lifeless, dull, uninteresting** That play has insipid characters.	**2.** *exciting, dynamic, provocative*
insist		*v.*	**require, order, command, expect** The teacher insisted on punctuality. *n.* We arrived punctually for class.	*waive, forgo, defer*
insolent		*adj.*	**rude, offensive, arrogant, impudent, contemptuous, impertinent** The students were suspended for their insolent behavior. *n.* Insolence is not tolerated in this school.	*polite, courteous, servile, meek, well-mannered, respectful, shy*
inspect		*v.*	**investigate, study, probe, examine, scrutinize, check** Who inspects the used cars to determine if they are safe to drive? *n.* The inspection of the cars is performed by official inspectors.	*ignore, overlook*
install	1.	*v.*	**establish, inaugurate** The board installed a new president.	**1.** *remove, withdraw*
	2.	*v.*	**set up, put in, place** Computers were installed in every classroom. *n.* Pedestrians asked for the installation of crossing lights at the busy junction.	**2.** *remove, take away*
instant	1.	*n.*	**moment, second, flash, minute, jiffy, twinkling** In an instant the squirrel was up the tree.	

2. *adj.* **immediate, rapid, prompt, fast, quick, sudden, direct, speedy, instantaneous**
Instant replays are a regular part of sports telecasts.
adv. Some pain can be relieved instantly.

2. delayed, slow, later

instantaneous *adj.* **instant, rapid, speedy, immediate, quick, fast, prompt**
This pill claims to provide instantaneous relief for headaches.

delayed, later

instruct **1.** *v.* **teach, guide, educate, direct, coach**
The flight attendant instructed the passengers about safety procedures.
n. She was a good instructor.

1. learn

2. *v.* **order, tell, command, direct, bid**
The captain instructed the crew to abandon ship.
n. The crew obeyed the captain's instructions.

2. ask, request

insufferable *adj.* **unbearable, intolerable, painful, unendurable, agonizing, excruciating**
The accident caused her insufferable pain.

bearable, tolerable, endurable

insufficient *adj.* **inadequate, meager, skimpy**
The trip was canceled because of insufficient funds.

sufficient, ample, enough, surplus, excess

insulate *v.* **protect, line, coat, cover, shield**
The builder insulated our house with modern insulation materials.

expose, uncover

insure *v.* **guarantee, protect**
Insure the car against theft.
n. Car insurance is mandatory.

intact *adj.* **together, whole, complete, sound, untouched, uninjured**
The car was intact after the accident.

damaged, in pieces, broken, dismantled

intangible **1.** *adj.* **indefinite, uncertain, unsure, vague, unspecific, abstract, hypothetical**
The suspect was released because of intangible evidence.

1. definite, sure, tangible, certain, specific

2. *adj.* **immaterial, untouchable**
Shadows are intangible.

2. material, real, physical

integrate *v.* **combine, join, unify, connect, blend**
The immigrants tried to integrate into the community.
adj. An integrated school accepts students of all races and religions.

separate, keep apart

intelligence **1.** *n.* **intellect, acumen, mental ability, discernment, cleverness**
The child's remarkable intelligence was obvious during the debate.

1. stupidity

	2.	*n.*	**vital information, secret information** The spy was jailed for disclosing military intelligence.	
intelligent	1.	*adj.*	**clever, bright, astute, smart, perceptive, quick, shrewd** The intelligent girl was top of her class.	**1.** *stupid, dull*
	2.	*adj.*	**sensible, rational** Is there intelligent life on other planets?	**2.** *irrational*
intend	1.	*v.*	**aim, plan, propose, hope to, resolve** I intend to do well in the examinations. *n.* It is my intention to do well.	
	2.	*v.*	**reserve, assign, mean, designate** Which gift did you intend for me?	
intense		*adj.*	**violent, strong, acute, keen, deep, extreme, exceptional, heightened** Intense heat drove back the firefighters.	*weak, dull, shallow*
intentional		*adj.*	**deliberate, prearranged, intended, premeditated, contemplated, planned** The cruel remarks were intentional. *adv.* The remarks were made intentionally to hurt you.	*accidental, unintentional, undesigned, unplanned, casual, haphazard*
interfere	1.	*v.*	**meddle, pry, intervene** Don't interfere in my affairs! *n.* Such interference is not wanted.	**1.** *neglect, ignore, leave alone*
	2.	*v.*	**prevent, stop, hinder, obstruct, hamper** The rain interfered with our plans for a picnic.	**2.** *assist, aid, support*
interior		*adj.*	**inner, inward, inside, internal, indoor** The interior walls were painted pink. *n.* The interior of the house is decorated opulently.	*exterior, outward, outside, outdoor*
intermediate		*adj.*	**middle, neutral, compromising, moderate, central, halfway** The politician held an intermediate stand on the dispute.	*extreme, uncompromising, immoderate*
intermittent		*adj.*	**periodic, broken, occasional, irregular, interrupted** The foghorn sounded on an intermittent basis. *adv.* It sounded intermittently.	*constant, lasting, incessant, regular*
interrogate		*v.*	**question, ask, probe, cross-examine** The lawyer interrogated the witness. *n.* The interrogation was stressful for the witness.	
interval	1.	*n.*	**intermission, break, interlude** There was a short interval in the middle of the show.	

	2.	*n.*	**period, hiatus, lapse, space** There is a one week interval between classes.

intervene — *v.* — **intercede, mediate**
The referee intervened in the dispute.

intimidate — *v.* — **scare, frighten, threaten**
The guard dog intimidated the intruder.
help, placate, encourage, reassure

intolerant — *adj.* — **prejudiced, biased, narrow-minded, bigoted**
The intolerant man was fired from his job.
n. His intolerance of people of different races was not acceptable.
tolerant, receptive, open-minded

intrepid — *adj.* — **courageous, bold, dauntless, brave, fearless**
The champion is an intrepid fighter.
cowardly, timid, cowering, fearful

intricate — *adj.* — **involved, complicated, complex, tricky, difficult, elaborate**
A spider spins an intricate web.
n. Intricacies of the law confuse us.
simple, plain, uncomplicated, uninvolved, easy

intrigue
1. *n.* **plot, scheme, conspiracy**
Spies are involved in intrigue.
2. *v.* **interest, fascinate**
The plot of the novel intrigued us.
2. bore, repel

intrude — *v.* — **interfere, meddle, interrupt**
Don't intrude on our meeting.
n. Intruders are not allowed at the meeting.
neglect, ignore, leave alone

invade
1. *v.* **attack, assail**
The troops invaded the enemy camp at sunrise.
n. The invaders attacked at sunrise.
n. The invasion took the enemy completely by surprise.
1. retreat, withdraw, surrender
2. *v.* **trespass, interfere with, meddle, encroach upon, violate**
Do not invade my privacy.
n. Reading someone's diary is an invasion of the person's privacy.
2. ignore, leave alone

invalid — *n.* — **patient, sick person**
He has been an invalid since his heart attack.

invalid — *adj.* — **unusable, void, worthless**
The check was invalid because it had no signature.
valid, usable

invent
1. *v.* **devise, conceive, design, create, discover, compose, plan, fashion**
Who invented the steam engine?
n. The invention is patented.
1. imitate, copy, reproduce

2. *v.* **fabricate, falsify, misrepresent**
They invent the most fantastic excuses
for not doing homework.

invert

1. *v.* **upset, overturn, tip, topple,
turn over**
The strong wave inverted the canoe.

2. *v.* **reverse, transpose, exchange**
To divide by a fraction, invert the fraction
and multiply.

1. *put upright,
straighten, stand up*

2. *maintain, keep*

investigation

n. **inquiry, search, study, examination,
probe**
There will be an investigation into the
cause of the accident.
v. The police will investigate the incident
thoroughly.

invigorating

adj. **bracing, exhilarating, refreshing,
stimulating**
The campers had an invigorating swim
before breakfast.

soft, mild, gentle

invincible

adj. **unconquerable, unbeatable,
unyielding, insurmountable**
No team is invincible.

*conquerable, weak,
surmountable*

involve

1. *v.* **implicate, incriminate, entangle**
Do not involve me in this crooked scheme.

2. *v.* **concern, include, encompass**
This event involves both students and
parents.

1. *exclude, separate,
disconnect, eliminate*

2. *exclude*

irate

adj. **furious, angry, incensed, enraged,
annoyed, irritated**
Irate fans booed when the concert was
canceled.

*calm, peaceful, quiet,
appeased, serene,
composed, soothed,
placated*

ire

n. **wrath, fury, rage, anger**
Public ire was aroused over the increase
in taxes.

*patience, calmness,
gentleness*

irk

v. **annoy, bother, pester, irritate,
harass, perturb**
The boy's whining irked us.
adj. Please stop your irksome whining.

*soothe, relax, calm,
please, satisfy,
placate*

irregular

1. *adj.* **uneven, occasional, infrequent,
sporadic, variable**
The alarm sounded at irregular intervals.

2. *adj.* **unusual, extraordinary, abnormal**
It is irregular for the guard to be absent.

3. *adj.* **uneven, broken, jagged, crooked,
zigzag, lopsided**
The brook followed an irregular course.

1. *regular, even,
scheduled,
predictable*

2. *usual, normal,
customary*

3. *straight, even,
uniform, equal,
symmetrical, regular*

irrelevant	*adj.*	**inappropriate, unrelated, unconnected** Irrelevant information is often given in court cases.	*relevant, related, appropriate, fitting, connected, apropos*
irritable	*adj.*	**bad-tempered, touchy, testy, peevish, cross, grouchy, fretful, irascible** People become irritable in hot weather.	*pleasant, calm, agreeable, good-natured*
irritate	1. *v.*	**provoke, irk, annoy, agitate, bother, pester, exasperate, disturb, nettle** Her loud whining irritated us. *n.* Her whining is a constant irritation.	**1.** *soothe, calm, quiet, comfort, placate*
	2. *v.*	**inflame, redden, chafe** Constant coughing irritates the throat.	**2.** *soothe, comfort, ease*
isolate	*v.*	**confine, detach, seclude, separate, withdraw, segregate, quarantine** The hospital isolates persons with contagious diseases. *n.* These patients are kept in isolation.	*desegregate, include, mix, combine, unite, merge*
isolated	*adj.*	**secluded, lonely, remote, desolate, inaccessible** Garbage dumps should be located in isolated areas.	*populated, crowded, populous*
issue	1. *n.*	**question, dispute, concern, problem** Equality is an issue of the day.	**1.** *solution, answer, remedy*
	2. *v.*	**emerge, appear, flow out, spurt** Blood issued from the wound.	**2.** *remain*
	3. *v.*	**circulate, announce, declare, publish, send out, broadcast** The government issued the report.	**3.** *retain, keep, withhold*
	4. *n.*	**printing, edition, copy, number** Did you read the last issue of the magazine?	

J

The tenth letter of our alphabet sounds the same as *g* in *gem*.

In the very early days of the English language, *I* and *J* were frequently interchanged in printing and writing. *J* developed a sound and a shape of its own about five hundred years ago.

jab	1.	*n.*	**punch, blow, poke, hit**	
			The boxer threw many quick jabs at his opponent.	
	2.	*v.*	**stab, dig, poke, thrust, pierce**	
			Ling jabbed her fork into her steak.	
jail	1.	*n.*	**prison, penitentiary, penal institution**	
			The robber was sentenced to one year in jail.	
	2.	*v.*	**imprison, confine, arrest, capture, impound, incarcerate**	**2.** *release, let go, discharge, liberate*
			The judged jailed the robber for a year.	
jam	1.	*n.*	**tie-up, crush, block, press**	
			Jen was late because she was caught in a traffic jam.	
	2.	*n.*	**difficulty, mess, trouble, fix, dilemma**	**2.** *solution*
			The company has been in a jam since the president retired.	
	3.	*v.*	**stuff, squeeze, pack, cram, shove**	**3.** *ease, remove, unpack*
			He jammed his notes into his binder.	
	4.	*v.*	**crush, wedge**	**4.** *release, let go*
			Mary jammed her finger in the door.	
jar	1.	*n.*	**bottle, container, jug**	
			The jam jars were empty.	
	2.	*v.*	**jolt, bump, shake, vibrate, joggle**	
			The vibrations from the passing train jarred the dishes.	
	3.	*v.*	**scrape, grate**	**3.** *calm, quiet, soothe, settle*
			Carlo's singing jars my nerves. *adj.* He has a jarring voice.	
jargon		*n.*	**cant, idiom, dialect, slang**	
			It is hard to understand the medical jargon of physicians.	
jealous	1.	*adj.*	**envious, resentful, covetous**	**1.** *loyal, tolerant, indifferent*
			Paul was jealous of Marco's success.	
	2.	*adj.*	**suspicious, possessive**	**2.** *trusting*
			The jealous man was unhappy when his wife danced with another man. *n.* His jealousy caused his wife pain.	
jeer		*v.*	**scoff, sneer, mock, taunt, boo, ridicule, laugh at, poke fun at**	*cheer, applaud, respect, honor, praise, encourage*
			The crowd jeered at the tennis player's unsporting behavior. *n.* Their jeers caused the player to leave the game.	
jeopardize		*v.*	**endanger, imperil, risk**	*protect*
			The refugees jeopardized their lives by escaping in crowded boats. *n.* Their lives were in jeopardy until a ship picked them up.	

jerk	*n.*	**tug, pull, twist** The sailor gave the rope a jerk. *v.* He jerked the door open and ran off. *adj.* The jerky movements of the bus made me feel ill.	*push, shove*
jiggle	*v.*	**joggle, shake, jerk, move, jostle** The hula dancer jiggled her hips.	*steady, hold firm,* *secure*
jittery	*adj.*	**nervous, jumpy, edgy, fidgety** Jan was jittery before giving her speech.	*calm, relaxed, serene,* *placid, peaceful*
jog	1. *n.* 2. *v.*	**push, shake, jerk, nudge** I gave Mike a jog with my elbow when he fell asleep during the opera. **trot, run** Helen and Steve jog daily. *n.* Jogging is good exercise. *n.* We often see joggers on our streets.	
join	1. *v.* 2. *v.* 3. *v.*	**link, couple, fasten** Join hands to form a circle. **meet, connect, combine, unite, merge** The highways joined outside the city. **sign up, enter, enroll in, become a** **member, associate with, enlist** Have you joined the debating club?	1. *separate,* *uncouple, unfasten* 2. *divide, disconnect,* *part, sever* 3. *resign, withdraw,* *quit*
jolly	*adj.*	**merry, cheerful, joyful, happy, festive** Christmas is a jolly time of year.	*solemn, sober, grave,* *serious, morose*
jostle	*v.*	**push, shove, shake, prod, bump** The children jostled each other as they rushed out for recess.	
journal	1. *n.* 2. *n.*	**record, diary, notebook, log** Do you keep a journal of your travels? **magazine, periodical, newspaper** Ken enjoys reading scientific journals.	
journey	*n.*	**trip, excursion, voyage, trek, tour,** **expedition, passage** We studied the journeys of Marco Polo. *v.* He journeyed across Asia.	
jovial	*adj.*	**merry, happy, cheerful, jolly** We all like our jovial teacher.	*sad, downcast, dour,* *gloomy, morose*
joy	*n.*	**pleasure, gladness, delight, happiness** Children bring joy to their parents. *adj.* Birthdays are joyous occasions. *adj.* Graduation is a joyful day.	*sorrow, sadness,* *misery, gloom,* *unhappiness,* *despair*
jubilant	*adj.*	**joyful, elated, happy, rapturous,** **delighted, overjoyed, triumphant** The team was jubilant after winning the Cup for the third time.	*sorrowful, sad,* *despondent, dejected,* *forlorn*

judge				
	1.	*n.*	**adjudicator, referee, umpire, critic** Ms. Mann was a judge at the art show.	
	2.	*n.*	**court justice, magistrate** She is a judge in the Supreme Court.	
	3.	*v.*	**appraise, evaluate, assess** Karen judged the quality of the wine. *n.* She is a good judge of wines.	
	4.	*v.*	**settle, try, rule on, hear, pass sentence** Her Honor has judged many difficult cases in this court. *n.* Her judgments are always fair.	4. *know, be certain*
	5.	*v.*	**guess, estimate, determine, suppose, believe, assume, conclude, surmise** I judge her age to be about thirty.	

jumble				
	1.	*n.*	**clutter, muddle, mess, confusion, chaos** My papers are all in a jumble.	1. *order, system, arrangement*
	2.	*v.*	**mix, confuse, disarrange** The children jumbled the cards.	2. *put in order, arrange*

jumbo				
		adj.	**huge, enormous, immense, mammoth, colossal** Have you ever flown on a jumbo jet? *n.* Elephants are called jumbos because of their size.	*small, tiny, little, wee, miniature, petite*

junction				
		n.	**intersection, crossroads, joining, connecting point, meeting** There is always heavy traffic at the junction of those two highways.	

junk				
	1.	*n.*	**rubbish, trash, scrap, clutter, litter, waste, debris, rummage, garbage** All that junk in the basement needs to be cleared out.	
	2.	*v.*	**scrap, discard, dump, throw away** Mark junked his old bicycle.	2. *save, keep, retain, hold*

just				
	1.	*adj.*	**honest, fair, impartial, righteous** We believe our laws are just.	1. *unjust, unfair, one-sided, biased*
	2.	*adv.*	**barely, hardly, scarcely** He was just in time to catch the bus.	2. *early, late*
	3.	*adv.*	**exactly, precisely** The apples weigh just two pounds.	3. *approximately, about*

justice				
		n.	**equity, fairness, honesty, the law** Justice was served when the criminal was sent to jail.	*injustice, dishonesty, unfairness, wrong*

jut				
		v.	**project, stick out, extend, protrude** Florida juts into the Gulf of Mexico.	

juvenile				
	1.	*n.*	**minor, youth, child** Some movies are not suitable for juveniles.	1. *adult, grown-up, elder*
	2.	*adj.*	**young, immature** We were surprised by the leader's juvenile behavior.	2. *mature, adult, grown-up, senile*

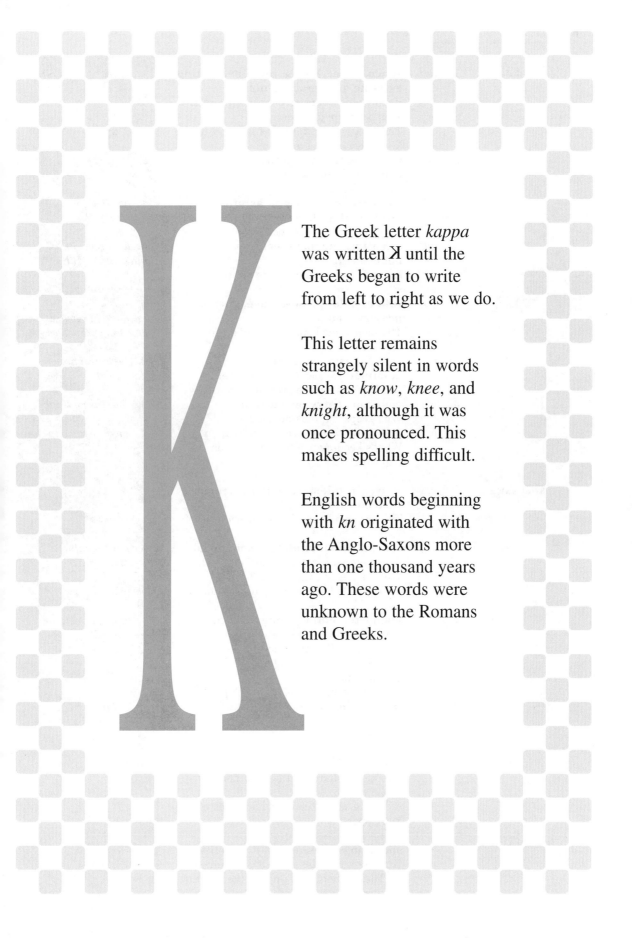

K

The Greek letter *kappa* was written Ƙ until the Greeks began to write from left to right as we do.

This letter remains strangely silent in words such as *know*, *knee*, and *knight*, although it was once pronounced. This makes spelling difficult.

English words beginning with *kn* originated with the Anglo-Saxons more than one thousand years ago. These words were unknown to the Romans and Greeks.

keen	1.	*adj.*	**sharp, bitter, biting, piercing, cutting, extreme, penetrating, nippy** Keen winds swept across the Antarctic.	1. *gentle, mild, soft*
	2.	*adj.*	**sharp, razor-like, pointed** The cook accidentally cut his finger on the keen edge of the knife.	2. *dull, blunt, unsharpened*
	3.	*adj.*	**enthusiastic, energetic, interested, eager, ardent, intent** Ray is a keen golfer.	3. *lazy, disinterested*
	4.	*adj.*	**shrewd, clever, bright, astute, intelligent, judicious, quick** Everyone enjoys his keen wit.	4. *unintelligent, stupid, dull*
	5.	*adj.*	**sensitive, sharp, perceptive, penetrating** Animals have a keen sense of hearing.	5. *unobservant, inattentive, dull*
keep	1.	*v.*	**retain, hold, possess, save, guard, preserve, maintain** The school has kept records of all its students.	1. *give away, relinquish, release, give up, throw away*
	2.	*v.*	**care for, run, maintain, operate, administer, direct, manage, tend** Gardeners keep the grounds beautiful.	2. *neglect, ignore, disregard*
	3.	*v.*	**continue, carry on, sustain** Who keeps that business going?	3. *end, discontinue, stop*
	4.	*v.*	**prevent, stop, restrain, detain** What's keeping you from coming on this trip with us?	4. *encourage, help*
keepsake		*n.*	**souvenir, token, reminder, memento, remembrance** This pin is a keepsake of our friendship.	
key		*adj.*	**crucial, chief, vital, basic, material, fundamental, salient, indispensable** Will the key witness testify? *n.* The code holds the key to the plot.	*secondary, minor, lesser, immaterial, insignificant, peripheral*
kid	1.	*n.*	**youngster, child, young person, juvenile, adolescent** The kids really enjoy the video games. *adj.* Tim has a cute kid brother.	1. *adult, grown-up, senior, elder*
	2.	*n.*	**young, yearling** The kids were gamboling in the pasture.	
	3.	*v.*	**tease, ridicule, rib, trick, bluff** Domo's friends kidded him about his new haircut.	3. *compliment, praise, laud, applaud*
kidnap		*v.*	**abduct, seize, carry off, take, steal** Two men kidnapped the child and asked for a ransom. *n.* Police saved the child and arrested the kidnappers.	*free, rescue, release*
kill		*v.*	**slay, murder, assassinate, slaughter** Hunters killed the animals for their fur. *n.* The police are looking for the killer of the security guard.	*preserve, protect, guard, rescue*

n. The killing of the villagers in the war zone shocked everyone.

kin		*n.*	**family, relatives, relations** Police are trying to find the kin of the injured driver.	*stranger*
kind	1.	*n.*	**sort, type, variety, class, brand, style** What kind of apple is this?	
	2.	*adj.*	**friendly, gentle, good, tender, loving, considerate, courteous, affectionate** The kind woman stopped to help the accident victims. *adv.* She treated everyone kindly.	**2.** *cruel, harsh, brutal, unkind, ruthless*
kindle		*v.*	**light, ignite, set fire to** The guide kindled the campfire. *adj.* The kindling wood burned rapidly.	*douse, quench, smother, stifle, extinguish*
kindness		*n.*	**goodness, generosity, friendliness, understanding, support** Thank you for your kindness during our trouble.	*harshness, cruelty, selfishness, brutality*
kingdom		*n.*	**dominion, domain, realm, empire, country, land** The news of the prince's birth spread throughout the kingdom.	
knack		*n.*	**flair, gift, skill, ability, faculty, talent, aptitude** Bob has a knack for carpentry.	*inability, ineptitude*
know	1.	*v.*	**understand, comprehend, realize** I know the answer to this problem.	**1.** *misunderstand*
	2.	*v.*	**be acquainted with, be friends with** Alex knows several people in his new school.	
	3.	*v.*	**be aware of, be informed** Kim's friends knew she was in trouble and offered to help.	**3.** *be ignorant of, be unaware of*
knowing		*adj.*	**shrewd, sharp, cunning, intelligent, clever, understanding, perceptive** The coach gave the team a knowing smile before the game began. *adv.* He smiled knowingly.	*ignorant, unintelligent, undiscerning*
knowledge	1.	*n.*	**learning, information, wisdom** Sue has a good knowledge of American history. *adj.* She is knowledgeable about famous people.	**1.** *ignorance, misinformation*
	2.	*n.*	**sense, memory, comprehension, awareness, realization** The victim had no knowledge of what had happened.	

L was shaped from the ancient symbol called *lamed* which meant *whip*. In hieroglyphics, the Phoenicians wrote this sign as ∠ or ⌃. The Greeks made it ⌐ and called it *lambda*. It was turned on its side to make the Roman *L*. In Roman numerals, the *L* represents 50.

labor	1.	*n.*	**work, toil, task, employment, effort** The workers were poorly paid for their labor.	**1.** *idleness, ease, relaxation, rest*
	2.	*n.*	**workers, workforce, employees** There is a shortage of skilled labor.	**2.** *bosses, employers*
	3.	*v.*	**work, toil, strive** The crew labored for hours in the heat. *n.* The crew consisted of ten laborers.	**3.** *idle, laze, rest, relax*
laborious	1.	*adj.*	**difficult, tough, arduous, grueling** The research project proved to be a laborious task.	**1.** *easy, light, simple, trivial*
	2.	*adj.*	**hard-working, industrious, diligent** The students were rewarded for their laborious effort on the project. *adv.* They worked laboriously on the project.	**2.** *lazy, indifferent, indolent*
lack	1.	*n.*	**absence, scarcity, shortage, deficiency** There is a lack of medical services in some Third World countries.	**1.** *plenty, excess, abundance, surplus, plethora*
	2.	*v.*	**need, require, be short of, fail to have, be without** The team lacked the dedication required to win.	**2.** *have, possess*
lag		*v.*	**loiter, linger, straggle, drag, straggle, trail** The exhausted child lagged behind the rest of the family.	*hasten, hurry, hustle*
lame	1.	*adj.*	**handicapped, crippled, disabled** The lame horse was put to sleep.	**1.** *fit, healthy*
	2.	*adj.*	**weak, poor, feeble, unconvincing, unsatisfactory** Everyone saw through their lame excuse for not completing the job.	**2.** *strong, excellent, convincing, satisfactory*
lament	1.	*n.*	**cry, sob, wail, moan, outcry** Loud laments were heard at the funeral.	**1.** *laughter, joy, celebration*
	2.	*v.*	**mourn, weep over, cry over, wail, weep, bemoan, regret, deplore** Alice lamented the loss of her dog. *adj.* It was a lamentable event.	**2.** *laugh, rejoice*
land	1.	*n.*	**real estate, property, terrain, realty, grounds** Land near the city is very expensive.	
	2.	*n.*	**dirt, soil, loam, earth, ground** The land in Iowa grows excellent corn.	
	3.	*n.*	**country, nation, region, state, homeland, realm, domain** Anna still misses her native land.	
	4.	*v.*	**alight, descend, touch down** Our plane landed at O'Hare Airport in Chicago.	**4.** *ascend, go up, takeoff*

	5.	*v.*	**catch, capture, get, secure, take** Glenn landed several large salmon.	**5.** *lose, release*
	6.	*v.*	**go ashore, dock, disembark** As we landed at New York we saw the Statue of Liberty.	**6.** *embark, leave, weigh anchor, cast off*
languid		*adj.*	**listless, lifeless, slow, weak, feeble, weary, exhausted, lethargic** Renee felt languid after a long illness.	*lively, tireless, energetic, vigorous, strong*
languish		*v.*	**weaken, fade, fail, droop** The roses languished in the heat.	*thrive, flourish, blossom*
lanky		*adj.*	**gangly, tall and lean** The lanky basketball player is the star of the team.	*husky, brawny, stocky*
large		*adj.*	**big, great, huge, enormous, vast, grand, towering, massive, spacious, bulky, plentiful, mighty** The family made a large donation to the university.	*small, tiny, petite, miniature, little, insignificant, meager, wee*
last	**1.**	*v.*	**endure, stay, remain, persist** The storm lasted several hours.	**1.** *cease, stop, end*
	2.	*adj.*	**final, latest** Our family was the last group to arrive. *adv.* We arrived last because of heavy traffic.	**2.** *first, foremost, initial*
lasting		*adj.*	**enduring, permanent, stable, durable, perpetual** This chair has a lasting finish on it.	*temporary, fleeting, short-lived*
late	**1.**	*adj.*	**past, dead, deceased, departed** The late President John F. Kennedy was a war hero.	
	2.	*adj.*	**tardy, slow, delayed** Yasmin was late for school. *adv.* She arrived late.	**2.** *early, prompt, on time, punctual*
lately		*adv.*	**recently** Have you seen Brenda lately?	
latent		*adj.*	**passive, dormant, sleeping, inactive, hidden, concealed, undiscovered** Mario has a latent talent in music.	*active, developed, expressed*
laugh		*v.*	**chuckle, giggle, guffaw, titter** The children laughed at the clown's jokes. *n.* Their laughter filled the circus tent.	*cry, weep, wail*
laughable		*adj.*	**funny, comical, humorous, ridiculous, absurd, amusing** That masquerade costume is laughable.	*serious, morbid, solemn, sad, melancholy*

lavish	1.	*v.*	**waste, squander, pour out** The millionaire lavished his money on expensive yachts.	1. *save, hoard, stint*
	2.	*adj.*	**extravagant, wasteful, excessive** The movie star leads a lavish life. *adv.* He spends his money lavishly on clothes and parties.	2. *thrifty, stingy, modest*
	3.	*adj.*	**generous, bountiful, abundant, liberal, profuse** Her lavish praise told us she was pleased with our work.	3. *meager, stingy, skimpy*
lawful		*adj.*	**legal, legitimate, permissible, allowed** It is lawful to drive at 55 miles per hour on some highways in the United States. *adv.* They were lawfully married by a judge.	*illegal, prohibited, unlawful*
lawless		*adj.*	**defiant, uncontrolled, unruly, rowdy, rebellious** Lawless mobs looted the stores.	*law-abiding, obedient, orderly*
lax		*adj.*	**loose, slack, careless, indifferent, remiss, soft** Discipline is lax in this school.	*firm, reliable, strict, careful, exact*
lazy	1.	*adj.*	**idle, shiftless, indolent** The lazy workers did not complete their work on time. *n.* The workers lost their jobs because of their laziness.	1. *industrious, energetic, active*
	2.	*adj.*	**sleepy, languid, sluggish, drowsy, lethargic** We all feel lazy on hot, humid days. *adv.* The cows grazed lazily in the fields.	2. *brisk, active, energetic*
lead	1.	*n.*	**main role, principal part, star** Roy has been chosen to play the lead in the play.	1. *supporting role, minor role*
	2.	*n.*	**clue, hint** Police are asking for leads on the robbery.	
	3.	*v.*	**guide, escort, pilot, steer** The guide led us through the forest.	3. *follow*
	4.	*v.*	**direct, command, supervise, head** She will lead the group on this mission.	4. *follow*
	5.	*v.*	**excel, surpass, come first** Reg leads the company in sales. *n.* He is in the lead in sales.	5. *trail*
leader		*n.*	**chief, head, director, master, conductor, commander** Police are looking for the leader of this gang.	*follower*
lean	1.	*v.*	**bend, slope, slant, incline, tilt** The fence leans to the right.	

	2.	*adj.*	**skinny, thin, slender, slim, wiry, sinewy, lank** His lean build is an asset as an athlete.	**2.** *stout, fat, obese, overweight*
	3.	*adj.*	**not fatty, fat-free** Our family eats only lean meat.	**3.** *fatty*
leap		*n.*	**jump, spring, bound, vault** The skater made several leaps into the air. *v.* The frog leapt into the pond.	
learn		*v.*	**acquire knowledge, understand, be educated, master** Lyanne is learning to read. *n.* She is a fast learner.	*teach, instruct*
learned		*adj.*	**educated, well-informed, scholarly, wise, cultured** Professor Smythe is a learned woman.	*ignorant, illiterate, uneducated*
leave	**1.**	*n.*	**permission, consent, approval** Jim was given leave to go on the trip.	**1.** *refusal, denial*
	2.	*n.*	**holiday, furlough, vacation, break** The soldier has a four-day leave.	
	3.	*v.*	**depart, go away, set out** Has Sue left for her holidays?	**3.** *stay, remain, arrive*
legal		*adj.*	**permitted, permissible, lawful, allowed, legitimate** Ravi is the children's legal guardian.	*illegal, unlawful, illicit, unauthorized*
legend		*n.*	**myth, tale** I enjoy reading the Greek legends.	
legendary		*adj.*	**fictitious, mythical** Paul Bunyan is a legendary hero.	*actual, true, factual*
legible		*adj.*	**plain, distinct, clear, neat, readable** Your writing is legible, but mine is illegible. *adv.* We all should write legibly.	*illegible, unreadable, indecipherable, obscure*
legitimate	**1.**	*adj.*	**lawful, legal, rightful** The family made a legitimate claim to the property.	**1.** *unlawful, illegal, invalid, illegitimate*
	2.	*adj.*	**true, real, genuine, authentic, valid** Illness is a legitimate reason for missing school.	**2.** *false, counterfeit*
leisure	**1.**	*n.*	**rest, ease, relaxation, recreation** We seem to have more time for leisure in the summer.	**1.** *work, toil, employment*
	2.	*adj.*	**free, idle, unoccupied, unemployed** We have too few leisure hours in a day. *adv.* We strolled leisurely through the park.	**2.** *busy, employed, occupied*
lengthen		*v.*	**extend, increase, stretch, elongate** The days lengthened as spring approached.	*shorten, reduce, lessen, decrease, shrink, contract*

lenient	*adj.*	**tolerant, gentle, merciful, compassionate, forgiving** The owner was lenient with the tenant when he was late with the rent.	*strict, harsh, severe, stern, merciless*
lessen	*v.*	**decrease, shorten, reduce, ease** Modern appliances lessen the amount of housework.	*increase, extend, stretch*
let	*v.*	**allow, permit, tolerate** "Please let me help you," she said.	*forbid, prohibit*
lethargic	*adj.*	**inert, sluggish, drowsy, listless, weary, slow, weak, lazy, languid** The lethargic person is sleepy all the time. *n.* Lethargy may be caused by illness.	*energetic, lively, tireless, vigorous, strong, active, vital, animated, spirited*
level	1. *n.*	**depth, height, altitude** The water level rose quickly in the flood.	
	2. *n.*	**grade, standard** Kai was promoted to the next level in computer class.	
	3. *n.*	**floor, story** Our apartment is on the first level.	
	4. *v.*	**aim, point, direct** The pilot leveled the missiles at the army camp.	
	5. *v.*	**destroy, demolish, knock down, raze, wreck, ruin** Wreckers leveled the old building.	*5. restore, build, erect, construct, reconstruct*
	6. *adj.*	**flat, smooth, horizontal, regular** An airplane runway must be level.	*6. uneven, rough, vertical, irregular*
liable	1. *adj.*	**prone, inclined, likely, apt** People are liable to fall on this icy sidewalk.	*1. unlikely*
	2. *adj.*	**responsible, accountable** The court found him liable for the accident.	*2. innocent, unaccountable*
liberal	1. *adj.*	**ample, generous, lavish, abundant** Alex receives a liberal allowance.	*1. stingy, frugal, miserly, small*
	2. *adj.*	**broad-minded, tolerant** Unlike his conservative brother, Andrew is a liberal thinker.	*2. prejudiced, narrow-minded, intolerant, bigoted*
liberate	*v.*	**free, release, discharge** The Allies liberated the prisoners when the war ended.	*hold, keep, confine, detain*
liberty	*n.*	**freedom, right, independence** The people fought for liberty and equality in the French Revolution.	*tyranny, restraint, bondage*
lie	1. *n.*	**fib, untruth, falsehood** They finally confessed that they had been telling lies. *v.* They lied about the stolen money. *n.* They admitted to being liars.	*1. truth, fact, veracity*

	2.	*v.*	**rest, recline** Dad lay on the couch to take a nap.	**2.** *sit up, stand up, rise, sit*
life	1.	*n.*	**human, person, soul, being** Many lives were lost in the plane crash.	
	2.	*n.*	**existence, way of living** They lead busy lives in the city.	**2.** *death, non-existence*
	3.	*n.*	**energy, spirit, vigor, vitality, drive** Christine is full of life and is always on the go.	**3.** *lethargy*
lift	1.	*v.*	**raise, hoist, boost, elevate** Who lifted that heavy box for you?	**1.** *lower, drop, bring down*
	2.	*v.*	**cancel, remove, rescind, withdraw** Will the government lift the ban on foreign imports?	**2.** *impose, establish, set*
light	1.	*n.*	**illumination, glow, glare, shine** The light of the moon turned the lake to silver.	**1.** *dark, shadow, darkness, shade*
	2.	*n.*	**lamp, source of light** We switched on the lights when it got dark.	
	3.	*v.*	**kindle, set fire to, ignite, spark** Rae lit the fire before we arrived.	**3.** *put out, extinguish*
	4.	*v.*	**illuminate, turn on, switch on** Have you lighted all the lamps in the living room?	**4.** *turn off, darken, switch off, dim*
	5.	*adj.*	**bright, illuminated, well-lit** It was still light enough to see the path.	**5.** *dark, dim, gloomy, dull*
	6.	*adj.*	**not heavy, lightweight** Let the child carry a light parcel.	**6.** *heavy*
	7.	*adj.*	**scanty, sparse, meager, simple, spare** We asked the waiter for a light meal.	**7.** *heavy, rich, large, substantial*
lighten	1.	*v.*	**ease, relieve, lessen** We lightened the load on the wagon before going up the hill.	**1.** *increase, enlarge, burden, overload*
	2.	*v.*	**brighten, clear** The sky lightened after the storm.	**2.** *darken*
likelihood		*n.*	**probability, chance** There is a likelihood of snow tomorrow. *adj.* It's likely to snow tomorrow.	
likeness		*n.*	**similarity, resemblance** There is a strong family likeness between the brother and the sister.	*difference, disparity*
limit	1.	*n.*	**maximum, restriction, ceiling** What is the speed limit on this highway?	**1.** *minimum*
	2.	*n.*	**boundary, border, edge, end** Small towns have sprung up just beyond the city limits.	
	3.	*v.*	**restrict, confine, restrain, check** Mom limited Yang to one hour of television a day.	**3.** *extend, increase, enlarge*

limp

1. *n.* **lameness, hobble**
   The injured man walks with a limp.
   v. He limped to the bench after he injured his ankle.
2. *adj.* **slack, lax, drooping, flabby, soft**   **2.** *stiff, rigid, firm*
   Limp vegetables make bad salads.

linger

1. *v.* **loiter, lag, tarry, dawdle, dally**   **1.** *hurry, speed, hasten, rush*
   Anne lingered at the park.
2. *v.* **endure, remain, persist, stay, survive**   **2.** *disappear*
   Memories of Elvis lingered in the hearts of his fans long after his death.

link

1. *n.* **connection, tie, bond, union, alliance, association**   **1.** *separation*
   There is a strong link between our families.
   v. Marriage links our families.
2. *v.* **join, fasten, bind, connect, attach**   **2.** *disconnect, untie, detach*
   The children linked hands and formed a circle.
   adj. Our computers are linked by a network.

liquid

1. *n.* **fluid, drink, beverage**   **1.** *solid, vapor, gas*
   The patient was allowed only liquids after surgery.
2. *adj.* **fluid, molten, thawed, melted**   **2.** *solid, gaseous, hard, frozen*
   An active volcano spews liquid rock called lava.

list

1. *n.* **record, roll, schedule, account, file, tally, inventory**
   The list of names seemed endless.
2. *v.* **record, arrange, set down, catalog**   **2.** *delete, cancel, erase, wipe out*
   The teacher listed our names on the first day of school.
3. *v.* **tilt, lean, tip, pitch, incline**   **3.** *remain even, level*
   The boat listed to one side in the strong winds.

listless

adj. **lazy, dull, indolent, languid, lethargic**   *active, lively, alert, energetic, vigorous*
I feel listless on hot, humid days.

literal

adj. **exact, accurate, precise, factual, close, correct, true, actual, verbatim**   *free, liberal, inexact*
The press requested a literal translation of the French minister's speech.

literate

adj. **educated, able to read and write, informed**   *illiterate*
Most people in this country are literate.

lithe

adj. **agile, supple, nimble, flexible**   *stiff, rigid, awkward*
Gymnasts are usually lithe and strong.

litter

1. *n.* **rubbish, trash, junk, refuse, clutter**
   There is a fine for throwing litter on the highway.

2. *n.* **offspring, young**
Ben's dog had a litter of six pups.

3. *v.* **scatter, strew, clutter, heap, pile**
People littered the park with trash.

3. clean up

little *adj.* **small, minute, wee, tiny**
Is this little puppy lost?

large, huge, big, colossal, gigantic

live **1.** *v.* **reside, dwell, inhabit, stay, lodge**
The Turners live on Maple Avenue.

2. *v.* **exist, subsist, survive**
Will you be able to live on your pension?

lively **1.** *adj.* **vigorous, spirited, active, festive**
The party was a lively affair.

2. *adj.* **bright, vivid, cheerful**
Red is a lively color.

1. inactive, listless, dull, boring
2. drab, dull, dreary, subdued

livid **1.** *adj.* **discolored, bruised, black-and-blue, purple, purplish**
The boxer's skin was livid from the many blows he received.

2. *adj.* **furious, angry, vexed, indignant, fuming, outraged**
Aminah was livid over the salesperson's dishonesty.

2. pleased, happy, content, forgiving

load **1.** *n.* **cargo, shipment, truckload, carload, planeload, freight**
How many loads of topsoil did you put on the garden?

2. *n.* **burden, pressure, trouble, worry, weight, drag**
"That's a load off my mind!" she said when she had completed her task.

2. support, help, consolation, solace

3. *v.* **fill, pile, heap, pack, stack, stow**
The movers loaded the van with the furniture.

3. unload, empty, unpack

loaf **1.** *n.* **shaped mass of dough or meat**
The chef baked two loaves of bread.

2. *v.* **take it easy, laze, waste time, idle**
Some workers were loafing on the job.
n. Some people are born loafers.

2. labor, work, toil

loan **1.** *n.* **advance, credit**
The bank arranged a loan for Al's new car.

2. *v.* **lend, permit to borrow**
We loaned the neighbors our ladder.

2. borrow, return, give back, repay

local *adj.* **neighborhood, regional, district**
The local theater shows good movies.
adv. People are pleased that these movies can be seen locally.

worldwide, international

locate **1.** *v.* **place, put, situate, establish, fix**
We located the library on Main Street.
n. The location is handy for everyone.

1. remove, dislodge, displace, move from

2. *v.* **find, discover, detect, uncover, track down**
The divers located the remains of the *Titanic* in the Atlantic Ocean.

2. lose, hide, conceal, displace

lofty **1.** *adj.* **high, elevated, tall**
Mountaineers scaled the lofty peak.

1. low, dwarfed

2. *adj.* **haughty, conceited, inflated, proud, exalted, grand**
Some people have lofty ideas of themselves.

2. meek, humble, lowly, ordinary, unassuming

log **1.** *n.* **lumber, timber, stump, block**
The trucks hauled the logs to the sawmill.

2. *n.* **diary, account, schedule, journal**
The captain made a daily entry in the ship's log.
v. He carefully logged all events.

log on *v.* **connect, link**
I logged on to my Internet server and browsed through the web.

disconnect, log off

logic *n.* **reasoning, deduction, organized thinking**
Mathematicians are skilled in logic.
adj. They are logical thinkers.

loiter *v.* **linger, dawdle, lag, dally, tarry, delay**
Several students loitered in the schoolyard after school was over.

hasten, hurry, hustle

lonely **1.** *adj.* **lonesome, forlorn, friendless, forsaken**
Kim was lonely when she first moved to a new town.

2. *adj.* **remote, secluded, isolated, deserted**
The children were warned against loitering in the lonely areas of town.

2. crowded, populated, busy

lonesome *adj.* **lonely, alone, forlorn**
Keith's pup is lonesome when his master is at school.

popular

long **1.** *v.* **yearn, crave, wish, hope**
Everyone longs for warm weather.

2. *adj.* **lengthy, prolonged, extended**
We listened politely to the long speech.

2. short, brief, concise, curt, terse

look **1.** *n.* **appearance, manner, air, expression**
The tired worker has a weary look.

2. *v.* **appear, seem**
She looks tired after a long day's work.

3. *v.* **see, view, observe, gaze, stare**
Tourists looked around the museum with interest.
n. They only had time for a quick look at the displays.

3. overlook, omit, pass over

loose	1.	*adj.*	**untied, unfastened** Your shoelace is loose. *adv.* Let the dog run loose.	1. *tied, fastened*
	2.	*adj.*	**not tight, unrestricted, slack** Loose clothes keep us cool on hot days.	2. *tight, restricting*
loosen		*v.*	**untie, free, release, unfasten, let go, undo, set free** Dad loosened his tie when he got home.	*tie, fasten, secure, hold, retain*
lopsided		*adj.*	**uneven, unbalanced** The lopsided table has one leg that is shorter than the others.	*balanced, even, upright*
lose	1.	*v.*	**mislay, misplace, drop** Marie lost her watch at the park.	1. *find, get, obtain, recover, locate*
	2.	*v.*	**be defeated, succumb** They lost the game after a tough match.	2. *win, triumph, be victorious*
lot	1.	*n.*	**property, plot, tract, field, land** Aunt Pat sold the lot she owned on Shadow Lake.	
	2.	*n.*	**great deal, abundance, large amount** There was a lot of food at the party.	2. *scarcity, shortage*
loud	1.	*adj.*	**noisy, blaring, boisterous** Loud music can be annoying.	1. *soft, quiet, faint, inaudible, gentle*
	2.	*adj.*	**flashy, garish, gaudy, showy** Pat's loud clothes drew much attention.	2. *conservative, subdued*
love		*n.*	**affection, tenderness, adoration, devotion** The parents were filled with love for their new baby. *v.* They loved the baby. *adj.* They were loving parents.	*hatred, aversion, dislike, loathing, malice*
lovely		*adj.*	**beautiful, attractive, pleasing, appealing, charming, handsome** Our neighbor has a lovely house.	*ugly, plain, unattractive*
low	1.	*adj.*	**short, squat, not high** There is a low hedge around the backyard.	1. *high*
	2.	*adj.*	**sunken, depressed, below sea level** Many of the low areas were flooded in the recent storm.	2. *high, elevated*
	3.	*adj.*	**mean, cruel, vile, base, cowardly** That was a low trick to pull on a friend.	3. *fine, good, kind, honorable*
	4.	*adj.*	**quiet, soft, whispered, gentle, hushed** We spoke in low voices so we wouldn't wake the baby. *v.* Lower your voices, please.	4. *loud, noisy, boisterous*
	5.	*adj.*	**depressed, downcast, unhappy, dejected, down, gloomy** The team felt low when they lost the final game.	5. *cheerful, happy, elated*
	6.	*adj.*	**small, little, paltry, trifling** The salary for a beginner is often low.	6. *high, big, above average*

loyal	*adj.*	**faithful, true, devoted, constant** Dogs are loyal to their masters. *n.* Workers are often rewarded for their loyalty to the company.	*disloyal, untrue, faithless, unfaithful*
lucid	*adj.*	**clear, precise, direct, accurate** The witness gave a lucid account of the accident.	*vague, inaccurate, muddled, obscure, fuzzy*
luck	1. *n.*	**good fortune, success** We wished Rudy luck before the job interview.	1. *misfortune, bad luck, ill-luck*
	2. *n.*	**fortune, chance, fate** They have had a run of good luck.	
lucky	*adj.*	**fortunate** The lucky couple won $1 million in the lottery.	*unlucky, unfortunate, ill-fated, luckless*
ludicrous	*adj.*	**ridiculous, crazy, absurd, farcical, preposterous, zany** People tell ludicrous stories about aliens.	*sensible, serious, somber*
lurch	*v.*	**swerve, stumble, sway, stagger, totter** The wounded soldier lurched forward and fell.	
lure	1. *n.*	**bait, decoy** They used plastic lures instead of worms to fish.	
	2. *n.*	**attraction, pull** We couldn't resist the lure of the seaside.	2. *repulsion*
	3. *v.*	**entice, bait, trap, persuade, coax, trick, tempt, attract** Hunters use decoys to lure the ducks to the marsh.	3. *repel, repulse, deter*
lurk	*v.*	**prowl, slink, sneak, skulk, hide** A prowler lurked among the bushes.	
luscious	*adj.*	**delicious, tasty, savory, delectable, succulent, appetizing** Some juice dribbled on my chin as I bit into a luscious apple.	*unsavory, unappetizing, tasteless, unpalatable*
luster	*n.*	**shine, glow, sparkle, brightness, gloss, glare, sheen** This silver dish has lost its luster.	*dimness, tarnish, dullness*
luxuriant	*adj.*	**abundant, profuse, lush, dense, thick** We couldn't get through the luxuriant undergrowth of the jungle.	*sparse, meager, thin, scanty*
luxury	*n.*	**extreme comfort, wealth, riches, extravagance, material abundance** The wealthy live in great luxury. *adj.* We stayed at a luxurious hotel on our holiday.	*poverty, need, want, penury, hardship*

M

In its earliest form *M* was but a wavy line 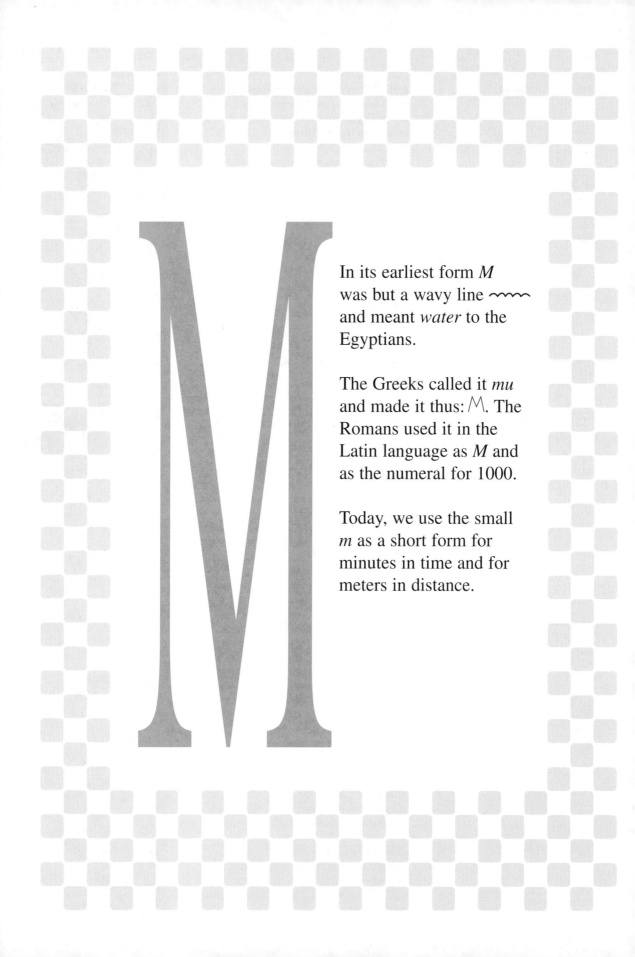 and meant *water* to the Egyptians.

The Greeks called it *mu* and made it thus: ᛖ. The Romans used it in the Latin language as *M* and as the numeral for 1000.

Today, we use the small *m* as a short form for minutes in time and for meters in distance.

mad	1.	*adj.*	**crazy, insane, deranged, demented** The dog was mad from rabies.	1. *sane, normal, rational, sound*
	2.	*adj.*	**angry, furious, irate, provoked** Len was mad when he missed the train. *v.* The violent fight between the hockey players maddened the spectators.	2. *glad, happy, pleased, composed*
magic	1.	*n.*	**sleight of hand, illusion, trickery** Magicians thrill us with their magic. *adv.* The statues were transformed magically into moving creatures.	
	2.	*n.*	**witchcraft, sorcery** Fairy tales feature magic spells.	
	3.	*adj.*	**unbelievable, stupendous, enchanting** Wonderland is a magic playground for children and adults. *adj.* The children were awed by the magical special effects in the movie	
magnetic		*adj.*	**inviting, attractive, fascinating, irresistible, captivating** No one can resist her magnetic personality.	*repulsive, repelling, unattractive, offensive*
magnificent		*adj.*	**imposing, splendid, fine, superb, grand, glorious** There are many magnificent old churches in Rome. *n.* Many tourists come to view the magnificence of the Sistine Chapel.	*ordinary, poor, unimposing*
magnify	1.	*v.*	**enlarge, increase, expand, amplify** Scientists use a microscope to magnify minute objects for study.	1. *reduce, minimize, lessen, condense*
	2.	*v.*	**exaggerate, overstate** Jim magnified his problems to gain sympathy.	2. *understate, minimize*
magnitude		*n.*	**measure, greatness, extent, size, consequence, significance** The San Francisco earthquake of 1989 was of great magnitude.	*insignificance, inconsequence*
maim		*v.*	**cripple, disable, impair, injure** The horse was maimed in an accident.	*heal*
main		*adj.*	**primary, essential, chief, central, principal, important, leading** State the main idea of your story.	*subordinate, lesser, secondary*
maintain	1.	*v.*	**assert, contend, claim, insist, declare** The suspect maintained that she was innocent.	1. *deny, reject*
	2.	*v.*	**uphold, preserve, keep** The police maintain law and order.	2. *ignore*
	3.	*v.*	**provide for, support, sustain** It is expensive to maintain a large family.	3. *abandon, neglect*

majestic	*adj.*	**grand, noble, dignified, stately, magnificent, splendid, imposing** The Rocky Mountains are majestic. *n.* Her Majesty Queen Victoria was a British monarch.	*lowly, common, ordinary*
major	1. *n.*	**military officer** The major ordered the troops to rest.	1. *private*
	2. *adj.*	**senior, superior, leading, chief** John had the major role in the play.	2. *minor, lesser, junior*
make	1. *n.*	**kind, brand, form** What make of computer do you prefer?	
	2. *v.*	**manufacture, produce, create, build** This company makes good cars.	2. *destroy, wreck, dismantle*
	3. *v.*	**force, press, compel, require** Our teachers made us work hard before the final examination.	3. *ask, beg*
	4. *v.*	**appoint, nominate, name, elect** The coach made her captain of the team.	
	5. *v.*	**arrive at, reach, catch, attain** Can we make the 9:30 train?	5. *miss*
malady	*n.*	**illness, sickness, ailment, disease** Kim suffers from an unusual malady.	*strength, vigor, health*
malice	*n.*	**spite, grudge, hate, resentment, ill will** Although he walked out on her, Pari bears him no malice.	*good will, kindness, benevolence*
malicious	*adj.*	**hateful, spiteful** Someone has been spreading malicious rumors about our new neighbors.	*kind, thoughtful*
malnourished	*adj.*	**undernourished, starved, emaciated** Many children in the Third World are malnourished. *n.* They suffer from malnutrition.	*overfed, sated, well-nourished*
mammoth	*adj.*	**giant, colossal, gigantic, enormous, huge** The school is in the middle of a mammoth fundraising project.	*tiny, little, small, minute, miniature*
man	1. *n.*	**male, fellow, chap, guy** Many men stayed home today because of the strike.	1. *woman, female*
	2. *v.*	**staff, attend, operate, maintain** Three astronauts will man the spacecraft.	2. *abandon, leave*
manage	1. *v.*	**direct, govern, administer, regulate, control, cope** She managed the company competently. *n.* Who is the manager here?	1. *mismanage, misdirect*
	2. *v.*	**cope, fare, make out** Did you manage to do the job alone? *adj.* It is a manageable job.	2. *fail*

management	1.	*n.*	**supervision, operation, guidance, conduct, command, control**	**1.** *mismanagement*
			The success of this company is due to good management.	
	2.	*n.*	**executive board, board of directors, administrators**	**2.** *labor, staff, employees, workers*
			The management turned down the union's request for more pay.	
mandate		*n.*	**order, command, directive, approval, authorization**	*request, appeal, petition*
			The county committee issued a mandate for immediate road repairs.	
mandatory		*adj.*	**compulsory, obligatory, necessary, required, forced**	*optional*
			It is mandatory to wear seatbelts in the car.	
manipulate	1.	*v.*	**operate, use, handle, control, manage**	
			I learned how to manipulate a computer.	
	2.	*v.*	**deceive, defraud, control, influence**	
			The cult leader manipulated the group into obeying him blindly.	
manner	1.	*n.*	**style, form, way, method, mode**	
			Her manner of speaking is clear and concise.	
	2.	*n.*	**kind, type, sort, variety**	
			What manner of book is this?	
	3.	*n.*	**bearing, conduct, deportment, demeanor, behavior**	
			The statesman has a noble manner.	
manners		*n.*	**conduct, behavior, deportment, bearing, etiquette**	
			It pays to watch your manners.	
manual	1.	*n.*	**handbook, guide, reference**	
			They read the manual to find out how to assemble the furniture.	
	2.	*adj.*	**physical, hand-operated**	**2.** *mechanical, automatic*
			The car is equipped with a manual transmission.	
			adv. The machine was operated manually.	
manufacture		*v.*	**make, build, construct, produce, assemble, form**	*destroy, demolish, scrap*
			Factories in Detroit manufacture cars.	
			n. Japan and the United States are major manufacturers of cars.	
many		*adj.*	**numerous, ample, abundant**	*few, several, some*
			We have seen this movie many times.	
map	1.	*n.*	**chart, plan, diagram**	
			The road map was most helpful when we drove across Europe.	

	2.	*v.*	**draw, illustrate, describe, plot, plan, chart** "Map a new route," ordered the leader.	

mar   *v.*   **blemish, damage, spoil, harm, stain**   *beautify, decorate, adorn*
Violence marred the hockey game.

margin
1. *n.*   **edge, border, boundary, limit**   *1. center, middle*
Keep inside the margins of your page.
2. *n.*   **allowance, leeway**
There is no margin for error in the space flights.

marginal   *adj.*   **insignificant, minor, slight, trivial, borderline, unimportant**   *principal, primary, major, compelling, important*
Marginal gains were made in some investments this year.

marine   *adj.*   **of the sea, nautical, oceanic, maritime**
Scuba divers examine marine life in the ocean depths.

mark
1. *n.*   **stamp, brand, proof, symbol, sign, impression, hallmark**
The artist put her mark on her work.
v. She marked her name on her work.
2. *n.*   **spot, stain, blotch, streak, blemish**
The spilt soup left a mark on my skirt.
3. *n.*   **target, goal**
The President is the mark of kidnappers.
4. *n.*   **grade, score, rating**
Boris got a good mark on the test.
v. The teacher marked the test papers and returned them to the students.
5. *v.*   **take notice, watch, note**   *5. ignore, disregard, disobey*
"Mark my words," said the teacher. "All those who don't work will fail."

marked   *adj.*   **definite, notable, outstanding, significant, prominent**   *insignificant, slight*
There is a marked improvement in Tracie's grades this year.

market
1. *n.*   **bazaar, store, shop, fair**
We buy fresh vegetables at the market.
2. *n.*   **demand, buyers, consumers**
There is a large market for home DVDs.
3. *v.*   **sell, exchange, trade, vend**   *3. buy*
Many companies market their goods on the Internet.

maroon   *v.*   **abandon, desert, strand, leave**   *rescue, save*
The shipwreck victims were marooned on an island.

martial   *adj.*   **military, warlike**   *civil, civilian*
The army imposed martial law after the coup.

marvelous		*adj.*	**wonderful, astonishing, remarkable, fabulous, splendid, superb, amazing** The world watched in awe as Neil Armstrong made his marvelous journey to the moon. *n.* Armstrong's journey was a marvel.	*ordinary, plain, common, terrible*
masculine		*adj.*	**manly, virile** Is there a masculine role model today? *n.* What is defined as masculinity?	*feminine, womanly*
mask	1.	*n.*	**false face, face guard, face cover** The children wore ghostly masks on Halloween.	
	2.	*v.*	**hide, disguise, cover, shroud, conceal, screen** The bank robbers masked their faces with nylon stockings.	**2.** *unmask, uncover, show, reveal, disclose, divulge, expose*
mass	1.	*n.*	**crowd, mob, great number** The mass of people prevented us from entering the building.	**1.** *small number, few*
	2.	*n.*	**size, bulk, extent** Please determine the mass of this shipment of books.	**2.** *paucity, smallness*
	3.	*v.*	**collect, gather, assemble, congregate** The protesters massed in front of the Senator's office.	**3.** *scatter, spread, disperse*
massacre		*n.*	**mass slaughter, killing, carnage, butchery** The massacre took place during the war. *v.* Innocent people are massacred in wars.	
massive	1.	*adj.*	**large, big, bulky, heavy** Massive rocks were hurled down the mountain during the landslide.	**1.** *tiny, small, minute, miniature*
	2.	*adj.*	**vast, widespread, immense** The police launched a massive search for the escaped convict.	**2.** *small scale*
mass media		*n.*	**information means, communications means** The mass media keep people abreast of events around the world.	
master	1.	*n.*	**leader, employer, director, boss** The workers obeyed their master's orders.	**1.** *subordinate, employee*
	2.	*n.*	**expert, teacher** The judo master demonstrated the steps to the students.	**2.** *novice, disciple, beginner, tyro, pupil*
	3.	*v.*	**tame, subdue, overpower, conquer, overcome** Susan finally mastered her fear of heights.	**3.** *be defeated, be overcome by, submit to, succumb*
	4.	*v.*	**become expert at, become skilled at, learn** She mastered the art of public speaking. *adj.* She is a masterful speaker.	**4.** *amateur*

	5.	*adj.*	**expert, skilled, able, gifted** A master artisan carved that statue.	
	6.	*adj.*	**main, chief, best, principal** The master bedroom has its own bathroom.	**6.** *lesser*

match	1.	*n.*	**contest, competition, game** The tennis match drew a large crowd of spectators.	
	2.	*n.*	**equal, equivalent, peer** Ray admitted he had met his match in Kevin when they tied in the golf game.	**2.** *superior, inferior*
	3.	*v.*	**fit together, join, pair** We matched the pieces of the puzzle.	**3.** *take apart, scatter*
	4.	*v.*	**be similar to, resemble** Your taste in clothes matches mine.	**4.** *differ from*
	5.	*v.*	**harmonize with, suit** The shoes match the outfit perfectly.	**5.** *clash with, mismatch*

material	1.	*n.*	**data, facts, notes, information, ideas, resources** I have enough material for my essay.	
	2.	*n.*	**fabric, textile, cloth** I chose a heavy material for the drapes.	
	3.	*adj.*	**physical, tangible, real** They place too much importance on the material comforts of life.	**3.** *spiritual, intangible*
	4.	*adj.*	**substantial, important, valuable** The company made a material gain in its sales of computers.	**4.** *unimportant, slight, small, trivial*

matter	1.	*n.*	**object, thing, material, substance, stuff** There is some foreign matter in the patient's eye.	
	2.	*n.*	**event, episode, affair, incident, topic, question, situation, subject, issue** This matter does not concern you.	
	3.	*n.*	**trouble, difficulty, cause of distress** What is the matter with the car?	
	4.	*v.*	**signify, count, be important** It matters a lot to me to do well.	**4.** *be unimportant*

mature	1.	*v.*	**ripen, bring to perfection, develop, mellow, age** Fruit matures in the sun.	
	2.	*adj.*	**adult, full-grown, developed** She has very mature views for one so young. *n.* She displayed her maturity in the way she handled the crisis.	**2.** *immature, young, adolescent*

maxim		*n.*	**proverb, motto, rule, adage, axiom** Have you heard this maxim: "Many hands make light work?"	

maximize		*v.*	**increase, intensify, amplify** The workers were asked to maximize their efforts to increase productivity.	*minimize, lessen*

maximum		*adj.*	**greatest, supreme, highest, utmost, top** The ambulance rushed off at maximum speed.	*least, smallest, minimum, lowest*
maybe		*adv.*	**possibly, perchance, perhaps** Maybe we can go with you.	*definitely, positively, probably not*
meager	1.	*adj.*	**sparse, scant, slight, short** The campers had a meager supply of food.	*1. ample, plentiful, abundant, bountiful*
	2.	*adj.*	**lean, slim, thin, spare** Mei's meager face caused us concern.	*2. full, fat, plump, stout*
meal		*n.*	**repast, food, nourishment, refreshment** Our evening meal is at six o'clock.	
mean	1.	*v.*	**intend, plan, propose, aim, want** Derek means to win this competition.	
	2.	*v.*	**denote, indicate, convey, signify** What does this symbol mean?	
	3.	*adj.*	**nasty, miserable, unkind, cruel** That circus trainer is mean to animals. *n.* Meanness to animals is not to be tolerated.	*3. generous, kind, noble, warm, good, humane*
	4.	*adj.*	**median, average, norm, middle, center, midpoint** The mean temperature in winter is thirty-two degrees Fahrenheit.	
meander		*v.*	**wander, ramble, roam** The tourists meandered through the streets of Paris.	*go straight*
meaning	1.	*n.*	**definition, explanation** Look up the meaning of the word in the dictionary.	
	2.	*n.*	**gist, point, substance, sense, aim, intention, significance** The meaning of the message was unclear.	
means	1.	*n.*	**ability, capability, capacity, machinery** The company has the means to produce the goods in a very short time.	
	2.	*n.*	**resources, funds, wealth, money** She has the means to buy the house.	
measure	1.	*n.*	**share, quota, allowance, portion, quantity** A full measure of aid was given to the flood victims.	
	2.	*n.*	**law, act, bill, proposal, plan** Congress will be debating that measure tomorrow.	
	3.	*n.*	**step, method, procedure, course, means** What measures have been taken to prevent further flooding?	

	4.	*n.*	**size, extent, dimension, quantity** A mile is a standard measure of distance.	
	5.	*v.*	**size, gauge, judge, assess** The decorator measured the windows for the new drapes. *n.* He wrote down the measurements.	
meddle		*v.*	**interfere, intervene, tamper with** Our neighbors constantly meddle in our affairs. *adj.* Meddlesome people cause trouble.	*ignore, shun*
mediocre		*adj.*	**passable, fair, common, ordinary** The lazy student handed in a mediocre essay. *n.* Don't settle for mediocrity.	*excellent, superior, extraordinary*
meditate		*v.*	**think, contemplate, ponder, deliberate, concentrate, reflect** Sue meditated on her dilemma for weeks. *n.* The monk sat in meditation at the temple.	*skip over, ignore*
meek		*adj.*	**mild, gentle, humble, yielding, docile, submissive** The supervisor bullied the meek worker. *adv.* The worker meekly did whatever he was told to do.	*bold, forward, domineering, bossy*
meet	1.	*v.*	**join, converge, intersect** An intersection is a point where roads meet.	1. *separate, divide*
	2.	*v.*	**convene, gather, assemble** The committee will meet to elect a chairperson. *n.* The athletic meet was canceled because of the rain.	2. *disperse, scatter, leave, disassemble*
	3.	*v.*	**fulfill, satisfy, answer** His work meets the standards required to graduate.	3. *fail, fall short of*
	4.	*v.*	**encounter, run into** Selma and I met at the exhibition.	4. *avoid, ignore, shun, miss*
meeting		*n.*	**gathering, discussion, assembly, rally, conference** The school called a meeting to discuss the new rules.	
melancholy	1.	*n.*	**unhappiness, gloom, despair, dejection, sorrow, grief** The bad news filled us with melancholy.	1. *happiness, joy, cheer, gladness, elation*
	2.	*adj.*	**sad, dismal, gloomy, sorrowful, glum, depressed, dispirited** Hamlet was known as the melancholy Dane.	2. *happy, bright, cheerful, joyous, jolly, merry*
mellow	1.	*adj.*	**smooth, soft, sweet, delicate** Some fruits have a mellow taste when ripe.	1. *harsh, bitter, acrid, sour*

	2.	*adj.*	**seasoned, matured** The cello has a mellow tone. *v.* The singer's voice mellowed with age.	2. *green, unripe, immature*
melody		*n.*	**tune, music, theme** This song has a lively melody. *adj.* The singer had a melodious voice.	
melt	1.	*v.*	**thaw, dissolve, liquefy** The snow melted quickly in the sunshine.	1. *freeze, set, harden, congeal, coagulate*
	2.	*v.*	**scatter, vanish, disappear, merge** The thugs melted into the night when they heard the police siren.	2. *gather, appear*
memento		*n.*	**souvenir, keepsake, token** Did you bring me a memento of your trip?	
memorable		*adj.*	**unforgettable, impressive, remarkable, outstanding, extraordinary, notable** The Browns often speak of their memorable holiday in China.	*ordinary, dull, mediocre, commonplace*
menace	1.	*n.*	**threat, danger, hazard, peril, risk** Hurricanes are a menace in the Caribbean.	1. *aid, blessing, benefit, advantage*
	2.	*v.*	**threaten, scare, terrify** The bully menaced the small boys into giving him their pocket money.	2. *aid, defend, help, support, protect*
mend	1.	*v.*	**repair, fix, overhaul, restore** Will the cobbler mend your shoes?	1. *break, damage, mar, tear*
	2.	*v.*	**sew, darn, patch** Chris mends his own clothes.	2. *rip, tear*
	3.	*v.*	**get well, heal, cure, recover** My cut will mend quickly. *n.* Ken is on the mend after a prolonged illness.	3. *deteriorate, get sick, relapse*
mention	1.	*n.*	**report, notice, reference, citation** The art display received little mention in the newspapers.	
	2.	*v.*	**declare, name, tell, state, speak of, refer to, cite** Nick mentioned that you are interested in a job.	2. *conceal, withhold, disregard, overlook*
merciful		*adj.*	**compassionate, humane, kind** The merciful villagers offered the starving man some food.	*cruel, merciless, ruthless, unforgiving, callous, inhumane*
mercy		*n.*	**kindness, tolerance, pity, compassion, sympathy** The guerrillas showed no mercy to their captives.	*severity, harshness, cruelty*
mere		*adj.*	**minor, paltry, insignificant** The bracelet was a mere trinket and of no real value.	*considerable, significant*

merely	*adv.*	**only, solely, simply** This car is not merely good, it is also affordable.	
merge	*v.*	**mix, mingle, blend, join, unite** Traffic merges into one lane here. *n.* Business mergers help companies grow faster.	*separate, divide, part*
merit	1. *n.* 2. *v.*	**value, worth, advantage, benefit, credit** Amos feels there is a great merit in studying hard. **deserve, earn, rate, warrant** He merited the high marks he received in every subject.	**1.** *weakness, fault, discredit* **2.** *be unworthy of*
merry	*adj.*	**jolly, festive, jovial, lively, vivacious, cheerful, happy** The children sang a merry tune.	*sad, unhappy, dejected, miserable, melancholy*
mess	1. *n.* 2. *n.* 3. *n.* 4. *v.*	**confusion, muddle, jumble, disorder, mayhem** The house was in a mess after the party. *adj.* The living room was especially messy after the party. **botch, bad job, bungle** She made a mess of her project by trying to focus on too many things. **difficulty, plight, dilemma, trouble** Delia was in a real mess when her car broke down on a deserted road. **dirty, soil, disorder** Try not to mess your clean clothes.	**1.** *order* **2.** *success* **4.** *clean, tidy*
meteoric	*adj.*	**brilliant, rapid, speedy, sudden, blazing, swift, flashing, explosive** The Beatles had a meteoric rise to fame.	*slow, gradual, steady*
method	*n.*	**way, process, means, manner, mode, procedure, system** What is the best method of cooking beans?	
methodical	*adj.*	**orderly, systematic, organized, disciplined** The methodical researcher organizes her findings very carefully. *adv.* She methodically checks every source of information.	*haphazard, random, disorderly*
meticulous	*adj.*	**fastidious, finicky, careful, exacting, scrupulous** Cliff is a meticulous dresser. *adv.* He dresses meticulously.	*inexact, sloppy, negligent, careless, slovenly*
mettle	*n.*	**courage, nerve, spirit, pluck, bravery, boldness, grit, stamina** Henry Hudson showed great mettle in his Arctic exploration.	*cowardice, timidity*

microscopic		*adv.*	**minute, atomic, infinitesimal, tiny, miniature** Many viruses are microscopic and can only be seen under a microscope.	*large, huge, immense, colossal, gigantic*
middle	1.	*n.*	**center, midpoint, main part, hub** The middle of our town is always busy.	**1.** *edge, outskirts, periphery, border*
	2.	*adj.*	**central, midway, intermediate** Don took the middle position on the issue.	**2.** *extreme*
might		*n.*	**strength, power, force, energy** The people fought with all their might to overthrow the dictator.	*weakness, frailty*
mighty		*adj.*	**powerful, strong, intense, great, forceful, vigorous** We moved the rock with a mighty push.	*weak, ineffective, gentle*
migrant		*adj.*	**nomadic, itinerant, roving** Migrant farm workers are hired during the harvest.	
migrate		*v.*	**move, relocate, resettle** People from the countryside migrate to the cities to look for jobs. *n.* The migration of people to the cities has left farms with no workers.	*remain, stay*
mild	1.	*adj.*	**gentle, easy, calm, placid, kind, serene, agreeable** The children like the mild manners of their babysitter.	**1.** *rough, cross, unkind, harsh, severe, disagreeable*
	2.	*adj.*	**temperate, warm, moderate** We enjoyed the mild spring day.	**2.** *cold, unpleasant, chilly, stormy, bitter*
milestone		*n.*	**turning point, significant event** Winning the scholarship was a milestone in Shannon's career.	
militant		*adj.*	**uncompromising, defiant, assertive, martial, resolute, warlike, aggressive** The speaker's militant views drew much criticism from the audience.	*moderate, peaceable, submissive*
mimic		*v.*	**imitate, impersonate, ape** The parrot mimicked my laugh. *n.* Parrots are good mimics.	
mind	1.	*n.*	**brain, intellect, intelligence** Alexander Graham Bell had an inventive mind.	
	2.	*v.*	**look after, tend, take care of** Who will mind the baby while we're out?	**2.** *ignore, neglect*
	3.	*v.*	**heed, attend to, obey** Competitors have to mind the rules of the game.	**3.** *disobey, forget, neglect*
	4.	*v.*	**object to, resent, detest** Do you mind the noise?	**4.** *approve of*

mingle	*v.*	**blend, mix, combine, merge, socialize, circulate, associate** The movie star mingled with his fans at the party.	*part, separate, divide, avoid, shun*
miniature	*adj.*	**small, tiny, petite, toy, minute** Yun collects miniature crystal animals.	*colossal, giant, huge, mammoth, large*
minimize	*v.*	**reduce, lessen, decrease** The carpenter added insulation to minimize the noise in the restaurant.	*maximize, increase, enlarge, expand*
minimum	*adj.*	**least, smallest, lowest, basic** He is paid a minimum wage as a waiter. *n.* Her patience was at a minimum after a sleepless night.	*maximum, largest, greatest*
minor	*adj.*	**less, smaller, lower, junior** Joel had a minor part in the play.	*major, large, senior, main*
minute	*adj.*	**microscopic, insignificant, tiny, small, slight, diminutive, petite** A minute speck of dust irritated her eye.	*large, massive, huge, bulky, immense, great, colossal*
miracle	*n.*	**marvel, surprise, wonder** It was a miracle they survived the crash. *adj.* They made a miraculous escape.	
mirror	1. *n.*	**glass, reflector, looking glass** Seth fixed his hair in front of the mirror.	
	2. *v.*	**reflect, show** The smooth lake mirrored the trees along the shore.	
mirth	*n.*	**merriment, festivity, gaiety, merrymaking, laughter** There was fun and mirth at her party.	*misery, sadness, depression*
misbehavior	*n.*	**misconduct, disorder, impudence** Misbehavior in class is not allowed. *v.* Some pupils deliberately misbehave.	*obedience, order, good conduct*
miscalculate	*v.*	**err, miscount, mistake** Andre miscalculated the time needed to drive to the airport. *n.* He missed his plane as a result of his miscalculation.	
miscellaneous	*adj.*	**various, mixed, diverse, assorted** A miscellaneous collection of old cards was in the box.	*uniform, identical*
mischief	*n.*	**prank, naughtiness, misbehavior, vandalism** The gang was up to mischief as usual. *adj.* Some children are more mischievous than others.	

misconduct		*n.*	**misbehavior, bad conduct, mismanagement, disorder** Joe was fired for professional misconduct.	*order, good conduct*
miserable	**1.**	*adj.*	**wretched, very poor, deplorable, mean, desperate, sorry** The refugees lived in miserable conditions.	**1.** *comfortable, good, luxurious*
	2.	*adv.*	**unhappy, distressed, sad, sorrowful, forlorn** Doug was miserable until he found his dog.	**2.** *happy, merry, glad, cheerful*
misery		*n.*	**sorrow, grief, suffering, agony, distress, trouble** A severe illness can cause much misery.	*joy, gladness, happiness, comfort, relief, contentment*
misfortune		*n.*	**disaster, calamity, hardship, trouble, mishap** Our holiday was marred by several misfortunes.	*fortune, good luck*
misgiving		*n.*	**anxiety, doubt, foreboding, fear, worry, apprehension** We had some misgivings about driving in the freezing rain.	*trust, confidence, assurance*
mishap		*n.*	**setback, misfortune, snag, upset, accident** An unfortunate mishap put that horse out of the race.	
miss	**1.**	*n.*	**blunder, slip, oversight, mistake, failure, fault, error** I lost because I had too many misses.	**1.** *success, hit*
	2.	*v.*	**fail to hit, overlook, lose** Did you miss your chance to score?	**2.** *get, obtain, gain*
	3.	*v.*	**long for, yearn for, desire, crave** The travelers missed their family back home.	**3.** *forget, be indifferent*
mission	**1.**	*n.*	**errand, task, assignment** The soldiers were sent overseas on a special mission.	
	2.	*n.*	**calling, vocation** Her mission in life is to help the poor.	
mist		*n.*	**moisture, dew, fog, haze** Mist forms when air is chilled. *adj.* His eyes were misty with tears when he heard the good news.	
mistake	**1.**	*n.*	**error, slip, blunder, oversight** The cashier made a mistake on our bill.	**1.** *correction*
	2.	*v.*	**confuse, mix up, misunderstand** Vera mistook the salt for sugar.	**2.** *be accurate*
mistaken		*adj.*	**wrong, incorrect, erroneous** He has a mistaken idea about what happened.	*correct, right, accurate*

mix	1.	*v.*	**blend, combine, unite** Mix the ingredients in a bowl. *n.* This mixture makes a better drink.	**1.** *separate, divide*
	2.	*v.*	**join, mingle, associate** John mixes well with everyone. *n.* He is a good mixer.	**2.** *segregate, separate, divide*
mob	1.	*n.*	**swarm, mass, crowd, rabble, throng, horde** The police were called to disperse the angry mob of demonstrators.	**1.** *small number, individual*
	2.	*v.*	**crowd, jostle, surround, swarm** Fans mobbed the singer after the show.	**2.** *ignore, overlook, pass by*
mobile		*adj.*	**movable, portable** The mobile library comes every week.	*immobile, fixed, immovable*
mock	1.	*v.*	**imitate, mimic, tease, jeer, ridicule** The rude audience mocked her singing.	**1.** *applaud, cheer, compliment, praise*
	2.	*adj.*	**fake, counterfeit, sham, false, imitation** Mona's mock fur coat looks real.	**2.** *real, actual, genuine*
mode		*n.*	**style, manner, fashion, method, custom, way, means** What will be our mode of travel in the year 2500?	
model	1.	*n.*	**pattern, replica, dummy, copy, duplicate, representation, facsimile** A model of the space shuttle was displayed at the science show.	
	2.	*n.*	**design, style, type, variety** What model is your new car?	
	3.	*n.*	**ideal, good example** The courageous and dedicated leader is a model for everyone. *adj.* She is a model citizen.	
	4.	*v.*	**shape, mold, form, design, build** Tim modeled a statue out of clay.	
moderate	1.	*v.*	**soothe, soften, quiet, quell, reduce, control, curb, check** The umpire's words moderated the tempers of the players. *adj.* His words had a moderating influence on the team.	**1.** *aggravate, excite, disturb, stir up, increase*
	2.	*adj.*	**reasonable, medium, average, modest** The Tangs are looking for a car with a moderate price. *adv.* They want a moderately priced car.	**2.** *outrageous, extreme, severe, excessive*
modern		*adj.*	**new, up-to-date, recent** The modern hospital has all the latest equipment.	*ancient, antique, old, old-fashioned, primitive*
modest	1.	*adj.*	**humble, meek, quiet, unassuming** Sue is modest about her achievements. *n.* Her modesty is to be applauded.	**1.** *showy, immodest, conceited*

2. *adj.* **chaste, decent, demure, discreet**
The modest girl dislikes short skirts.
adv. She dresses modestly in long skirts.

3. *adj.* **moderate, reasonable**
They paid a modest price for their house.

modify   *v.*   **change, alter, revise**
Adjectives and adverbs modify the
meaning of other words.

moist   *adj.*   **damp, humid, wet, watery**
The moist grass smelled sweet.
v. She moistened her parched lips by
licking them.
n. Moisture in the carpet caused it to
turn moldy.

moment   *n.*   **second, jiffy, flash, minute, instant**
I can only stay for a moment as I'm late.
adj. There was a momentary silence
when the bad news was announced.

momentous   *adj.*   **eventful, important, notable,
memorable, outstanding**
The inauguration of a new President is a
momentous occasion.

momentum   *n.*   **force, energy, impetus, thrust, drive,
push, velocity, speed**
The bobsled gathered momentum as it
sped down the icy slope.

monarch   *n.*   **sovereign, emperor, king, queen**
The United States has no monarch.

money   **1.** *n.*   **cash, funds, currency, coin,
legal tender**
Paul deposited his money at the bank.

2. *n.*   **wealth, riches, large income,
affluence, capital**
She made her money in the stock market.

monitor   **1.** *n.*   **detector, scanner, sensor**
The heart monitor indicated that the
patient's heart rate was high.

2. *n.*   **screen, video display terminal**
I bought a larger monitor for my computer.

3. *v.*   **watch over, inspect, overlook,
observe, scrutinize, supervise**
The nurse monitored the amount of
medicine given to the patient.
n. The class monitor helped the teacher
distribute the new books.

monopolize   *v.*   **control, corner, take over, dominate**
It is against the law to monopolize any
commodity.

---

2. *indecent, gaudy*

3. *extravagant*

*keep, maintain,
uphold*

*dry, arid, parched,
dehydrated*

eternity, age

*insignificant,
unimportant, trivial,
common, ordinary*

subject, follower

3. *ignore*

share, divide, include

monopoly	*n.*	**control, cartel, exclusive right, exclusive possession, corner** No one firm should have a monopoly on any kind of industry.	*open market*
monotonous	*adj.*	**tedious, dull, boring, tiresome, wearisome, routine** Workers in monotonous jobs require frequent breaks. *n.* Some people find the monotony of the prairie scenery unbearable.	*stimulating, interesting, pleasing, diversified, changing, varying*
mood	*n.*	**feeling, temper, frame of mind, disposition** The students were in a holiday mood on the last day of school.	
moody	*adj.*	**unhappy, dejected, melancholy, gloomy, sullen, brooding, despondent** Sheen is moody because she lost the match.	*happy, cheerful, amiable, high-spirited*
morale	*n.*	**confidence, self-assurance, spirit, resolution, mental attitude** The debating team's morale was boosted when they won the trophy.	
morbid	*adj.*	**gruesome, sickening, unwholesome, grim, depressing** What a morbid movie that was!	*wholesome, pleasant, uplifting*
more	1. *adj.*	**extra, additional, spare, reserve, other, supplementary** There are more sandwiches in the refrigerator. *n.* Would you like more of the same?	**1.** *less, fewer*
	2. *adv.*	**to a greater degree, to a greater extent** She reads more than anyone else does.	**2.** *less than, fewer than*
morose	*adj.*	**sad, moody, mournful, depressed, melancholy, glum** What a morose ending to that movie!	*cheerful, happy, pleasant*
mortal	1. *n.*	**human being, person, creature** Will mortals ever set foot on Mars?	
	2. *adj.*	**human, temporal, earthly** There are mortal limitations to what we can do.	**2.** *immortal, eternal, everlasting, perpetual*
	3. *adj.*	**fatal, lethal, deadly** The warrior dealt his enemy a mortal blow. *adv.* The soldier was mortally wounded in battle.	**3.** *lifesaving, life-giving*
	4. *adj.*	**intense, enormous, extreme** The child was in mortal fear of the dog.	

motion	1.	*n.*	**movement, passage, action, flow** The motion of the ship made some passengers ill.	1. *stillness, calm, rest, repose*
	2.	*n.*	**suggestion, recommendation, request, proposition** Tina made a motion to adjourn the meeting.	
	3.	*v.*	**signal, gesture, wave, beckon, nod** The police officer motioned us to proceed around the stalled vehicle.	
motionless		*adj.*	**still, stationary, unmoving** The motionless cat watched the mouse.	*moving, shifting*
motivate		*v.*	**induce, drive, prompt, stimulate, incite, impel** The chance to win a scholarship motivated Yen to work hard. *n.* Her motivation was strengthened by the competition she faced.	*dissuade, thwart, deter, discourage*
mount	1.	*v.*	**climb, rise, ascend, go up, scale** Grandpa mounted the stairs slowly.	1. *descend, go down*
	2.	*v.*	**swell, grow, multiply, increase, rise** Unemployment figures mounted last year.	2. *lessen, decline, fall*
	3.	*v.*	**get on, climb on** The cowboy mounted his horse and rode away.	3. *dismount, get down*
	4.	*v.*	**prepare, set, fix, place, install** The photographer mounted our pictures in suitable frames.	
mourn		*v.*	**grieve, sorrow, regret, lament** We mourned the loss of the astronauts in the space shuttle Columbia. *adj.* The funeral was a mournful occasion.	*rejoice, be glad, cheer, delight in, celebrate*
move	1.	*v.*	**shift, go, proceed, travel** The procession moved slowly through the city. *n.* The movement of troops to the border worried everyone.	1. *remain, halt, stand, pause, stay, stop*
	2.	*v.*	**transfer, carry, shift** The company moved our furniture to Milwaukee. *n.* Nothing was broken in the move!	
	3.	*v.*	**suggest, recommend, propose** John moved that we adjourn the meeting.	
	4.	*v.*	**affect, touch, arouse, stir** His letter moved me to tears.	4. *pacify, quiet, allay*
movie		*n.*	**film, cinema, show, motion picture, picture** My brother enjoys horror movies.	
much	1.	*n.*	**great deal, lots, large amount** There's much to be done before a wedding.	1. *little, nothing*

2. *adj.* **plentiful, ample, sufficient, abundant**
There was much food at the picnic.

2. little, scarce, sparse, scant

3. *adv.* **greatly, exceedingly, extremely**
Terry Fox is much admired for his "Marathon of Hope."

3. not much, scarcely, hardly

4. *adv.* **nearly, somewhat, almost, about, approximately**
The old house looks much the same as it did five years ago.

4. hardly, barely

muddy *adj.* **cloudy, unclear, murky**
We didn't want to swim in the muddy water of the pond.

clear, transparent, lucid, unclouded

muffle
1. *v.* **cover, wrap, enclose, swathe**
We muffled our faces with scarves against the bitter cold.

1. uncover, lay bare, expose

2. *v.* **silence, mute, stifle, suppress**
The thick walls muffled the captive's cries for help.

2. magnify, increase

multiply *v.* **reproduce, increase, expand**
The world population multiplies each year.

decrease, lessen, diminish, reduce

multitude *n.* **crowd, swarm, mass, horde, flock, throng, host**
A multitude of gulls rested on the beach.

small number

mumble *v.* **whisper, murmur, mutter**
Tim mumbled that he was sorry.

speak clearly, enunciate, articulate

murky
1. *adj.* **gloomy, dim, cloudy, dreary, overcast**
Murky weather is usual in the winter.

1. sunny, bright, clear

2. *adj.* **muddy, cloudy, dirty**
I refused to drink the murky water.

2. clear, unclouded, clean

murmur *n.* **low sound, whisper, undertone**
There was a murmur of approval at the mayor's suggestion.
v. We murmured our approval.

shout, yell

muse *v.* **ponder, meditate, reflect, deliberate, contemplate**
"Shall I buy that stereo," he mused, "or save the money?"

musty *adj.* **stale, damp, mildewed, moldy**
There was a musty smell in the attic.

fresh, new

mutiny *n.* **rebellion, revolt, riot, insurrection**
There was a mutiny on the ship.
v. The sailors mutinied against their violent captain.
adj. The mutinous sailors took control of the ship.

mutter	*v.*	**mumble, growl, grumble** No one can hear you if you mutter.	*speak clearly, enunciate, articulate*
mutual	*adj.*	**common, shared, joint** Sylvia is a mutual friend of ours.	*exclusive*
myriad	*adj.*	**countless, innumerable, infinite, endless, limitless, immeasurable** Myriad stars are found in the Milky Way.	*few, limited*
mysterious	*adj.*	**puzzling, secretive, strange, unnatural** The mysterious disappearance of the scientist caused much concern. *adv.* He disappeared mysteriously while he was out for a walk.	*obvious, definite, evident, clear, explained*
mystery	*n.*	**riddle, puzzle, secret** Sherlock Holmes solved many mysteries.	*answer, clarity, solution*
mystify	*v.*	**perplex, puzzle, bewilder, baffle** Our neighbor's sudden disappearance mystified us.	*clarify, explain*
myth	1. *n.*	**story, tale, fable, parable, legend** The ancient Greeks invented myths to explain natural occurrences. *adj.* A unicorn is a mythical creature.	**1.** *fact, real life, happening*
	2. *n.*	**illusion, delusion, false belief** Tales of his riches turned out to be mere myth.	**2.** *truth, fact, actuality*

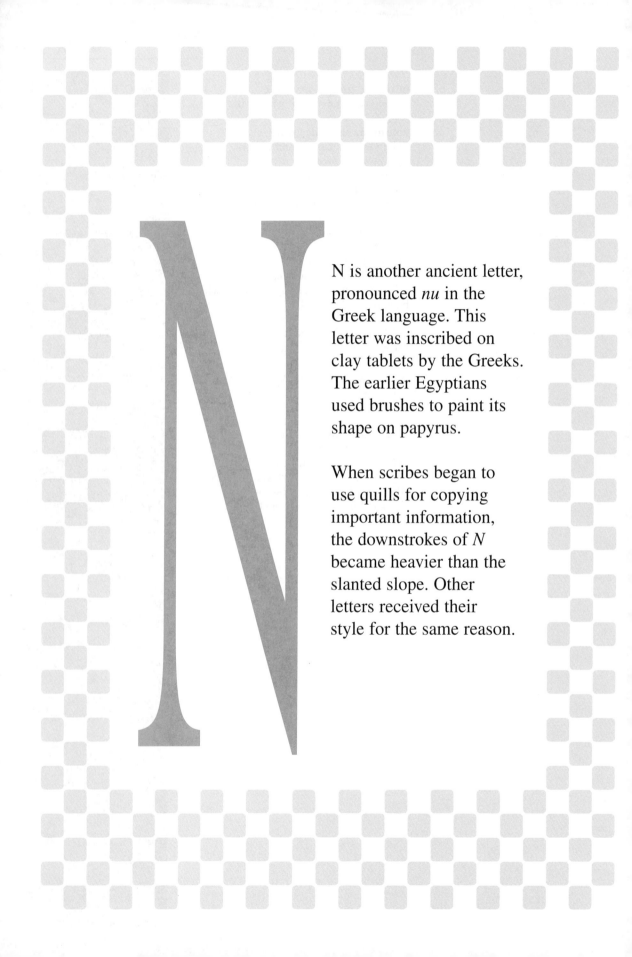

N is another ancient letter, pronounced *nu* in the Greek language. This letter was inscribed on clay tablets by the Greeks. The earlier Egyptians used brushes to paint its shape on papyrus.

When scribes began to use quills for copying important information, the downstrokes of *N* became heavier than the slanted slope. Other letters received their style for the same reason.

nab	*v.*	**seize, grab, arrest, snatch, catch** The police nabbed the robber in the alley.	*release, set free*
nag	*v.*	**hassle, pester, badger, scold** Mom nagged Jim about his messy room.	*praise, compliment*
naked	*adj.*	**nude, bare, undressed, exposed** The child ran out of his bath stark naked.	*covered, clothed, dressed, clad, robed*
name	1. *n.*	**title, term, first name, surname** The baby's full name is Jane Smith. *v.* They named the baby after her grandmother.	
	2. *n.*	**reputation, renown, repute** A good name is earned by good deeds.	**2.** *disrepute*
	3. *v.*	**mention, speak of, indicate** The author named our family in his book.	
	4. *v.*	**choose, appoint, select, nominate** The school named a new principal.	
nap	1. *n.*	**short sleep, siesta, snooze, catnap** The baby takes a nap each afternoon.	
	2. *v.*	**doze, slumber, drowse** Our dog napped in front of the fire.	
narrate	*v.*	**tell, describe, recite, recount, relate** Nan narrated her story to the class. *n.* She is a good narrator. *n.* Her powerful narration kept the audience spellbound.	*conceal, withhold*
narrative	*n.*	**story, chronicle, tale** Joe wrote a gripping narrative of his experiences in the war.	
narrow	1. *v.*	**restrict, contract, limit, close** We narrowed the distance between us and the group ahead by running faster.	**1.** *broaden, widen, enlarge*
	2. *adj.*	**compressed, cramped, slender, tight** We couldn't crawl through the narrow space in the cave.	**2.** *wide, broad, spacious*
	3. *adj.*	**bigoted, limited, prejudiced, biased, shallow, intolerant, dogmatic** The politician lost the election because of his narrow views on the issue.	**3.** *liberal, tolerant, open-minded, broad-minded*
nasty	1. *adj.*	**offensive, mean, vicious, unkind** Tim shocked us with his nasty remarks.	**1.** *pleasant, kind, nice, sweet*
	2. *adj.*	**foul, dirty, offensive, disagreeable** Nasty odors came from the chemical plant.	**2.** *agreeable, clean, pleasant, savory*
native	1. *n.*	**original inhabitant, aborigine** The Maoris are the natives of New Zealand.	**1.** *invader, intruder*
	2. *n.*	**lifetime inhabitant, one born there** William Shakespeare was a native of England.	**2.** *foreigner, alien, immigrant*

	3.	*adj.*	**inborn, innate, natural, inherent** The pianist had native musical ability.	**3.** *acquired, learned*
	4.	*adj.*	**local, domestic, indigenous** We should support the economy by buying native products.	**4.** *imported, foreign*
natural	**1.**	*adj.*	**original, close to nature, pure** Many poets have praised the natural beauty of England's Lake District.	**1.** *artificial, created, manufactured*
	2.	*adj.*	**spontaneous, unforced, unaffected** Sally is a natural actress. *adv.* She acts quite naturally.	**2.** *affected, unnatural*
	3.	*adj.*	**normal, usual, typical, common** It's natural to feel depressed when things go wrong.	**3.** *abnormal, odd, unusual*
	4.	*adj.*	**inborn, innate, native, intrinsic** She should be encouraged to develop her natural artistic ability.	**4.** *acquired, learned*
nature	**1.**	*n.*	**natural world, environment, cosmos** Human beings have destroyed much of nature through industrialization.	
	2.	*n.*	**personality, character, disposition, temperament** Simone is a pleasure to be with because of her sunny nature.	
	3.	*n.*	**instinct, spirit** Leo is by nature a hard worker.	
	4.	*n.*	**sort, kind, variety, type** What is the nature of your problem?	
naughty		*adj.*	**mischievous, bad, ill-behaved, unruly, disobedient** The naughty child was not allowed to watch television.	*good, well-behaved, obedient*
navigate		*v.*	**steer, direct, guide, pilot, cruise, sail** The contestants navigated their bikes through the obstacle course. *n.* Sandy was the best navigator. *n.* Her expert navigation earned her first prize.	
near	**1.**	*v.*	**approach, come up to, come toward** We were happy as we neared home.	**1.** *recede, depart, leave*
	2.	*adj.*	**close, approaching, impending, imminent, looming** Those dark clouds mean a storm is near. *adv.* Tension rises as examinations draw near.	**2.** *distant, far off*
	3.	*adj.*	**close, next door, close by, alongside** I walk to school as it is quite near.	**3.** *distant, far, remote*
	4.	*prep.*	**close to, not far from, in sight of** Herb lives near the school.	**4.** *far from*
nearly		*adv.*	**almost, just about, about, practically** The work on the new house is nearly finished.	*totally, fully, completely*

neat		*adj.*	**tidy, groomed, well-kept, trim, orderly**	*unkempt, messy, untidy*

neat   *adj.*   **tidy, groomed, well-kept, trim, orderly**   *unkempt, messy, untidy*
Mei always has a neat appearance.
n. Neatness is a desirable habit.
adv. Mark is neatly dressed for school.

necessary   *adj.*   **essential, needed, indispensable,**   *unnecessary, optional*
vital, required, mandatory, requisite
She was hired as she had all the
necessary qualifications for the job.
n. Water is a necessity for survival.

need
1. *n.*   **hardship, poverty, distress**   **1.** *plenty, comfort, luxury*
Some families live in great need.
adj. The needy ones must be helped.
2. *n.*   **necessity, requirement, want**
Bev is in need of medical help.
3. *v.*   **require, want**   **3.** *possess, own, hold, have*
I need two more credits to graduate.

negative
1. *adj.*   **antagonistic, contrary, pessimistic**   **1.** *positive, helpful, encouraging*
Sam's negative attitude dampened the
team's morale.
2. *adj.*   **opposing, dissenting, opposed**   **2.** *affirmative, positive, assenting*
The vote was altogether negative.

neglect
1. *n.*   **lack of care, disregard, inattention**   **1.** *care, attention*
Years of neglect had left the house in ruins.
v. The parents neglected their children
because of their hectic jobs.
2. *v.*   **miss, skip, omit, ignore, disregard**   **2.** *attend to, take care of*
He neglected his work and lost his job.

negligent   *adj.*   **careless, inattentive, thoughtless,**   *careful, watchful, keen, alert, attentive*
heedless, reckless
Sam was charged with negligent driving
after the accident.

negotiate   *v.*   **bargain, set terms, confer, discuss**
Ray negotiated a better price for the car.
n. The negotiations saved him money.

neighborhood   *n.*   **area, vicinity, district, community**
We live in a quiet neighborhood.
adj. I attend the neighborhood school.

neighboring   *adj.*   **nearby, adjacent, next, bordering**   *distant, remote, far off*
Our house is on a neighboring street.

nerve
1. *n.*   **daring, vigor, courage, pluck**   **1.** *cowardice, weakness*
It takes a lot of nerve to skydive.
2. *n.*   **audacity, gall, cheek, impudence**   **2.** *politeness, courtesy, refinement*
He had the nerve to jump queue.

nervous   *adj.*   **agitated, anxious, uneasy, tense,**   *calm, poised, at ease, steady*
jumpy, jittery, fearful
The nervous student bit her nails.
adv. The suspect stuttered nervously.

net	1.	*n.*	**snare, mesh, web, trap, screen** Pierre used a net to catch the butterfly.	
	2.	*n.*	**Internet, web, worldwide web** We surfed the Net to find the information for our project.	
	3.	*v.*	**bag, capture, catch, seize** Jay netted three fish from the pond.	3. *release, set free*
	4.	*v.*	**earn, gain, acquire, take in, clear** The business netted a good profit.	4. *lose*
neutral		*adj.*	**non-partisan, impartial, unbiased, indifferent, dispassionate** Switzerland has been neutral in all foreign wars since 1815. *n.* The country has a policy of neutrality.	*biased, partisan, prejudiced*
neutralize		*v.*	**offset, check, block, halt, cancel, annul, overcome, counterbalance** The doctor neutralized the effects of the poison with an antidote.	*exaggerate, aggravate*
nevertheless		*adv.*	**yet, but, however, regardless, anyhow, even so, notwithstanding** The weather was terrible, nevertheless we set out for Winnipeg.	
new	1.	*adj.*	**unused, fresh** The Chinese wear new clothes to celebrate the Chinese New Year.	1. *old, used, worn*
	2.	*adj.*	**novel, latest, revolutionary, original, innovative, ultramodern** This new software can do amazing things.	2. *out-of-date, dated, obsolete, passe*
	3.	*adj.*	**different** Todd will attend a new school next fall.	3. *same*
	4.	*adj.*	**strange, unexplored, unfamiliar** All this technology is new to me.	4. *familiar, known*
news		*n.*	**information, report, dispatch, account, announcement, bulletin** Did you watch the news on television?	
next		*adj.*	**following, succeeding, subsequent, ensuing** Please turn to the next page. *adv.* Next, let's read chapter two.	*previous, preceding, prior*
nice	1.	*adj.*	**pleasant, agreeable, fine, wonderful** We had a nice time at Jose's party. *adv.* The room was nicely decorated.	1. *unpleasant, awful, disagreeable, horrid, revolting, dreadful*
	2.	*adj.*	**charming, delightful, friendly, kind, amiable, pleasant** Everyone likes him because he is such a nice person.	2. *obnoxious, rude, awful, unpleasant*
nimble		*adj.*	**active, spry, agile, sprightly, supple** The nimble gymnast leapt gracefully onto the bar.	*slow, awkward, sluggish, clumsy, uncoordinated*

noble	1.	*n.*	**nobleman, noblewoman, aristocrat, peer, lord, lady** We visited the castle of an ancient noble.	*1. commoner, plebeian*
	2.	*adj.*	**dignified, majestic, grand, glorious, magnificent, worthy, honorable** The soldiers died for a noble cause.	*2. inferior, lowly, ignoble, dishonorable*
noise		*n.*	**din, clatter, discord, sound, tumult, racket, clamor** The baby was awakened by a loud noise. *adj.* The boys had a noisy argument.	*silence, stillness, hush, peace, quiet*
nominate		*v.*	**propose, name, recommend, appoint, suggest** We nominated Karen for class president. *n.* She accepted the nomination.	
non-renewable		*adj.*	**irreplaceable, irrecoverable** Oil and coal are non-renewable sources of energy.	*renewable, replaceable*
nonsense		*n.*	**drivel, folly, absurdity, foolishness, balderdash** Their claims about seeing a Martian were dismissed as utter nonsense. *adj.* At parties we play nonsensical games.	*wisdom, sense, reality, fact*
normal		*adj.*	**usual, typical, regular, natural, ordinary, customary, average** Our normal work hours are 9 to 5. *adv.* The letter carrier normally comes in the morning.	*unusual, odd, peculiar, irregular, uncommon, abnormal*
notable		*adj.*	**great, outstanding, momentous, remarkable, important, significant** Neil Armstrong's walk on the moon was a notable event.	*insignificant, obscure, unimportant, unknown*
note	1.	*n.*	**letter, message, memo** Mom sent a note to my teacher to let him know that I was ill.	
	2.	*v.*	**write, put down, record** The monitor noted our names on the board.	
	3.	*v.*	**observe, notice, regard, perceive, see** Note the colors of that bird.	*3. disregard, ignore, overlook*
noted		*adj.*	**famous, well-known, renowned, acclaimed, celebrated** Glenn Gould was a noted pianist.	*unknown, obscure*
notice	1.	*n.*	**announcement, poster, circular, advertisement, communication** Where did you see the notice for the game?	
	2.	*v.*	**note, observe, regard, see** Did you notice my new shoes?	*2. disregard, ignore*

notify	*v.*	**inform, let know, acquaint, tell** The university notified Lara that she had been accepted. *n.* The notification came in the mail.	*conceal, keep silent, withhold*
notion	*n.*	**opinion, impression, idea, thought** Where did he get the notion that he had won the scholarship?	
notorious	*adj.*	**infamous, ill-famed, scandalous** Have you read about the notorious Jack the Ripper?	*reputable, respected*
nourish	*v.*	**feed, sustain, nurture, support** Birds nourish their young. *n.* All living things need nourishment. *adj.* Have a nourishing meal before you set off on your trip.	*starve, deprive, weaken*
novel	**1.** *n.*	**fiction, tale, story** *Treasure Island* is a famous novel.	
	2. *adj.*	**fresh, new, original, unusual, different** The scientist's novel ideas met with ridicule. *n.* The novelty of the game made it a success.	**2.** *common, ordinary, hackneyed*
novice	*n.*	**beginner, newcomer, neophyte, tyro** I'm a novice when it comes to snowboarding.	*professional, master, old hand, veteran*
numb	*adj.*	**dulled, deadened, unfeeling, paralyzed** Ed's fingers were numb from the cold. *v.* The anaesthetic numbed his pain.	*sensitive*
number	**1.** *n.*	**amount, volume, quantity, total** A large number of people attended our concert.	
	2. *n.*	**figure, digit, integer, numeral** Pick a lucky number.	
	3. *n.*	**song, tune, piece** The choir sang a merry number.	
	4. *v.*	**assign a number, count, total** Ben numbered the pages of his essay.	
numerous	*adj.*	**many, abundant, various, copious** Selene received numerous job offers after graduating at the top of her class.	*few, hardly any*
nutrient	*n.*	**nourishment, food, sustenance** There are excellent nutrients in whole grain cereals.	
nutritious	*adj.*	**nourishing, healthful, wholesome** Whole wheat bread is a nutritious food. *n.* What other foods give us nutrition?	*harmful*

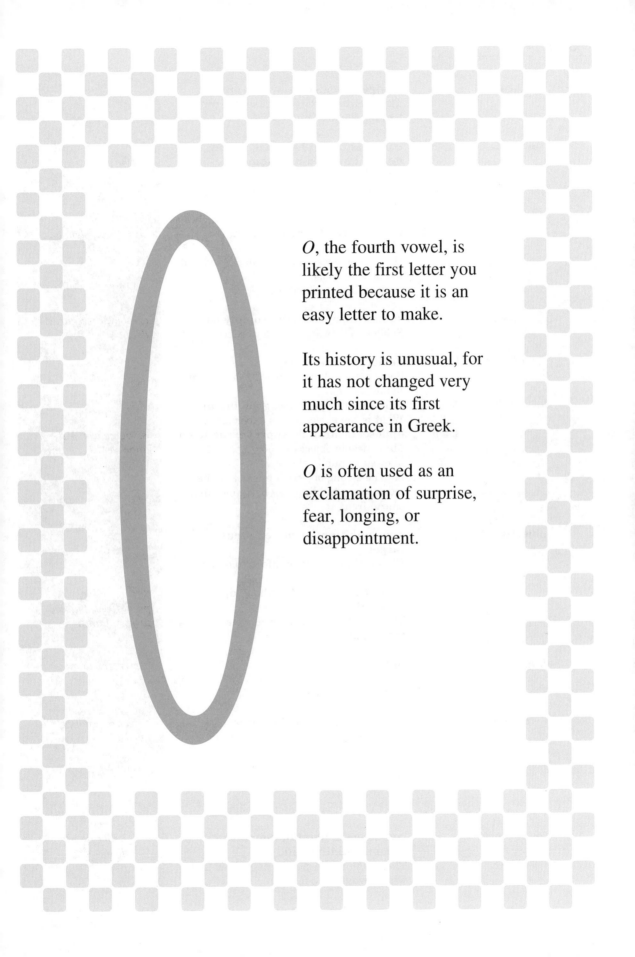

O, the fourth vowel, is likely the first letter you printed because it is an easy letter to make.

Its history is unusual, for it has not changed very much since its first appearance in Greek.

O is often used as an exclamation of surprise, fear, longing, or disappointment.

oath   *n.*   **pledge, promise, vow, guarantee**
The scientists who worked on the project had to take an oath of secrecy.

obedient   *adj.*   **compliant, well-behaved, dutiful, docile, law-abiding, submissive**
The obedient dog came when called.
n. Our new dog has been trained in obedience.
disobedient, unruly, defiant

obese   *adj.*   **fat, overweight, heavy, stout, plump, chubby, corpulent**
He became obese from too much food and too little exercise.
n. Obesity is unhealthy.
slim, thin, slender, lean, gaunt, skinny

obey   *v.*   **submit to, agree with, comply with**
Soldiers are trained to obey orders.
disobey, disregard, defy

object
1. *n.* **device, article, thing**
Some people claim to have seen strange flying objects.
2. *n.* **motive, aim, purpose, goal, intent**
What is the object of this experiment?
3. *v.* **oppose, protest, disapprove, condemn**
Many people object to smoking being allowed in public places.
n. The strong objection to smoking has led to many public areas being declared smoke-free.
3. *agree, consent, approve, like, admire*

objective
1. *n.* **aim, ambition, purpose, intent, target**
Kai's main objective in life is to become extremely rich.
2. *adj.* **impartial, fair, just, unbiased, rational, detached**
The reporter wrote an objective account of the situation.
2. *subjective, prejudiced, biased, unjust, unfair*

obligation   *n.*   **duty, task, responsibility**
Each of us has an obligation to help clean up the environment.
choice, freedom

oblige
1. *v.* **require, compel, make, force, bind**
The rules obliged the group to attend the seminar.
2. *v.* **accommodate, help, cooperate**
Please oblige me with an immediate e-mail response.
adv. The secretary replied obligingly.
1. *spare, exempt, free, release*

obliging   *adj.*   **considerate, helpful, thoughtful, accommodating, kind**
The obliging salesperson helped me find what I wanted.
inconsiderate, rude, discourteous

obliterate	1.	*v.*	**erase, wipe out, delete, rub out, abolish, cancel, blot out** Someone obliterated important evidence from the audio tapes.	**1.** *keep, preserve, add, restore, create*
	2.	*v.*	**destroy, level, ravage, eradicate, pulverize, crush** A volcanic eruption obliterated the ancient city of Pompeii. *adj.* The obliterated city was buried in lava.	**2.** *construct, build*
oblivious		*adj.*	**unmindful, unaware, heedless, unconcerned, forgetful** The pianist was oblivious to everything except the music.	*aware, concerned, conscious, attentive, observant*
obnoxious		*adj.*	**offensive, repulsive, displeasing, distressing, disagreeable, unpleasant** Obnoxious odors came from the chemical plant.	*pleasing, inviting, pleasant, delightful, agreeable*
obscure	1.	*v.*	**block, hide, conceal, cover, veil** Clouds obscured the tops of the mountains.	**1.** *reveal, show, display*
	2.	*adj.*	**little-known, unknown, minor** An obscure person wrote the book. *n.* She has since risen from obscurity to fame.	**2.** *famous, renowned, well-known*
	3.	*adj.*	**unclear, indefinite, hidden, vague, hazy, ambiguous** We were puzzled by the book's obscure ending.	**3.** *evident, plain, obvious, definite, clear*
observant		*adj.*	**attentive, alert, watchful, perceptive** The observant guard stopped the shoplifter from leaving the store.	*unobservant, heedless, careless, inattentive, oblivious*
observation		*n.*	**view, theory, opinion, comment, remark, finding** Share your observations of the experiment with us.	
observe	1.	*v.*	**obey, keep, follow, respect, comply with, conform to** Our team observed all the rules of the game.	**1.** *violate, break, disobey, disregard, flaunt*
	2.	*v.*	**notice, see, detect, watch, perceive** We observed two strangers loitering in the street.	**2.** *ignore, overlook, miss*
	3.	*v.*	**commemorate, celebrate, solemnize, keep, respect** We observe Christmas on 25 December.	**3.** *overlook, neglect, ignore*
obsolete		*adj.*	**outdated, outmoded, old-fashioned, worn-out, archaic** The company replaced its obsolete equipment with the latest computers.	*recent, new, current, modern, avant-garde, up-to-date*

obstacle	*n.*	**obstruction, barrier, hindrance** All traffic had to detour around the obstacles on the road.	*aid, assistance, help, support*
obstinate	*adj.*	**stubborn, determined, persistent, willful, inflexible** The obstinate man refused to change his mind. *adv.* He obstinately refused to make way for us.	*willing, obliging, cooperative, flexible*
obstruct	*v.*	**hinder, bar, block, impede, retard, restrict, stop** The new building obstructed our view of the lake. *n.* The obstruction of traffic was caused by a stalled car.	*aid, help, speed, assist, clear, open*
obtain	*v.*	**get, secure, acquire, procure, gain** How did you obtain this information?	*forfeit, lose, give*
obvious	*adj.*	**plain, clear, apparent, evident** It was obvious from the start that our team was better. *adv.* The better team obviously won.	*doubtful, unclear*
occasion	1. *n.* 2. *n.*	**affair, event, episode, happening, circumstance, situation** The baby shower was a happy occasion. **cause, reason, motive, grounds** We had occasion to celebrate after we heard the test results.	
occasional	*adj.*	**infrequent, irregular, rare, uncommon** Reg enjoys an occasional game of golf. *adv.* We play occasionally.	*regular, frequent*
occupant	*n.*	**resident, tenant, inhabitant** Who is the occupant of the next apartment?	
occupation	1. *n.* 2. *n.*	**profession, employment, work, job, trade, calling, business, craft, vocation** He's been in the same occupation for years. **ownership, possession** The new owners will take occupation of the house soon.	**1.** *hobby, avocation, pastime*
occupy	1. *v.* 2. *v.* 3. *v.*	**inhabit, reside in, live in** Who occupied this house before you? **fill, engage, employ, absorb** My aunt occupies her time with skiing. **conquer, control, possess** Enemy troops occupied the territory.	**1.** *abandon, desert, leave, move from* **3.** *liberate, free, withdraw*

occur	*v.*	**happen, befall, take place, transpire** A serious accident occurred yesterday.	
occurrence	*n.*	**episode, event, experience, happening, incident, occasion** The sudden storm was an unusual occurrence in this region.	
odd	1. *adj.*	**strange, queer, peculiar, irregular, unusual, abnormal** Peng has an odd habit of twitching his nose. *adv.* He has been behaving oddly lately.	*1. normal, usual, ordinary, common, customary*
	2. *adj.*	**sundry, various, casual, occasional** Our students do odd jobs for retired people.	*2. regular, steady, full-time*
	3. *adj.*	**uneven, irregular** One, three, and five are odd numbers.	*3. even, even-numbered*
odor	*n.*	**smell, scent, aroma, fragrance, stench** There was a stale odor in the kitchen.	
offense	*n.*	**crime, error, fault, wrong, violation** The suspect was accused of a serious offense.	
offend	*v.*	**insult, displease, anger, hurt, irritate** Hank offended his friend with his rude remarks.	*please, satisfy, help, calm*
offensive	1. *adj.*	**impudent, impertinent, insulting, rude, obnoxious** The tennis player was disqualified for his offensive manners.	*1. courteous, polite, charming, mannerly*
	2. *adj.*	**foul, unpleasant, nasty, revolting** Rotten eggs produce offensive odors.	*2. agreeable, pleasant, delightful*
offer	1. *n.*	**proposal, tender, bid** Dad put in an offer on the house.	
	2. *v.*	**suggest, volunteer, propose** We offered to help build the fence.	*2. deny, withhold*
	3. *v.*	**give, serve, pass, hand** We offered our guests some tea.	*3. refuse, decline*
official	1. *n.*	**officer, executive, administrator** Government officials made the decisions regarding tax exemptions.	
	2. *adj.*	**authorized, appointed, endorsed, sanctioned, approved** Canada has two official languages — English and French.	*2. unauthorized, unofficial*
often	*adv.*	**frequently, generally, regularly, constantly, habitually** We often stop at the restaurant on our way home.	*never, rarely, seldom, occasionally*

old	1.	*adj.*	**ancient, antique** This old piece of furniture belonged to my grandmother.	1. *modern, recent, new*
	2.	*adj.*	**aged, elderly** Old people need to keep active.	2. *young, youthful*
	3.	*adj.*	**outdated, out-of-date** Who wants to read an old newspaper?	3. *current, up-to-date*
	4.	*adj.*	**worn, used, aged** We reupholstered our old sofa and it looks new again.	4. *new*
	5.	*adj.*	**former, previous** I visited my old school recently.	5. *current, present*
ominous		*adj.*	**threatening, sinister, menacing, unfavorable, dire, grim, foreboding** The ominous rumors about nuclear war make people anxious.	*encouraging, promising, favorable, auspicious*
omit		*v.*	**exclude, overlook, leave out, disregard** Ron omitted one question on the test. *n.* The omission cost him some marks.	*include, insert, put in*
onlooker		*n.*	**spectator, witness, bystander, observer** Curious onlookers crowded around the scene of the accident.	*participant*
only	1.	*adj.*	**sole, single, lone** Eugene is an only child.	1. *one of many*
	2.	*adv.*	**exclusively, just, solely, merely** He comes only on Saturdays.	
open	1.	*v.*	**unfasten, release, unlock** Please open the door.	1. *close, fasten, lock, shut, seal*
	2.	*v.*	**commence, start, initiate, begin** The meeting opened with the singing of the national anthem.	2. *conclude, end, close, finish*
	3.	*adj.*	**unlocked, unobstructed** We entered through the open door.	3. *closed, shut, fastened, locked*
	4.	*adj.*	**free, unrestricted, accessible** The open border beckoned the refugees.	4. *closed, blocked, inaccessible*
opening	1.	*n.*	**opportunity, chance, occasion, possibility** He had a good opening to score in the last period of the hockey game.	
	2.	*n.*	**clearing, gap, hole, break, chink** The snowmobile fell through the opening in the ice.	2. *barrier, block, blockade*
	3.	*n.*	**vacancy, space, place, job, position** The company has an opening for an editor.	
	4.	*adj.*	**beginning, starting, initial, first** The opening ceremony of the Olympic Games was most impressive.	4. *final, concluding, closing, ending*
operate		*v.*	**work, manage, drive, run, manipulate** Jane operates this machine very well.	

n. Telephone operators at the police station are trained to handle emergency calls.

operation   *n.*   **action, performance, process, procedure**
Liz is responsible for the smooth operation of the company.

opinion   *n.*   **viewpoint, idea, impression, judgment, notion, conclusion**
What's your opinion on this issue?

opponent   *n.*   **antagonist, rival, competitor, enemy**   *ally, partner, friend, colleague, helper, supporter, associate*
The two opponents faced each other in a debate.

opportunity   *n.*   **chance, occasion, opening, time**
Here is your opportunity to learn a new language.

oppose   *v.*   **object to, dispute, challenge, defy**   *support, approve, defend, accept*
Who opposes this plan?

opposite   1.   *adj.*   **conflicting, contrary, opposed**   *1. same, similar, agreeable, identical*
We have entirely opposite political views.
n. "Left" is the opposite of "right."
         2.   *prep.*   **facing, across from**   *2. beside, next to, side by side*
Sit opposite me.

opposition   *n.*   **defiance, antagonism, resistance**   *cooperation, support, approval, assistance*
There was strong opposition to the government's proposals.

oppressive   1.   *adj.*   **harsh, cruel, brutal, despotic**   *1. just, kind, humane, benevolent*
Oppressive leaders are often overthrown.
         2.   *adj.*   **overwhelming, overpowering, unbearable**   *2. comfortable, soothing*
Many people fainted from the oppressive heat in the stadium.

optimistic   *adj.*   **hopeful, confident, upbeat, encouraging**   *pessimistic, gloomy, cynical*
We are optimistic about our chance of winning the championship.
n. The senator expressed optimism about the economy.
n. She is an optimist.

option   *n.*   **choice, selection, alternative**
Weigh your options carefully.
adj. Is it optional to wear seatbelts?

orbit   1.   *n.*   **path, circuit, course, trajectory, revolution**
Many satellites have been put into orbit around the Earth.

	2. *v.*	**circle, revolve around, travel around** Artificial satellites orbit the Earth.	
order	1. *n.*	**quiet, calm, control, discipline** The police were called in to restore order among the rioters.	**1.** *disorder, chaos*
	2. *n.*	**command, instruction, decree** The mayor gave orders to evacuate the town because of a chemical leak. *v.* The mayor ordered the evacuation of the town.	
	3. *n.*	**system, form, arrangement, rank, sequence, progression** List the names in alphabetical order.	**3.** *disorder, chaos, confusion*
	4. *v.*	**request, ask for, obtain, purchase** We ordered some dessert after the meal. *n.* We placed an order for a new car.	
orderly	1. *adj.*	**well-behaved, calm** People left in an orderly fashion after the play.	**1.** *disorderly, unruly*
	2. *adj.*	**tidy, neat, systematic, organized, methodical, regulated** The chairs were arranged in orderly rows.	**2.** *chaotic, confused, jumbled*
ordinary	*adj.*	**common, usual, normal, customary, regular** We had another ordinary day at school. *adv.* We ordinarily leave for school by eight o'clock.	*extraordinary, unusual, exceptional*
organization	1. *n.*	**company, firm, establishment, business** Mom works for a large organization.	
	2. *n.*	**system, arrangement** The students were responsible for the organization of the dance.	
organize	*v.*	**arrange, establish, coordinate** Who organized the science fair? *n.* The organizer of the fair did a great job.	*disorganize, upset, disturb*
origin	1. *n.*	**source, beginning, cause, base** Ideas, like rivers, often have hidden origins.	**1.** *end, finish, close, conclusion*
	2. *n.*	**descent, family, ancestry, lineage, race, stock, parentage** The Koyata family is of Japanese origin.	
original	1. *adj.*	**first, earliest, primary** Native Americans were the original inhabitants of North America.	**1.** *last, latest, final, most recent, ultimate*
	2. *adj.*	**unique, novel, creative, fresh, imaginative, unusual, inventive** John has an original idea for the poster. *n.* His idea shows originality.	**2.** *unoriginal, imitative*

originate   *v.*   **start, introduce, begin, create, invent**
The idea for this book originated from a childhood experience.

ornate   *adj.*   **showy, fancy, elaborate, lavish, adorned, ornamented**   *simple, plain, unadorned*
The visitors admired the ornate decorations.

ought   *v.*   **should, be obliged, must**
Ling ought to study for the test.

oust   *v.*   **remove, expel, dismiss, eject, throw out, fire, discharge, evict**   *admit, welcome, reinstate, restore*
The members ousted the unethical director from the board.

outbreak
1. *n.*   **rebellion, uprising, mutiny, riot**   *1. peace, harmony*
The army is busy keeping down the outbreaks by the rebels.
2. *n.*   **eruption, explosion, outburst**
A sudden outbreak of laughter echoed down the hall.

outcome   *n.*   **consequence, effect, end, result**   *cause, origin, beginning*
The outcome of the game was surprising.

outfit
1. *n.*   **supplies, equipment, apparatus, gear, provisions**
Is your camping outfit ready?
2. *n.*   **group, organization**
He works for a large medical outfit.
3. *n.*   **ensemble, clothes, garb**
Susie chose a red outfit for her vacation.
4. *v.*   **equip, supply**   *4. strip*
The owner outfitted the motorhome with a television.

outlaw
1. *n.*   **bandit, criminal, desperado, fugitive**
The sheriff arrested the outlaw.
2. *v.*   **ban, forbid, make illegal**   *2. allow, make legal, permit*
The city outlawed smoking in restaurants.

outline
1. *n.*   **plan, scheme, framework, draft**
First, make an outline for your story.
2. *n.*   **edge, frame, boundary**
She drew a black outline around her picture.
3. *v.*   **describe, summarize, draft**
The teachers outlined their plans for the class trip.
4. *v.*   **draw, sketch**
George outlined a map on the board.

outlook
1. *n.*   **view, viewpoint, attitude, perspective, frame of mind**
Her outlook on life has changed since she became ill.

2. *n.* **prospect, forecast, expectation, probability**
The outlook for the economy is promising.

2. *retrospect*

3. *n.* **view, vista, sight, scene, panorama**
The outlook from the top of the tower is spectacular.

outrageous   *adj.* **awful, atrocious, indecent, offensive, shocking, shameful**
We were embarrassed by their outrageous behavior at the party.

honorable, decent, moderate

outset   *n.* **beginning, start, origin, inception, commencement, opening**
We had a flat tire at the very outset of our trip.

end, finish, closing, conclusion, termination

outspoken   *adj.* **blunt, direct, frank, candid, forthright, straightforward**
The coach was most outspoken in his criticism of the players.

tactful, guarded, diplomatic

outstanding   **1.** *adj.* **leading, notable, famous, great, prominent, celebrated**
Marie Curie was an outstanding scientist.

1. *commonplace, ordinary*

2. *adj.* **exceptional, superior, great, remarkable, excellent**
Shi-Lan is an outstanding student.

2. *inferior, poor*

3. *adj.* **unpaid, due, payable, owing**
All outstanding accounts are charged twenty percent interest.

3. *paid, settled*

over   **1.** *adj.* **finished, complete, done, ended**
School is over by four o'clock.

1. *beginning*

2. *prep.* **across, above**
Jump over the fence.

2. *under, beneath, below*

3. *prep.* **more than, beyond**
The tickets cost over a dollar.

3. *less than, under*

overcast   *adj.* **cloudy, dull, gloomy, sunless, gray**
The skies have been overcast all day.

cloudless, clear, sunny, bright

overcome   *v.* **conquer, overpower, subdue, vanquish, defeat**
Patsy overcame her fear of spiders.

yield, give in to, submit to, surrender to

overdue   **1.** *adj.* **unpaid, owing, outstanding**
The account was long overdue.

1. *paid, settled*

2. *adj.* **delayed, belated, late**
Many people were worried about the overdue flight.

2. *early, prompt, on time*

overload   **1.** *n.* **excessive load, undue amount, surplus**
The overload on the circuit blew the fuses.

2. *v.* **burden excessively, load excessively, weigh down**
The workers overloaded the truck.

overlook	1.	*v.*	**ignore, disregard, excuse, forgive** Please overlook my being late.	*1. heed, pay attention to, notice, criticize*
	2.	*v.*	**forget, neglect, miss, slight** The waiter overlooked my request for a glass of water.	*2. remember, heed, notice*
overt		*adj.*	**apparent, visible, plain, obvious, evident, easily seen, clear, open** There was no overt evidence of fraud in the deal.	*hidden, secret, invisible, covert*
overthrow	1.	*n.*	**downfall, defeat, undoing, upset, destruction** The overthrow of the tyrant brought peace to the land.	*1. protection, preservation*
	2.	*v.*	**overcome, overpower, defeat, crush, abolish, topple** The rebels overthrew the dictator after a short battle with his troops.	*2. preserve, maintain, keep, support, guard, uphold, protect*
overwhelm	1.	*v.*	**vanquish, subdue, conquer, crush, defeat, beat** The other team overwhelmed us in spite of our best efforts.	*1. yield, submit to, surrender*
	2.	*v.*	**swamp, bury, engulf** Huge waves overwhelmed the canoe. *adj.* Her friends suffered overwhelming sorrow when they heard the news of her death.	*2. float, bring up*
	3.	*v.*	**astonish, puzzle, confound, confuse, bewilder, disconcert** Technology overwhelms many people.	*3. clarify*
own	1.	*v.*	**possess, have, hold** Our family has owned this house for three generations.	
	2.	*adj.*	**personal, private, individual** Donna has her own car now.	*2. another's*

P is the first letter of "punctuation." The Greeks and Romans did not use punctuation or spaces between words. Their writing WASALLINCAPITALS SMALLLETTERSWERE UNKNOWNUNTILTHE MIDDLEAGES.

A scholar named Alcuin, of York, England, taught church writers how to punctuate the Gospels. He taught in Europe between 796 and 814. Alcuin also gets much credit for introducing the "small-letter" alphabet.

pace	1.	n.	**speed, tempo, rate** Sam could not keep up the pace with the other runners.	
	2.	n.	**step, stride, footstep** Take three paces forward.	
	3.	v.	**walk, march, tread** The couple paced up and down the hall during their son's operation.	
pacify		v.	**settle, appease, calm, quieten, soothe** No amount of rocking could pacify the screaming baby.	*antagonize, anger, enrage, provoke, irritate, aggravate*
pack	1.	n.	**bundle, package, parcel, load** The hiker carried a large pack on her back.	
	2.	n.	**group, horde, gang, mob** A pack of wolves attacked the sheep.	
	3.	v.	**fill, load, cram, stuff** I've packed my suitcases for the trip.	**3.** *empty, unload, unpack*
package	1.	n.	**bundle, crate, case, parcel** The courier delivered a package today.	
	2.	v.	**wrap, encase, pack, display** Mom packaged a gift basket for Grandpa.	**2.** *unwrap, unpack*
pact		n.	**contract, agreement, bond, treaty, bargain, deal, settlement** Canada has signed a major trade pact with the United States.	
pain	1.	n.	**ache, twinge, pang, suffering, agony** The pain in his tooth kept him up all night.	**1.** *pleasure, joy, enjoyment, delight*
	2.	v.	**hurt, distress, trouble** Her hurtful remarks pained me. *adj.* Losing our cat was a painful experience.	**2.** *relieve, comfort, ease*
pains		n.	**care, trouble, consideration, effort** The students took great pains to make sure the science fair was a success.	*neglect, indifference, negligence*
painstaking		adj.	**thorough, careful, exacting, precise, meticulous, attentive** It took years of painstaking research to discover insulin.	*careless, uncaring, haphazard, negligent, sloppy*
pal		n.	**chum, friend, companion, buddy** We have been pals since kindergarten.	*enemy, antagonist, opponent, rival, foe*
pale	1.	adj.	**ashen, pasty, wan, pallid, colorless** People are often pale after an illness. *v.* Pam paled visibly when she heard the bad news.	**1.** *radiant, rosy*
	2.	adj.	**light, faint, weak** We painted the room a pale green.	**2.** *dark, deep, bright, strong*
pamper		v.	**spoil, coddle, humor, indulge** The whole family pampered the baby.	*mistreat, abuse, oppress*

pandemonium		*n.*	**uproar, din, tumult, chaos, disorder** There was pandemonium when our team won the game.	*silence, quiet, order, calm, peace*

panic		*n.*	**fright, alarm, terror, dread, fear** Everyone was in a panic when the fire alarm sounded. *v.* The teachers panicked when they realized a child was missing. *adj.* They could not think clearly because they were panicky.	*peace, calm, quiet, security, contentment*

parade	**1.**	*n.*	**procession, display, motorcade, show** There were many floats in the parade.	
	2.	*v.*	**strut, swagger, exhibit, flaunt** The models paraded on the catwalk.	
	3.	*v.*	**march, file, pass** The demonstrators paraded through the city.	

paralyze	**1.**	*v.*	**cripple, disable, incapacitate** The diving accident paralyzed Tim.	
	2.	*v.*	**make powerless** A heavy snowstorm paralyzed the city.	**2.** *enliven, make active*

paramount		*adj.*	**utmost, greatest, main, chief, highest, supreme, leading** The student's paramount concern is to get into a good university.	*least, slight, trifling, minor, smallest*

pardon	**1.**	*n.*	**forgiveness** I beg your pardon for the trouble I caused.	**1.** *blame, conviction, condemnation*
	2.	*n.*	**discharge, acquittal, release, reprieve** The prisoner was granted a full pardon by the government. *v.* The government pardoned the prisoner.	**2.** *conviction, imprisonment, condemnation, punishment*
	3.	*v.*	**forgive, excuse, overlook** Please pardon my lateness.	**3.** *punish, accuse, sentence*

part	**1.**	*n.*	**share, piece, portion, fraction, fragment, section** They sold us a part of their business.	**1.** *whole, all, total*
	2.	*n.*	**function, role, capacity, task, duty** What was your part in the project?	
	3.	*n.*	**role, character** Ed has a small part in the play.	
	4.	*v.*	**detach, separate, divide, split** The crowd parted to make way for the ambulance.	**4.** *join, unite*
	5.	*v.*	**take leave, say goodbye** We parted at the back door.	**5.** *meet, arrive, stay, remain*

partial	**1.**	*adj.*	**limited, incomplete** He suffered partial paralysis after a stroke. *adv.* He was partially paralyzed.	**1.** *whole, complete, entire*
	2.	*adj.*	**biased, prejudiced** The crowd booed at the partial umpire.	**2.** *fair, impartial*

participate   *v.*   **take part, perform, join in, engage in**
Only amateurs are allowed to participate in this tournament.
n. Participation is limited to those under the age of eighteen.
n. Jean is a keen participant in these tournaments.

particular

1. *adj.*   **special, outstanding, exceptional**
Your health is of particular concern to me.
2. *adj.*   **distinct, unique, individual**   *2. vague*
The particular aroma of Indian food wafted through the house.
3. *adj.*   **choosy, careful, selective, fussy**   *3. careless, reckless, heedless*
Sue is particular in making friends.

particularly   *adv.*   **especially, exceptionally, unusually**
Yang is particularly fond of science fiction.

partner   *n.*   **co-worker, colleague, ally, associate**   *rival, competitor, opponent*
Jennifer and Martine are partners on this project.

party

1. *n.*   **gathering, reception, celebration**
We threw a surprise birthday party for Helen.
2. *n.*   **group, force, band, company**
Several search parties were out looking for the missing child.

pass

1. *n.*   **permit, ticket**
Bill has a free pass to the movies.
2. *n.*   **gap, passageway, path, opening**   *2. barrier, obstacle*
The railway runs through a narrow pass in the mountains.
3. *v.*   **overtake, go ahead**   *3. follow, trail, stay behind*
The truck passed us on the highway.
4. *v.*   **hand over, deliver, give, present, share**   *4. receive, hold, retain*
Please pass the drinks to the guests.
5. *v.*   **approve, authorize, allow, sanction, legislate, confirm**   *5. disallow, reject, disapprove, deny, veto, defeat*
Congress passed the new Security Act.
6. *v.*   **spend, use, occupy, fill, employ**
My uncle passes his time reading.

passage

1. *n.*   **corridor, passageway, hall, route, access, course, thoroughfare**
We walked down a long passage to the rear of the museum.
2. *n.*   **voyage, journey, trip**
The ship had a rough passage across the Atlantic.
3. *n.*   **portion, part, selection, excerpt**   *3. whole, entirety*
Read a passage from this essay.
4. *n.*   **approval, enactment, legislation**   *4. veto, defeat*
Passage of the new bill took a long time.

	5.	*n.*	**passing, advance, movement** His wounds healed with the passage of time.	**5.** *stoppage, cessation*
passion	**1.**	*n.*	**ardor, desire, love, craving, longing, obsession, lust** Romeo's passion for Juliet led to tragedy.	
	2.	*n.*	**zest, gusto, enthusiasm, energy** The violinist performed with passion.	
passionate	**1.**	*adj.*	**ardent, fervent, intense, avid** He has a passionate interest in golf.	**1.** *calm, cool*
	2.	*adj.*	**fiery, inflamed, impassioned** Her passionate speech excited the crowd.	**2.** *dull, boring, listless*
past	**1.**	*n.*	**history, previous times** Anton is secretive about his past.	**1.** *future*
	2.	*adj.*	**gone by, ended, elapsed** Archaeologists try to find out about times past.	**2.** *forthcoming*
	3.	*adj.*	**former, earlier, previous** She is the past president of the club.	**3.** *future, present*
paste	**1.**	*n.*	**glue, gum, cement, adhesive** Where do you keep the paste?	
	2.	*v.*	**stick, glue, fasten, insert** Paste the labels on the parcel.	**2.** *peel off, remove, cut*
	3.	*v.*	**insert** The ability to cut and to paste text is an excellent word processing tool.	**3.** *cut, delete*
pastime		*n.*	**recreation, amusement, hobby, diversion, play** Fishing is Grandpa's favorite pastime.	*job, labor, occupation, work, profession*
patch	**1.**	*n.*	**plot, lot, piece, tract, area, spot** There is a patch of grass in the front.	
	2.	*v.*	**fix, mend, repair, sew, darn** Alex patched the rip in her skirt.	**2.** *tear, rip, break, damage*
patent	**1.**	*n.*	**right, license, trademark, copyright** The inventor took out a patent on his creation. *v.* He patented his invention.	
	2.	*adj.*	**obvious, evident, apparent, clear, indisputable, open, plain** It was a patent case of bribery.	**2.** *obscure, hidden, ambiguous, questionable*
path		*n.*	**route, way, road, trail, lane** We always take the same path to school.	
pathetic		*adj.*	**miserable, sad, wretched, pitiful, tragic, distressing, moving, poignant** The starving child was a pathetic sight.	*happy, cheerful*
patience		*n.*	**composure, calm, endurance, tolerance** The man lost his patience when told that his suit was still not ready.	*impatience*

patient	1.	*n.*	**invalid, convalescent, sick person**	
			The nurse cared for the patient.	
	2.	*adj.*	**tolerant, long-suffering, easygoing, uncomplaining, accommodating**	*2. impatient, hasty, restless, irritable*
			Fiona is very patient with children.	
			adv. Tina waited patiently for her turn.	
patrol	1.	*n.*	**police, soldiers, scouts, guards**	
			The patrol was on guard for looters.	
	2.	*v.*	**watch, guard, protect, inspect, police**	*2. neglect, ignore*
			Police patrolled the streets after the riots.	
patron	1.	*n.*	**supporter, sponsor, benefactor**	
			The patrons of the museum donated money for its renovation.	
	2.	*n.*	**customer, purchaser, buyer, client**	
			The store keeps its patrons happy with excellent service.	
pause	1.	*n.*	**rest, recess, intermission, interlude**	
			Television programs have many pauses for advertisements.	
	2.	*v.*	**stop, halt, rest, linger, delay**	*2. continue, advance, proceed*
			We paused for a quick lunch.	
pay	1.	*n.*	**salary, earnings, allowance, wages, remuneration, income**	*1. expense, outlay*
			The workers asked for higher pay.	
	2.	*v.*	**reimburse, remunerate, compensate**	
			Mina's new job paid well.	
	3.	*v.*	**give, extend, grant, present**	*3. withhold, retain*
			Pay attention to this announcement.	
peace	1.	*n.*	**calm, quiet, harmony, tranquility, serenity, silence**	*1. uproar, racket, pandemonium, chaos*
			I enjoy the peace of the countryside.	
	2.	*n.*	**armistice, concord, amity**	*2. war, warfare, battle*
			The signing of the treaty ended the war and brought peace to the two nations.	
peaceful	1.	*adj.*	**restful, calm, quiet, serene, tranquil**	*1. noisy, disturbed, restless*
			We spent a peaceful day by the lake.	
	2.	*adj.*	**friendly, agreeable, harmonious**	*2. hostile, bitter, unfriendly*
			The strike was settled in a peaceful way.	
			adv. It was settled peacefully.	
peak	1.	*n.*	**tip, top, pinnacle, summit, crest**	*1. base, bottom, foundation*
			The mountain peak is snow-capped.	
	2.	*n.*	**height, highest level, top, apex**	*2. bottom, lowest level*
			She is at the peak of her career.	
			adj. Airplanes are packed during the peak holiday season.	
peculiar	1.	*adj.*	**odd, unusual, curious, strange, quirky**	*1. usual, common, ordinary, normal*
			The teenager has a peculiar hairstyle.	
	2.	*adj.*	**distinctive, particular, unique**	*2. common, ordinary, universal, global*
			She has a peculiar way of talking.	
			n. We all recognize her peculiarity.	

peek		*v.*	**look, peep, peer, glance** Lionel peeked around the corner. *n.* We saw him take a quick peek.	

peer
1. *n.* **equal, companion, match**
His peers in school encouraged him to work hard.
2. *v.* **stare, gaze, inspect, scrutinize**
The scientist peered through the microscope to study the specimen.

pelt
1. *n.* **skin, hide, fleece**
The hunters sold their beaver pelts.
2. *v.* **beat, strike, hit, knock**
Rain pelted against the windows.

penalty   *n.* **punishment, fine**   *reward, payment*
He was given a penalty for foul play.
v. The referee penalized the player.

penetrate
1. *v.* **puncture, enter, pierce**
A nail penetrated the tire and caused it to go flat.
2. *v.* **seep into, permeate**
Cold air penetrated the room from a crack in the window.
3. *v.* **infiltrate, enter, probe, violate**
Hackers penetrated the computer systems of many businesses.

penetrating
1. *adj.* **sharp, piercing**   *1. soft, gentle, soothing*
A penetrating scream alarmed us.
2. *adj.* **keen, acute, insightful**   *2. insensitive, unaware*
Reiko's penetrating essay on racism inspired many students.

pensive   *adj.* **thoughtful, reflective, dreamy, serious**   *frivolous, carefree*
Jules was in a pensive mood after he received a letter from home.
adv. He stared pensively out the window all day.

people
1. *n.* **humans, human beings, mortals, persons, humanity**
Will people ever learn to live in peace?
2. *n.* **inhabitants, citizens, populace, public**
The people of the city elected a new mayor.
3. *n.* **family, relatives, ancestors, kin**
Patrick's people came from Ireland.

perennial
1. *adj.* **continuing, enduring, constant**   *1. temporary, short-lived, fleeting*
For many people, music is a perennial source of joy.
2. *adj.* **long-lasting, durable, permanent**   *2. annual, yearly*
Perennial plants last for many years.
n. Dandelions are perennials.

perfect
1. *adj.* **faultless, flawless, impeccable**
The student wrote a perfect test.
2. *v.* **accomplish, achieve, fulfill, polish**
She perfected her skating skills through years of practice.
3. *adj.* **entire, absolute, complete**
A good driver has perfect control of the car.
4. *adj.* **exact, strict, precise, accurate**
The soldiers marched in perfect order.
adv. The coat fit perfectly.

1. *imperfect, incorrect*

3. *inadequate, incomplete*
4. *imperfect, haphazard*

perfection
n. **excellence, ideal, precision**
She strives for perfection in everything she does.

perform
1. *v.* **do, accomplish, execute**
Surgeons perform operations.
2. *v.* **act, present, exhibit**
The acrobats performed at the circus.
n. It was a superb performance.
n. The other performers were magicians.

perhaps
adv. **maybe, possibly**
Perhaps it will rain tonight.

definitely, certainly

peril
n. **danger, risk, hazard, menace**
They were warned of the perils of skating on thin ice.
adj. The racers drove at a perilous speed.

safety

perish
v. **die, wither, pass away**
Thousands of people perished in the war.
adj. Perishable foods must be refrigerated.

live, grow, thrive, flourish

permanent
adj. **enduring, lasting, durable, abiding, eternal, everlasting**
The accident left a permanent scar on his arm.
adv. The arm was permanently scarred.

temporary, brief, short-lived, impermanent

permission
n. **consent, approval, authorization**
The pilot was given permission to take off.

refusal, denial

permit
1. *n.* **license, warrant, sanction**
We applied for a building permit to build an extension on the house.
2. *v.* **allow, let, authorize**
I permitted him to use my car.

1. *prohibition, veto, denial*

2. *deny, refuse, prevent, prohibit*

perpendicular
adj. **upright, vertical, steep, sheer**
It was difficult climbing up the perpendicular path.
adv. The path runs perpendicularly to the top of the cliff.

horizontal, level

perpetual
1. *adj.* **everlasting, eternal, endless**
A perpetual flame burns at the grave of John F. Kennedy.

1. *momentary, brief, temporary, transitory*

2. *adj.* **constant, incessant, continual**
The city is a perpetual hive of activity.
adv. They are perpetually striving to help the poor.

2. *temporary, transitory*

perplex *v.* **puzzle, confuse, baffle, bewilder, mystify**
Carlo's strange behavior perplexed us.
adj. The students' perplexed faces told us they had not understood the lesson.

enlighten, explain

persecute *v.* **torment, plague, harass, oppress, abuse, molest**
Some governments persecute people for their religious beliefs.
n. Many people leave their homeland because of religious persecution.

encourage, help, aid, support, endorse

persevere *v.* **persist, endure, continue, keep on**
All the runners persevered to the end of the race.
n. They were applauded for their perseverance.

yield, give up, quit, stop

persist *v.* **stand fast, persevere, continue**
Despite setbacks, she persisted at medical school.
adj. She was the most persistent student in the class.
n. Her persistence was rewarded when she became a doctor.

stop, cease, give up, change, falter, quit

personal *adj.* **private, individual, intimate**
The movie star asked reporters not to pry into her personal affairs.

public

persuade *v.* **convince, influence, urge, coax, induce, cajole, entice**
Hazel persuaded us to go skiing.
n. We agreed to go after some persuasion.

dissuade, discourage, deter

pervade *v.* **fill, penetrate, permeate**
The aroma of baking bread pervaded the house.

perverse *adj.* **contrary, stubborn, willful, obstinate, headstrong, dogged**
She took a perverse delight in being cruel.

agreeable, amiable, obliging

pessimistic *adj.* **gloomy, hopeless, downhearted, glum, discouraging, despairing, cynical**
Tom has a pessimistic view of the future.
n. The pessimist predicted that it would rain on our sports day.
n. There was pessimism about our chances of winning the game.

optimistic, cheerful, hopeful, confident, encouraging

pest	1.	*n.*	**nuisance, annoyance, irritation** All his classmates avoid him because he is such a pest.	1. *help, assistance*
	2.	*n.*	**parasite, vermin, harmful insect** The gardener uses insecticides to control pests.	
pester		*v.*	**vex, bother, annoy, irk, aggravate, irritate, torment, disturb, harass** I was pestered by a cough all winter.	*comfort, help, aid*
petite		*adj.*	**tiny, small, little, wee, dainty** The petite gymnast amazed everyone with her skill.	*large, huge, big, tall, enormous, immense*
petrify	1.	*v.*	**fossilize, harden, solidify** It took millenniums for the trees to petrify in Arizona's Petrified Forest.	
	2.	*v.*	**frighten, terrorize, alarm, scare** The rioting mob petrified the tourists. *adj.* The petrified child stood frozen on the spot.	2. *calm, comfort, soothe*
petty	1.	*adj.*	**mean, narrow-minded, shabby** His petty remarks upset the team. *n.* Pettiness makes others unhappy.	1. *generous, tolerant, broad-minded*
	2.	*adj.*	**small, trivial, insignificant, minor** How could such a petty matter cause a quarrel?	2. *significant, important, major*
petulant		*adj.*	**cross, sulky, grumpy, irritable, sullen, huffy, peevish** Gord was petulant when he couldn't have his way. *adv.* He argued petulantly all night. *n.* His petulance got him nowhere.	*agreeable, cheerful, good-natured, content*
phantom		*n.*	**ghost, apparition, mirage, illusion, vision, specter** Was the figure that he saw in the drifting fog real, or was it a phantom?	
phenomenal		*adj.*	**exceptional, outstanding, amazing, extraordinary, unusual, remarkable, marvelous, incredible, sensational** Nelson Mandela showed phenomenal courage in his fight against apartheid.	*ordinary, common, normal, usual, average*
phenomenon		*n.*	**wonder, marvel, oddity** The Dionne Quintuplets were considered a phenomenon at birth.	
phony		*adj.*	**imitation, fake, counterfeit, false, bogus, forged** The customer tried to pay with a phony hundred-dollar bill. *n.* It was difficult to detect that the bill was a phony.	*legal, real, actual, honest, genuine*

phrase	1.	*n.*	**saying, expression, proverb, maxim, cliche** Who coined the phrase, "Might is right?"	
	2.	*v.*	**express, state, say, put, declare, utter** "I'll phrase the question another way," she suggested.	
pick	1.	*v.*	**select, elect, choose** The class picked Mary as president.	**1.** *reject, refuse*
	2.	*v.*	**gather, harvest, pluck, collect** The workers picked the ripe peaches.	
picture	1.	*n.*	**painting, portrait, illustration** The artist painted a picture of the school.	
	2.	*n.*	**photograph, snapshot, likeness, resemblance, image** This camera takes excellent pictures.	
	3.	*v.*	**describe, illustrate, portray, depict, represent** The media pictured the dictator as a ruthless tyrant.	
	4.	*v.*	**visualize, fantasize, imagine** Marie pictured herself receiving the Nobel Prize.	
picturesque		*adj.*	**scenic, attractive, quaint, charming** We drove through picturesque countryside in Austria.	*unattractive, unsightly, uninteresting*
piece	1.	*n.*	**portion, fragment, share, quantity, part, amount, fraction, segment** Did you get a piece of cake?	**1.** *entirety, whole*
	2.	*n.*	**selection, composition, work, study, creation, article** The orchestra played a piece by Mozart.	
	3.	*v.*	**put together, assemble, combine** The detective pieced together the evidence and solved the mystery.	**3.** *break apart*
pierce		*v.*	**stab, penetrate, perforate, puncture** The doctor pierced my ear with a needle.	
piercing		*adj.*	**shrill, keen, penetrating, strident** Sally's piercing shriek brought everyone running.	*soft, soothing, faint, muffled, calm*
pile	1.	*n.*	**heap, mass, quantity, stack, mound** The children romped in a pile of leaves.	
	2.	*v.*	**stack, collect, load, assemble** Pile the books on the shelf.	**2.** *spread, scatter*
pilfer		*v.*	**steal, embezzle** The cashier pilfered money from the cash register. *n.* She was arrested for the pilferage.	
pilot	1.	*n.*	**aviator, flier** The pilot skillfully landed the plane.	

	2.	*v.*	**steer, direct, guide, lead, handle** Mag piloted the canoe safely through the rapids.	
pinnacle		*n.*	**top, crest, summit, crown, peak** The mountain climbers placed a flag on the pinnacle.	*bottom, foot, depths, base*
pinpoint	1.	*n.*	**dot, spot, speck** The giant plane was now only a pinpoint in the distance.	
	2.	*v.*	**locate, zero in on, detect, identify** Engineers are trying to pinpoint the cause of leaks in the spacecraft.	
pioneer	1.	*n.*	**settler, colonist, immigrant** Pioneers from around the world settled in North America.	
	2.	*v.*	**start, begin, lead** The Americans and the Russians pioneered space exploration.	
piquant		*adj.*	**spicy, sharp, biting, pungent** Indian cuisine is piquant.	*bland, insipid, tasteless, flat*
pirate	1.	*n.*	**buccaneer, marauder, raider** Pirates attacked and looted the ship.	
	2.	*v.*	**copy, imitate, reproduce, plagiarize** The recording company pirated many old songs. *adj.* The store was closed down for selling pirated compact discs.	
pitch	1.	*n.*	**tone, sound** The choir sang off pitch.	
	2.	*n.*	**tar, asphalt** Black pitch is very sticky.	
	3.	*v.*	**hurl, throw, toss, fling, sling** Tom pitched the ball at the batter. *n.* Tom is a good pitcher.	*3. catch*
	4.	*v.*	**erect, set up, place, fix, raise, hoist** We pitched our tents near the lake.	*4. take down, disassemble*
pitcher		*n.*	**container, jug, jar** Where is the milk pitcher?	
pitiful	1.	*adj.*	**sad, sorry, pathetic, wretched, miserable, piteous, moving** The wet puppy was a pitiful sight. *adv.* It howled pitifully.	*1. cheerful, happy, contented, noble, joyful*
	2.	*adj.*	**small, meager, scanty, paltry** The appeal raised only a pitiful sum of money for the refugees.	*2. plentiful, abundant, large*
pity	1.	*n.*	**mercy, compassion, sympathy** The starving children aroused our pity.	*1. cruelty, harshness*
	2.	*v.*	**feel sorry for, sympathize with** We pitied the animals in the small cage.	*2. disdain, scorn*

place	1.	*n.*	**region, spot, location, site, space**
			Can we find a better place for our tent?
	2.	*n.*	**shop, store, business, restaurant**
			That place serves good food.
	3.	*v.*	**lay, deposit, set, arrange, put**
			Who placed the dishes that way?

placid

1. *adj.* **calm, even-tempered, docile, steady, composed**
Her placid nature makes her a wonderful babysitter.
1. excitable, restless, temperamental, agitated

2. *adj.* **peaceful, restful, serene, tranquil**
The boat drifted on the placid river.
2. rough, turbulent, stormy

plague

1. *n.* **epidemic, contagion, disease, affliction**
A cholera plague killed many people.

2. *v.* **bother, annoy, torment, worry, pester, trouble, irk**
Mosquitoes plagued us at the cottage.
2. please, leave alone, satisfy

plain

1. *n.* **level land, prairie, grassland**
Buffalo used to live on the plains of North America.

2. *adj.* **obvious, clear, evident**
It was plain to everyone that he was ill.
2. obscure

3. *adj.* **simple, clear, distinct, direct**
Use plain English so we can understand.
adv. Speak plainly, please.
3. complicated, difficult, indistinct, obscure

4. *adj.* **ordinary, homely, simple, modest**
She wore plain but comfortable clothes.
4. fancy, ornate, intricate, frilly

plaintive

adj. **mournful, sad, doleful, melancholy**
The plaintive sound of a violin filled the air.
adv. The puppy howled plaintively all night.
merry, cheerful, happy, bright

plan

1. *n.* **program, course, design, scheme, arrangement, formula, method**
Our club meetings follow a regular plan.
v. We plan our projects together.

2. *n.* **scheme, project, strategy, blueprint**
The government announced a new plan to improve education.

3. *n.* **map, chart, design, drawings, diagram**
These are the plans for our new house.

4. *v.* **intend, aim, propose**
We plan to leave early tomorrow.

plant

1. *n.* **shrub, tree, bush, weed, seedling**
Young plants need much water.

2. *n.* **factory, shop, mill, business**
Dad works at an automobile plant.

3. *v.* **sow, deposit, seed**
Who planted the pumpkin seeds?
3. remove, uproot, dig out

4. *v.* **place, put, establish, infiltrate**
The secret service planted a spy in the organization.
4. remove, take away

plaque   *n.*   **plate, disc, slab, tablet**
A plaque on the wall tells the history of the building.

plastic   1. *n.*   **synthetic compound, moldable substance, pliable material**
The mug is made of plastic.
adj.   We used plastic cups for the party.
2. *adj.*   **pliable, yielding, soft, pliant, moldable**   *2. hard, stiff, rigid*
Clay and dough are plastic materials.

plateau   1. *n.*   **highland, level region, elevation, mesa, tableland**   *1. valley, ravine, lowland*
Our camp was on a small plateau overlooking the valley.
2. *n.*   **stable level**
House prices reached a plateau last year.

plausible   *adj.*   **likely, probable, sound, reasonable, logical, sensible, believable, valid**   *unlikely, unreasonable, improbable*
That isn't a plausible explanation for your absence.

play   1. *n.*   **drama, show, theatrical production**
Shakespeare wrote many plays.
2. *v.*   **act, perform**
Peter played the piano at the concert.
n.   He is a good player.
3. *v.*   **frolic, make merry, romp**   *3. work, toil, labor*
The children rushed out to play at recess.
n.   All work and no play makes one dull.

playful   *adj.*   **frisky, frolicsome, jolly, lively**   *serious, earnest, sad, sedate*
The playful child would not sit still.
adv.   The puppy playfully nipped Rani's ankles.

plea   *n.*   **appeal, request, entreaty, petition**
The lawyer entered a plea of "not guilty" for his client.
v.   The accused pleaded his innocence in court.

plead   *v.*   **beg, implore, beseech**
Tanya pleaded for permission to go to the rock concert.

pleasant   *adj.*   **agreeable, cheerful, delightful, lovely, enchanting, enjoyable**   *unpleasant, dreary, disagreeable, obnoxious*
We spent a pleasant week at the cottage.

please   1. *v.*   **satisfy, suit, delight, enchant, cheer, gladden, content, gratify**   *1. displease, offend, anger*
It pleases me to help others.
2. *v.*   **want, will, choose, wish, desire, like, prefer**
You are free to do as you please.

pleasing		*adj.*	**pleasant, agreeable, inviting** Pleasing aromas drifted from the kitchen.	*unpleasant,* *disagreeable*
pleasure		*n.*	**joy, delight, thrill, satisfaction,** **enjoyment, happiness** Music gives pleasure to many people.	*pain, sorrow,* *displeasure*
pledge	1.	*n.*	**promise, agreement, vow, oath** The new citizens made a pledge of allegiance to the country.	
	2.	*v.*	**promise, assure, vow, swear** I pledge my loyalty to this country.	
plentiful		*adj.*	**large, abundant, ample** We had a plentiful harvest this year.	*insufficient, scarce,* *sparse, scant, small*
plenty		*n.*	**ample amount, abundance** We have plenty to do before we leave.	*scarcity, lack,* *shortage*
pliable	1.	*adj.*	**plastic, flexible, supple, pliant, limber** Soaking reed and cane makes them pliable for weaving.	**1.** *stiff, rigid*
	2.	*adj.*	**easily persuaded, easily influenced** He is too pliable to be an effective leader.	**2.** *firm, obstinate*
plight		*n.*	**condition, state, dilemma, distress,** **difficulty, predicament** The government is trying to improve the plight of the homeless.	
plot	1.	*n.*	**scheme, conspiracy, plan, stratagem** The police uncovered a plot to kidnap the President. *v.* The suspects had carefully plotted the kidnapping.	
	2.	*n.*	**structure, design, development, story** This book has an interesting plot.	
	3.	*n.*	**land, lot, field, tract** Are they building on this plot?	
	4.	*v.*	**draw, map, chart, mark** The travelers plotted their route before setting off.	
ploy		*n.*	**maneuver, move, stratagem, trick** That clever ploy won him the chess game.	
plucky		*adj.*	**brave, daring, courageous** The plucky girl rescued the two children from the fire.	*cowardly, timid*
plump		*adj.*	**stout, chubby, fat, obese, rotund** The plump child should exercise more.	*lean, thin, scrawny,* *skinny, slender*
plunder	1.	*n.*	**stolen goods, loot, booty** Rioters broke into stores and took off with their plunder.	
	2.	*v.*	**rob, loot, steal, raid** Pirates plundered many ships.	

plunge	1.	*v.*	**thrust, drive, force** The cook plunged the knife into the roast.	1. *withdraw, remove*
	2.	*v.*	**dip, submerge, dive, leap into** The divers plunged into the pool. *n.* We took a plunge in the lake to cool off.	2. *emerge*
plus	1.	*n.*	**benefit, boon, advantage** Some people consider it a plus to live close to the subway line.	1. *disadvantage, handicap*
	2.	*prep.*	**added to** Three plus four equals seven.	2. *minus, less, subtracted from*
poetry		*n.*	**verse, rhyme, poem, song** Good poetry can lift the spirits.	*prose*
point	1.	*n.*	**nib, tip, end** Who broke the point of your pen?	
	2.	*n.*	**spot, place, dot, location, position** Find the right point on the map for San Francisco.	
	3.	*n.*	**detail, feature, item, aspect** Don't overlook this important point in your answer.	
	4.	*n.*	**purpose, reason** What's the point of buying it if you don't need it?	
	5.	*v.*	**aim, level, direct** Bill pointed his gun at the target.	
	6.	*v.*	**show, indicate, steer, guide** The child pointed the way to the principal's office.	
pointed	1.	*adj.*	**sharp, pronged** Use a pointed stick to hold the marshmallows over the fire.	1. *blunt, dull*
	2.	*adj.*	**barbed, biting, sarcastic, hurtful** Her pointed remarks hurt her friends.	2. *bland, gentle*
pointless		*adj.*	**meaningless, useless** It is pointless to attend school and not do your homework.	*meaningful, useful*
poise	1.	*n.*	**assurance, self-confidence, calm, composure** The child star showed poise during the press conference. *adv.* He remained poised throughout the interview.	1. *insecurity, bewilderment*
	2.	*v.*	**balance, brace** Steve poised himself on the diving board before diving.	
poison	1.	*n.*	**toxic chemical, toxin, venom, harmful drug** Poisons should be kept out of the reach of children. *adj.* Many insecticides and weed killers are poisonous to humans.	1. *antidote*

	2.	*v.*	**pollute, taint, contaminate** Industrial waste has poisoned our waters.	**2.** *purify, cleanse, refresh*
poke	1.	*n.*	**thrust, jab, punch, hit, push** Someone gave him a poke from behind and he fell over.	
	2.	*v.*	**jab, nudge, jostle, prod** I poked her in the side to wake her up.	
pokey		*adj.*	**slow, dull** A pokey old horse pulled our wagon.	*speedy, agile*
police	1.	*n.*	**police officer, constable, sheriff** The police rushed to the scene of the robbery.	
	2.	*v.*	**patrol, guard, monitor, supervise** Soldiers policed the streets after the riots.	
polish	1.	*n.*	**gloss, shine, glaze, finish, wax** Apply the polish to your shoes.	
	2.	*v.*	**buff, rub, shine** Polish the silver before the party.	**2.** *tarnish, dull*
polite		*adj.*	**courteous, well-mannered, refined** The polite girl offered her seat to the old man. *n.* He appreciated her politeness.	*impolite, rude, boorish, insulting, discourteous*
poll	1.	*n.*	**census, count, survey, referendum** A poll was taken to find out how many people supported the new bill.	
	2.	*n.*	**voting place, vote, tally, returns** The polls for the election open at eight o'clock.	
	3.	*v.*	**canvass, survey, question** The company polled its employees about working on Sundays.	
pollute		*v.*	**contaminate, taint, infect, dirty, defile** The waste from the plant pollutes the lake. *adj.* Fish are dying in the polluted lakes. *n.* Laws are being passed to stop environmental pollution.	*cleanse, purify, refresh*
pomp		*n.*	**ceremony, splendor, grandeur, magnificence, pageantry** The graduation ceremony was conducted with pomp.	
pompous		*adj.*	**affected, grandiose, haughty, showy, arrogant, pretentious** The media poked fun at his pompous manners.	*modest, simple*
ponder		*v.*	**think over, study, consider, reflect on, examine, deliberate** We pondered over the problem all day.	*ignore, forget, overlook, bypass*

poor	1.	*adj.*	**impoverished, destitute, needy, broke** The scholarship is designed to help children from poor families. *n.* We raised money to help the poor.	*1. rich, wealthy, affluent, well-to-do*
	2.	*adj.*	**bad, inferior, deficient** Su-min was told to work hard to improve his poor marks.	*2. superior, fine, excellent*
	3.	*adj.*	**unfortunate, pitiful** Those poor children lost their parents in an automobile accident.	*3. fortunate, lucky*
popular		*adj.*	**admired, well-liked, in demand** Betty is a popular student. *n.* Her popularity has not made her conceited.	*unpopular, offensive, disliked*
populate		*v.*	**inhabit, live in, settle** Hardy immigrants populated the prairies in the 19th century. *adj.* The cities are usually the most heavily populated areas.	*desert, vacate, abandon*
population		*n.*	**inhabitants, citizenry, residents** The world population grows at a tremendous rate.	
porous		*adj.*	**absorbent, permeable** The spill was quickly absorbed by the porous paper towel.	*non-porous*
portable		*adj.*	**transportable, handy, movable** Laptop computers are portable.	*fixed, immovable, stationary*
portion		*n.*	**piece, fragment, fraction, share, slice, segment, section** Save me a portion of the cake.	*all, whole, total*
position	1.	*n.*	**spot, site, location, place** Show me the exact position of the village on the map. *v.* We positioned ourselves in front of the window to watch the parade.	
	2.	*n.*	**job, situation, office, rank, post, role** I hold a good position in this company.	
	3.	*n.*	**opinion, viewpoint, perspective** What is your position on this matter?	
positive	1.	*adj.*	**absolute, confident, assured, definite, certain, firm, sure** Are you positive you saw him?	*1. doubtful, uncertain, unsure, vague, indefinite*
	2.	*adj.*	**optimistic, progressive, cooperative** The coach encouraged us to be positive. *adv.* "Think positively," he said.	*2. negative, pessimistic, dubious*
possess	1.	*v.*	**have, own** The family possesses many books. *n.* They lost all their possessions when their house burnt down.	*1. relinquish, give up, lose*

2. *v.* **occupy, control, acquire, seize**
Enemy forces possessed the town after a day of fighting.

possible *adj.* **likely, probable, conceivable**
There are three possible answers to the question.
n. There is a possibility of rain today.
adv. You possibly could be right.

impossible, unlikely, unthinkable

post **1.** *n.* **pole, support, beam, prop**
Do not lean on the post.
2. *n.* **place, position, job, office**
Rita was elected to the post of chairperson.
3. *n.* **mail, postal service**
Please send this by express post.
v. I posted the letter yesterday.
4. *v.* **place, display, put**
I posted the announcement on my website.

4. conceal, remove, edit

poster *n.* **placard, bill, handbill**
Election campaign posters were displayed around the school.

postpone *v.* **delay, put off, defer, shelve, suspend**
Fred postponed the meeting for a week.
n. He informed the committee members of the postponement.

move ahead, hasten, expedite

potent *adj.* **strong, forceful, powerful, influential**
Television is a potent force in our lives.

impotent, weak, ineffective, mild

potential **1.** *adj.* **ability, possibility, capability**
Min has potential for success in music.
2. *adj.* **possible, concealed, likely, probable**
Are you aware of the many potential dangers in riding a motorcycle?

2. actual, real

pound **1.** *n.* **trap, enclosure, cage, pen**
The stray dog was put in the pound.
2. *v.* **strike, hammer, beat, thump, hit, batter**
The worker pounded the metal into the required shape.

poverty *n.* **want, destitution, need, penury**
Some people live in utter poverty.

luxury, wealth, riches, affluence, prosperity

power **1.** *n.* **force, energy**
Some submarines use nuclear power.
2. *n.* **authority, control, influence, right**
The government has the power to declare holidays.
3. *n.* **strength, might, vigor, brawn**
He has amazing power in his hands.
adj. The singer has a powerful voice.

3. weakness

practical	*adj.*	**efficient, sensible, workable, effective** Harry has many practical ideas about helping the homeless.	*impractical, ineffective, unsound*
practically	*adv.*	**almost, nearly, essentially, virtually** We were practically home when the car broke down.	
practice	1. *n.*	**habit, custom, routine, tradition** It is our practice to eat out on Sundays.	
	2. *n.*	**drill, preparation, rehearsal, training** Keep up your practice if you wish to excel.	
	3. *n.*	**business, profession** Dr. Lee has a busy practice.	
	4. *v.*	**rehearse, train, drill, prepare** Musicians practice every day.	
	5. *v.*	**work at, employ oneself in** Tasha practices law.	
practiced	*adj.*	**experienced, trained, skilled** Jill is a practiced dancer.	*inexperienced, untrained, unskilled*
praise	1. *n.*	**acclaim, commendation, approval, appreciation, applause, ovation** Glenn received praise for his work.	**1.** *contempt, scorn, disapproval, blame*
	2. *v.*	**acclaim, applaud, cheer, compliment** Everyone praised the firefighters for their bravery.	**2.** *scold, blame, criticize*
precarious	*adj.*	**risky, hazardous, insecure, dangerous** The worker was cleaning windows at a precarious height. *adv.* He was perched precariously on the ramp.	*safe, secure*
precaution	*n.*	**safeguard, protection, provision, security, safety, care, measure** Every precaution was taken to ensure the children's safety.	*carelessness*
precede	*v.*	**lead, go before** The band preceded the majorettes in the parade.	*follow, come after*
preceding	*adj.*	**previous, earlier, prior, former** Reread the preceding paragraph.	*following, later, succeeding*
precious	*adj.*	**valuable, costly, priceless, treasured** Precious gems should be insured against theft and loss.	*worthless, cheap, trashy, common*
precipitation	*n.*	**condensation, rain, snow, hail** The weather forecast calls for some precipitation today.	
precise	*adj.*	**accurate, exact, specific, correct** Scientists work with precise data. *n.* Everything is calculated with precision.	*inaccurate, erratic, incorrect, inexact, vague*

predict	*v.*	**anticipate, forecast, foretell, prophesy** I predict our team will win tomorrow.	
predominant	*adj.*	**major, chief, main, leading, supreme, principal, prevalent** The predominant reason for his success is hard work.	*minor, unimportant, secondary*
preface	1. *n.*	**introduction, foreword, prelude** The preface of a book helps people to understand it.	**1.** *appendix, addendum, epilogue, postscript*
	2. *v.*	**precede, introduce, start, usher** The principal prefaced her speech with a welcome to the parents.	**2.** *follow, end, conclude*
prefer	*v.*	**choose, select, fancy, favor** Luke prefers pizza to salad. *n.* Mom's preference was a salad. *adj.* Is steak preferable to a roast?	
prejudice	1. *n.*	**bias, intolerance, discrimination** Avoid prejudice in judging others.	**1.** *impartiality, fairness, tolerance*
	2. *v.*	**sway, bias, influence** The critical review prejudiced my opinion of the movie.	
preliminary	*adj.*	**introductory, preparatory** The preliminary races will be run a day before the finals.	*final, concluding*
preoccupied	*adj.*	**engrossed, inattentive, absent-minded, lost in thought** Dad seemed preoccupied at supper.	*attentive, alert*
preparation	*n.*	**arrangement, precaution, groundwork, rehearsal** The crew underwent intensive preparations for the space flight.	
preparatory	*adj.*	**introductory, preliminary** The council made a preparatory plan for the building.	*final, concluding*
prepare	*v.*	**arrange, provide, get ready, fix** Dan prepared a delicious dinner for us.	
preposterous	*adj.*	**absurd, ridiculous, outrageous, unreasonable, silly** Do you expect me to believe that preposterous story about a talking dog?	*reasonable, believable, sensible*
prerequisite	1. *n.*	**qualification, need, necessity, requirement, demand, condition** A pass in Level I is a prerequisite for the Level II course.	**1.** *option*
	2. *adj.*	**required, essential, necessary** The prerequisite deposit for the purchase of the land has been paid.	**2.** *unessential, optional*

presence		*n.*	**attendance, existence, being** Is your presence at school checked daily?	*absence*
present	1.	*n.*	**gift, donation, award** She received many farewell presents.	
	2.	*n.*	**today, now, nowadays** We are too busy at present to take on another project.	**2.** *past, future,* *yesterday,* *bygone days*
	3.	*adj.*	**current, contemporary, existing** The present generation is concerned about preserving the environment for future generations.	**3.** *past, future*
present	1.	*v.*	**give, offer, award, proffer** David presented flowers to the soloist after the concert.	**1.** *receive, obtain, get*
	2.	*v.*	**exhibit, display, act, perform** The group presented a concert to raise money for the homeless.	
presently	1.	*adv.*	**soon, shortly, before long** The train will arrive presently.	
	2.	*adv.*	**currently, now** They are presently on holiday.	
preserve	1.	*n.*	**shelter, sanctuary, refuge** National parks are preserves for wildlife.	
	2.	*n.*	**jam, jelly, conserve** Doug makes delicious preserves.	
	3.	*v.*	**protect, guard, keep, conserve, save,** **maintain** Measures have been taken to preserve wildlife. *n.* The preservation of our natural resources is of great importance.	**3.** *destroy, spoil, kill,* *exterminate*
press	1.	*n.*	**news media, journalists, reporters,** **newspapers** The scientists announced their discovery to the press.	
	2.	*v.*	**squeeze, crush, compress** We press fruit to get the juice.	
	3.	*v.*	**iron, smooth, flatten** Bill pressed his trousers for the dance.	**3.** *wrinkle, crease*
	4.	*v.*	**hurry, hasten, rush, push on** "Press on," said the leader.	**4.** *slow down, delay*
	5.	*v.*	**urge, encourage, implore, force** Tony's friends pressed him to stay longer.	**5.** *discourage, check,* *restrain, prevent*
pressing		*adj.*	**urgent, important, demanding** A pressing matter at work forced her to miss the party.	*unimportant, trivial*
pressure	1.	*n.*	**strain, tension, stress** Some athletes don't perform well under pressure.	**1.** *release, relief*

	2.	*v.*	**force, compel, press, coerce** The salesperson pressured the customer into buying the car.	**2.** *discourage*
prestige		*n.*	**fame, distinction, importance, note, reputation, esteem** Glenn Gould was a pianist of international prestige.	*obscurity*
presume		*v.*	**assume, suppose, surmise** The law presumes everyone is innocent until proven guilty. *n.* My presumption that Jordan would do well proved correct.	*doubt, distrust*
pretend	**1.**	*v.*	**imagine, fancy, suppose, make-believe** Jay pretended he was an astronaut.	*reality, fact*
	2.	*v.*	**fake, sham, feign, affect, hoodwink** She pretended she was sick to gain our sympathy.	
pretense		*n.*	**hoax, invention, make-believe, trick, deception, fabrication** Her illness was only a pretense.	
pretentious		*adj.*	**showy, ostentatious, ornate, garish, gaudy, overdone** The star lives in a pretentious home.	*modest, plain, simple*
pretty	**1.**	*adj.*	**attractive, lovely, beautiful, pleasing** Shirley Temple was a pretty child actress.	**1.** *homely, ugly, plain, unattractive*
	2.	*adv.*	**moderately, fairly, rather** The debate went pretty well.	**2.** *extremely, exceptionally*
prevalent		*adj.*	**frequent, common, general, abundant** Mosquitoes and black-flies are prevalent during the summer.	*rare, unusual, uncommon, infrequent*
prevent		*v.*	**obstruct, stop, hinder, prohibit** A storm prevented the plane from landing.	*aid, assist, permit, allow, help, encourage*
prevention		*n.*	**restraint, hindrance, inhibition** Vaccination is prevention against measles.	*assistance, encouragement*
previous		*adj.*	**earlier, prior, former, foregoing** I did better on a previous test than on this one.	*later, subsequent, following*
price		*n.*	**cost, expenditure, rate, charge, value, expense, outlay** The price of the car is too high for me.	
priceless		*adj.*	**rare, prized, valuable, precious, costly, invaluable** There are priceless antiques at the show.	*worthless, cheap, inexpensive, common*

primary	1.	*adj.*	**elementary, first, beginning, introductory** The primary school children leave first.	1. *secondary, later*
	2.	*adj.*	**basic, principal, main, chief, essential, most important, central** The primary aim here is to learn to speak French.	2. *lesser, unimportant*
prime	1.	*n.*	**peak, best time, best part** The athlete was in the prime of her career when she was injured.	1. *decline*
	2.	*adj.*	**superior, first-class, splendid, superb, first-rate, choice** Nick's old car is still in prime condition.	2. *poor, inferior, second-rate*
	3.	*adj.*	**chief, main, first, primary** The prime reason for the team's success is its excellent coach.	3. *secondary, unimportant*
primitive	1.	*adj.*	**beginning, early, first, original, primary, fundamental** Plans for commercial space journeys are still in the primitive stage.	1. *advanced, latter*
	2.	*adj.*	**crude, simple, rough, rude** Living conditions at the hunting camp are quite primitive.	2. *developed, sophisticated*
principal	1.	*n.*	**headmistress, headmaster, leader, chief, administrator** The school principal is admired for her leadership and understanding.	
	2.	*adj.*	**leading, main, foremost, most important, paramount** Who has the principal part in the play?	2. *minor, small, trivial, peripheral*
principle		*n.*	**regulation, rule, law, truth** We follow certain principles in scientific research.	
prior		*adj.*	**earlier, previous, former** A prior engagement prevented the speaker from coming here.	*following, later*
prisoner		*n.*	**captive, convict, hostage** The prisoner served his full sentence.	
private	1.	*adj.*	**remote, isolated, secluded** Jan prefers to read in a private place.	1. *crowded, busy, populated*
	2.	*adj.*	**secret, confidential, personal** Please do not pry into my private diary.	2. *public, open*
privilege		*n.*	**advantage, right, benefit, favor** Club membership entitles you to many privileges.	
prize	1.	*n.*	**reward, award, trophy** Jon won first prize for public speaking.	1. *penalty, punishment*
	2.	*v.*	**value, cherish, treasure, love** Tracy prizes her swimming awards.	2. *abhor, dislike*

probable		*adj.*	**likely, reasonable, possible** It is probable there will be snow today. *n.* There is a probability of snow today. *adv.* The snowfall probably will be heavy.	*improbable, unlikely, impossible*
problem	1.	*n.*	**puzzle, riddle, question** The problem was easily solved.	**1.** *answer, solution*
	2.	*n.*	**difficulty, trouble** Mita has lots of problems in school. *adj.* The problem child is getting special assistance.	
procedure		*n.*	**method, process, plan, system** The procedure must be followed exactly if the experiment is to work.	
proceed		*v.*	**advance, progress, continue** Finish the first book before you proceed to the next one.	*retreat, retire*
proceeds		*n.*	**yield, income, returns, gain, profit** All proceeds from the cookie sales will go to charity.	*expenses, costs*
process	1.	*n.*	**method, plan, scheme, project, system** Please explain the printing process.	
	2.	*n.*	**evolution, development, experience** Building a house is a long process.	
	3.	*v.*	**prepare, preserve, treat, dry, can, dehydrate** Chemicals are used to process foods.	
	4.	*v.*	**deal with, fill, ship, handle** The order clerk processed our book order.	
proclaim		*v.*	**announce, declare, inform, tell** The rebel leader proclaimed himself the new president of the republic. *n.* The proclamation was announced over television and radio.	*retract, cancel*
procure		*v.*	**secure, pick up, gather, win, gain, get, acquire, obtain** The candidate procured votes by making grand promises.	*lose, squander, waste, spend*
prod		*v.*	**stimulate, move, urge, drive, spur, prompt, encourage** The coach prodded the team to make a greater effort.	*discourage, hinder*
produce		*n.*	**yield, fruits and vegetables, products** Produce from our farm is sold at the market.	
produce		*v.*	**make, create, cause, originate** Leonardo da Vinci produced many great masterpieces.	*destroy, demolish*

producer	1.	*n.*	**creator, originator** The producer of the movie accepted the award for Best Film of the Year. *n.* The movie was an excellent production.	
	2.	*n.*	**grower, breeder** Fruit growers in the California are the producers of fine apples.	
product		*n.*	**result, effect, consequence** Success is the product of hard work.	*cause, origin*
productive		*adj.*	**rich, fruitful, luxuriant, prolific, fertile** Good climate has made this a productive area for farming.	*barren, poor, unproductive*
profession		*n.*	**occupation, career, calling, business, field, vocation** She is a journalist by profession. *adj.* Professional athletes can now compete in the Olympic Games.	
proficient		*adj.*	**confident, skillful, expert, able** Kelly is a proficient pianist. *adv.* He plays the piano proficiently. *n.* Proficiency comes with practice.	*incapable, incompetent, unskilled*
profile	1.	*n.*	**side view, silhouette, outline, shape** A profile of George Washington appears on our coins.	1. *full face*
	2.	*n.*	**biography, character sketch, summary** A profile of the student was included in her university application.	
profit		*n.*	**return, proceeds, gain, benefit, yield** The company made good profits this year. *v.* We all profited from the deal.	*loss*
profitable	1.	*adj.*	**lucrative, money-making, fruitful** Our club had a profitable bake sale.	1. *unprofitable*
	2.	*adj.*	**beneficial, enriching, rewarding** The training session was a profitable experience for all of us.	2. *unrewarding*
profound	1.	*adj.*	**deeply felt, great, intense, heartfelt** Sam sent his profound apologies for forgetting our date.	1. *light, shallow*
	2.	*adj.*	**wise, shrewd, penetrating, intellectual** Einstein was a profound thinker.	2. *simple, shallow, superficial, flighty*
profuse		*adj.*	**lavish, ample, generous, plentiful, abundant, bountiful** There is a profuse growth of ferns in the woods. *n.* It was difficult to walk through the profusion of ferns in the woods. *adv.* We thanked our hosts profusely.	*scanty, sparse, meager*

program	1.	*n.*	**outline, schedule, plan, agenda, design** The program for the concert looks good.	
	2.	*n.*	**concert, performance, presentation, show** Acrobats were included in the program.	
	3.	*v.*	**arrange, direct, control, instruct** The technician programmed the computer. *n.* The computer program searched through the entire database in seconds.	
progress	1.	*n.*	**advancement, development, improvement, growth, headway** Todd shows much progress in his writing.	**1.** *decline, decrease, recession, stay, relapse, stoppage*
	2.	*v.*	**advance, proceed, gain, develop** Su-Lin is progressing well at school.	**2.** *retreat, regress*
progressive	1.	*adj.*	**mounting, increasing, rising, advancing, continuing, accelerating** The chart showed progressive improvement in sales.	**1.** *decreasing, deteriorating, declining*
	2.	*adj.*	**modern, up-to-date, forward, advanced** Our leader has many progressive ideas.	**2.** *backward, old-fashioned, outdated*
prohibit		*v.*	**forbid, deny, ban, prevent** The law prohibits drinking and driving.	*permit, allow, let, tolerate*
project		*n.*	**plan, design, enterprise, task, scheme, undertaking** Our science projects are well displayed.	
project	1.	*v.*	**overhang, extend, jut out, protrude** The roof projects beyond the walls.	**1.** *withdraw*
	2.	*v.*	**throw, shoot, hurl, thrust, fire, fling, discharge, eject, propel, launch** Jet propulsion projects missiles into space. *n.* Projectiles may be fired from submarines.	**2.** *catch, receive*
prolific	1.	*adj.*	**fertile, fruitful, productive** Rabbits are prolific animals.	**1.** *barren, unproductive*
	2.	*adj.*	**creative, very productive** Agatha Christie was a prolific writer.	**2.** *unproductive*
prolong		*v.*	**lengthen, stretch, continue, extend** Heated debate on the dumpsite prolonged the meeting into the night. *adj.* The councilors were exhausted after the prolonged debate.	*shorten, reduce, limit, lessen*
prominent	1.	*adj.*	**famous, outstanding, notable, distinguished, well-known** Several prominent writers were at the conference.	**1.** *unknown, obscure, minor, secondary*
	2.	*adj.*	**conspicuous, noticeable** The award was displayed in a prominent place in the school. *adv.* It was prominently displayed.	**2.** *inconspicuous, obscure*

promise	1.	*n.*	**pledge, vow, guarantee, pact** One should never break a promise. *v.* Dad promised to take us skiing today.	
	2.	*n.*	**hope, expectation, indication** The child shows promise of being an outstanding musician.	
promising		*adj.*	**favorable, budding, encouraging** She has a promising future in music.	*discouraging, unfavorable*
promote	1.	*v.*	**advance, upgrade** The company promoted Hugo to manager. *n.* His promotion was well-deserved.	*1. demote, reduce, downgrade*
	2.	*v.*	**advance, encourage, help, assist, aid, further, sponsor, support** The organization promotes the preservation of the environment.	*2. hinder, deter, discourage, check*
prompt	1.	*v.*	**encourage, prod, inspire, spur, motivate, provoke** What prompted him to quit school?	*1. discourage, deter*
	2.	*v.*	**help, assist, advise, aid, cue** The audience was told not to prompt the contestant.	*2. hinder*
	3.	*adj.*	**punctual, ready, swift, quick** Customers appreciate prompt service. *adv.* Answer this letter promptly.	*3. slow, late, negligent, lax*
prone	1.	*adj.*	**inclined, liable, apt, predisposed** Alvin is prone to accidents.	*1. disinclined, unaccustomed*
	2.	*adj.*	**face down, horizontal, prostrate** The child was lying prone in bed, sound asleep.	*2. face up, erect, vertical, upright*
pronounce	1.	*v.*	**articulate, speak, say, utter, state, voice, vocalize** Actors must pronounce their words clearly.	*1. mispronounce, mutter, mumble*
	2.	*v.*	**proclaim, declare, assert** The judge pronounced the defendant guilty as charged.	
pronounced		*adj.*	**conspicuous, evident, obvious, marked, noticeable, striking** Everyone commented on Tasha's pronounced weight loss.	*unnoticeable, slight, insignificant*
proof		*n.*	**evidence, verification, confirmation** The car rental company asked Lin for proof of her identity.	
prop	1.	*n.*	**support, reinforcement, brace, buttress** Props kept the roof from collapsing. *v.* The workers propped the roof with beams and braces.	
	2.	*v.*	**stand, lean, rest, set, place** The painters propped their ladders against the wall.	

propel	*v.*	**launch, push, thrust forward, drive, project, force ahead** Rockets propelled the spaceship into space.	*repel, hold*
proper	1. *adj.*	**correct, suitable, fitting, right** Wear proper shoes when jogging. *adv.* Dress properly for the cold.	**1.** *improper, incorrect, unsuitable*
	2. *adj.*	**customary, conventional, standard, accepted, respectable, appropriate** Proper table manners are expected at mealtime.	**2.** *improper, unconventional, unacceptable*
property	1. *n.*	**land, lot, holdings, real estate, realty, grounds, buildings** Dad hired an agent to take care of the family property in Florida.	
	2. *n.*	**possessions, assets, belongings, resources** Personal property can be insured against theft or fire.	
	3. *n.*	**quality, characteristic, attribute, trait** The foal has all the properties of a champion.	
proportion	*n.*	**part, share, ration, dimension, size, measurement, extent** A large proportion of the students will be going on to university.	
proposal	*n.*	**suggestion, recommendation, offer, proposition** The town rejected a proposal to build a large nuclear plant in the area.	*rejection*
propose	*v.*	**suggest, put forward, offer, present, submit, recommend, tender** The students proposed a new system for choosing prefects. *n.* The class voted on the proposition.	*oppose, protest, reject*
prospect	1. *n.*	**outlook, hope, chance, likelihood** What are the prospects for getting out early today?	
	2. *n.*	**view, picture, spectacle, scene, sight, outlook, panorama, vista** There is a good prospect of the town from that hill.	
	3. *n.*	**expectation, hope, proposal, promise, anticipation** The children were excited at the prospect of visiting the Grand Canyon.	
prosper	*v.*	**succeed, thrive, grow, gain, flourish, progress** Japan prospered after World War II.	*fail, decline, deteriorate*

prosperity	*n.*	**abundance, success, affluence** Dad's business has enjoyed prosperity for many years. *adj.* We hope for a prosperous future.	*failure, misfortune, adversity*
protect	*v.*	**shield, guard, preserve, care for, keep, defend, shelter** The bear protected its cub from the hunter.	*attack, expose, betray, mistreat, abandon, forsake, imperil*
protection	*n.*	**care, shelter, defense, security** The frightened people asked for police protection. *adj.* Animals are protective of their young.	*exposure, danger*
protest	*v.*	**complain, object, disagree, oppose** The captain protested the umpire's decision. *n.* He later wrote an official protest.	*agree, assent, consent*
proud	1. *adj.*	**conceited, vain, arrogant, boastful, haughty, imperious** The proud president was defeated in the election. *n.* His pride was one cause of his downfall.	*1. humble, modest, meek, lowly*
	2. *adj.*	**self-satisfied, pleased, appreciative** We are proud of our school.	*2. ashamed, embarrassed*
prove	*v.*	**verify, confirm, justify, support, demonstrate, show, substantiate** Shen proved his skill in writing by winning the essay competition. *n.* His victory was proof of his ability.	*disprove, contradict, refute, invalidate*
provide	*v.*	**supply, give, contribute, donate, allot** We provided aid for the flood victims. *n.* The victims were grateful for the provision of aid.	*withhold, refuse, deprive, deny, take away*
provoke	1. *v.*	**arouse, incite, induce, spark, stimulate** The movie provoked lots of excitement. *n.* Manuel loses his temper at the slightest provocation.	*1. calm, soothe, pacify*
	2. *v.*	**irritate, enrage, anger, vex, infuriate, annoy, exasperate, incense** Vic provoked us by being late again.	*2. please, satisfy*
prowl	*v.*	**rove, roam, wander, slink, lurk** Wolves prowled through the forest.	
prudent	*adj.*	**thoughtful, shrewd, cautious, careful, wise, thrifty** He made a prudent decision when he bought a coat instead of skis.	*careless, wasteful, unwise, reckless, rash*
pry	1. *v.*	**peer, spy, snoop, inquire, poke, investigate** Don't pry into other people's affairs.	*1. ignore, neglect*

2. *v.* **raise, lift, force, lever**
Jim pried the lid off the can of paint.

2. press, push

public   **1.** *n.* **people, society, community**
Let the public decide whether it wants
Sunday shopping.

2. *adj.* **common, general, universal, open,
unrestricted**
The museum is a public building.

*2. private, personal,
restricted*

publish   **1.** *v.* **announce, make known, disclose,
reveal, communicate, circulate**
The results of the draw will be published
next week.
adj. The published list is eagerly awaited.

*1. conceal, suppress,
withhold*

2. *v.* **print, issue, bring out, produce**
The company published a successful
dictionary last year.
n. The publisher was pleased with the
success of the dictionary.

pull   **1.** *n.* **attraction, magnetism**
The pull of gravity makes things stay on
the ground.

2. *v.* **haul, tow, drag, lug**
Tom pulled his chair to the front of the
classroom.

2. push, shove

pulsate   *v.* **throb, beat, shake, palpitate, tremble,
shudder, pound, vibrate**
The healthy heart pulsates with a steady,
even beat.
n. The pulsations of the heart can be felt
in the neck and wrists.

punch   **1.** *n.* **poke, blow, wallop, jab, hit**
The boxer got a punch on the nose.

2. *n.* **beverage**
There was fruit punch at the party.

3. *v.* **pierce, puncture, perforate**
The train conductor checked and punched
our tickets.

punctual   *adj.* **on time, prompt, on schedule,
not late**
We can rely on Sonia to be punctual.
adv. She arrives punctually at school
every day.
n. The school is strict about punctuality.

late, tardy

punish   *v.* **discipline, chastise, correct, rebuke,
penalize**
Who will punish the offender?
n. They had to stay in after school as
punishment.

*reward, excuse,
exonerate*

puny		*adj.*	**tiny, insignificant, undersized, feeble, inferior, delicate, weak** The boxer scoffed at his opponent's puny muscles.	*large, giant, oversized, great, strong*
purchase		*v.*	**buy, acquire, get, invest in** They purchased their house after years of saving. *n.* The purchase of a new house is an exciting event.	*sell, dispose of*
pure	1.	*adj.*	**clean, immaculate, untainted, spotless, uncontaminated** We should get pure water from the spring. *n.* The water is tested for purity.	1. *impure, dirty, contaminated, tainted*
	2.	*adj.*	**absolute, complete, sheer, utter** It is pure folly to drink and drive.	
purify		*v.*	**distill, cleanse, refine, filter** Filtration plants purify water.	*soil, spoil, dirty, contaminate*
purpose		*n.*	**function, aim, intention, ambition, object, objective, goal, motive** The group's purpose is to entertain.	
purposely		*adv.*	**intentionally, deliberately, knowingly** The paragraph was left out purposely.	*accidentally, by chance*
pursue		*v.*	**follow, chase, seek, track, trail** Hounds pursued the fox. *n.* The hunters watched the pursuit.	*avoid, shun*
push	1.	*v.*	**press, nudge, shove** The runner pushed the pedestrian out of the way.	1. *draw, pull*
	2.	*v.*	**encourage, prod, urge, drive, impel, force, coerce** The salesperson pushed them to buy a stereo.	2. *discourage, hinder, prevent*
put	1.	*v.*	**place, deposit, rest, lay, set** Please put the dishes on the table.	1. *remove, transfer*
	2.	*v.*	**state, express, word, phrase** Can you put the problem another way?	
	3.	*v.*	**present, pose, submit, propose, offer** The chairperson put the plan to the committee members.	3. *withdraw, remove*
puzzle	1.	*n.*	**mystery, confusion, enigma, riddle** How the house caught fire is a puzzle to everyone.	1. *answer, solution*
	2.	*v.*	**bewilder, confuse, baffle, confound, embarrass, perplex** His strange answer puzzled me.	2. *make clear, enlighten*

Q is the only letter that has a constant partner. In English, *Q* is always followed by a *u*.

Q has two sounds. In *quote*, *equal*, and *quick*, it is like *kw*. In words like *conquer* or *antique* (which we borrowed from the French), the sound is the same as *k*.

quack	*n.*	charlatan, rogue, fake, cheat, impostor, fraud, pretender The doctor turned out to be a quack. *adj.* The quack doctor was arrested.	
quaint	*adj.*	old, old-fashioned, antiquated, charming, curious Tourists like to visit quaint places.	*up-to-date, modern, modish*
quake	1. *n.*	tremor, shock, earthquake The quake ruined many buildings.	
	2. *v.*	tremble, shiver, shake, quiver, heave, shudder, vibrate The mouse quaked with fear at the sight of the cat.	2. *be stable, be firm*
qualified	1. *adj.*	professional, trained, certified, competent, experienced, skilled Qualified instructors will train the athletes at the camp.	1. *amateur*
	2. *adj.*	limited, conditional, restricted, guarded The mayor gave a qualified "yes" to the proposal.	2. *unlimited, unconditional*
qualify	1. *v.*	pass, meet the demands Our team qualified for the finals.	1. *fail, be unsuited*
	2. *v.*	change, modify, alter, moderate, temper, limit, restrain, reduce The driver qualified his statement when questioned by the police.	2. *retain, solidify*
quality	1. *n.*	grade, rank, class, standard, level We use top quality beef in our pies.	
	2. *n.*	characteristic, feature, trait Suni was chosen as captain of the team because of her leadership qualities.	
qualm	*n.*	doubt, anxiety, misgiving, uncertainty Marie had qualms about staying out late.	*confidence, assurance*
quandary	*n.*	plight, dilemma, predicament, puzzle The tourist was in a quandary when she lost her passport.	*ease, certainty, assurance*
quantity	*n.*	amount, number, extent, portion, volume, measure, stock, supply A large quantity of food is required for the party.	
quarrel	*n.*	disagreement, dispute, argument, feud, squabble, dissension, conflict, clash The sisters had a quarrel over money. *v.* They quarreled over many things. *adj.* They were a quarrelsome pair.	*agreement, harmony, understanding, conciliation*

quarry	1.	*n.*	**shaft, vein, mine, pit** Abandoned quarries are dangerous.	
	2.	*n.*	**game, prey, victim** Rabbits are quarry for foxes.	
queasy		*adj.*	**sick, uneasy, squeamish, nauseated** I had a queasy feeling as the plane took off.	*comfortable, well, hearty, relaxed*
queer		*adj.*	**strange, unusual, odd, peculiar, curious, abnormal, extraordinary** Queer sounds could be heard inside the empty house.	*usual, common, ordinary, familiar, customary*
quell	1.	*v.*	**subdue, suppress, stop, vanquish** The army quelled the uprising.	*1. yield, give up, concede*
	2.	*v.*	**calm, check, allay, quiet, overcome** The singer quelled his stage fright and walked on stage.	*2. incite, excite, agitate, arouse*
quench	1.	*v.*	**satisfy, satiate, allay** She quenched her thirst with a large glass of water.	
	2.	*v.*	**douse, extinguish, smother** Kim quenched the fire with an extinguisher.	*2. fan, replenish, renew, promote*
query		*n.*	**question, inquiry** Several queries were made about the accident at the factory. *v.* The police queried the witnesses about the accident.	*answer, reply, response*
quest		*n.*	**search, pursuit, hunt, crusade** Prospectors rushed to the West in quest of gold.	
question	1.	*n.*	**query, inquiry** Each contestant was asked one question.	*1. reply, response, answer, solution*
	2.	*v.*	**ask, inquire, interrogate, quiz, query** Lawyers question witnesses in court.	*2. answer, reply, respond, state*
	3.	*v.*	**dispute, doubt, suspect, distrust** Tom questioned the referee's decision.	*3. trust, believe, affirm, reinforce*
questionable		*adj.*	**doubtful, uncertain, dubious, suspicious, debatable, disputable** This work of art is of questionable value.	*certain, definite, unquestionable, proven*
quick	1.	*adj.*	**fast, rapid, speedy, fleet, swift, brisk** The soldiers marched at a quick pace. *adv.* They marched quickly.	*1. sluggish, slow, gradual*
	2.	*adj.*	**prompt, immediate, sudden, instant** The car came to a quick stop.	*2. slow, tardy, gradual*
	3.	*adj.*	**impatient, hasty, rash, impetuous** Her quick temper often lands her in trouble.	*3. easygoing, calm, cool, level-headed, patient*
	4.	*adj.*	**intelligent, clever, alert, bright, sharp** The quick student is top of the class.	*4. stupid, dull, slow*

quiet

1. *adj.* **noiseless, still, silent, hushed**
Patients need quiet surroundings.
n. The dog's howl broke the quiet of the night.

    1. *noisy, loud*

2. *adj.* **still, placid, motionless, calm, smooth**
The boat drifted on the quiet lake.

    2. *turbulent, moving*

3. *v.* **soothe, calm, relax, pacify, console, comfort, ease**
Lullabies can quiet babies.
adv. Lullabies are sung quietly.

    3. *agitate, excite, disturb*

quit

1. *v.* **abandon, surrender, relinquish, renounce**
Which soldier quit the battle?

    1. *invade, attack*

2. *v.* **end, cease, stop**
Mike has quit smoking.

    2. *start, begin, commence, continue*

3. *v.* **leave, cease work, resign, discontinue**
Those workers quit their jobs.

    3. *seek, apply for*

4. *v.* **vacate, depart, leave**
When will the tenants quit the apartment?

    4. *move in*

quite

1. *adv.* **entirely, wholly, totally, completely**
You're quite right about the matter.

    1. *partially, somewhat*

2. *adv.* **really, truly, very, positively, genuinely, actually, indeed**
I am quite astounded at your remarks!

    2. *somewhat, barely, hardly*

quiver

v. **tremble, shake, shudder, quaver, shiver, flutter, vibrate**
Dan's lips quivered as he bit back his tears.
n. Do you see the quiver in Dan's lips?

stay still, be stable, stay calm

quiz

n. **test, query, interrogation, probe, examination, review**
We sat through a rigorous math quiz.
v. Police quizzed the witnesses on the events of the robbery.

quota

n. **share, allotment, proportion, part, percentage, apportionment, portion**
That company has exceeded its quota of imported textiles.

quotation

1. *n.* **selection, citing, citation, excerpt, passage, extract**
Many people begin a speech with a quotation from a famous person.

2. *n.* **market price, current price, price**
Stock market quotations are published in the newspapers and on the Internet.

quote

1. *v.* **repeat, recite, extract, cite, echo**
She quoted some lines from Robert Frost.

    1. *misquote*

2. *v.* **give a price, name a price**
The seller quoted the price of the car.
n. Bob gave a low quote for the job.

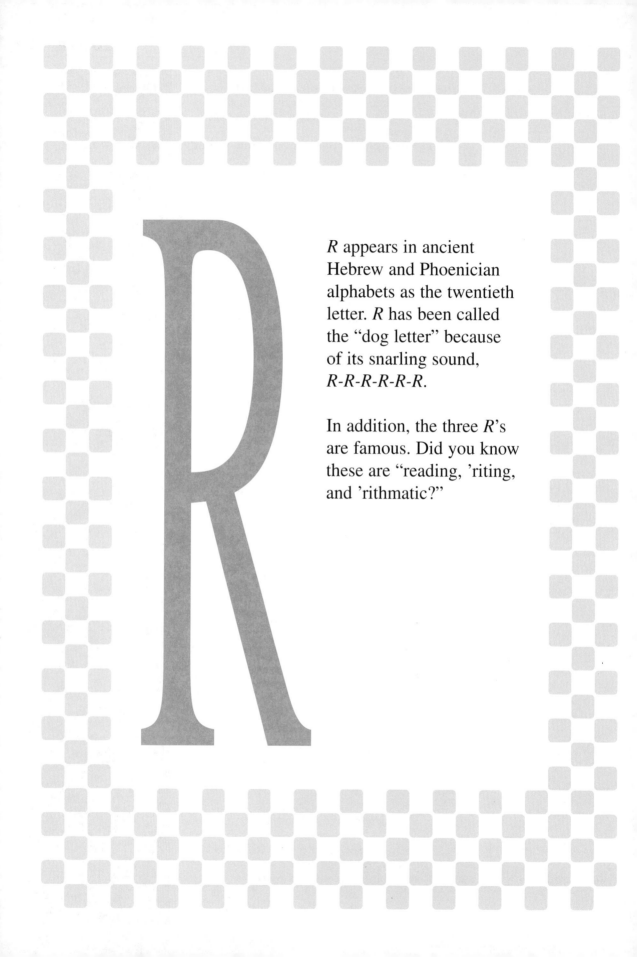

R appears in ancient Hebrew and Phoenician alphabets as the twentieth letter. *R* has been called the "dog letter" because of its snarling sound, *R-R-R-R-R-R*.

In addition, the three *R*'s are famous. Did you know these are "reading, 'riting, and 'rithmatic?"

rabid	1.	*adj.*	**mad, insane, frenzied, hydrophobic** Rabid animals are dangerous to humans.	**1.** *sane, normal, well*
	2.	*adj.*	**fanatical, zealous, ardent, fervent, obsessed** Rabid fans rushed onto the soccer field after the match.	**2.** *indifferent, neutral, lukewarm, half-hearted*
race	1.	*n.*	**species, type, strain, breed** Is the human race more developed than the other animal races?	
	2.	*n.*	**nationality, tribe, clan, people, ethnic group, cultural group** Many races form the melting pot of American society. *adj.* The people live in racial harmony.	
	3.	*n.*	**competition, speed contest, run, meet, match** Sena won the race on Sports Day. *v.* Many drivers raced in the Grand Prix.	
	4.	*v.*	**run, hurry, hasten, speed, hustle, dash, sprint, bolt, scamper, rush** People raced for cover when the storm hit.	**4.** *delay, creep, crawl, plod, amble, stroll, saunter*
racism		*n.*	**prejudice, discrimination, intolerance, bias, bigotry** Racism is not tolerated in our society.	
racket		*n.*	**uproar, tumult, din, noise, disturbance** The protesters made a racket during the meeting.	*quiet, peace, harmony, calmness, tranquility*
radiant	1.	*adj.*	**luminous, shining, bright, glowing, brilliant, sparkling, resplendent** The queen wore a radiant diamond tiara. *n.* The travelers were blinded by the radiance of the sun.	**1.** *dull, dim, drab, tarnished, lackluster*
	2.	*adj.*	**bright, happy, glowing** The skaters flashed radiant smiles when they won the Olympic medal. *adv.* They smiled radiantly all day.	**2.** *solemn, glum, downcast, sad, miserable, dejected*
radiate	1.	*v.*	**shed, emit, give out, send out, transmit, disseminate, discharge** The sun radiates heat and light. *n.* Electric radiators give off heat.	**1.** *absorb, take in, assimilate, consume, digest*
	2.	*v.*	**spread out, diverge** Many roads radiate from the center of town.	**2.** *converge, meet*
radical	1.	*adj.*	**fundamental, basic, original** Ore is the radical form of metal.	**1.** *derived, acquired*
	2.	*adj.*	**complete, extreme, entire, drastic, thorough** After his heart attack, Uncle Ken made a radical change in his lifestyle. *adv.* Uncle Ken radically changed his lifestyle.	**2.** *partial, superficial, extraneous*

3. *adj.* **revolutionary, rebellious**
The French Revolution was started by radical citizens.
n. The radicals changed France from an imperial society to a democracy.

3. *patriotic, loyal, tempered*

4. *adj.* **original, novel, advanced, different, unusual, unconventional, progressive**
Sigmund Freud was regarded as a radical thinker.

4. *imitative, ordinary, conservative, conventional, moderate*

rage

1. *n.* **anger, wrath, fury, frenzy**
We were filled with rage when we saw the man kick his dog.

1. *serenity, gentleness*

2. *n.* **fashion, fad, vogue, style, trend**
Which color is the rage this season?

3. *v.* **rave, fume, rant, show anger**
The crowd raged at the umpire's unfair call.

3. *be calm, remain quiet*

ragged

1. *adj.* **torn, tattered, shabby, worn, frayed, threadbare, patched, ripped**
The refugees arrived in ragged clothing.

1. *new, well-kept, repaired*

2. *adj.* **disorganized, sloppy, jagged, uneven**
They stood in ragged rows outside waiting for help.

2. *smooth, even*

raid

1. *n.* **invasion, assault, attack, onset, strike, incursion, foray**
The army launched a surprise raid on the enemy camps at dawn.

1. *retreat, withdrawal*

2. *v.* **attack, invade, strike, storm**
Police raided the kidnapper's hideout and saved the victim.

2. *surrender, defend, protect*

3. *v.* **ransack, loot, rob, pillage, plunder**
Vikings raided the coastal towns.

rain

n. **downpour, shower, drizzle, rainfall, thunderstorm, storm**
After a long drought, everyone was happy when the rain came.
v. It rained all day yesterday.
adj. It was the start of the rainy season.

raise

1. *n.* **increase**
Cindy had a large raise in her salary when she was promoted.

1. *decrease, cutback*

2. *v.* **lift, hoist, heave, elevate, boost**
The crane raised the girder to the top of the building.

2. *lower, bring down, take down, drop*

3. *v.* **hold up, lift, put up**
Raise your hand if you agree with this.

3. *lower*

4. *v.* **arouse, stir up, boost, excite, kindle**
Jean's good marks raised her hopes of winning a scholarship.

4. *quell, subdue, lull, quiet, compose, calm*

5. *v.* **grow, breed, cultivate, rear, produce, nurture, bring up**
The rancher raises cattle.

5. *retard, destroy*

6. *v.* **increase, inflate, put up**
Why did the store raise the price of fruit?

6. *lower, drop, reduce*

	7. *v.*	**collect, gather, procure, accumulate** The students are washing cars to raise money for computers.	**7.** *disperse, scatter*
	8. *v.*	**erect, build, construct, put up** Citizens raised monuments to honor the war veterans.	**8.** *tear down, demolish, destroy*
	9. *v.*	**suggest, bring up, mention, propose, broach** Raise the matter at the next meeting.	
	10. *v.*	**promote, advance, upgrade** The navy raised the seaman's rank.	**10.** *demote, lower, downgrade, degrade*
ram	*v.*	**run into, butt, strike, slam, bump, hit, pound, smash, crash** The drunk driver rammed his car into a pole.	*avoid, dodge*
ramble	**1.** *v.*	**stroll, walk, saunter, wander, roam, amble, hike** It's fun to ramble through the park. *n.* We were tired after our ramble in the park.	**1.** *run, bound, dash, dart, rush*
	2. *v.*	**digress, get off the point, babble, drift** The speaker rambled on, unaware that the audience had fallen asleep.	**2.** *focus*
	3. *v.*	**twist, turn, spread, wind** Vines ramble in all directions.	
ramshackle	*adj.*	**dilapidated, neglected, shabby, rickety, decrepit, crumbling** The ramshackle cottage will be demolished.	*well-kept*
rancid	*adj.*	**stale, rank, sour, putrid, tainted, impure, contaminated, polluted** Rancid tuna should not be eaten.	*fresh, pure, untainted, fragrant*
random	*adj.*	**haphazard, chance, aimless, irregular** Lottery numbers were chosen in random order.	*selective, specified, designated*
range	**1.** *n.*	**extent, spread, distance, scope, reach** The search covered a range that spread over ten miles.	
	2. *n.*	**selection, variety, spectrum** The store offers a wide range of goods.	
	3. *n.*	**pasture, meadow, grassland, field, prairie, plain, grazing land** Cattle graze on the range.	**3.** *wasteland, tundra, forest, desert*
	4. *v.*	**fluctuate, spread, vary** Temperatures range from very hot to very cold in desert regions.	**4.** *remain constant*
rank	**1.** *n.*	**order, grade, position, standing, level, station, status** She holds a position of high rank in the armed forces.	
	2. *v.*	**arrange, classify, grade, categorize** We ranked ourselves according to height.	**2.** *disarrange, disorder, disorganize*

3. *adj.* **smelly, putrid, foul, disagreeable, offensive, rotten, obnoxious, rancid**
Decaying produce has a rank odor.

3. *fragrant, sweet, fresh, pleasant, agreeable*

ransack *v.* **plunder, raid, loot, pillage, ravage**
Robbers ransacked the house while the owners were on vacation.

protect, defend

rap *n.* **knock, thump, blow, tap**
There was a loud rap on the window.
v. Someone rapped on the door in the middle of the night.

rapid *adj.* **quick, fast, speedy, fleet, swift, accelerated**
Ann had a rapid recovery from surgery.
adv. She recovered rapidly.

slow, sluggish, languid, tardy

rare
1. *adj.* **unusual, uncommon, extraordinary**
That pianist has a rare talent!
n. Such talent is a rarity.

1. *usual, ordinary, common, typical*

2. *adj.* **sparse, few, scanty, meager, limited**
We were happy to see Dan on one of his rare visits.

2. *abundant, plentiful*

3. *adj.* **select, choice, superlative, matchless**
Rare gems are among the crown jewels.

3. *inferior, mediocre, cheap, tawdry, vulgar*

4. *adj.* **thin, light, tenuous**
Rare air is found at high altitudes.

4. *dense, heavy*

5. *adj.* **nearly raw, underdone**
Many people enjoy eating rare steaks.

5. *well-done, overdone*

rarely *adv.* **seldom, not often, infrequently**
Robins are rarely seen in winter.

frequently, often

rascal *n.* **imp, rogue, scoundrel, troublemaker, scamp, rapscallion**
He was a rascal to pull that trick on me.

model, paragon, saint

rash *adj.* **reckless, hasty, impetuous, impulsive, unthinking, foolhardy**
He made a rash decision to quit school.

level-headed, prudent, cautious, safe, wary

rate
1. *n.* **speed, tempo, pace**
Some cities have seen a tremendous rate of growth in recent years.

2. *n.* **cost, price, fee, value, amount**
What is the monthly rate to park the car?

3. *n.* **ratio, percent, proportion**
Interest rates rise and fall.

4. *v.* **rank, judge, evaluate, grade, assess**
A panel of international judges rated the skaters' performances.

rational *adj.* **level-headed, logical, sound, thoughtful, reasonable, sensible**
Let's find a rational solution to the problem.

irrational, rash, reckless, unsound, absurd, emotional

rattle	1.	*n.*	**racket, noise, clatter, clack** The rattle of machine guns sent everyone dashing for safety. *v.* The car rattled on the bumpy road.	1. *silence, quiet*
	2.	*v.*	**unnerve, confuse, fluster, bewilder, bother, disconcert** Hecklers rattled the speaker.	2. *aid, help, assist, calm, soothe*
ravage	1.	*v.*	**wreck, destroy, devastate, ruin** An atomic bomb ravaged Hiroshima. *n.* We were horrified when we saw the ravages of the war.	1. *build, improve, rehabilitate, restore*
	2.	*v.*	**loot, pillage, plunder, raid, sack** Looters ravaged the stores during the riots.	
rave	1.	*v.*	**babble, jabber, rant, rail** The delirious patient raved all night.	1. *speak coherently*
	2.	*v.*	**enthuse, praise, cheer** He raved about the amazing special effects in the movie.	2. *criticize, degrade*
	3.	*v.*	**rage, rant, fume** Lee raved and ranted when he lost.	3. *cheer*
ravenous		*adv.*	**starved, hungry, famished, voracious** We were ravenous after our hike. *adj.* We dug ravenously into our dinner.	*satisfied, full, sated, satiated*
ravine		*n.*	**gully, gorge, gap, chasm, gulch** There is a variety of wildlife in the ravine.	
ravish	1.	*v.*	**charm, delight, please, enchant, captivate, fascinate, enthrall** The singer ravished the audience with a stunning performance. *adj.* The audience was bewitched by her ravishing beauty.	1. *repel, offend, disgust, displease*
	2.	*v.*	**violate, ravage, spoil** Fire ravished the forest.	2. *respect, protect, restore*
raw	1.	*adj.*	**uncooked, unprepared** Raw carrots are crunchy.	1. *cooked, prepared*
	2.	*adj.*	**unfinished, crude, natural** Canada exports raw materials like lumber and minerals.	2. *manufactured, processed, refined*
	3.	*adj.*	**undisciplined, inexperienced, new, untrained** The armed forces train raw recruits.	3. *experienced, trained, expert, seasoned*
	4.	*adj.*	**cold, biting, cutting, piercing** Raw winds forced the cancellation of the outdoor meet.	4. *balmy, pleasant, moderate, warm*
	5.	*adj.*	**chafed, scraped** The mountain climber's hands were raw from clutching the rope.	5. *healed, smooth*
reach	1.	*n.*	**range, scope, distance, proximity** We live within easy reach of the school.	
	2.	*v.*	**arrive, get to** We finally reached home at midnight.	2. *set off, start, leave*

	3.	*v.*	**contact, communicate with** You can reach me at this number.	*3. avoid, shun*
	4.	*v.*	**stretch, extend** I reached for the book on the top shelf.	*4. crouch, shrink*
react		*v.*	**respond, reply, answer, reciprocate** She reacted rudely when asked to help. *n.* There was a violent reaction from the fans when the concert was canceled.	*ignore, shun*
ready	1.	*adj.*	**prepared, fit, equipped, primed** I studied hard and was ready for the test.	*1. unprepared, unfit*
	2.	*adj.*	**complete, finished, available** Your wedding gown is ready.	*2. incomplete, unfinished*
	3.	*adj.*	**willing, eager, enthusiastic, keen** Mark is ever ready for adventure.	*3. reluctant*
	4.	*adj.*	**zealous, prompt, quick, fast, swift, immediate, instant** Ready help arrived at the scene of the crash. *adv.* The workers readily accepted the company's proposal.	*4. slow, hesitant*
real	1.	*adj.*	**genuine, authentic, true** Real diamonds are hard enough to cut glass.	*1. false, fake, artificial, counterfeit*
	2.	*adj.*	**actual, factual, concrete, tangible** Non-fiction books deal with real life situations. *adv.* Is she really the owner of the car?	*2. fictitious, false, imaginary, hypothetical*
realistic	1.	*adj.*	**sensible, feasible, viable, rational** Dan was advised to set realistic goals.	*1. unrealistic, idealistic, irrational*
	2.	*adj.*	**lifelike, convincing, authentic** The wax museum has realistic models of famous people.	*2. unnatural, unconvincing*
realize	1.	*v.*	**comprehend, understand, recognize, grasp, see, appreciate, know** Do you realize what you are doing?	*1. misunderstand, not know, be ignorant of*
	2.	*v.*	**fulfill, achieve, accomplish** After years of struggle she realized her dream of success. *n.* The realization of her dreams brought her much happiness.	*2. fail, abandon, give up*
	3.	*v.*	**earn, obtain, receive, net, fetch** We realized a good profit from the sale of our house.	*3. lose*
rear	1.	*n.*	**back, background** Park at the rear of the building.	*1. front, foreground*
	2.	*v.*	**raise, lift, elevate** The bull reared its head and charged at the matador.	*2. lower, bow, drop*
	3.	*v.*	**bring up, raise, breed** The farmer rears pigs.	
reason	1.	*n.*	**purpose, aim, objective, motive, explanation, rationale** The reason for this meeting is to clear up some misunderstandings.	

2.　*n.*　**logic, sense, judgment, intelligence**
She is a person of reason and can be trusted to do the right thing.

3.　*v.*　**think, contemplate, reflect, consider, conclude, deduce**
The detective reasoned that the suspect was innocent.
n. His reasoning was based on the many clues he had examined.

reasonable

1.　*adj.*　**fair, moderate, just, sensible, average, inexpensive, modest**
That's a reasonable price for a car.

2.　*adj.*　**feasible, sound, plausible, rational, logical, credible**
John won the debate with his reasonable arguments.

3.　*adj.*　**sensible, rational, realistic, thoughtful**
Jan is a reasonable leader who always helps us with our problems.

1. *excessive, extreme, exorbitant, outlandish*

2. *unreasonable, implausible, unsound*

3. *unreasonable, irrational*

rebel

1.　*n.*　**revolutionary, agitator, rioter, guerrilla, insurgent**
The rebels attacked the palace.

2.　*n.*　**individualist, independent, innovator**
Picasso was considered to be a rebel in the art world.

3.　*v.*　**revolt, mutiny, rise up, resist**
The army rebelled against the government.
n. The rebellion was a success.

1. *loyalist*

2. *follower, imitator*

3. *submit, obey, follow*

rebuke

n.　**reprimand, reproach, reproof, disapproval, criticism**
The coach's rebuke upset the skater.
v. The coach rebuked the skater for his lack of concentration.

compliment, praise, congratulations, applause, approval, encouragement

recall

1.　*v.*　**recollect, remember, think of**
Can you recall her name?

2.　*v.*　**withdraw, call back, summon**
Auto manufacturers sometimes recall their vehicles for safety checks.

1. *forget*

2. *send out, dispatch*

recede

1.　*v.*　**withdraw, retreat, go back**
The troops receded under heavy attack.
adj. Dad has a receding hairline.

2.　*v.*　**sink, fall, drop, lessen, abate, decline, ebb, subside**
The floodwaters receded after a week.

1. *go forward, go ahead, advance*

2. *rise, increase, flow*

receive

1.　*v.*　**get, accept, take, gain, acquire, collect, procure, come by, secure, win**
We received praise for our performance.

2.　*v.*　**greet, welcome, admit, entertain, meet**
Who received the guest-of-honor?

1. *give, donate, contribute, discard, decline*

2. *reject, refuse, oust, banish*

recent		*adj.*	**current, modern, up-to-date, fresh, new, contemporary** I read about it in a recent magazine.	*outdated, old, stale*

recess
1. *n.* **intermission, pause, break, interruption, respite, rest period**
We have a short recess at school in the morning.
2. *n.* **opening, hole, indentation, alcove, niche, nook, hollow**
The children hid in a recess in the rock.

2. protrusion

recite
v. **relate, tell, repeat, recount, narrate**
The student recited a comical poem.
n. Everyone gave recitations of their favorite poem in class.

ad lib

reckless
adj. **rash, inconsiderate, careless, wild, thoughtless, foolhardy**
Reckless drivers are a menace to society.
adv. Tom ran recklessly across the road.

careful, cautious, considerate, wary, prudent

reckon
1. *v.* **calculate, estimate, figure, count, gauge, total, compute, enumerate**
The cashier reckoned the change correctly.
2. *v.* **think, consider, judge**
I reckon he's the best student in our class.

1. guess, miscount, miscalculate

reclaim
1. *v.* **retrieve, redeem, salvage**
After the war, the family returned to reclaim their property.
2. *v.* **regenerate, renew, restore, remodel**
Singapore has reclaimed much of its land from the sea.
adj. Whole towns have been built on reclaimed land in Singapore.

2. exhaust, waste, abandon

recognize
1. *v.* **identify, know, distinguish**
We recognized our relatives even though we hadn't seen them in years.
2. *v.* **perceive, realize, see, admit, detect, understand**
Robert recognized that he had made a mistake in not working harder.
3. *v.* **acknowledge, take notice of, consider**
The judges recognized Linda as the best debater of the competition.

1. misidentify

2. miss, overlook

3. ignore, overlook

recollect
v. **recall, remember**
Can you recollect her e-mail address?
n. I have no recollection of where I left my glasses.

forget

recommend
1. *v.* **endorse, vouch for, approve, commend, favor**
Kim recommended Amy for the job.
n. Her recommendation helped Amy get the job.

1. disapprove, censure, denounce, disparage

	2.	*v.*	**advise, suggest, urge, counsel, propose** I recommend that you stay home and rest.	
record	1.	*v.*	**note, register, enter, chronicle, catalog** Record the information in the notebook.	**1.** *obliterate, delete, leave no trace*
	2.	*v.*	**report, journal, chronicle, log, account** Dad kept a record of his experiences in the war.	
records		*n.*	**documents, chronicles, registers, archives, accounts, diaries** Historical records are kept in museums.	
recover	1.	*n.*	**get well, rally, improve, recuperate** Atif recovered from the accident. *n.* We are pleased with his recovery.	**1.** *relapse, decline, become worse, fail*
	2.	*v.*	**restore, reclaim, regain, redeem, retrieve, rescue, repossess, save** Police recovered the stolen goods from a warehouse.	**2.** *lose, mislay, misplace*
recreation		*n.*	**amusement, sport, pastime, relaxation, diversion** Our family's favorite recreation is golf. *adj.* The town offers good recreational facilities.	*labor, work, toil, employment, drudgery*
rectify		*v.*	**correct, revise, amend, remedy, redress** The cashier rectified the error on my bill.	*disregard, set aside, ignore, overlook*
recur		*v.*	**return, reappear, repeat, reoccur** The flood recurs each year. *adj.* Rani is plagued by a recurring nightmare about exams.	*end, terminate, stop, cease*
reduce	1.	*v.*	**diminish, lessen, decrease, lower** The store reduced the price of books. *n.* We welcomed the price reductions.	**1.** *increase, magnify, enlarge, inflate, extend*
	2.	*v.*	**subdue, overcome, humiliate** The judge's comments reduced the young offender to tears.	**2.** *exalt, praise, flatter*
reflect	1.	*v.*	**think, ponder, consider, contemplate** Grandpa often reflects on the past.	**1.** *disregard, neglect, ignore, overlook*
	2.	*v.*	**mirror, reproduce** The lake reflected the full moon. *n.* The baby smiled at his own reflection in the mirror.	
	3.	*v.*	**demonstrate, reveal, show, display** Their manners reflect their good upbringing.	
reform	1.	*v.*	**revise, amend, change, alter, remodel** The government voted to reform the existing tax laws.	**1.** *perpetuate, keep, maintain*
	2.	*v.*	**correct, improve** The young offender was warned to reform his ways.	

refrain	1.	*n.*	**verse, song, theme, phrase, chorus** "Auld Lang Syne" is a refrain often heard on New Year's Eve.	
	2.	*v.*	**abstain, avoid, forgo, cease** Refrain from talking in class.	**2.** *indulge, partake, join*
refresh		*v.*	**revive, restore, renew, invigorate** The runners refreshed themselves with cold drinks. *adj.* That was a refreshing shower!	*debilitate, tire, weary, enervate, exhaust*
refrigerate		*v.*	**chill, cool, freeze** Refrigerate all dairy products. *n.* Always keep milk in the refrigerator.	*heat, warm*
refuge		*n.*	**shelter, sanctuary, haven, retreat** The millionaire built a refuge for homeless children.	*hazard, trap, peril*
refund		*v.*	**give back, pay back, rebate, return, repay, reimburse** The storekeeper refunded the customer's money. *n.* How much is the refund?	*take away, keep*
refuse		*n.*	**waste, garbage, rubbish, trash, debris** Much refuse can be recycled.	*treasure, valuables*
refuse	1.	*v.*	**deny, withhold, deprive of** The principal refused to give the students permission to hold a dance. *n.* The students were upset with the refusal by the principal.	**1.** *allow, consent*
	2.	*v.*	**decline, turn down, reject, spurn** Jill refused my invitation to dinner.	**2.** *accept, agree*
regain		*v.*	**recover, retrieve, get back, recapture** The patient regained his health after months of convalescence.	*lose*
regard	1.	*n.*	**esteem, respect, admiration** Gandhi was held in high regard.	**1.** *disrespect, dishonor*
	2.	*v.*	**consider, view, look at, think of, deem** I regard my teacher as a friend.	**2.** *dismiss, disregard*
region		*n.*	**area, district, territory, section, locality, sector, zone, vicinity** The Niagara region is noted for its fruits. *adj.* Regional elections will be held soon.	
register	1.	*v.*	**show, reveal, disclose, express, display** The winner's face registered joy.	**1.** *hide, conceal*
	2.	*v.*	**enroll, enlist, sign in, check in** Sam registered for summer school.	**2.** *drop out, withdraw*
	3.	*v.*	**indicate, point to, designate** Thermometers register the temperature.	

4. *n.*   **directory, list, catalog, record, roll**
We checked the school's register for our records.

regret   **1.** *n.*   **remorse, repentance, sorrow**
The driver expressed regret for the accident.
adv. The driver spoke regretfully of the accident.   **1.** *satisfaction, pleasure, solace, contentment*

2. *v.*   **be sorry for, rue, lament, mourn, grieve, repent, bemoan, deplore**
He regretted the outcome of the accident.   **2.** *be satisfied with, celebrate, be glad of, rejoice*

regular   **1.** *adj.*   **customary, usual, normal, routine**
Our regular business hours are from nine to five.
adv. We eat regularly at six o'clock.   **1.** *irregular, unusual, odd*

2. *adj.*   **consistent, methodical, steady, patterned, uniform, rhythmic**
We were hypnotized by the regular beat of the drums.   **2.** *sporadic, erratic, irregular, uneven, broken, interrupted*

regulate   **1.** *v.*   **manage, direct, control, govern**
The council regulates the business of the city.

2. *v.*   **adjust, set, standardize**
A thermostat regulates the heat in the building.   **2.** *upset, confuse*

regulation   *n.*   **rule, order, law, ordinance, statute, command**
Please observe all traffic regulations when driving.

rehearse   *v.*   **practice, prepare**
The dancers rehearsed for the concert.
n. The dress rehearsal was a hectic affair.

reject   **1.** *v.*   **discard, throw out, eliminate**
The sorters rejected all imperfect produce.   **1.** *choose, keep, maintain, accept*

2. *v.*   **deny, refuse, decline, rebuff**
The injured cyclist rejected all offers of help.   **2.** *accept, welcome, endorse, hail*

rejoice   *v.*   **revel, enjoy, exult, celebrate**
Everyone rejoiced when peace was declared.   *lament, mourn, grieve, weep, sorrow*

relate   **1.** *v.*   **tell, narrate, state, describe, report, recount**
Pin related the events of his holiday to his friends.   **1.** *conceal, keep silent*

2. *v.*   **connect, link, associate**
Marriage relates the two families.
n. People who are related are known as relatives or relations.   **2.** *estrange, separate*

relax	1.	*v.*	**loosen, slacken, let go** The doctor told me to relax my arm before she gave me the injection.	*1. tighten, strengthen*
	2.	*v.*	**rest, take it easy, lounge** Let's relax at home this weekend. *n.* Everyone needs some relaxation after hard work.	*2. work, struggle, toil, labor*
release	1.	*n.*	**freedom, liberation, discharge** News of the hostage's release spread quickly.	*1. restraint, constraint, captivity*
	2.	*v.*	**let go, free, liberate** The kidnappers released the hostage after they were paid a ransom.	*2. confine, hold, constrain*
relentless		*adj.*	**merciless, ruthless, hard, pitiless, harsh, remorseless, unyielding** The suspect was subjected to relentless interrogation.	*merciful, kind, forgiving, compassionate*
relevant		*adj.*	**appropriate, pertinent, related, applicable, associated, connected** All relevant information will be considered in court.	*inapplicable, incongruous, inappropriate*
reliable		*adj.*	**dependable, staunch, steady, loyal, true, faithful, reputable, trustworthy, responsible** The news came from a reliable source.	*unreliable, insincere, false, irresponsible, undependable*
relieve	1.	*v.*	**alleviate, comfort, soothe, lessen, lighten, aid, allay, diminish, help** Cold compresses relieved the swelling. *n.* The rain was a relief from the heat.	*1. aggravate, worsen, increase*
	2.	*v.*	**replace, take over for, substitute for** New troops were sent in to relieve the tired soldiers. *adj.* How many relief pitchers were used during the game?	*2. reinstate, restore, put back*
relinquish		*v.*	**give up, surrender, yield, abandon, quit, cede** The prince relinquished all claims to the throne.	*keep, hold, retain, possess, maintain*
relish	1.	*n.*	**condiment, seasoning, sauce** Try some relish on the hot dog.	
	2.	*n.*	**liking, zest, gusto, enjoyment, appetite** The children dug into their food with relish. *v.* Certain people relish vegetarian meals.	*2. aversion, dislike, distaste*
reluctant		*adj.*	**unwilling, hesitant, averse** The scientist was reluctant to talk to the press about his discovery. *n.* His reluctance to discuss his discovery aroused much curiosity. *adv.* After much badgering he reluctantly agreed to come.	*anxious, keen, eager, willing, disposed*

rely	*v.*	**depend on, count on, trust** We rely on the mass media for accurate and up-to-date news. *adj.* Is television a reliable news source?	*be wary of, distrust*
remain	*v.*	**stay, linger, settle, continue on** The tourists remained on the island for another day.	*leave, go, depart*
remainder	*n.*	**leftover, balance, excess, surplus** The remainder of the money was spent on food.	
remarkable	*adj.*	**exceptional, extraordinary, noteworthy, notable, striking** She is admired for her remarkable achievements in science.	*unremarkable, ordinary, common, everyday, undistinguished*
remedy	*n.*	**cure, treatment, relief, antidote** Many new remedies for illnesses are now available. *v.* Physiotherapy remedied Vern's back ailment.	
remember	1. *v.*	**recall, recollect** Do you remember your former neighbors?	1. *forget*
	2. *v.*	**keep in mind, call to mind** Remember to turn off the oven before you leave.	2. *overlook, forget, disregard*
remind	1. *v.*	**prompt, call to mind** She reminded me that it was my turn to do the dishes.	
	2. *v.*	**caution, warn, point out, prompt** Signs remind drivers to go slowly. *n.* Reminders are given on the radio.	
remorse	*n.*	**grief, regret, anguish, self-reproach** The murderer showed no remorse.	*complacency, self-satisfaction*
remote	1. *adj.*	**distant, far away, far-off, removed, isolated, secluded** We vacationed on a remote island.	1. *near, close, accessible*
	2. *adj.*	**unrelated, irrelevant, indirect** The suspect was released because all evidence proved to be remote.	2. *relevant, related*
	3. *adj.*	**slight, faint, small, negligible** Our team only has a remote chance of winning as the other team is strong.	3. *strong*
remove	1. *v.*	**take away, carry off, clear, withdraw** Truckers removed the goods from the warehouse. *n.* Removal of the goods was quick.	1. *deposit, put in, install*
	2. *v.*	**dismiss, discharge** The council removed the president from office.	2. *install, establish, reinstate*

renew	1.	*v.*	**refresh, revive, restore, rebuild, regenerate, rejuvenate, refurbish** The city renewed its downtown core. *n.* Urban renewal is changing the appearance of many cities. *adj.* Some natural resources are renewable.	**1.** *deteriorate, exhaust, empty, spend, consume, weaken, debilitate, impair, kill, destroy*
	2.	*v.*	**resume, repeat, continue** The committee renewed its efforts to raise funds for a health center. *adj.* The committee's renewed efforts got some results.	**2.** *stop, discontinue, end*
renounce		*v.*	**forgo, relinquish, abandon, quit, forsake, give up, surrender** The king renounced his throne to marry the woman he loved.	*hold, defend, retain, own, claim, assert*
renown		*n.*	**fame, distinction, eminence** Marie Curie was a scientist of great renown.	*obscurity, anonymity*
renowned		*adj.*	**famous, noted, celebrated, notable, well-known, distinguished, illustrious** The world's most renowned authors were present at the conference.	*unknown, obscure, undistinguished*
repair		*v.*	**remedy, correct, fix, mend, overhaul, refurbish, renew, put in order** Dad repaired the car after the accident. *n.* The repairs were costly.	*break, destroy, wreck, damage, smash*
repay		*v.*	**refund, return, pay back, reimburse, give back, recompense** She promised to repay the loan soon.	
repeat		*v.*	**do again, say again, duplicate** Please repeat what you just said. *n.* Work that requires repetition can be boring.	*discontinue, stop, do once, say once*
repel	1.	*v.*	**rebuff, repulse, resist, force back** Troops repelled the invaders at the border.	**1.** *accept, surrender, yield, withdraw, retire*
	2.	*v.*	**disgust, revolt, offend, nauseate** The smell of dead fish repelled us.	**2.** *attract, please, invite, entice, charm*
replace	1.	*v.*	**return, restore, reinstate** Li replaced the library books he had lost. *n.* Replacement of lost books is costly for libraries.	**1.** *remove, take away, take*
	2.	*v.*	**take the place of, substitute for** Robots have replaced humans on many assembly lines.	
reply		*v.*	**answer, respond, retort** When asked to join us for dinner she replied that she was busy. *n.* We were disappointed with her reply.	*ask, question, query, ignore, be silent*

report

1. *n.* **record, account, statement**
The treasurer's report is accurate.
2. *n.* **bang, blast, noise, detonation**
The report of guns frightened us.
3. *v.* **announce, publish, proclaim, reveal, disclose, communicate, tell**
The scientists reported their astounding discovery at a press conference.

2. *silence*

3. *suppress, conceal, hide, withhold*

reporter

n. **journalist, correspondent, columnist, broadcaster, commentator, writer**
Reporters hounded the movie stars everywhere they went.

reproach

1. *n.* **blame, reproof, disgrace, discredit, dishonor, rebuke**
Is your conduct beyond reproach?
2. *v.* **condemn, censure, upbraid, reprove, rebuke**
The teacher reproached Jim for bullying the new student.

1. *credit, honor, commendation, praise*

2. *laud, praise, commend, approve*

repulsive

adj. **disgusting, odious, offensive, ugly, forbidding, revolting, repugnant**
Rotten fish has a repulsive odor.
v. The smell repulsed the diners.

agreeable, attractive, winning, alluring, seductive, pleasant, captivating

request

v. **ask, petition, solicit, appeal, seek**
Pam requested help in math.
n. Requests for aid poured in daily.

require

1. *v.* **want, need**
Animals require food and water.
2. *v.* **demand, command, expect**
The school requires students to wear a school uniform.
n. The school uniform is a requirement.

required

adj. **compulsory, necessary, essential, imperative, mandatory**
Which are the required subjects for the diploma?

voluntary, optional, discretionary, elective

rescue

1. *v.* **salvage, save, recover, retrieve, redeem, extricate**
Divers rescued the cargo from the sunken hulk.
2. *v.* **free, deliver, liberate, release, extricate**
Who rescued the hostages from the terrorists?
n. It was a daring rescue.

1. *lose, relinquish, surrender, abandon*

2. *capture, jail, imprison, incarcerate*

research

v. **study, examine, investigate, explore, inquire into, analyze**
Authors research their topics before writing stories.
n. Do your research on the Internet.

| resemble | v. | **look like, be similar to, approximate**
Does the baby resemble her mother?
n. The child bears a slight resemblance
to her mother. | *differ from, be unlike* |

| resentment | n. | **anger, ill will, malice, displeasure,
animosity, bitterness, indignation**
The people have a deep resentment
toward the cruel dictator.
v. We resent cruelty to animals. | *friendship, affection,
gratitude* |

reserve	1. n.	**provisions, store, supply, resources, stock, hoard** Squirrels have a reserve of nuts for the winter.	
	2. n.	**substitute, standby, replacement** When Jo hurt herself, the coach called in a reserve to take her place.	
	3. n.	**shyness, aloofness, restraint, reticence** The new student spoke with reserve.	*3. boldness, confidence*
	4. n.	**park, sanctuary, reservation** We went camping in the nature reserve.	
	5. v.	**book, order, retain, keep, save, hold** Sue reserved a table for dinner. adj. I have reserved seats for the show.	

| reserved | adj. | **shy, modest, retiring, reticent,
restrained, sedate, soft-spoken**
That normally reserved person becomes a
dynamo when she is on stage. | *loud, flashy,
boisterous,
ostentatious,
immodest* |

| reside | v. | **live, dwell, occupy, inhabit, stay**
Millions of people reside in Shanghai.
n. They are residents of the city. | |

| residence | n. | **home, abode, dwelling, living quarters**
The White House is the official residence
of the President. | |

| residue | n. | **remainder, leavings, remnant, dregs**
There was a black residue in the test-tube
after our experiment. | |

| resign | v. | **quit, step down, leave, vacate, retire**
She resigned from her job after a
disagreement with her boss.
n. Her resignation was accepted. | *retain, keep, remain* |

| resist | v. | **oppose, defy, withstand,
strive against**
The people resisted attempts by the new
government to make changes. | *submit, give in, yield,
surrender* |

| resistance | 1. n. | **opposition, defiance**
The government's proposals met with
strong resistance. | *1. submission,
acceptance* |
| | 2. n. | **immunity, endurance**
The weak have low resistance to illness. | |

resourceful		*adj.*	**ingenious, inventive, creative, imaginative, enterprising** The resourceful boy succeeded in raising money for college.	*unimaginative*
resources	1.	*n.*	**riches, assets, wealth, reserves** America is rich in natural resources.	
	2.	*n.*	**reserve, supply, source, stock** The Middle East has large resources of oil.	
respect	1.	*n.*	**esteem, admiration, deference, honor, reverence** The firefighters of New York City won the respect of the nation for their bravery on September 11, 2001.	*1. ridicule, scorn, disrespect, derision*
	2.	*v.*	**admire, value, honor, revere** We respect Christopher Reeve for his courage and determination.	*2. scorn, despise, mock, deride*
respectable	1.	*adj.*	**decent, honorable, upright, proper** She comes from a respectable family.	*1. disreputable, dishonorable*
	2.	*adj.*	**good, impressive, worthy** She makes a respectable income.	*2. bad, poor*
respectful		*adj.*	**polite, considerate, courteous** The people stood in respectful silence during the funeral.	*rude, impolite, disrespectful, contemptuous*
respond		*v.*	**answer, reply, acknowledge** Has the university responded to your application? *n.* Was it a favorable response?	*ignore, overlook, disregard, neglect*
responsible	1.	*adj.*	**dependable, reliable, trustworthy, competent** He is a responsible babysitter. *adv.* He always behaves responsibly.	*1. irresponsible, unreliable, flighty*
	2.	*adj.*	**liable, accountable, answerable** She is responsible for the safety of the children. *n.* Taking care of the children is a big responsibility.	*2. not responsible, not accountable*
rest	1.	*n.*	**break, breather, interlude** After an hour of hiking we stopped for a short rest.	
	2.	*n.*	**nap, snooze, sleep** The baby is having a rest.	
	3.	*n.*	**remainder, surplus, excess, balance** You may have the rest of the money.	
	4.	*v.*	**relax, laze, lounge, doze, snooze, nap** We rested after a busy week at school.	
	5.	*v.*	**lean, support, place, stand, balance** I rested my bicycle against the fence.	
restful		*adj.*	**peaceful, placid, tranquil, soothing** What a restful place for a holiday!	*irritating, loud, agitating, disturbing*

restless

1. *adj.* **agitated, fidgety, jumpy, flustered**
The crowd became restless after the long wait for the rock star to appear.

2. *adj.* **unsettled, uneasy, sleepless**
The baby was teething and had a restless night.

1. *calm, relaxed, placid, contented*

2. *peaceful*

restore

1. *v.* **replace, put back, return**
Restore the toys to the proper box.

2. *v.* **repair, recondition, refurbish, renew, reconstruct**
The new owners restored the old mansion to its former grandeur.
n. The restoration of the old manor took two years to complete.

3. *v.* **reinstate, reinstall, re-establish**
The police quickly restored law and order after the riots.

1. *remove, take, take away*

2. *destroy, ruin, spoil, wreck*

3. *expel, remove, dismiss, discharge*

restrain

v. **hold back, check, curb, bridle, repress, inhibit, confine, restrict**
The police formed a human chain to restrain the rowdy protesters.
n. They exercised restraint in dealing with their unpleasant neighbors.

encourage, urge, incite, free, let loose

restrict

v. **restrain, curb, check, confine, limit, control**
Bylaws restricted parking in the downtown core.
n. There is a restriction on the watering of lawns during the drought.

encourage, allow, permit, extend, expand, increase

result

n. **effect, consequence, conclusion, outcome, product**
Their success was the result of many years of hard work.
v. Their hard work resulted in success.

cause, origin

resume

v. **continue, go on, proceed with, recommence**
The transit workers resumed work after a long strike.
n. The resumption of transit service was much welcomed.

stop, cease, quit, discontinue

retain

1. *v.* **hold, keep, maintain**
The house is designed to retain heat.

2. *v.* **employ, engage, hire**
The accused man retained a lawyer.

3. *v.* **remember, recall, recollect, memorize**
Do you retain facts easily?

1. *relinquish, let go, drop, yield, give up*

2. *fire, let go, release*

3. *forget*

retaliate

v. **get even with, repay, pay back, avenge**
The leader vowed to retaliate against the soldiers who attacked the town.
n. The retaliation was swift and successful.

forgive, pardon

retard		*v.*	**delay, slow down, check, hinder, impede, hold up** Road works retarded traffic all day.	*expedite, promote, hasten, speed up*

retire	**1.**	*v.*	**withdraw, leave, depart, retreat, quit** She retired from the race when she became injured.	**1.** *join, take part in*
	2.	*v.*	**go to bed, lie down, rest, sleep** At what time did the guests retire?	**2.** *get up, rise, awaken*
	3.	*v.*	**resign, give up work** She retired at the age of sixty-five. *n.* She has been traveling since her retirement.	**3.** *work*

retort		*v.*	**reply, respond, answer, react** "No way!" the child retorted when she was asked to go to bed. *n.* What a rude retort!	*remain silent, question, ask, listen, reply calmly*

retract	**1.**	*v.*	**remove, draw in, withdraw** The cat retracted its claws.	**1.** *extend, put forth*
	2.	*v.*	**withdraw, recant, revoke, rescind** The witness retracted the statement she had made to the police.	**2.** *reaffirm, proclaim, admit, insist, assert, repeat*

retreat	**1.**	*n.*	**shelter, refuge, haven, sanctuary** The cottage is our summer retreat.	
	2.	*n.*	**withdrawal, evacuation, flight** Heavy bombing forced the rebels' retreat into the mountains. *v.* Troops retreated from the front lines after a day of heavy fighting.	**2.** *advance, progress, front*

retrieve		*v.*	**regain, reclaim, bring back, recover** Police retrieved the stolen goods from the robber's car.	*lose, give up, relinquish*

return	**1.**	*v.*	**come back, arrive, reappear** The astronauts returned after a long mission in space. *n.* Everyone cheered their safe return.	**1.** *go forward, advance, leave, depart*
	2.	*v.*	**restore, replace, send back, give back** I returned the books to the library.	**2.** *keep, hold back, retain*
	3.	*n.*	**profit, gain, yield, income** *n.* We made a handsome return on our investment.	**3.** *loss*

reveal	**1.**	*v.*	**expose, divulge, make known, disclose, tell, make public, publish** The report revealed secret information. *n.* The revelations shocked the nation.	**1.** *hide, keep secret, withhold, be silent*
	2.	*v.*	**expose, show, display, exhibit** She took off her hat and revealed her new hairdo.	**2.** *conceal, hide, veil, cover*

revenue		*n.*	**income, returns, earnings, yield** The business brings us a good revenue.	*expenses, expenditures*

reverse	**1.**	*n.*	**opposite, converse, antithesis** The true story is the reverse of what was described.
	2.	*v.*	**overturn, revoke, repeal, retract** The judge reversed the decision of the lower court.
review	**1.**	*n.*	**critique, evaluation, appraisal** The film received critical reviews. *n.* Only one reviewer liked the film.
	2.	*n.*	**study, analysis, survey, inspection** The school conducts a review of the students' progress each year. *v.* The teachers review students' progress.
revise	**1.**	*v.*	**edit, correct, rewrite, improve** The writer revised her story before submitting it to a publisher. *n.* The revision process greatly improved the story. *adj.* A revised edition of our science textbook has just been published.
	2.	*v.*	**change, alter, amend** The school revised its policy about Saturday classes.

revive	**1.**	*v.*	**enliven, renew, refresh, regenerate, invigorate, vivify, energize, restore** A cold drink revived the runners.	**1.** *wither, weaken*
	2.	*v.*	**rouse, recover, awaken** The patient surprised everyone when she revived from her coma. *n.* Her revival was a wonderful surprise.	
revolt		*n.*	**rebellion, revolution, uprising, mutiny** The protesters stirred up a revolt against the government. *v.* They revolted against the harsh laws.	*submission, obedience*
revolting		*adj.*	**disgusting, offensive, unpleasant** Revolting smells came from the dump.	*appetizing, pleasant, pleasing, appealing*
revolution	**1.**	*n.*	**rebellion, revolt, uprising, mutiny** The army put down a revolution by rebels.	**1.** *law, order, stability*
	2.	*n.*	**rotation, whirl, spin, turn, twirl, orbit** Wheels make many revolutions per minute.	
revolve		*v.*	**rotate, spin, whirl, twirl, turn** Car wheels revolve on axles. *adj.* Be careful with the revolving door.	
reward		*n.*	**payment, bonus, recompense, compensation, remuneration** A reward has been offered for information on the missing child. *v.* The police rewarded Simon for his help in finding the child.	*penalty, punishment, fine*

rhythm		*n.*	**tempo, beat, swing, cadence, meter, accent** This dance music has a Latin rhythm.	
rich	1.	*adj.*	**wealthy, prosperous, affluent** Rich countries should help the poorer nations. *n.* Some people are generous about sharing their riches. *n.* The rich live a life of luxury.	**1.** *poor, needy, destitute*
	2.	*adj.*	**fertile, luxuriant, fruitful, productive** This region is a rich farming area.	**2.** *sterile, barren, infertile*
	3.	*adj.*	**abundant, lush, copious, plentiful, profuse, luxuriant** Rich undergrowth is found in equatorial regions.	**3.** *inadequate, deficient*
	4.	*adj.*	**opulent, luxurious, sumptuous, extravagant, lavish, magnificent** The windows were draped in rich velvet. *adv.* The house is richly furnished.	**4.** *dull, drab, bland, cheap, simple, plain*
	5.	*adj.*	**deep, resonant, sonorous, mellow, full** The singer has a rich voice.	**5.** *thin, weak*
rickety		*adj.*	**wobbly, shaky, unsteady, feeble, fragile, weak** Don't climb the rickety fence!	*stable, secure, steady, firm*
riddle		*n.*	**puzzle, mystery, conundrum, enigma** It's a riddle as to who stole the painting.	*explanation, answer, solution*
ridicule	1.	*n.*	**derision, mockery, scorn, sarcasm** The critics heaped ridicule on the new play.	**1.** *respect, honor, praise, commendation*
	2.	*v.*	**laugh at, jeer, mock, make fun of, deride, snigger at, lampoon** Hecklers ridiculed the candidate's speech.	**2.** *respect, honor, approve, praise, applaud, encourage*
ridiculous		*adj.*	**absurd, silly, unreasonable, foolish, odd, preposterous, ludicrous, funny** It's ridiculous to spend so much money on a wedding.	*sensible, proper, respectable, usual*
right	1.	*n.*	**justice, truth, propriety** Children must be taught right from wrong.	**1.** *wrong, injustice, impropriety*
	2.	*n.*	**claim, liberty, privilege, authority** You had no right to drive my car without my permission.	
	3.	*v.*	**correct, repair, remedy, rectify, mend** Hopefully, the new laws will right some injustices.	**3.** *wrong, hurt, harm*
	4.	*v.*	**straighten, set upright, turn** Please right the garbage can.	**4.** *upset, overturn*
	5.	*adj.*	**suitable, apt, appropriate, proper** Make sure you wear the right clothes for the occasion.	**5.** *unsuitable, improper, inappropriate*
	6.	*adj.*	**true, correct, valid, accurate, precise** That is the right answer!	**6.** *invalid, wrong, incorrect, inaccurate*
	7.	*adj.*	**right-hand, right side** Make a right turn at the junction.	**7.** *left-hand, left side*

rigid	1.	*adj.*	**solid, stiff, firm, hard, unyielding** The tent is held up by a rigid frame.	1. *flexible, soft, yielding, pliant*
	2.	*adj.*	**strict, severe, exacting, harsh, firm** Rigid rules were in place at the school.	2. *lax, lenient, accommodating*
	3.	*adj.*	**fixed, set, definite, determined** World time zones are rigid.	3. *indefinite, changeable*
rigorous	1.	*adj.*	**severe, harsh, austere, rugged, extreme** Early settlers faced rigorous conditions.	1. *luxurious*
	2.	*adj.*	**exact, precise, accurate, meticulous** Each recruit was given a rigorous test.	2. *lax, slack, imprecise, inaccurate*
ring	1.	*n.*	**loop, circle, rim** Circus horses galloped around the ring.	
	2.	*n.*	**tinkle, chime, peal, jingle, jangle, clang** Everyone heard the ring of the doorbell. *v.* The phone rang in the middle of the night. *adj.* What is that ringing sound?	
	3.	*n.*	**band, group, gang, crew** The police finally succeeded in breaking up the smuggling ring.	
	4.	*v.*	**enclose, encircle, circle, surround, rim, gird, encompass** Tall trees ringed the garden.	
riot		*n.*	**revolt, uprising, tumult, protest** Riots resulted from a shortage of food. *v.* The citizens rioted in the streets. *adj.* Police quelled the riotous crowd.	*peace, harmony*
ripe		*adj.*	**mature, developed, ready, fit, mellow** These apples are ripe enough to eat. *v.* Fruit ripens on the trees.	*green, unripe, unfit, undeveloped, immature*
rise	1.	*n.*	**growth, increase, climb, inflation, ascent, upsurge** What is causing the rise in prices? *v.* Prices rose last month.	1. *fall, drop, decrease, reduction*
	2.	*v.*	**ascend, climb, lift, soar** The sun rises in the east.	2. *descend, set*
	3.	*v.*	**arise, stand up, get up** Please rise for the national anthem.	3. *sit down*
	4.	*v.*	**wake up, get out of bed** We rise at dawn at our summer camp.	4. *retire, go to sleep, go to bed*
	5.	*v.*	**begin, spring, issue, originate, start** Rivers rise in the hills. *n.* The invention of machines led to the rise of the Industrial Revolution.	5. *end, terminate*
risk	1.	*v.*	**venture, chance, gamble** He risked his life savings on his business. *n.* The risks are high when one gambles. *adj.* Gambling is a risky business.	1. *be safe, be secure*
	2.	*v.*	**jeopardize, endanger** She risked her life to save her child.	

rival	1.	*n.*	**opponent, competitor, antagonist** The sisters were rivals for the match.	**1.** *partner, colleague, ally, friend, mate*
	2.	*v.*	**match, equal, vie with, approximate, compare with, approach** These fireworks rival those of last year.	**2.** *cooperate, be unequal to*
rivalry		*n.*	**competition, opposition** There is a rivalry between the two sisters.	*cooperation*
road		*n.*	**street, thoroughfare, highway, route, path, track, passage, trail** Be careful when crossing the road.	
rob		*v.*	**burglarize, plunder, steal, loot, pillage** An armed man robbed the bank. *n.* Security at the bank has been tightened since the robbery.	*give, donate, return*
robber		*n.*	**thief, burglar, bandit, pirate** The robbers were caught in the act.	
robe		*n.*	**gown, cloak, mantle, cape, wrap** The judge wore a black robe.	
robust		*adj.*	**vigorous, sturdy, hardy, athletic, strong, healthy, hearty, hale** The robust athletes practiced all day.	*weak, frail, puny, feeble*
rock	1.	*n.*	**stone, boulder, pebble** Move the rocks out of the way. *adj.* The rocky road is bad for my car.	
	2.	*v.*	**sway, pitch, lurch, teeter, wobble, roll, swing, reel, shake, move** The boat rocked back and forth in the choppy waters.	**2.** *remain still, be stationary, be fixed*
rogue		*n.*	**scoundrel, rascal, villain, scamp** The rogue was arrested by the police.	
role	1.	*n.*	**task, function, duty, job** My role is to help new students settle into the school.	
	2.	*n.*	**part, character** Pina has the lead role in the play.	
roll	1.	*n.*	**record, list, register, catalog, index** Yang made the honor roll in school.	
	2.	*v.*	**rotate, spin, turn over, revolve** The golf ball rolled into the hole.	**2.** *stay still*
	3.	*v.*	**flatten, press, level** My brother rolled the lawn.	**3.** *fluff up*
	4.	*v.*	**tilt, sway, rock, pitch** The canoe rolled on the large waves. *n.* The roll of the waves made me sick.	
	5.	*v.*	**wrap up, curl up** She rolled up the poster and put it away in a cardboard tube.	

romantic		*adj.*	**dreamy, fanciful, idyllic, sentimental** They had a romantic honeymoon.	*realistic, unromantic, down-to-earth*
rookie		*n.*	**beginner, novice, recruit, tyro** Taka was chosen as the best rookie in the hockey league this year.	*veteran, expert*
root	1.	*n.*	**reason, cause, origin, source** The mechanic found the root of the problem.	**1.** *consequence, result*
	2.	*n.*	**bottom, base, lower part** Plants absorb water through their roots.	**2.** *top, upper part*
rot		*v.*	**decay, spoil, decompose, putrefy** Vegetables rot in the heat. *adj.* Rotten food must be thrown out.	
rotate		*v.*	**revolve, turn, twirl, whirl, spin, circle** The Earth rotates on its axis. *n.* The rate of the Earth's rotation can be measured.	
rough	1.	*adj.*	**uneven, bumpy, irregular, coarse, jagged** She cut her knee when she fell on the rough driveway.	**1.** *smooth, even, regular, polished, level, flat*
	2.	*adj.*	**coarse, crude, disorderly, rude, vulgar, uncivil, boorish** The rough behavior of the audience upset the performers.	**2.** *polite, courteous, orderly, civil, mannerly*
	3.	*adj.*	**approximate, inexact, imprecise** The plumber gave us a rough estimate of the cost. *adv.* It takes roughly two hours to drive to the cottage.	**3.** *exact, precise*
round		*adj.*	**circular, spherical, globular** The Earth is round.	*square, flat, straight, angular*
rouse	1.	*v.*	**arouse, waken** Loud noises roused the sleeping family.	**1.** *lull, soothe*
	2.	*v.*	**excite, stir up, incite, provoke** The politician roused his supporters into action with his passionate speech.	**2.** *lull, soothe, calm, placate*
route		*n.*	**path, road, track, course, way, direction** We marked our route on the map before setting off on our trip.	
routine	1.	*n.*	**habit, program, practice, system, regimen, procedure** We have a busy routine at school.	
	2.	*adj.*	**customary, usual, general, regular, habitual, scheduled** The children are due for their routine dental checkup.	**2.** *irregular, unusual, rare, unscheduled*

row		*n.*	**quarrel, disturbance, brawl, fight, squabble, disagreement, hassle** They had a row over who should cut the grass.	*harmony, agreement*

| **row** | 1. | *n.* | **line, queue, file, column**
The children stood in a neat row. |
| | 2. | *v.* | **paddle**
We rowed down the river in our canoe. |

| **rowdy** | | *adj.* | **noisy, loud, boisterous, disorderly, rebellious, unruly**
Rowdy crowds disrupted the soccer game. | *orderly, quiet, mannerly, lawful* |

| **royal** | | *adj.* | **regal, majestic, grand, superb, august, splendid, magnificent, noble**
Queen Elizabeth's coronation was celebrated with royal pomp. | *mean, lowly, base, humble* |

| **rub** | | *v.* | **scrape, scour, grate, chafe, polish**
Rub the tarnished brass with this cloth.
n. Give it a good rub. |

| **rubbish** | | *n.* | **trash, litter, refuse, garbage, waste, debris, junk, dregs, dross**
Dump the rubbish in these bags. | *treasure, valuables* |

rude	1.	*adj.*	**discourteous, impolite, impudent, boorish, insolent, disrespectful** The rude child was told to leave the class. *n.* Rudeness is not to be tolerated.	**1.** *polite, courteous, refined, cultured, civil*
	2.	*adj.*	**harsh, rough, violent** The company's bankruptcy came as a rude shock to the workers.	**2.** *gentle, mild*
	3.	*adj.*	**coarse, crude, obscene, vulgar, offensive** We were shocked by his rude jokes.	**3.** *refined, decent*

| **rugged** | 1. | *adj.* | **tough, strong, sturdy, robust, vigorous, hale, healthy, hardy**
Rugged pioneers braved the harsh conditions of the territory. | **1.** *weak, frail, puny* |
| | 2. | *adj.* | **rough, uneven, harsh, severe, hilly, broken, mountainous**
Guerrillas often hide in rugged terrain. | **2.** *even, smooth, flat* |

| **ruin** | | *v.* | **wreck, raze, demolish, destroy, damage**
A fire ruined the historic building.
n. The building was a ruin after the fire. | *build, erect, save, protect, restore, renew* |

rule	1.	*n.*	**law, regulation, edict, code, act, decree, statute, canon** We have to observe the school's rules.
	2.	*n.*	**custom, habit, practice, routine** As a rule, we eat out on Sunday.
	3.	*v.*	**govern, administer, lead, direct** Queen Victoria ruled England for many years.

	4.	*v.*	**order, decree, command, direct, judge** The government ruled it necessary to wear seat belts in the car.	**4.** *suggest, request*
rumor		*n.*	**gossip, talk, hearsay, tale** Rumors of his arrival proved to be false.	*fact, truth*
run	**1.**	*n.*	**sprint, lope, amble** Dogs need a daily run.	
	2.	*v.*	**hurry, speed, race, gallop, sprint, dart, dash, rush, bolt, scamper** We ran all the way to school as we were late.	**2.** *walk, stroll, saunter*
	3.	*v.*	**flow, gush, glide, pass through** The river runs through the town.	**3.** *stagnate, stop, end*
	4.	*v.*	**manage, direct, supervise, operate, control, govern, command** Who runs the local radio station?	
	5.	*v.*	**depart, flee** The dog ran away when the skunk tried to spray him.	**5.** *stay, remain, stand firm*
	6.	*v.*	**move, travel, go** The bus runs by our house every fifteen minutes.	
	7.	*v.*	**work, function, perform, operate** The car runs better after the tune-up.	
rural		*adj.*	**rustic, countrified, suburban, agricultural, pastoral** Rural areas have a smaller population than urban areas.	*urban, industrial, commercial, metropolitan*
ruse		*n.*	**trick, wile, subterfuge, gimmick, device** Police used a ruse to capture the crook.	*truth, honesty, sincerity*
rush	**1.**	*n.*	**haste, speed, scramble, hurry, dash** There was a rush to get home before the storm.	**1.** *delay*
	2.	*n.*	**stampede, charge, onslaught, dash** There was a rush for seats when the theater doors opened. *v.* The patrons rushed for the seats.	
rustic	**1.**	*adj.*	**countrified, rural, pastoral** The tourists enjoyed the rustic charm of the village.	**1.** *urban, industrial, commercial, citified, metropolitan*
	2.	*adj.*	**simple, plain, unsophisticated, natural** The rustic furniture suited the decor of the chalet.	**2.** *urbane, complex, sophisticated*
ruthless		*adj.*	**brutal, cruel, harsh, pitiless, merciless, vicious, savage** The dictator launched a ruthless attack on his enemies.	*merciful, kind, tender, compassionate*

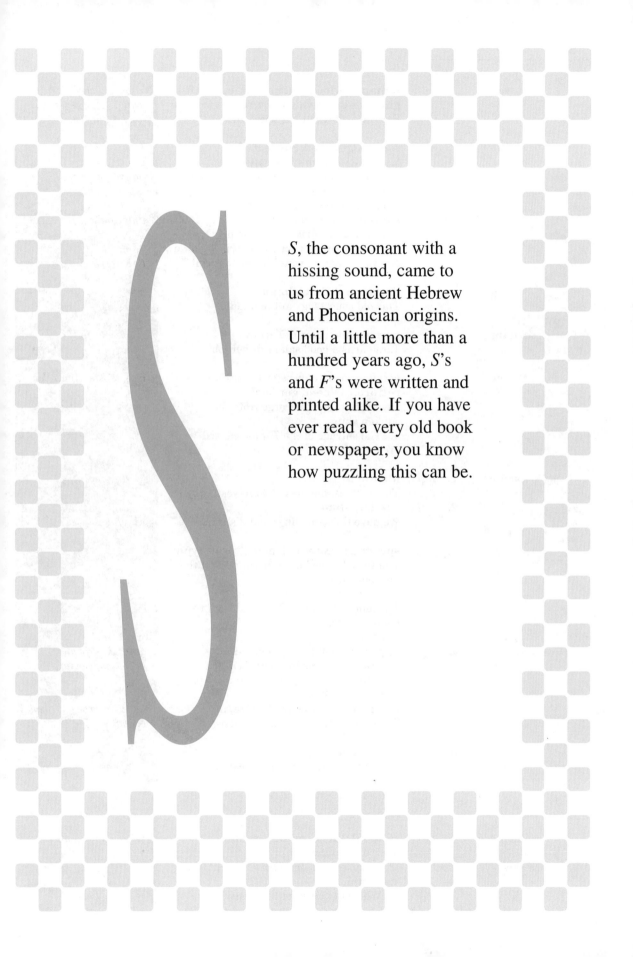

S, the consonant with a hissing sound, came to us from ancient Hebrew and Phoenician origins. Until a little more than a hundred years ago, *S*'s and *F*'s were written and printed alike. If you have ever read a very old book or newspaper, you know how puzzling this can be.

sad		*adj.*	**unhappy, gloomy, dejected, mournful, glum, depressed, sorrowful, downcast** Pat was sad when her dog died.	*happy, cheerful, joyous, glad, spirited, jolly, light-hearted*
safe	1.	*adj.*	**secure, guarded, protected** Keep the valuables in a safe place. *adv.* We made sure the door was safely locked before we left.	*1. unsafe, risky, unprotected, dangerous, exposed*
	2.	*adj.*	**careful, reliable, dependable, cautious, responsible** The school bus driver is a safe driver.	*2. reckless, unreliable*
	3.	*adj.*	**harmless, pure, non-toxic, wholesome** Are you sure this water is safe to drink?	*3. harmful, hazardous*
sag		*v.*	**droop, dip, sink, slump** This old couch sags in the middle.	*rise*
salary		*n.*	**pay, wages, remuneration** Tara earns a good salary at her job.	
salvage		*v.*	**retrieve, recover, regain, rescue, restore, redeem, get back** Divers salvaged the cargo from the sunken ship. *n.* The salvage of the *Titanic* caused great excitement.	*lose, waste, squander*
same	1.	*adj.*	**identical** This is the same dress I wore yesterday.	*1. different*
	2.	*adj.*	**similar, alike** We have the same likes and dislikes.	*2. different, unrelated*
sample	1.	*n.*	**specimen, example, model, prototype** The store handed out free samples of the new perfume.	
	2.	*v.*	**test, try, taste, examine, inspect** The judges sampled all the cakes in the baking contest.	
sanction	1.	*n.*	**approval, consent, permission, assent, approbation, ratification** The students were granted sanction to hold a school dance.	*1. disapproval, objection, censure*
	2.	*v.*	**confirm, endorse, authorize, approve** The school board sanctioned plans for a new school building.	*2. disapprove, censor, object*
	3.	*n.*	**ban, embargo, penalty, fine, injunction, punishment, restraint, restriction** The United Nations voted to place trade sanctions against that country.	*3. reward, compensation*
sane		*adj.*	**rational, lucid, sound, stable, mentally balanced** The accused was declared sane and fit to stand trial. *n.* Who will vouch for his sanity?	*insane, irrational, mad*

sanitary		*adj.*	**clean, hygienic, purified, disinfected, sterile, germ-free** Hospitals must be kept in a sanitary condition.	*dirty, contaminated, unsanitary*
sap		*v.*	**undermine, weaken, drain, exhaust** The intense heat sapped our energy.	*revive, revitalize, improve, increase*
satisfaction		*n.*	**contentment, pleasure, pride** She smiled with satisfaction when she heard that she had won first prize.	*dissatisfaction, dismay, frustration*
satisfactory		*adj.*	**adequate, acceptable, pleasing** Bev cooked a satisfactory meal.	*unsatisfactory, unacceptable*
satisfy		*v.*	**please, gratify, make happy** The salesclerks are trained to satisfy all customers.	*dissatisfy, displease, disappoint, vex, annoy*
saturate		*v.*	**drench, soak, permeate** Heavy rains saturated the fields.	*dry, parch*
saucy		*adj.*	**impudent, rude, flippant, bold, impertinent, brazen, insolent** Sally's saucy remarks upset us.	*polite, courteous, shy, modest*
savage	1.	*adj.*	**wild, untamed, unrestrained** Lions are savage animals.	1. *tame, civilized, domesticated*
	2.	*adj.*	**cruel, brutal, ferocious, furious, violent, merciless, ruthless** The huge beast made a savage attack on the hunter.	2. *kind, gentle, humane, merciful*
save	1.	*v.*	**rescue, deliver, extricate, free, liberate, release, salvage** Firefighters saved the person trapped in the burning house.	1. *desert, leave, abandon*
	2.	*v.*	**protect, shield, safeguard, preserve** Seat covers save the upholstery from damage.	2. *destroy, dirty, mar, damage*
	3.	*v.*	**hoard, gather, reserve, lay aside, set aside, collect, store** Joe saved all his money for a new computer.	3. *throw away, give up, waste, spend, squander*
savory		*adj.*	**appetizing, delectable, scrumptious, tasty, palatable, delicious, luscious** Everyone loves Grandma's savory pies.	*tasteless, insipid, unpalatable, unappetizing*
say		*v.*	**utter, speak, tell, express, declare, assert, announce** Did you hear what she said?	*keep quiet, remain silent*
scale	1.	*n.*	**covering, layer, coating, encrustation** Do all fish and reptiles have scales?	
	2.	*v.*	**climb, mount, ascend** Sir Edmund Hillary was the first man to scale Mount Everest.	2. *descend*

	3. *v.*	**scrape, peel, skin, flake, strip off, husk, shell, shuck, pare, exfoliate** The dentist scaled the plaque from the patient's teeth.	**3.** *cover, wrap, encase, envelop*
scales	*n.*	**balance** Weigh the bananas on the scales.	
scan	**1.** *v.*	**scrutinize, study, examine, survey** Searchlights scanned the sky for enemy aircraft.	**1.** *ignore, overlook, neglect*
	2. *v.*	**glance at, thumb through, browse, skim, flip through** Patients scan magazines in the waiting room of the doctor's office.	**2.** *study, peruse, examine, scrutinize, concentrate*
	3. *v.*	**reproduce or copy electronically** She scanned a photo of herself to e-mail to her friends. *n.* She bought a new scanner for her computer.	
scanty	*adj.*	**meager, sparse, little, skimpy, insufficient, limited** There was a scanty supply of food during the war. *adv.* The scantily dressed child was shivering in the cold.	*ample, sufficient, adequate, full, unlimited, copious*
scarce	*adj.*	**rare, insufficient, uncommon** Some of our natural resources are becoming scarce from overuse.	*plentiful, ample, sufficient, common, abundant*
scare	*v.*	**frighten, alarm, terrify** The violent storm scared the children. *n.* The loud knock in the middle of the night gave everyone a scare. *adj.* Rob wore a scary mask for Halloween.	*soothe, calm, comfort*
scatter	**1.** *v.*	**sow, strew, spread, sprinkle** The farmer scattered the seeds in the field.	**1.** *reap, collect, gather*
	2. *v.*	**separate, disperse, disband, diverge** The demonstrators scattered when the police arrived.	**2.** *assemble, collect, congregate, gather, convene*
scene	**1.** *n.*	**landscape, view, vista, panorama, spectacle** The tourists photographed the beautiful scene from the mountaintop. *adj.* They drove along the scenic route. *n.* The scenery along the route was spectacular.	
	2. *n.*	**location, site, place, position** Police rushed to the scene of the crime.	
	3. *n.*	**act, part, episode** The movie is unsuitable for children because it has violent scenes.	

scent	1.	*n.*	**perfume, pleasant smell, fragrance, aroma, odor** Roses have a lovely scent.	**1.** *stench, stink*
	2.	*n.*	**trail, smell** Police dogs were used to follow the scent of the robbers.	
schedule	1.	*n.*	**program, plan, agenda, timetable** According to the airline schedule, the first flight is at nine o'clock.	
	2.	*v.*	**book, plan, arrange, set a time** I scheduled a meeting for tomorrow.	
scheme	1.	*n.*	**plan, design, project** The class drew up a scheme to raise money for the trip.	
	2.	*n.*	**plot, conspiracy** The terrorists' scheme to kidnap the President was uncovered by the FBI. *v.* The terrorists had schemed to take over the government.	
scintillate		*v.*	**sparkle, flash, glitter, gleam, glint, twinkle, shimmer, shine, glimmer** The singer's beaded costume scintillated under the stage lights.	*remain dull*
scoff		*v.*	**sneer, jeer, mock, taunt, deride, ridicule, be contemptuous of, belittle** Ian scoffed at Lee for losing the game.	*admire, respect, sympathize with, praise*
scold		*v.*	**reprimand, rebuke, reprove** Ben scolded Jon for being rude. *n.* He was upset by the scolding.	*praise, encourage, extol, laud*
scope		*n.*	**extent, amount, size, degree, measure, range, magnitude** Forecasters are unsure of the scope of the storm.	
scorch		*v.*	**char, blacken, burn, parch, wither, shrivel, sear** Flames scorched the wheat fields as the fire raged. *adj.* The scorched fields were a dreadful sight.	
score	1.	*n.*	**points, marks, tally, rating** Yun got a good score in her science test.	
	2.	*v.*	**gain a point, win a point** Jan scored the winning goal in the final seconds of the game. *n.* Wayne Gretzky was a leading scorer for his hockey team.	**2.** *lose a point*
	3.	*v.*	**scratch, damage, mar, deface, mark, disfigure** The cook accidentally scored the table with a sharp knife.	**3.** *protect, save, shield, guard, preserve*

scorn	1.	*v.*	**despise, disdain, have contempt for, look down upon** The public scorned the traitors. *n.* The press heaped scorn on the traitors during their trial. *adj.* People were scornful of the traitors for betraying their country. *adv.* The traitor was treated scornfully.	*1. respect, honor, admire, flatter*
	2.	*v.*	**reject, spurn, shun, renounce, mock** The company scorned the inventor's idea.	*2. welcome, accept, acknowledge*
scoundrel		*n.*	**scamp, rogue, rascal, villain** The scoundrel disappeared with the money raised for charity.	
scowl		*v.*	**glower, frown, glare** The librarian scowled at the noisy students. *n.* The students settled down when they saw the librarian's scowl.	*smile, grin, beam*
scrap	1.	*n.*	**particle, piece, portion, fragment, crumb** After dinner, Fred cleaned the scraps off the table.	*1. whole*
	2.	*n.*	**iota, jot, speck, bit** Police could not find a scrap of evidence at the scene of the crime.	
	3.	*n.*	**junk, garbage, waste, trash, refuse** The dealer said my old car should be sold for scrap. *v.* I scrapped my car at the junkyard.	*3. valuables, treasure*
	4.	*v.*	**discard, abandon, cancel, reject** Rain caused us to scrap our plans for a picnic.	*4. keep, retain, save, maintain*
scrape		*v.*	**rub, scour, scratch, grate** Pat scraped the ice off the windshield. *n.* She used an ice scraper for the job.	
scrawl		*n.*	**scribble, scratch** The pharmacist could not read the doctor's illegible scrawl. *v.* Vandals scrawled all over the walls.	
scrawny		*adj.*	**lean, thin, skinny, gaunt, lanky** Pictures of the scrawny war orphans touched the hearts of everyone.	*brawny, muscular, heavy-set*
scream		*n.*	**shriek, cry, screech, squeal, yell** The victim's frightened screams could be heard a block away. *v.* The robbers dashed off when the victims screamed for help.	*sob, sigh, whisper*
screech		*n.*	**scream, shriek, cry, squeal, yell** We were awakened by the screech of tires. *v.* The parrot screeched for attention.	

screen	1.	*v.*	**hide, veil, conceal, mask, shield, guard** A high fence screened the movie star's house from curious fans. *n.* Use a sun screen to prevent sunburn.	1. *expose, uncover*
	2.	*v.*	**choose, select, sort, examine, analyze** The hiring team screens all applicants.	
	3.	*n.*	**curtain, partition, divider** The nurse put a screen between the beds.	
scrimp		*v.*	**save, economize** They scrimped to put their daughter through college.	*spend, waste, splurge, squander*
scrutinize		*v.*	**examine, watch carefully, view, study, inspect** The detectives scrutinized all the clues at the scene of the robbery. *n.* The suspects were held under close scrutiny.	*glance at*
search		*v.*	**look for, probe, hunt, seek** The children searched for Easter eggs. *n.* They were successful in their search.	*find, discover, uncover*
season	1.	*n.*	**term, period, spell, interval, time** Fall is the most beautiful season of the year.	
	2.	*v.*	**condition, age, cure, dry out** Bob seasoned the wood before building the cabinet. *adj.* Seasoned firewood burns well.	
	3.	*v.*	**marinate, spice, make tasty** Season the steaks with salt and pepper. *n.* Soya sauce is a seasoning used in Chinese cooking.	
seasoned		*adj.*	**trained, prepared, experienced** Jacques is a seasoned diver.	*inexperienced, untrained, green*
secret	1.	*n.*	**mystery, confidence** Can you keep a secret? *adv.* They left the country secretly.	1. *disclosure, exposure*
	2.	*adj.*	**concealed, hidden, secluded** The money is kept in a secret place.	2. *open, revealed, obvious, public*
	3.	*adj.*	**confidential, intimate, private** The captives made secret plans to escape.	3. *public*
secretive		*adj.*	**veiled, concealed, covert, furtive, mysterious** Their secretive behavior aroused everyone's curiosity.	*open, frank, overt, public, aboveboard*
section	1.	*n.*	**part, share, piece, slice, segment, portion, division** They divided the cake into sections.	1. *whole, entirety, aggregate*
	2.	*n.*	**region, area, sector, district** Traffic is heavy in this section of the city.	

sector		*n.*	**area, quarter, section, part, portion**	*whole, entirety*

sector   *n.*   **area, quarter, section, part, portion**   *whole, entirety*
We hurried through the rough sector of town.

secure
1. *v.* **guard, defend, protect, shield**   **1.** *abandon, forsake*
The soldiers secured the fort against the enemy.
2. *v.* **obtain, get**   **2.** *be refused*
Lara secured permission to attend the lecture.
3. *v.* **fasten, tighten**   **3.** *loosen, untie, unfasten*
The skipper secured the boat with ropes.
adv. The boat was tied securely.

sediment   *n.*   **residue, dregs, silt, deposit**
A delta is formed from the sediment at the mouth of a river.

see
1. *v.* **watch, perceive, observe, regard, notice, look at, pay attention to**   **1.** *disregard, miss*
Maria slipped because she did not see the ice on the sidewalk.
2. *v.* **understand, comprehend, discern**   **2.** *misunderstand*
I see what you mean.
3. *v.* **ensure, make sure, take care**
See that you do your homework before you watch television.
4. *v.* **visit, meet**
I'm going to see my aunt next week.
5. *v.* **imagine, consider, envision**
I see him as a leader some day.

seek
1. *v.* **look for, search, hunt, pursue**   **1.** *ignore, neglect, disregard, find*
Police sought the escaped convict.
2. *v.* **try, endeavor, attempt, strive**   **2.** *ignore, abandon, discard*
Three persons seek to hold the position of mayor.

seize
1. *v.* **hang onto, take hold of, grasp, clutch, grip, catch, clench**   **1.** *release, let go, relinquish*
The bully seized Todd by the arm.
2. *v.* **grab, snatch, take by force, apprehend, capture, impound, commandeer**   **2.** *return, restore, replace, reimburse*
Customs officers seized the smuggled goods.

seldom   *adv.*   **rarely, not often, hardly ever, infrequently**   *often, frequently, regularly*
This team seldom loses.

select
1. *v.* **choose, pick out, designate, elect, decide on**   **1.** *reject, decline, refuse*
Have you selected your courses for this semester?
adj. Only a select few will be admitted to the meeting.
n. This store has a good selection of books.

	2.	*adj.*	**exclusive, superior, choice** This company manufactures a select line of sportswear.	**2.** *inferior, common*
send	**1.**	*v.*	**dispatch, forward, transmit, convey** Please send the check by express mail.	**1.** *get, receive, import*
	2.	*v.*	**throw, cast, fling, propel, hurl** The pitcher sent the ball to first base.	**2.** *clutch, grasp, hold, grab, retain*
sensation	**1.**	*n.*	**feeling, response, sentiment, emotion** Love is a wonderful sensation.	
	2.	*n.*	**sensitiveness, feeling, sensitivity, response** That patient has no sensation in his legs.	**2.** *numbness*
sensational		*adj.*	**spectacular, astonishing, exciting, incredible, marvelous, thrilling** The play was a sensational success.	*dull, uninteresting, boring, tedious, humdrum, banal*
sense		*n.*	**understanding, reason, appreciation, judgment, perception** Artists have an excellent sense of color.	*ignorance, misunderstanding*
senseless	**1.**	*adj.*	**foolish, absurd, silly, ridiculous, stupid, illogical** His senseless talk bored everyone.	**1.** *wise, sensible, intelligent, logical*
	2.	*adj.*	**unconscious** The senseless boxer was rushed to the hospital.	**2.** *conscious*
sensible	**1.**	*adj.*	**discerning, sane, rational, level-headed** The sensible girl chose to study for her exam instead of going out with friends.	**1.** *foolish, stupid, silly, scatterbrained, absurd, thoughtless*
	2.	*adj.*	**logical, prudent, reasonable** Taking an umbrella was a sensible thing to do.	
sensitive	**1.**	*adj.*	**delicate, sore, tender, painful** Sunburned skin is sensitive to the touch.	**1.** *insensitive, comfortable*
	2.	*adj.*	**touchy, high-strung, nervous, irritable** The sensitive actor stormed off the stage when the audience booed.	**2.** *impervious, indifferent, apathetic*
	3.	*adj.*	**alert, aware, perceptive** Police dogs are highly sensitive to smell.	**3.** *unaware, oblivious*
sentiment		*n.*	**feeling, emotion, thought** Romantic sentiments are expressed in Valentine's Day cards.	
sentimental		*adj.*	**emotional, romantic** The family reunion was a sentimental affair for everyone.	*hard, callous, unemotional*
separate	**1.**	*v.*	**keep apart, part, divide, disconnect** The driveway separated the two houses.	**1.** *join, connect, fasten, link, integrate*
	2.	*v.*	**divorce, uncouple, undo** The couple separated after a brief marriage.	**2.** *unite*

n. Their separation surprised us.

3. *adj.* **distinct, individual, unconnected, unrelated** | 3. *connected, related, linked*
Each group will work on a separate project.

sequence

1. *n.* **order, progression, flow, succession** | 1. *disorder, jumble*
The names were listed in alphabetical sequence.

2. *n.* **series, chain, string, set** | 2. *one*
The actor appeared in a sequence of films.

serene

adj. **calm, tranquil, composed, placid, peaceful, unruffled** | *ruffled, excited, tempestuous, turbulent, agitated*
We picnicked at a serene spot by the lake.

serious

1. *adj.* **thoughtful, earnest, sincere** | 1. *light-hearted, frivolous*
That issue requires serious thought.

2. *adj.* **sober, solemn, thoughtful, grave** | 2. *happy, joyful*
The doctor's serious expression told us something was wrong.

3. *adj.* **important, significant** | 3. *unimportant, insignificant*
That's a serious mistake!

4. *adj.* **grave, critical, dangerous** | 4. *trivial, minor*
Cancer is a serious disease.
adv. Mavis is seriously ill with cancer.

service

1. *n.* **aid, help, assistance** | 1. *hindrance, opposition*
She was awarded a medal for services rendered during the war.

2. *n.* **work, duty**
The company offers service with a smile.

3. *v.* **repair, care for**
The mechanic serviced the car.

settle

v. **determine, decide, confirm, agree on, resolve, end** | *argue, debate, discuss, disagree*
Have the neighbors settled their dispute over the fence?

settlement

1. *n.* **agreement, arrangement, compact, contract** | 1. *disagreement, impasse*
A settlement was reached in the dispute between the two teams.

2. *n.* **payment, compensation, reimbursement** | 2. *non-payment*
The injured worker received a large settlement from the insurance company.

3. *n.* **colony, community, establishment**
Quebec City was one of the first settlements in North America.

severe

1. *adj.* **harsh, rigid, strict, stern, exacting, austere, grim, forbidding, relentless** | 1. *lax, lenient, merciful, genial*
The judge handed the traitor a severe sentence.

2. *adj.* **intense, sharp, cutting, extreme, keen** | 2. *slight, moderate*
Grandpa suffered severe chest pains.

shabby	1.	*adj.*	**ragged, worn, threadbare, dilapidated, poor, run-down, seedy** The beggar wore shabby clothes. *adv.* He was shabbily dressed.	**1.** *new, well-kept*
	2.	*adj.*	**mean, miserable, unkind, low, contemptible, thoughtless** Oliver Twist received shabby treatment in the orphanage.	**2.** *kind, generous, noble, considerate*
shady		*adj.*	**shaded, dusky, shadowy, dim, sheltered** Some plants grow best in shady places.	*sunny, bright*
shake		*v.*	**tremble, quiver, shiver, quake, shudder, vibrate** Earthquakes cause the ground to shake.	*remain still*
sham		*n.*	**counterfeit, fake, imitation, pretense** The thief replaced the famous painting with a sham.	*original, fact, reality*
shame		*n.*	**disgrace, dishonor, embarrassment, discredit, humiliation, disrepute** The traitor brought shame upon his family. *v.* His behavior shamed the family. *adj.* What a shameful thing to do.	*pride, honor, credit, respect, praise, approval, glory*
shameless	1.	*adj.*	**brazen, bold, rude, forward, vulgar, impudent, immodest** The rowdy guests were told to stop their shameless behavior. *adv.* He behaved shamelessly at the party.	**1.** *polite, cultured, courteous, modest*
	2.	*adj.*	**unashamed, unabashed** Lee was expelled from school for his shameless cheating.	**2.** *repentant, sorry*
shape	1.	*n.*	**form, figure, outline, mold, contour, appearance, frame** Some sails have a triangular shape.	
	2.	*v.*	**form, fashion, mold, make, build, construct, pattern** The sculptor shaped a horse out of the clay.	
share	1.	*n.*	**part, portion, quota, lot, section, allotment, allowance, division, helping, serving, ration, fraction, percentage** Divide the money into equal shares.	**1.** *whole, total, entirety, aggregate*
	2.	*v.*	**divide, allot, distribute, apportion** The winners shared the prizes.	**2.** *unite, combine*
	3.	*v.*	**participate, take part in** The teachers shared in the discussion with their pupils.	**3.** *take no part in, avoid, shun*
sharp	1.	*adj.*	**keen, acute, razor-edged, honed, sharpened** A sharp knife is needed to cut roast beef.	**1.** *blunt, dull, unsharpened*
	2.	*adj.*	**severe, harsh, piercing, intense** Sharp winds made skiing impossible.	**2.** *mild, gentle*

	3.	*adj.*	**cutting, biting, sarcastic, caustic** Sharp remarks can hurt a person's feelings.	3. *thoughtful, pleasing, kind, complimentary*
	4.	*adj.*	**clever, bright, alert, shrewd, intelligent** Luke is the sharpest student in the class.	4. *unintelligent, stupid, dull*
	5.	*adj.*	**watchful, alert, vigilant, attentive, close, observant** Keep a sharp eye on the luggage!	5. *inattentive, careless, negligent*
	6.	*adj.*	**pointed, spiked, peaked, barbed** The vet was scratched by the cat's sharp claws.	6. *rounded, smooth*
	7.	*adj.*	**bitter, pungent, biting, acrid, acidic** Lemons have a sharp taste.	7. *bland, insipid, tasteless*
shatter		*v.*	**burst, break, split, splinter, smash, disintegrate, destroy** Windows shattered during the earthquake.	*remain intact, keep intact*
shear	1.	*v.*	**cut, shave, trim, clip** Who will shear the lamb's wool in the spring? *adj.* Shorn lambs are a sorry sight. *n.* Shears are used to trim bushes.	
	2.	*v.*	**remove, withdraw, deprive, strip** The commander sheared the officer of his rank for improper conduct.	
	3.	*v.*	**cleave, sever** The truck sheared the car into two parts in the accident.	
sheer	1.	*adj.*	**steep, abrupt, precipitous** There's a sheer drop from the top of the bluff to the sea.	1. *gradual, slight, gentle*
	2.	*adj.*	**thin, flimsy, transparent, delicate, fine, diaphanous** The actress wore sheer nylon stockings.	2. *thick, heavy, coarse*
	3.	*adj.*	**absolute, utter, complete, total** Many rescuers were ill from sheer exhaustion.	3. *mild, slight, partial*
shelter	1.	*n.*	**refuge, haven, sanctuary, retreat, cover, protection, safety** Don't take shelter under trees during an electrical storm.	1. *peril, hazard, danger*
	2.	*v.*	**protect, shield, screen, guard, safeguard** Umbrellas shelter us in rainy weather.	2. *expose, endanger*
	3.	*v.*	**cover, conceal, secure, preserve, house, hide** He sheltered a fugitive in his barn.	3. *reveal, evict, turn out*
shield		*v.*	**protect, cover, preserve, shelter, guard, defend** The bear shielded its cub from the hunter's bullets. *n.* The warrior's shield saved him from the enemy's spear.	*expose, uncover, endanger*

shift

1. *n.* **turn, spell, working time, working period**
Are you working the day or night shift?

2. *n.* **change, transfer, substitution, alteration, variation**
A shift in the winds brought rain.

2. permanence, steadiness

3. *v.* **move, relocate, transfer**
We shifted the old furniture to the cottage.

3. stay

shiftless

adj. **lazy, indolent, inactive**
The shiftless worker was told to pull up his socks.

industrious, active, hard-working

shifty

adj. **sly, cunning, tricky, elusive, evasive**
The stranger's shifty looks aroused our suspicion.

open, frank, candid, undesigning, straightforward

shimmer

v. **gleam, glow, scintillate, glisten, shine**
Water shimmers in the moonlight.
adj. The singer wore a shimmery gown.

shine

1. *n.* **luster, polish, gleam, gloss, brilliance**
The table looked beautiful with the shine of polished silver.

1. tarnish, dullness

2. *v.* **glow, gleam, scintillate, beam, radiate, sparkle**
The sun shone on their wedding day.

2. remain dull

3. *v.* **polish, scour, wax, burnish, clean**
The cadets shined their shoes before the parade.

3. tarnish, scuff

ship

v. **send, dispatch, transport, deliver**
Tankers ship oil across the oceans.

receive, import

shiver

v. **shake, shudder, tremble, quake, quiver**
The skaters shivered in the cold.
n. The scary movie sent shivers down my spine.
adj. Joe was shivery with a high fever.

shock

1. *n.* **blow, jolt, jar, impact, crash, collision**
The buildings tumbled from the shock of the earthquake.

2. *v.* **startle, agitate, disturb**
The burst of gunfire shocked us.

2. calm, quieten

3. *v.* **insult, outrage, horrify, revolt, anger, astound, dismay, appall**
The vandalism caused by the gangs shocked the community.
adj. The gang members were punished for their shocking behavior.

3. please, delight, comfort, relieve

shore

1. *n.* **coast, bank, beach, coastline**
The house sits on the shores of a lake.

2. *v.* **support, prop up**
Ted shored the sagging roof with a pillar.

2. let down, collapse

short	1.	*adj.*	**brief, curtailed, short-lived, fleeting, concise, limited** The whole family spent a short vacation in Bermuda.	**1.** *long, extended, prolonged, extensive*
	2.	*adj.*	**not tall, little, low, tiny, small** Who is the shortest basketball player?	**2.** *tall, long, large*
	3.	*adj.*	**inadequate, deficient, lacking, insufficient** The charity will be short of funds this year because of poor contributions. *n.* This year's drought will cause a shortage of fruit.	**3.** *abundant, adequate, sufficient, ample, copious*
	4.	*adj.*	**curt, sharp, abrupt, terse** His short answer to my question made me wonder what was wrong.	**4.** *friendly, kind, expansive*
shortcoming		*n.*	**fault, failing, weakness, foible, defect, deficiency** Kay's biggest shortcoming is her carelessness.	*strength, virtue*
shout		*n.*	**cry, yell, call, bellow, scream, roar** The rescuers heard the shouts of the trapped people. *v.* The victims shouted for help.	*whisper, whimper, moan*
show	1.	*n.*	**exhibition, exhibit, display, presentation** Automobile shows are popular. *v.* Manufacturers showed their latest cars.	**1.** *concealment, suppression, secrecy*
	2.	*n.*	**sham, pretense, affectation, simulation, pretext** The child's tears were just a show to win our sympathy.	**2.** *sincerity, honesty*
	3.	*v.*	**explain, tell, guide, direct** "I'll show you how to use the computer program," said the teacher.	**3.** *confuse, confound*
	4.	*v.*	**register, indicate, reveal, record, point out, designate, disclose** These marks show that you'll have to work harder if you want to graduate.	**4.** *conceal, hide, deny, contradict, obscure*
showy		*adj.*	**bright, vivid, striking, ornate, gaudy, glaring, flashy, garish, colorful, florid, pretentious, ostentatious** Jim wears showy clothes to attract attention.	*dull, drab, colorless, simple, unnoticeable, inconspicuous, subdued, quiet*
shred	1.	*n.*	**fragment, piece, scrap, bit, trace, snippet** There's not a shred of evidence to prove who committed the murder.	
	2.	*v.*	**tear, rip** I shredded the cabbage for the coleslaw.	
shrewd		*adj.*	**keen, sharp, clever, knowing, astute, discerning, observant** Nat is a shrewd businesswoman.	*stupid, silly, foolish, unthinking*

shrill	*adj.*	**piercing, high-pitched, sharp, penetrating, strident** The campers were awakened by the shrill cries of the birds.	*low-pitched, soft, faint, muffled, low*
shrink	*v.*	**compress, diminish, contract, become less, shrivel** My silk blouse shrank in the wash.	*enlarge, stretch, expand, increase*
shrivel	*v.*	**dry up, wither, contract, wrinkle** Plants shrivel without water.	*expand, spread, develop, unfold*
shun	*v.*	**avoid, evade, ignore, neglect, dodge, keep away from, elude** Some famous people shun publicity.	*seek, look for, accept, adopt*
shut	1. *v.* 2. *v.*	**close, fasten, lock, seal** The stores shut their doors at six. **enclose, confine** We shut the dog in the backyard before we left.	1. *open, unfasten, unlock* 2. *release, liberate*
shuttle	*v.*	**alternate, come and go, go back and forth** The bus shuttles between the hotel and the amusement park. *adj.* The hotel provides a shuttle bus service. *n.* The space shuttle returned safely to Earth after its mission.	
shy	1. *adj.* 2. *adj.*	**bashful, timid, reserved, retiring, timorous** The shy author refused to be interviewed by the press. *n.* After some persuasion, he overcame his shyness and met the reporters. **cautious, wary, fearful, timid, suspicious, skittish** Deer are shy of humans.	1. *bold, brazen, impudent, confident* 2. *heedless, careless, fearless*
sick	*adj.*	**ill, unwell, unhealthy, ailing, impaired, indisposed, diseased** Doctors tend to sick people. *n.* Meg's sickness is not serious.	*well, healthy, sound, hearty, robust, strong*
sign	1. *n.* 2. *n.* 3. *v.*	**indication, clue, trace** There was no sign of life in the desert. **symbol, mark, insignia, badge** The car screeched to a halt at the stop sign. **authorize, endorse, approve, confirm, acknowledge** Both parties signed the contract.	 3. *condemn, censure, denounce*
signal	*n.*	**sign, indication, cue, beacon, alarm, warning** A flashing red light is a signal of danger. *v.* The driver signalled that he was turning.	

significant	*adj.*	**important, notable, vital, prominent, meaningful, momentous** The fourth of July is a significant date for Americans. *n.* Do you know the significance of that date?	*unimportant, trivial, trifling, insignificant*
signify	*v.*	**mean, imply, show, indicate, denote, express, declare** The conductor's arrival on stage signified the start of the concert.	
silent	*adj.*	**noiseless, still, quiet, hushed, soundless, calm** We quietly entered the silent room. *n.* The silence was broken by a cough. *adv.* We left as silently as we had arrived.	*noisy, loud*
silly	*adj.*	**foolish, stupid, ridiculous, inane, absurd, senseless, irrational, witless** The teacher told the students to stop being silly.	*sensible, rational, prudent, wise, sound, clever*
similar	*adj.*	**alike, like, much the same** The twins are very similar in looks. *n.* Their similarity is quite remarkable.	*different, unlike, dissimilar*
simple	1. *adj.* 2. *adj.*	**easy, uncomplicated, straightforward** How could you fail such a simple test? **plain, unadorned, untrimmed, unaffected, ordinary, unsophisticated** Simple designs are often the most beautiful.	**1.** *difficult, hard, complicated, complex* **2.** *adorned, showy, flashy, ornate, garish, sophisticated*
simulate	1. *v.* 2. *v.*	**imitate, mimic, duplicate, replicate** Laugh tracks on television shows simulate the laughter of a live audience. *n.* Astronauts train in simulations of conditions in outer space. **pretend, feign** Wendy simulated illness so she could stay home.	**1.** *originate* **2.** *reveal, speak the truth*
sincere	*adj.*	**genuine, true, reliable, honest, trustworthy, forthright, candid** Sincere friends should be valued. *n.* Sincerity is an admirable quality.	*unreliable, false, insincere, hypocritical*
site	*n.*	**place, spot, situation, location, position** A hospital is to be built on this site.	
situation	1. *n.*	**place, spot, site, location, position** This cottage is in an ideal situation. *v.* The builder situated the house close to the lake.	

	2.	*n.*	**condition, circumstance**
			Ron was in an awkward situation when he was unable to pay the bill.

skillful — *adj.* — **skilled, trained, accomplished, efficient, capable**
The skillful gymnast amazed everyone at the tournament.
adv. The gymnast performed skillfully on the bar.

unskilled, incompetent, clumsy, inept, awkward, unqualified

skip
1. *v.* **jump, hop, spring, leap**
Skipping rope is good exercise.
2. *v.* **omit, pass over, overlook, exclude**
Bea skipped a difficult question in the test.

2. *include, put in*

slack
1. *adj.* **relaxed, limp, lax, loose**
They tightened the slack tennis net before starting the game.
v. Who slackened the rope?

1. *taut, tight*

2. *adj.* **careless, lazy, indifferent, negligent, lax, sluggish, slow**
The salesclerks were dismissed for their slack work habits.

2. *diligent, careful, industrious*

3. *adj.* **slow, sluggish**
Business was slack at the stores after Thanksgiving.

3. *brisk, busy, active, bustling, lively*

sleek
1. *adj.* **glossy, velvety, lustrous, slick, silken, satiny, smooth**
Horses are groomed daily to keep their sleek appearance.

1. *rough, coarse, rugged, harsh, dull, drab*

2. *adj.* **streamlined, trim**
Peng arrived in his sleek sports car.

2. *bulky, broad, wide*

sleepy
1. *adj.* **drowsy, dozy, tired**
The sleepy child fell asleep in the car.

1. *wide-awake, alert, lively*

2. *adj.* **quiet, inactive, boring**
Joe couldn't wait to move out of his sleepy hometown.

2. *busy, bustling*

slender
1. *adj.* **slim, slight, thin, svelte**
Ann exercises to keep her slender figure.

1. *fat, stout, thick, wide, obese, pudgy*

2. *adj.* **meager, small, scanty**
They have difficulty living on their slender income.

2. *ample, massive, considerable, large, copious*

slick
1. *adj.* **glossy, slippery, oily, sleek, smooth**
Roads are slick when wet.

2. *adj.* **clever, smooth, ingenious, tricky**
The company used slick gimmicks to attract customers.

2. *mundane, dull, unimaginative*

slight
1. *adj.* **frail, slender, dainty, delicate, slim**
Although she has a slight build, the ballerina is very strong.

1. *stocky, heavy, stout, obese, pudgy*

	2.	*adj.*	**small, trivial, insignificant, trifling, meager** The company made slight profits this year.	**2.** *significant, large*
	3.	*v.*	**ignore, overlook, neglect, snub, rebuff, disdain, scorn** After he was elected, he slighted those who had helped him.	**3.** *favor, include, court*
slim	**1.**	*adj.*	**slender, thin, slight, svelte** She stays slim by eating the right foods.	**1.** *fat, chubby, stout, obese*
	2.	*adj.*	**small, narrow, tight** She won the race by a slim margin.	**2.** *large, wide, broad*
slip	**1.**	*n.*	**error, fault, mistake, blunder, indiscretion, faux pas** The cashier was fired for making too many slips in her calculations.	**1.** *correction*
	2.	*v.*	**bungle, err** Su-Lin slipped when she told Victor about the surprise party.	
	3.	*v.*	**glide, slide** Judy slipped on the ice and broke her elbow.	
	4.	*v.*	**decline, fall** House prices have slipped this year.	**4.** *rise*
slope		*n.*	**incline, grade, hill** Skiers glided down the steep slopes.	*flat, plain*
slow	**1.**	*adj.*	**sluggish, gradual, torpid, leisurely** We went for a slow walk after dinner. *adv.* We walked slowly to the park.	**1.** *fast, swift, rapid*
	2.	*adj.*	**delayed, belated, overdue, late** Transit service will be slow during the transit strike.	**2.** *early, prompt*
	3.	*v.*	**slacken, decrease speed** The car slowed as it approached the intersection.	**3.** *accelerate, quicken, speed up*
	4.	*v.*	**retard, hinder, impede, delay, decrease, reduce** Inefficient machinery slowed production at the plant.	**4.** *increase, aid, assist*
sluggish		*adj.*	**slow, torpid, languid, lethargic** His sluggish performance told us he was not feeling well.	*active, lively, fast, swift, rapid*
sly		*adj.*	**crafty, shrewd, cunning, foxy, tricky, wily, subtle** The politician's sly tactics won many votes.	*direct, sincere, open, straightforward, frank*
small	**1.**	*adj.*	**little, tiny, miniature, minute, petite, wee, diminutive** It's easy to lose a small child in a crowd.	**1.** *big, large, great, bulky, gigantic*
	2.	*adj.*	**scanty, meager, inadequate** There were only small quantities of food at the refugee camp.	**2.** *large, ample, adequate, abundant, extensive*

	3.	*adj.*	**trivial, insignificant, unimportant, unessential, minor** I have a small part in the play.	*3. significant, important, essential, major, weighty*
	4.	*adj.*	**modest, poor, humble, simple, unassuming, unpretentious** Abraham Lincoln was raised in a small cabin.	*4. grand, splendid, pretentious, spacious*
smart	1.	*adj.*	**clever, bright, intelligent, sharp, keen, alert** The smart student won a full scholarship.	*1. stupid, dull, unintelligent, slow*
	2.	*adj.*	**stylish, fashionable** Maria wore a smart suit for her interview. *adv.* She dressed smartly for the interview.	*2. unfashionable, out-of-date, dowdy*
	3.	*adj.*	**sharp, severe, stinging** The boxer took a smart uppercut to the jaw.	*3. mild, gentle, slight, inoffensive*
	4.	*adj.*	**active, vigorous, energetic, lively** The soldiers marched at a smart pace.	*4. slow, sluggish, languid*
	5.	*adj.*	**impudent, rude, bold, brazen** Smart remarks are not appreciated.	*5. polite, refined, courteous*
smell	1.	*n.*	**aroma, odor, fragrance, scent, perfume, bouquet** The smell of roast turkey filled the house at Thanksgiving.	
	2.	*n.*	**stench, stink** The smell of dead fish made us ill. *v.* Dead fish smell.	*2. fragrance, perfume, scent, aroma*
	3.	*v.*	**sniff, scent, detect an odor** I smell cookies baking in the oven.	
smooth		*adj.*	**even, level, flat, plane, sleek, lustrous, unvarying, glossy, uniform, unruffled** The smooth surface of the lake resembled a mirror. *v.* Workers smoothed the lawn tennis court with rollers.	*irregular, jagged, rough, uneven, broken, sharp*
smug		*adj.*	**self-satisfied, complacent, egotistical, self-righteous** The team members accepted their award with smug smiles.	*modest, humble, meek*
snatch		*v.*	**seize, grab, take, grasp** Thieves snatched the woman's purse and dashed off.	*return, restore, give back*
sneer		*v.*	**mock, jeer, gibe, taunt, scorn, belittle, scoff, disparage, ridicule** The contestants sneered at each other before the match.	*cheer, applaud, compliment, praise*
snobbish		*adj.*	**snooty, arrogant, ostentatious, pretentious** The snobbish man would only associate with the rich and famous. *n.* The snob would only talk to the rich people at the party.	*humble, modest, unassuming, gracious*

snub	*v.*	**shun, disdain, disregard, ignore, slight, rebuff** The singer snubbed the audience by refusing a curtain call. *n.* The snub hurt everyone's feelings.	*flatter, fuss over, pay attention to*
snug	1. *adj.*	**cozy, comfortable, sheltered, protected** The children nestled in their snug, warm beds.	*1. exposed, uncomfortable, unprotected*
	2. *adj.*	**tight, close, compact** Jack complained that the jacket was too snug.	*2. loose, lax*
soak	*v.*	**saturate, wet, drench, moisten** May soaked the flowerbeds after she had planted the bulbs.	*dry*
sober	*adj.*	**serious, solemn, grave, earnest, quiet, staid** We could tell from their sober faces that something was wrong.	*light-hearted, happy, loud, boisterous*
sociable	*adj.*	**affable, genial, friendly, social, hospitable** Sociable people usually enjoy parties.	*unsociable, distant, unfriendly, aloof*
soft	1. *adj.*	**pliable, flexible, yielding, malleable, pliant** Soft leather is used in making gloves.	*1. rigid, stiff, hard, unyielding*
	2. *adj.*	**gentle, mild, tender** The nurse's soft manner calmed the child.	*2. stern, severe, harsh, brutal*
	3. *adj.*	**low, mellow, subdued** The band played soft music while we dined.	*3. loud, harsh, piercing*
	4. *adj.*	**pale, pastel, delicate, faint** The nursery was decorated in soft colors.	*4. bright, glaring, brilliant, bold*
	5. *adj.*	**smooth, velvety, satiny, silky, fine, downy** Soft fabrics are pleasant to touch.	*5. rough, harsh dry, parched, arid*
soggy	*adj.*	**wet, damp, soaked, mushy, saturated** Cedar trees thrive in soggy soil.	
solemn	1. *adj.*	**sober, serious, grave** There were many solemn faces at the funeral.	*1. light-hearted, happy, joyful, merry*
	2. *adj.*	**ceremonial, formal, imposing, ritualistic, ceremonious** Veteran's Day services are solemn occasions.	*2. informal, unceremonial*
solid	1. *adj.*	**rigid, stable, sound, fixed** All buildings need solid foundations.	*1. unstable, weak, fragile, flimsy*
	2. *adj.*	**firm, hard, dense** The patient is not allowed solid food.	*2. fluid, liquid, soft*
	3. *adj.*	**sound, wise, valid, sensible, genuine** The graduates were given solid advice.	*3. invalid, foolish, ridiculous, unsound*

solitary	1.	*adj.*	**alone, lonesome, lonely, separate, unsocial** A hermit lives a solitary life. *n.* Hermits live in solitude.	*1. social, accompanied*
	2.	*adj.*	**sole, only, lone, single, one** There is a solitary passenger on the bus.	*2. several, many, numerous*
	3.	*adj.*	**remote, secluded, desolate, isolated, deserted** That cottage is on a solitary stretch of beach.	*3. populated, dense, crowded*
soluble		*adj.*	**dissolvable, solvable** Sugar is soluble in water.	*insoluble*
solution	1.	*n.*	**answer, resolution, explanation, key** Do you have the solution to the problem?	*1. question, problem*
	2.	*n.*	**fluid, liquid, mixture** Salt and water makes a saline solution.	
solve		*v.*	**figure out, decipher, unravel, resolve, answer** It took us a long time to solve the puzzle.	*leave unanswered, misunderstand*
somber	1.	*adj.*	**dark, gloomy, overcast, cloudy, drab, dull, murky** Somber winter days can be depressing.	*1. bright, sunny, cloudless*
	2.	*adj.*	**sad, depressing, melancholy, dire, funereal** Somber music is played at funerals.	*2. cheerful, merry, happy, joyous, festive*
soothe	1.	*v.*	**relieve, help, comfort** She soothed the pain of her twisted ankle with a cold compress.	*1. aggravate, irritate, hurt, worsen*
	2.	*v.*	**pacify, console, quieten, calm** Dad soothed the cranky baby by gently rocking him.	*2. agitate, irk, bother*
sordid		*adj.*	**dirty, filthy, wretched, abject, squalid** The refugees lived in sordid conditions at a camp.	*fresh, clean, uplifting, spotless, immaculate*
sore	1.	*n.*	**wound, infected spot** The mosquito bites turned into itchy sores.	
	2.	*adj.*	**painful, tender, smarting, aching** Lyn couldn't sing because of a sore throat.	*2. painless, healed*
sorrow		*n.*	**sadness, grief, woe, suffering, distress, anguish, heartache** War causes great sorrows.	*joy, happiness*
sorry	1.	*adj.*	**sad, grieved, mournful, melancholy** I'm sorry that your dog has died.	*1. happy, delighted, gleeful, pleased, glad*
	2.	*adj.*	**penitent, apologetic, regretful, remorseful** Sam was sorry for breaking his promise.	*2. unapologetic, unremorseful*
	3.	*adj.*	**poor, dismal, pitiful, pathetic** The house was in a sorry condition when we bought it.	*3. adequate, fine, acceptable, excellent*

sort		*n.*	**kind, class, type, species, variety, group, classification, category** There are many sorts of apples. *v.* Machines can sort goods by size.	
sound	1.	*n.*	**noise** Don't make a sound!	**1.** *silence, quiet*
	2.	*adj.*	**healthy, well, hearty, strong, sturdy, robust** Athletes have sound bodies.	**2.** *weak, diseased, sick*
	3.	*adj.*	**stable, durable, substantial, safe, secure, sturdy, firm, solid** The bridge is supported on sound bases.	**3.** *unsafe, flimsy, defective, fragile*
	4.	*adj.*	**reliable, wise, sensible, rational, prudent, reasonable** Take the counselor's sound advice.	**4.** *foolish, stupid, ridiculous*
	5.	*adj.*	**thorough, deep** Jim fell into a sound sleep after the test. *adv.* He slept soundly for a day.	**5.** *fitful, light, restless, uneasy*
sour	1.	*adj.*	**pungent, acid, bitter, tart** She winced when she bit into the sour lemon.	**1.** *sweet, sugary, mild, bland, mellow*
	2.	*adj.*	**grouchy, irritable, grumpy, peevish, disagreeable** Pat was in a sour mood after losing the game.	**2.** *good-humored, good-natured, cheerful, happy*
	3.	*v.*	**turn bad, spoil, curdle, ferment** Milk sours if not refrigerated.	**3.** *stay fresh*
source		*n.*	**origin, rise, beginning** Where is the source of the Nile River?	*end, finish, conclusion*
spacious	1.	*adj.*	**large, roomy, extensive, vast, ample** The rooms are spacious in this apartment.	*cramped, small, tiny, limited, confined*
	2.	*n.*	**measure, extent, spread** The span of an eagle's wings is spacious.	
span		*v.*	**stretch over, extend across, ford** A suspension bridge spanned the river.	*tunnel, burrow*
spare	1.	*v.*	**save, relieve, omit, exempt from** Please give me a ride and spare me from a long walk.	**1.** *condemn*
	2.	*adj.*	**extra, additional, superfluous, reserve, supplementary** Spare tires are stored in trunks of cars.	**2.** *necessary, wanting, lacking*
	3.	*adj.*	**scanty, meager, lean** The students survived on their spare budgets. *adv.* Apply the ointment sparingly.	**3.** *abundant, ample, liberal, generous, plentiful*
sparkle		*v.*	**glitter, gleam, twinkle, glisten, shine, flash, scintillate** The children's eyes sparkled when they saw the Christmas tree. *n.* There was a sparkle in their eyes.	*remain dull*

sparse	*adj.*	**scanty, thin, meager** Vegetation is sparse in the desert. *adv.* Vegetation grows sparsely in deserts.	*ample, adequate, thick, luxurious*
speak	*v.*	**talk, utter, tell, say, express, declare, voice** Laurel spoke about her trip to Asia. *n.* The speaker kept the audience entertained.	*remain silent, be quiet*
special	1. *adj.*	**particular, specific, definite, distinct, certain** Each instrument has a special purpose in the orchestra.	**1.** *general, unrestricted, indefinite*
	2. *adj.*	**unusual, extraordinary, exceptional** A fiftieth wedding anniversary is a special occasion.	**2.** *ordinary, common, usual, everyday, regular*
species	*n.*	**class, variety, kind, sort, category** Endangered species of birds and animals must be protected.	
specific	*adj.*	**particular, definite, exact, explicit, precise, distinct** We left specific instructions for the babysitter.	*vague, indefinite, general*
specimen	*n.*	**example, sample** The museum has rare specimens of fossils on display.	
speck	*n.*	**spot, fleck, bit, particle, iota, dot** There's not a speck of dust in May's home.	
spectacle	*n.*	**scene, sight, view, display, exhibition, show** The opening ceremonies of the Olympic Games were a spectacle.	
spectacular	*adj.*	**sensational, striking, impressive, magnificent, thrilling** Under certain atmospheric conditions, the Northern Lights are a spectacular sight.	*dull, boring, dreary, uninteresting*
spectrum	*n.*	**range, variety, array, extent** A wide spectrum of views was offered at the meeting.	
speed	1. *n.*	**swiftness, quickness, rapidity, velocity, rate, pace** The car reached a speed of ninety miles per hour.	**1.** *slowness, tardiness*
	2. *v.*	**hurry, hasten, move swiftly** Cars sped along the highway.	**2.** *slow*
speedy	*adj.*	**fast, quick, rapid, swift, prompt** The dry cleaners give speedy service.	*slow, tardy, sluggish*

spellbound		*adj.*	**mesmerized, entranced, amazed, enthralled, fascinated, captivated** The violinist held the audience spellbound with her performance.	*disgusted, offended, bored, disinterested, unmoved*
sphere	1.	*n.*	**orb, globe** Earth is a sphere. *adj.* Earth is a spherical planet.	
	2.	*n.*	**region, field, range, circle** Sports are not within our sphere of interest.	
spin	1.	*n.*	**ride, short trip** We went for a spin in Jo's new car.	
	2.	*v.*	**gyrate, swirl, twist, rotate, revolve, whirl, turn** Cars spun around on the icy roads. *n.* The skater made some spectacular spins on the ice.	
spite		*n.*	**malice, hatred, contempt, animosity, resentment, ill will, vindictiveness** Kyle spread vicious rumors about Tom out of spite. *adj.* The spiteful gossip caused Tom pain.	*love, affection, sympathy, good will, benevolence*
splendid		*adj.*	**glorious, grand, magnificent, superb, marvelous, resplendent, sumptuous** The royal family lives in splendid surroundings. *n.* The tourists admired the splendor of the Taj Mahal.	*ordinary, dull, unimposing, inferior, mediocre*
spoil	1.	*v.*	**decay, rot, decompose, putrefy, ferment, deteriorate** Fruit spoils when it is kept too long.	*1. stay fresh, purify, refresh, improve*
	2.	*v.*	**ruin, destroy, damage, harm, injure, impair** Heavy rains spoiled the crops.	*2. save, preserve, keep, renovate, repair, rectify*
spoils		*n.*	**booty, plunder, loot, pillage** Invaders carried off the spoils from the ransacked city.	
spontaneous		*adj.*	**automatic, instinctive, natural, unforced, uninhibited, impulsive** Spontaneous applause greeted the star.	*deliberate, intended, intentional, imposed, premeditated*
sporadic		*adj.*	**infrequent, occasional, irregular, spasmodic, uncommon, unscheduled** Alex makes sporadic visits to the mall. *adv.* She goes sporadically to shop.	*frequent, regular, scheduled, unlimited, continuous*
sport	1.	*n.*	**diversion, game, recreation, entertainment, amusement, play, pastime, pleasure, enjoyment** Skiing is a popular winter sport.	*1. work, business, seriousness, toil, labor*

	2.	*n.*	**mockery, joke, ridicule** The rude student made sport of the newcomer's accent.
	3.	*v.*	**show off, wear, exhibit, display** Jake proudly sported his Olympic medal around his neck.

2. *praise, approval*

spread
- **1.** *v.* **scatter, disperse, sow, strew, cast, circulate, disseminate, distribute**
  Machinery spreads seeds in the fields.
  1. *reap, gather, collect*
- **2.** *v.* **unfold, stretch, extend, unroll, expand, open, unfurl**
  We spread a rug on the ground.
  2. *gather up, furl, pick up, roll up*
- **3.** *v.* **proclaim, tell, divulge, circulate, broadcast, publish, declare, advertise**
  She spread the good news on the Internet.
  3. *suppress, hide, conceal, hush*
- **4.** *v.* **cover, coat, daub, smear, diffuse**
  Spread the paint over the entire wall.
  4. *spot, localize*

spring
- *v.* **leap, bound, vault, jump**
  The gymnast sprang over the bar.
  n. The cat made a spring for the bird.
  settle, drop, land, alight

spry
- *adj.* **nimble, active, agile, lively, vigorous**
  Some elderly people remain spry.
  inactive, infirm

spunk
- *n.* **courage, pluck, spirit**
  The runner showed spunk by finishing the race despite an injured leg.
  timidity, fear, cowardice, weakness

spurn
- *v.* **reject, repudiate, scorn, shun**
  The wrestler spurned his opponent's demand to surrender.
  accept, welcome

squabble
- *v.* **bicker, quarrel, fight, argue, disagree, dispute**
  The twins squabbled over the bicycle.
  n. They have squabbles over their toys.
  agree, cooperate

squalid
- *adj.* **dirty, filthy, unclean, foul, wretched**
  Some people live in squalid conditions in the cities.
  n. No one should have to live in squalor.
  clean, spotless, pleasant, welcoming, immaculate

squander
- *v.* **waste, throw away, lavish**
  He squandered his lottery winnings.
  economize, keep, preserve, save, hoard

squirm
- *v.* **wriggle, wiggle, writhe, twist, fidget**
  Babies are difficult to hold when they squirm.
  be still

stable
- **1.** *n.* **shelter, barn, pen, corral**
  Horses are kept in stables.
  v. The groom stabled the colt.
- **2.** *adj.* **steady, solid, firm, balanced**
  Her temperature is stable now.
  2. *unstable, changeable*

	3.	*adj.*	**permanent, durable, certain, enduring, constant, continuing** A stable government is good for a country.	*3. intermittent, spasmodic, irregular, uncertain*
stage	1.	*n.*	**platform, rostrum** The graduates walked up to the stage to receive their diploma.	
	2.	*n.*	**degree, grade, step, period, level** The egg is the first stage in the insect's life cycle.	
	3.	*v.*	**present, show, execute** The people staged a demonstration to protest the new taxes.	
stagnant	1.	*adj.*	**still, inert, inactive** Mosquitoes breed in stagnant waters.	*1. active, lively, moving*
	2.	*adj.*	**dormant, lifeless, idle, sluggish** The assembly line is stagnant during the strike.	*2. active, busy, productive*
stain	1.	*n.*	**blot, blotch, mark, spot, smear, blemish, splotch, smudge** Dan removed the stains on the tablecloth with bleach.	
	2.	*v.*	**mark, soil, spot, dirty, discolor** Blueberries stain teeth.	*2. clean, scour, whiten, bleach*
	3.	*v.*	**color, dye, tint, varnish, lacquer, paint** We will stain the wooden deck in the spring. *n.* We will use a dark brown stain.	
stall	1.	*n.*	**booth, compartment, cubicle** The horses were kept in stalls in the barn.	
	2.	*v.*	**break down, stop working, malfunction** Cars stalled in the extreme cold.	*2. go, function, work*
stalwart	1.	*adj.*	**strong, sturdy, robust, vigorous** A stalwart crew is needed on an ocean schooner.	*1. weak, puny, frail, sickly*
	2.	*adj.*	**brave, bold, valiant, resolute, staunch, reliable** The stalwart soldiers fought to the very end.	*2. cowardly, fearful, timid*
stamina		*n.*	**endurance, perseverance, strength, vigor** Long distance runners need stamina.	
standard	1.	*n.*	**flag, pennant, colors, banner** The standard waved in the breeze.	
	2.	*n.*	**emblem, insignia, symbol** Each uniform displayed the battalion's standard.	
	3.	*n.*	**measure, criterion, norm** This country has a high standard of living.	

4. *n.* **model, type, pattern, prototype**
A Stradivarius is the standard for violin makers.

5. *adj.* **regular, usual**
In this school, the standard class has twenty pupils.

5. irregular, unusual

staple *adj.* **essential, main, principal, chief, standard**
Rice is a staple food for millions of people.

non-essential, extra, secondary

stark **1.** *adj.* **severe, austere, unyielding, bare, barren, desolate, harsh**
Photographs showed the stark landscape of the tundra.

1. soft, gentle, yielding, welcoming

2. *adj.* **complete, absolute, utter, sharp**
There is a stark contrast between the lives of the rich and the poor.

2. fine, small

start **1.** *n.* **beginning, opening, commencement**
The start of the summer is most exciting.

1. end, ending, finale, conclusion

2. *v.* **begin, commence, set out**
When will the band start to play?

2. end, finish, stop, conclude, cease

startle *v.* **alarm, frighten, surprise, shock**
The loud noise startled the baby.
adj. The startling news left us in shock.

soothe, comfort

state **1.** *n.* **condition, situation, status**
This old house is in a ramshackle state.

2. *v.* **tell, say, inform, express, declare, announce, pronounce, assert, affirm**
The witness was asked to state only the facts.

2. remain silent, suppress, repress

stately *adj.* **dignified, majestic, grand, imposing, magnificent**
Many stately old homes have been converted into hotels.

modest, unimposing, unpretentious, commonplace

static *adj.* **immobile, inactive, dormant, inoperative, sedentary, latent**
Stock markets remained static during the holidays.

active, operative, mobile

status **1.** *n.* **rank, station, standing, position**
The singer achieved celebrity status with her first album.
adj. She bought a sleek car as a status symbol.

2. *n.* **condition, state, stage**
What is the status of Grandpa's health?

staunch *adj.* **loyal, faithful, trustworthy, true, steadfast, firm, strong, stalwart**
The mayor's staunch supporters turned out for the rally.

undependable, unreliable, faithless

stay
1. *v.* **remain, wait, linger**
We were asked to stay for supper.
2. *v.* **visit, dwell, live, reside, lodge, sojourn**
We will be staying with friends overnight.
3. *v.* **delay, postpone, defer, suspend**
The star's illness stayed the opening of the show.

1. leave, go
2. depart, leave, go
3. advance, hasten, bring forward

steady
1. *adj.* **unvarying, uniform, regular, constant, continuous**
Most people have a steady heartbeat.
2. *adj.* **sure, firm, dependable, secure, stable**
Pouring coffee requires a steady hand.

1. irregular, variable, inconstant, changeable
2. unsure, unsteady, wobbly, wavering

stealthy
adj. **furtive, sly, evasive, shrewd, cunning, wily**
Cats are stealthy creatures when they stalk their prey.
adv. The cat crept stealthily toward the bird.

straightforward, obvious, direct

steep
adj. **sheer, abrupt, precipitous, sharp**
Steep cliffs rose from the sea.

gradual

step
1. *n.* **pace, stride**
Take one step forward.
v. Please step forward.
2. *n.* **rung, level**
How many steps are on the ladder?
3. *n.* **stage, phase**
I was involved with every step of the production process.

stereotyped
adj. **conventional, typical, customary, indistinctive, routine**
Television shows tend to be filled with stereotyped characters.

atypical, original

stern
adj. **severe, rigid, strict, austere, harsh, forbidding, unyielding**
The security guard's stern expression frightened the students.

genial, lenient, easy, flexible, kindly, compassionate

stiff
1. *adj.* **rigid, inflexible, unbending, firm, unyielding, hardened**
The stiff collar made me most uncomfortable all day.
v. I stiffened the collar with starch.
2. *adj.* **hard, severe, exact, strict, difficult**
Only a few students passed the stiff examination.
3. *adj.* **formal, stilted, constrained, unnatural**
The speaker's stiff speech showed he was nervous.
4. *adj.* **potent, strong, powerful, hard**
Stiff winds caused high waves on the lake.

1. limp, flexible, pliant, soft, yielding
2. easy, lax, simple
3. relaxed, unceremonious
4. gentle, soft

still	1.	*adj.*	**hushed, quiet, silent, calm, tranquil, peaceful, serene** An owl's hoot broke the still night.	**1.** *noisy, turbulent*
	2.	*adj.*	**motionless** The boat couldn't sail in the still waters of the lake. *adv.* The child was told to stand still.	**2.** *moving, turbulent, undulating*
stimulate		*v.*	**stir, rouse, excite, kindle, foster, spur, invigorate, exhilarate** That movie stimulated my curiosity about the Orient.	*curb, restrict, hinder, impede*
stimulus		*n.*	**incentive, motive, inducement** Winning the first game of the season was a stimulus to the team.	*limitation, preventive, restraint, obstruction, obstacle, deterrent*
stingy		*adj.*	**miserly, close-fisted, tight-fisted, grasping, penny-pinching** At the outset of the famous novel, Scrooge is a stingy person.	*liberal, generous, lavish, unsparing, bountiful*
stop	1.	*v.*	**cease, quit, terminate, halt, discontinue** Please stop complaining. *n.* Police are trying to put a stop to drunk driving.	**1.** *begin, start, commence, continue*
	2.	*v.*	**stay, pause, rest, remain** Let's stop at this restaurant.	**2.** *continue, proceed, advance*
	3.	*v.*	**halt, arrest, block, suspend, detain** Will the police stop the fugitive?	**3.** *expedite, assist, release*
	4.	*v.*	**prevent, obstruct, hinder** A severe storm stopped all incoming flights from landing.	**4.** *promote, advance, assist*
stormy	1.	*adj.*	**blustery, inclement, turbulent, rough** The canoe capsized in the stormy weather.	**1.** *clement, mild*
	2.	*adj.*	**wild, fierce, violent, raging, turbulent** There was a stormy meeting about the proposal to close down the school.	**2.** *gentle, composed, serene, peaceful*
story		*n.*	**tale, narrative, article, account, report, anecdote** Have you read the story of Rapunzel?	
stout	1.	*adj.*	**fat, plump, corpulent, portly, heavy, thickset** Shakespeare's famous character Falstaff was stout.	**1.** *slender, thin, lean, slight, frail, puny*
	2.	*adj.*	**sturdy, strong, well-built, firm, durable, tough, solid** Stout beams support the weight of the building.	**2.** *fragile, weak*
	3.	*adj.*	**brave, bold, courageous, valiant, dauntless, resolute** The soldier praised those of stout heart who died in battle.	**3.** *timid, fearful, cowardly, irresolute*

straight	1.	*adj.*	**unbent, plumb, even, level, unswerving** Draw a straight line.	**1.** *bent, curved, crooked*
	2.	*adj.*	**clear, direct, frank, honest, reliable** Give me a straight answer to the question.	**2.** *indirect, evasive*
	3.	*adj.*	**undiluted, unmixed, pure** That glass contains straight orange juice.	**3.** *diluted, mixed*
	4.	*adv.*	**directly, without interruption** Stefanie went straight home after school.	**4.** *circuitous*
strange	1.	*adj.*	**unusual, bizarre, weird, peculiar, odd** The rock star wore strange clothes.	**1.** *normal, standard, common*
	2.	*adj.*	**peculiar, mysterious, queer, unnatural, abnormal** People report seeing strange flying objects in the night.	**2.** *usual, natural, normal, customary*
	3.	*adj.*	**foreign, alien, unknown, unfamiliar** Marco Polo traveled to strange lands. *n.* He was a stranger in Cathay.	**3.** *familiar, known*
strategy		*n.*	**tactics, plan, procedure** Napoleon was brilliant with regard to military strategies.	
stray	1.	*adj.*	**abandoned, homeless, lost** We took the stray cat home and fed it.	
	2.	*v.*	**wander, roam, drift** We strayed too far and lost our way.	
strength		*n.*	**vigor, vitality, robustness, sturdiness, power, force** Much strength is required to swim across the English Channel.	*weakness, frailty, feebleness*
strenuous		*adj.*	**vigorous, arduous, demanding, exhausting, laborious** Strenuous exercise was part of the daily routine for the trainee soldiers.	*easy, relaxing, undemanding*
stress	1.	*n.*	**importance, significance, weight, emphasis** How much stress is put on academic achievement? *v.* The school program stressed the arts.	**1.** *insignificance, irrelevance*
	2.	*n.*	**pressure, strain, tension, anxiety** He quit the job because he couldn't cope with the stress. *adj.* The job was too stressful.	**2.** *peace, quiet, tranquility, ease*
	3.	*n.*	**tension, strain, pressure, pull, force** Constant stress on the cable made it snap.	**3.** *relaxation, slack, play*
stretch	1.	*n.*	**expanse, tract, extent, length** The travelers drove across a vast stretch of desert.	
	2.	*v.*	**expand, extend, increase** Some stockings stretch to fit any size.	**2.** *contract, shrink*
	3.	*v.*	**occupy, spread over, extend** The land stretches as far as the ocean.	

strict		*adj.*	**severe, stern, rigid, stringent, austere, exact** Schools must have strict safety rules.	*easy, lax, loose, inexact, lenient*
strife	1.	*n.*	**quarrel, discord, disagreement, dispute, altercation, dissension** The building of a fence caused much strife between the neighbors.	**1.** *agreement, concurrence, harmony*
	2.	*n.*	**war, battle, fight, struggle** Many lives were lost in the strife between the nations.	**2.** *peace*
strike	1.	*n.*	**walkout, boycott, work stoppage** Will there be a strike by the employees? *v.* The employees struck for better working conditions.	
	2.	*n.*	**blow, hit, slap, punch, stroke, thump** The boxer landed many strikes to his opponent's body. *v.* The fighter struck her opponent.	**2.** *caress, pat, touch*
	3.	*v.*	**find, discover, uncover, expose** The prospectors finally struck gold. *n.* What a lucky strike!	**3.** *miss, overlook, lose*
	4.	*v.*	**begin, start, establish** They quickly struck a firm friendship.	**4.** *end, terminate*
	5.	*v.*	**impress** That strikes me as a bad plan.	
	6.	*v.*	**light, kindle, ignite, scratch** Strike a match and light the candles.	**6.** *extinguish, douse, put out, squelch*
strive		*v.*	**try, endeavor, attempt, aim, venture, compete, aspire** Sue strives to be an honor student.	*give up, quit*
strong	1.	*adj.*	**robust, sturdy, powerful, vigorous, hardy, forceful, mighty, brawny** Three strong horses hauled the load.	**1.** *feeble, weak, powerless, delicate*
	2.	*adj.*	**solid, firm, durable, stable, tough, steady, well-made, substantial** Space vehicles are made of strong materials.	**2.** *flimsy, insubstantial*
	3.	*adj.*	**powerful, potent, acute, intense** This cheese has a strong smell.	**3.** *mild, bland, delicate*
stubborn		*adj.*	**obstinate, unyielding, pigheaded, determined, headstrong** The stubborn child would not budge when told to go to bed.	*pliant, flexible, agreeable, docile*
student		*n.*	**pupil, trainee, learner** The college students are preparing for their final examinations.	*teacher, instructor, trainer, coach*
stumble		*v.*	**trip, fall, falter, lurch, flounder, topple, slip** The skater stumbled and fell. *n.* The stumble cost him some marks.	*be steady*

stun	1.	*v.*	**knock out, daze** The boxer stunned his opponent with a punch to the head.	**1.** *stimulate, revive*
	2.	*v.*	**surprise, astonish, amaze** The win stunned everyone. *adj.* It was a stunning win.	
stupendous	1.	*adj.*	**breathtaking, marvelous, amazing, overwhelming** The Egyptian pyramids are a stupendous sight.	**1.** *unimpressive, ordinary, mediocre*
	2.	*adj.*	**enormous, immense, colossal** We hope to be able to pay off our stupendous debt.	**2.** *minute, tiny, small, insignificant, paltry*
stupid	1.	*adj.*	**dull, dense, unintelligent** Is any one animal more stupid than another?	**1.** *bright, quick, sharp, clever, intelligent*
	2.	*adj.*	**foolish, silly, senseless, absurd, ridiculous, daft, ill-advised, inane, unwise, nonsensical** It is stupid to cross a street without looking in both directions. *adv.* The child stupidly dashed across the street without checking for traffic. *n.* He was punished for his stupidity.	**2.** *wise, sensible, judicious, sane*
sturdy	1.	*adj.*	**hardy, husky, robust, strong, powerful** Athletes have sturdy bodies.	**1.** *weak, frail, fragile, delicate*
	2.	*adj.*	**durable, tough, long-wearing** Hotels need sturdy furniture.	**2.** *fragile, delicate, unsubstantial*
	3.	*adj.*	**firm, stubborn, unyielding, resolute, determined, steadfast, steady, definite, unchanging** The witness' sturdy denial convinced the jury of his innocence.	**3.** *inconstant, fickle, vacillating, shifting, changeable, capricious, uncertain*
style	1.	*n.*	**way, form, manner, method, technique** The Beatles had a distinctive style of singing.	
	2.	*n.*	**fashion, vogue, mode, habit, custom** Models always dress in the latest styles. *adj.* These people are stylish.	
subdue	1.	*v.*	**tame, master, overcome, quell, conquer, suppress, vanquish** Alexander the Great subdued many enemies.	**1.** *yield, succumb, surrender, give up*
	2.	*v.*	**hold in check, handle, repress, restrain, contain, control, curb** He subdued his temper and spoke calmly.	**2.** *release, liberate, free, be overcome by*
subject	1.	*n.*	**topic, theme, matter, substance** Decide on the subject of your essay.	
	2.	*v.*	**control, tame, subordinate, subjugate, dominate, suppress** The dictator subjected the people into subservience.	**2.** *liberate, free, release, rescue*

submerge	1.	*v.*	**engulf, swamp, inundate, flood, immerse, submerse** The tidal wave submerged the village.	
	2.	*v.*	**sink, descend into water** Scuba divers submerged to explore the coral reef.	*2. rise, emerge, surface*
submit	1.	*v.*	**offer, tender, present, send in** Applicants submitted their resumes.	*1. withdraw, take back, withhold*
	2.	*v.*	**surrender, yield, cede, obey** The company submitted to the workers' demand for a pay raise. *n.* The submission by the company prevented a strike.	*2. hold fast, oppose, disobey, retaliate*
subsequent		*adj.*	**following, succeeding, later, ensuing** A new cast will perform at subsequent shows.	*previous, prior, former, earlier*
subside		*v.*	**dwindle, ebb, recede, sink, fall, abate, wane** The sea became calm as the winds subsided.	*increase, rise, swell*
substance	1.	*n.*	**material, matter** The new sink is made of a strong substance that will not scratch.	
	2.	*n.*	**essence, main point** The substance of the President's speech was that peace is vital.	
	3.	*n.*	**wealth, property, affluence, means** He comes from a family of substance.	
substantial	1.	*adj.*	**strong, solid, firm** Tall buildings require substantial foundations.	*1. insubstantial, weak, fragile*
	2.	*adj.*	**considerable, ample, large, abundant, plentiful** Substantial donations were given to the charity.	*2. small, meager, insignificant, paltry*
	3.	*adj.*	**important, valuable, principal, major** Ron has a substantial role in the play.	*3. unimportant, trivial, minor*
	4.	*adj.*	**wealthy, rich, well-to-do, affluent** A millionaire is a person of substantial means.	*4. poor, humble, ordinary*
substitute		*v.*	**replace, represent, stand for, take the place of** The designated hitter substituted for the weak batter. *n.* Margarine is a substitute for butter.	
subtle	1.	*adj.*	**inferred, indirect, implied, insinuated** Her subtle frown told us she was displeased with the situation.	*1. open, frank, blunt, obvious*
	2.	*adj.*	**faint, light, delicate, fine, slight** There is a subtle difference between the styles of these two writers.	*2. heavy, strong*

	3.	*adj.*	**discerning, acute, keen** His subtle observations made him a well-respected journalist.	**3.** *rough, simple*
	4.	*adj.*	**sly, cunning, crafty** He has a subtle way of getting what he wants.	**4.** *artless, direct, straightforward*
succeed	1.	*v.*	**prosper, thrive, flourish, score, gain, triumph** This business will succeed. *n.* The reason for her success is hard work. *adj.* Running a successful business takes a lot of time.	**1.** *fail, deteriorate, decline, diminish, lessen*
	2.	*v.*	**follow, come after, supplant, replace, displace, become heir to** Queen Elizabeth II succeeded her father as sovereign. *n.* She was the successor to the throne.	**2.** *precede, come before*
sudden		*adj.*	**hasty, quick, abrupt, swift, fast, impromptu, rapid, unexpected, unpremeditated, instantaneous** Our car came to a sudden stop when the light turned amber.	*slow, sluggish, premeditated*
suffer	1.	*v.*	**endure, bear, sustain, undergo, put up with, experience** Many people suffered hardships during the war.	**1.** *be relieved, be restored, recover*
	2.	*v.*	**allow, permit, authorize** "I will not suffer any laziness from my students," said the teacher.	**2.** *forbid, reject, exclude, expel, disallow*
sufficient		*adj.*	**enough, adequate, satisfactory** There's sufficient food for all the guests.	*inadequate, deficient, insufficient*
suggestion	1.	*n.*	**proposal, plan, proposition, recommendation** The teacher listened to the students' suggestions. *v.* They suggested ways to raise funds for new computers.	
	2.	*n.*	**hint, trace, insinuation, tinge** Everyone was shocked when the company collapsed because there had been no suggestion of trouble.	
suitable		*adj.*	**becoming, proper, fitting, appropriate** Suitable attire is required at the dance. *adv.* Guests must be suitably dressed.	*inappropriate, improper, unbecoming*
sullen		*adj.*	**glum, morose, grouchy, grumpy, sour, surly, unsociable** We left him alone when we saw his sullen face.	*friendly, happy, sociable, pleasant*

summit		*n.*	top, zenith, apex, crown, peak, pinnacle, culmination, climax Winning an Oscar is the summit of an actor's career.	*low point, starting point, bottom, start, beginning, nadir*
sunny	1.	*adj.*	bright Plants grow best in sunny areas.	1. *dark, dull, shady, overcast, gloomy*
	2.	*adj.*	cheerful, cheery, happy Jen is well liked because of her sunny disposition.	2. *miserable, sullen, morose, grouchy, grumpy, glum*
superb		*adj.*	magnificent, splendid, elegant, grand, terrific, wonderful, exquisite The band put on a superb performance.	*plain, ordinary, common, unimposing*
superficial	1.	*adj.*	exterior, shallow, surface The cat's claw made a superficial scratch.	1. *deep, deep-seated, serious, internal*
	2.	*adj.*	shallow, cursory Superficial friends disappear in times of trouble.	2. *profound, deep, sincere, true*
superfluous		*adj.*	excessive, redundant, surplus, unnecessary He was told to edit the superfluous words in his essay.	*essential, necessary, wanting*
supple		*adj.*	flexible, pliable, pliant, yielding, elastic, limber The gymnast has a supple body.	*firm, inflexible, rigid, unyielding, stiff*
supplement		*v.*	augment, add to, fortify, enrich, increase, strengthen Dot supplemented her income with a second job. *adj.* She needed the supplementary income to put herself through school. *n.* Some breakfast cereals contain vitamin supplements.	*lessen, deplete*
supply		*v.*	provide, give, furnish, outfit, contribute, fulfill, satisfy The people supplied the victims of the tornado with food and clothes. *n.* Supplies poured in from all regions.	*withhold, retain, withdraw, demand*
support	1.	*n.*	aid, assistance, help, cooperation The project succeeded because of the support of many volunteers. *v.* They support charities with donations.	1. *opposition, hindrance, discouragement*
	2.	*v.*	hold up, prop, sustain, bear, shoulder, shore up, uphold, brace The legs of a table support its weight. *n.* Legs are supports for tabletops.	2. *drop, let go, release, let fall*
	3.	*v.*	nourish, maintain, provide for, sponsor, subsidize, finance, nurture Ellie makes enough money to support herself and her child.	3. *abandon, neglect, hinder, fail, ignore, thwart*

4. *v.* **defend, stand by, promote**
How many voters will support this candidate?
n. Her supporters cheered when she won the election.

4. *oppose, disfavor, discourage, subvert*

suppose *v.* **assume, conjecture, surmise, believe, theorize, presume, deem, think**
I suppose that you will need some help with your homework.

be certain, know, prove, substantiate

suppress 1. *v.* **crush, defeat, overpower, put down, subdue, quell**
Troops were sent to suppress the revolt.

1. *surrender, submit, join, support*

2. *v.* **ban, withhold, conceal, hide**
The government suppressed the news about the uprising.

2. *disclose, release, publish*

3. *v.* **check, hold back, restrain**
Nan suppressed a yawn during the show.

3. *release, let out*

supreme *adj.* **highest, chief, paramount, top, principal, prime, utmost**
Final judgments are made by the supreme court of the land.

lowest

sure 1. *adj.* **certain, assured, confident, convinced, positive**
I'm sure that she will do well in the test.
adv. She will surely do well in the test as she has studied hard for it.

1. *doubtful, dubious, unsure, uncertain*

2. *adj.* **inevitable, unavoidable, certain, indisputable, unmistakable**
Coastal areas are sure to be hit by the hurricane.

2. *avoidable, uncertain, dubious, disputable, doubtful*

surf *v.* **scan, skim, search, check out, explore**
Mom surfed the Internet to find a vacation package for the summer.

study, inspect, concentrate, peruse, fix on, scrutinize

surface 1. *n.* **outside, exterior, facade, covering**
The surface of the house is covered with cedar siding.

1. *inside, interior, center*

2. *v.* **cover, coat**
The carpenter surfaced the countertop with waterproof material.

3. *v.* **emerge, arise, appear**
The tourists were thrilled when a dolphin surfaced beside their boat.

3. *submerge*

surly *adj.* **sullen, morose, irritable, uncivil, testy, discourteous, irascible**
We did not leave a tip for the surly waiter.

affable, sociable, civil, courteous, pleasant

surplus *n.* **excess, extra, glut, oversupply**
There was a surplus of corn in this year's harvest.
adj. The surplus corn was donated to the poor nations.

insufficiency, dearth, scarcity, deficiency

surprise	1.	*n.*	**astonishment, amazement, wonder, shock, bewilderment** She gasped in surprise when she saw her long lost friend.	**1.** *expectation, anticipation*
	2.	*v.*	**shock, startle, astonish, stun, amaze, astound** We surprised everyone when we won. *adj.* It was a surprising win for our team. *adv.* The other team was surprisingly easy to beat.	**2.** *predict, expect*
surrender		*v.*	**give in, give up, submit, yield, capitulate, cede, relinquish** The escaped convict surrendered to the police. *n.* News of the surrender was reported on television.	*fight, conquer, subdue, win, suppress*
surround		*v.*	**enclose, encircle, circle, girdle, shut in, envelop, hem in, wall in** Bodyguards surrounded the President.	*free, open, liberate*
surroundings		*n.*	**area, neighborhood, vicinity, environment, setting** We were enchanted by the beautiful surroundings of the Lake District.	
survey		*n.*	**review, study, examination, critique, investigation** A survey will be made to determine the needs of the elderly. *v.* A committee will survey their needs.	
suspicious	1.	*adj.*	**questionable, doubtful, suspect, open to question** There's something suspicious about that person!	**1.** *dependable, reliable, trustworthy*
	2.	*adj.*	**distrustful, doubting, doubtful, wary, dubious, uneasy** Ben was suspicious when the stranger offered him a ride home.	**2.** *trusting, undoubting*
sustain	1.	*v.*	**bear, support, hold up** Bridges sustain the weight of heavy traffic.	**1.** *drop, abandon, collapse, let fall*
	2.	*v.*	**nourish, feed, maintain, prolong** Soil, water, and sunlight sustain plant life.	**2.** *starve, neglect*
	3.	*v.*	**suffer, experience, undergo, endure** The company sustained major losses in the recession.	
sweet	1.	*adj.*	**pleasant, agreeable, pleasing, winning, engaging, considerate, gentle, gracious** Ly-Anne has a sweet disposition.	**1.** *disagreeable, repulsive, inconsiderate*
	2.	*adj.*	**sugary, candied, rich** Sweet foods are not good for the teeth.	**2.** *sour, bitter, sharp*

swell	*v.*	**inflate, rise, expand, bloat, dilate, distend, increase, enlarge, grow, inflate, amplify, extend, augment** Heavy rains swelled the rivers. *adj.* The swollen rivers overflowed their banks.	*shrink, deflate, contract, recede, decrease, shrivel, diminish, lessen, reduce, condense*
swift	*adj.*	**quick, fast, rapid, fleet, speedy** Sam could not keep up with Tim's swift pace in the race. *adv.* The deer ran swiftly when it heard a noise.	*slow, tardy, sluggish*
sympathy	*n.*	**compassion, understanding, pity, condolence, empathy, commiseration** People often express their sympathy by sending flowers. *v.* Everyone sympathized with Todd when he broke his collarbone.	*antipathy, coldness, antagonism, harshness*
synthetic	*adj.*	**chemically made, fabricated, artificial, manufactured** Synthetic rubber was invented when there was a shortage of natural rubber.	*natural*
system	1. *n.*	**method, mode, way, scheme, routine, custom, practice, procedure** The coach has a unique system for training our swim team.	1. *confusion, muddle, tangle*
	2. *n.*	**organization, order, sequence, network, arrangement** Earth is one planet in the solar system.	
	3. *n.*	**constitution, policy, philosophy, regime, organization** This state has an excellent education system.	
systematic	*adj.*	**organized, orderly, structured, logical, methodical** The systematic worker has never missed a deadline.	*confused, jumbled, disorganized*

T

In Greek, the letter with the name *tau* meant *mark*. From it came *T*, which in earliest times was made like an *X*.

T sometimes sounds like *sh* as in *nation*. Occasionally, *T* is soundless as in *listen* or *whistle*.

taboo		*v.*	**prohibit, forbid, disallow, ban** Some religions taboo the eating of meat. *n.* The eating of meat is a taboo for the followers of some religions. *adj.* Going out unclothed is taboo in our society.	*allow, permit, sanction, legalize*
tacky		*adj.*	**cheap, gaudy, crude, tasteless** Please remove those tacky plastic flowers.	*elegant, stylish, tasteful*
tact		*n.*	**discretion, delicacy, feeling, finesse, diplomacy, subtlety, sensitivity** Some situations must be handled with a great deal of tact. *adj.* Sara is such a tactful person. *adv.* She handles people tactfully.	*indiscretion, bluntness, tactlessness*
tactic		*n.*	**way, method, policy, scheme, approach, maneuvers, strategy** He used delaying tactics to avoid paying his bills.	
talent		*n.*	**skill, gift, ability, capability, aptitude, flair, faculty** Jin has a talent for drawing. *adj.* She is a talented artist.	*inability, incapability*
talk	1.	*n.*	**conversation, chat, discussion** They had a long talk about their plans.	
	2.	*n.*	**gossip, chatter, hearsay, rumor** There has been a lot of talk about building a new school.	
	3.	*n.*	**speech, address, oration, lecture** The science talk was about amphibians.	
	4.	*v.*	**lecture, deliver a speech** The missionary talked about his work in Africa.	4. *listen, hear*
	5.	*v.*	**discuss, chat, speak, converse** The former classmates talked about old times at the school reunion.	5. *be silent*
talkative		*adj.*	**chatty, gabby, wordy, loquacious** The talkative child was told to keep quiet in the library.	*quiet, silent, taciturn, mute, reserved, laconic*
tall	1.	*adj.*	**high, lofty, elevated, towering** The city is crowded with tall buildings.	1. *low, short, squat*
	2.	*adj.*	**far-fetched, outlandish, exaggerated** His claim that he had found a pot of gold was dismissed as a tall tale.	2. *realistic, believable, probable*
tame		*adj.*	**domesticated, docile, obedient** Dogs and cats are tame animals. *v.* The trainer tamed the wild tiger. *n.* The lion tamer cracked his whip.	*wild, fierce, uncontrollable, undomesticated*
tangible	1.	*adj.*	**material, solid, physical, concrete** Houses and cars are tangible assets.	1. *intangible, spiritual, ethereal*

	2.	*adj.*	**actual, definite, real, positive** The police had no tangible proof that the suspect was the robber.	**2.** *imaginary*
tantalize		*v.*	**tease, torment, plague, taunt, entice** Do not tantalize me with chocolate.	*soothe, comfort*
tardy		*adj.*	**late, slow, sluggish** The tardy salesclerk annoyed us. *n.* Many customers left because of the salesclerk's tardiness.	*prompt, punctual, quick, early*
tasteful		*adj.*	**exquisite, beautiful, pleasing, elegant** The designer's tasteful clothes are popular. *adv.* Their home is tastefully decorated.	*displeasing, inappropriate, unbecoming, tasteless*
tasty		*adj.*	**palatable, savory, delicious, delectable, appetizing** Dad baked a tasty pie for dessert.	*tasteless, insipid, unappetizing*
taunt		*v.*	**insult, tease, mock, jeer, scoff, ridicule** The children taunted Terry because he couldn't swim.	*applaud, praise, encourage, humor*
tear	**1.**	*n.*	**rip, split, slit, rent, hole** There is a tear in your green shirt.	
	2.	*v.*	**rip, split, slit, shred, lacerate** She angrily tore up the letter.	**2.** *patch, sew, mend*
	3.	*v.*	**snatch, grab, pull, yank, seize** The thief tore the purse from her hand.	
	4.	*v.*	**race, run, rush, dash, hustle, speed** The boys tore down the street to catch the bus.	**4.** *stroll, saunter, walk*
tease		*v.*	**taunt, tantalize, annoy, irritate, goad, irk, badger, aggravate, disturb, mock, torment, bother** The bully teased the children and made them cry.	*comfort, please, calm, soothe, encourage, console*
tedious		*adj.*	**tiresome, wearisome, dull, boring, slow, monotonous, humdrum** Tom quit his tedious job on the assembly line. *n.* He could not bear the tedium of the job.	*entertaining, amusing, interesting, fascinating, exciting*
teenager		*n.*	**adolescent, teen, youth, juvenile** Teenagers are people between the ages of thirteen and nineteen.	
tell	**1.**	*v.*	**reveal, inform, disclose, say, mention** Mom told us that she was expecting a baby.	**1.** *keep secret, be silent, hide*
	2.	*v.*	**narrate, relate, recite** Tell me the story again.	
	3.	*v.*	**distinguish, identify, differentiate** We cannot tell the twins apart.	**3.** *confuse, mix up*

temper	1.	*n.*	**calm, composure, balance** Rita lost her temper when she saw the tramp kick the puppy.	
	2.	*n.*	**anger, rage, fury, irritation, wrath** He needs help to control his temper.	**2.** *composure, good humor, patience*
	3.	*v.*	**moderate, soften** The judge tempered justice with mercy in passing sentence on the thief.	**3.** *violate, injure, attack*
	4.	*v.*	**harden, strengthen, toughen** Intense heat and sudden cooling is required to temper steel.	**4.** *weaken, soften, melt, dissolve*
temperamental		*adj.*	**excitable, moody, high-strung, erratic, unpredictable, emotional** The temperamental movie star stormed off the set in a huff.	*steady, easygoing, even-tempered, calm, cool*
temperate		*adj.*	**moderate, gentle, mild, clement, pleasant, balmy** Florida has a temperate climate in the winter.	*severe, harsh*
temporary	1.	*adj.*	**brief, transient, short-lived** There was a temporary power failure during the thunderstorm.	**1.** *permanent, lasting, perpetual, eternal*
	2.	*adj.*	**interim, stop-gap, short term** We had a temporary teacher while our teacher was ill.	**2.** *permanent, long term*
tempt		*v.*	**entice, lure, attract, captivate** The witch tempted Snow White with a red apple. *n.* Snow White could not resist the temptation.	*repulse, discourage, repel*
tenacious		*adj.*	**persistent, determined, stubborn, obstinate, steadfast, resolute, firm** Matt clings to the tenacious belief that he will recover soon.	*irresolute, wavering, flexible*
tendency		*n.*	**inclination, habit, disposition, leaning** Jay has a tendency to act rashly.	*reluctance, aversion*
tender	1.	*adj.*	**gentle, kind, loving, sympathetic, solicitous, compassionate** The nurse treats her patients with tender care.	**1.** *harsh, severe, unkind, cruel*
	2.	*adj.*	**delicate, fragile, frail, weak, soft** Young plants have tender stems.	**2.** *strong, sturdy, tough*
	3.	*adj.*	**painful, sore, sensitive** The pitcher's arm was tender after the long game.	**3.** *painless*
	4.	*adj.*	**youthful, immature, young, callow** Min started playing the violin at the tender age of two.	**4.** *mature, elderly, advanced*
	5.	*v.*	**give, submit, proffer, present** The frustrated employee tendered his resignation.	**5.** *withhold, withdraw, retain, retract*

tense	1.	*adj.*	**anxious, nervous, strained, on edge, jittery, excited** Everyone was tense as we waited for the election results to be announced.	1. *relaxed, calm, unconcerned, indifferent*
	2.	*adj.*	**tight, taut, stiff, rigid** The athlete did exercises to relax his tense muscles.	2. *relaxed, flaccid*
tension	1.	*n.*	**stretch, stress, pressure, tautness** The sewing machine has a device for adjusting the tension of the thread.	1. *slackness, looseness, flexibility*
	2.	*n.*	**strain, anxiety, apprehension, stress, pressure, nervousness** The class was under much tension on the day of the examination.	2. *relief, ease, calm, relaxation*
terminate	1.	*v.*	**end, conclude, finish, close, stop** The lease on our apartment terminates in September.	1. *open, begin, start, commence*
	2.	*v.*	**cancel, discontinue, annul, revoke, invalidate** We terminated our contract with the company because of poor service. *n.* The company sued us for the termination of the contract.	2. *validate, sanction, permit*
terrible	1.	*adj.*	**horrible, frightful, dreadful, ghastly, foul, shocking, terrifying, hideous** The world was stunned by the terrible terrorist attack in New York City.	1. *pleasing, welcome, appealing, pleasant*
	2.	*adj.*	**awful, disgraceful, poor, abysmal** My teacher told me to rewrite my terrible essay.	2. *wonderful, excellent, terrific*
terrific	1.	*adj.*	**terrible, frightening, terrifying** Terrific waves pounded the shore during the hurricane.	1. *mild, insignificant*
	2.	*adj.*	**excellent, wonderful, marvelous, great** Thank you for doing such a terrific job!	2. *awful, terrible, disgraceful, poor*
terrify		*v.*	**upset, frighten, scare, alarm, shock, horrify** The huge dog terrified the little boy.	*reassure, encourage, comfort, calm*
terror		*n.*	**panic, anxiety, dread, fear, fright, alarm, horror** The eruption of the volcano filled the villagers with terror.	*courage, unconcern, security, comfort, calm, reassurance*
test	1.	*n.*	**examination, trial, quiz, analysis, inspection** Vera passed the driver's test and got a license to drive.	
	2.	*v.*	**try, examine, inspect, analyze** Dad tested the well water before the family drank it.	

thankful		*adj.*	**grateful, obliged, appreciative** We are so thankful for your help.	*ungrateful,* *unappreciative*
thaw	1.	*v.*	**melt, liquefy, dissolve, soften, defrost** The snow thawed when the temperature rose. *n.* The thaw caused flooding.	**1.** *freeze, harden,* *solidify, congeal*
	2.	*v.*	**open up, relent, grow genial** Relations between the two countries thawed after the leaders met.	**2.** *harden, grow cool*
theft		*n.*	**robbery, burglary, piracy, stealing, thievery, pilfering** The suspect was charged with the theft of the famous painting.	
theory		*n.*	**concept, idea, plan, scheme, hypothesis** Darwin's theory of evolution is still debated today.	*proof*
thick	1.	*adj.*	**heavy, dense, close, profuse, packed** Thick rain forests cover many parts of Africa.	**1.** *thin, sparse,* *scanty, scattered,* *wide-open*
	2.	*adj.*	**deep, voluminous** It will take me many days to read this thick book.	**2.** *thin, slight,* *shallow*
thin	1.	*v.*	**dilute, reduce** The painter thinned the paint with turpentine.	**1.** *thicken, strengthen*
	2.	*adj.*	**slim, slender, slight, lean, lank, gaunt, skinny** Jan is quite thin since her illness.	**2.** *fat, bulky, obese,* *pudgy, plump, heavy*
	3.	*adj.*	**skimpy, light, flimsy** Mina shivered under her thin dress.	**3.** *thick, ample*
	4.	*adj.*	**weak, flimsy** No one believed his thin excuse for missing school. *adv.* We were not worried by his thinly veiled sneer.	**4.** *solid, substantial,* *valid*
	5.	*adj.*	**sparse, meager, scanty** How can I fluff up my thin hair?	**5.** *thick, dense,* *packed*
think	1.	*v.*	**ponder, meditate, reflect, consider, reason** Ken thought carefully about his choice of a university.	**1.** *act rashly*
	2.	*v.*	**believe, feel, judge, deem** I think that you should tell the truth.	
thorough	1.	*adj.*	**complete, full, perfect** Do you have a thorough understanding of this play? *adv.* The students were thoroughly drilled in safety procedures.	**1.** *incomplete,* *imperfect, partial*
	2.	*adj.*	**careful, meticulous, detailed** Pat did thorough research on the subject before writing her paper.	**2.** *careless*

thought	1.	*n.*	**idea, view, notion, opinion, conclusion** What are your thoughts about the future?	
	2.	*n.*	**concern, caring, kindness, regard, consideration** The thought is more important than the gift.	2. *disregard*
thoughtful		*adj.*	**considerate, kind, caring** My thoughtful neighbor brought me some soup when I was ill.	*thoughtless, inconsiderate*
thrifty		*adj.*	**frugal, economical, prudent, sparing** The thrifty man only buys things when they are on sale.	*wasteful, extravagant, spendthrift*
thrill	1.	*n.*	**glow, tingle, rush, quiver, tremor** We felt a thrill of excitement as the roller coaster took off.	
	2.	*v.*	**excite, arouse, stir, delight** The baby's birth thrilled the whole family.	2. *calm, soothe, bore*
thrive	1.	*v.*	**flourish, bloom, grow well** Most plants thrive in sunny areas.	1. *die, fade, wither, fail*
	2.	*v.*	**succeed, prosper, flourish, boom** The store thrived in the new location. *adj.* It should be a thriving business.	2. *fail, collapse*
throw		*v.*	**hurl, fling, pitch, toss, sling, cast, heave** The pitcher threw the ball wildly. *n.* It was a wild throw.	*catch, receive, grab, trap*
thwart		*v.*	**stop, hinder, foil, obstruct, prevent** The club members thwarted Rick's plans to become president.	*help, aid, support, encourage, facilitate*
tidy	1.	*v.*	**clean up, arrange, straighten** Did you tidy your room this morning?	1. *mess up, disarrange*
	2.	*adj.*	**neat, orderly, trim, well-kept** Rashid has a tidy desk.	2. *sloppy, messy, unkempt, untidy*
tight	1.	*adj.*	**firm, taut, secure, fast** The police held onto the robber with a tight grip. *v.* He tightened his grip when the robber struggled. *adv.* He clutched the robber tightly.	1. *slack, loose, shaky, relaxed, insecure*
	2.	*adj.*	**snug, close, narrow, small** Jim's new shoes are too tight.	2. *loose, large, oversized, wide*
	3.	*adj.*	**scarce, scant, deficient** We canceled the trip as money was tight.	3. *ample, plentiful, abundant*
timely		*adj.*	**well-timed, suitable, appropriate, opportune** The timely arrival of the firefighters prevented the fire from spreading.	*inopportune, untimely, unsuitable, inconvenient*

timid		*adj.*	**shy, afraid, fearful, cowardly** The timid child would not play with the other children. *n.* He must overcome his timidity. *adv.* He hid timidly behind his parents.	*brave, daring, confident, outgoing, fearless*
tiny		*adj.*	**small, little, wee, minute** Just look at the baby's tiny toes!	*immense, large, enormous, huge, big*
tip	1.	*n.*	**top, peak, apex, pinnacle, summit** We could see the tip of the iceberg from the deck of the ship.	**1.** *pit, bottom*
	2.	*n.*	**hint, suggestion, clue, pointer** Our teacher gave us a tip about the test.	
	3.	*n.*	**gratuity, reward** We left the waitress a large tip for her excellent service. *v.* We tipped her well.	
	4.	*v.*	**empty, dump, unload** Jane tipped the garbage into the dump.	**4.** *fill, load*
	5.	*v.*	**capsize, overturn, topple** The boat tipped because there were too many people in it.	
tire	1.	*v.*	**weary, exhaust, fatigue, wear out** The long flight from Hong Kong to Vancouver tired the travelers. *adj.* The tired travelers went to bed.	**1.** *refresh, invigorate, stimulate, awake*
	2.	*v.*	**bore, irritate, annoy, disgust** He tires us with his constant complaining.	**2.** *excite, inspire, interest, please*
tiresome		*adj.*	**irksome, wearisome, tedious, annoying** Please stop your tiresome whining.	*pleasing, stimulating, invigorating*
toil		*n.*	**work, labor, task, effort, drudgery, hardship** The workers are poorly paid for their toil. *v.* The workers toil all day long.	*leisure, rest, play*
tolerate	1.	*v.*	**permit, allow, condone** The school tolerates no alcohol or drugs.	**1.** *disallow, prohibit, prevent, oppose, ban*
	2.	*v.*	**bear, endure, handle** She tolerates her pain with courage.	
top	1.	*n.*	**summit, head, crown, zenith, apex, crest, tip, peak** They climbed to the top of the tower.	**1.** *base, bottom, foundation*
	2.	*n.*	**lid, cap, cover** Did you tear off the box top?	**2.** *bottom*
	3.	*v.*	**surpass, exceed, better, outdo** To date, no one has topped Elliot's backstroke record.	**3.** *fall short, approximate*
	4.	*adj.*	**highest, uppermost** Put the books on the top shelf.	**4.** *lowest, bottom*
	5.	*adj.*	**best, foremost, leading** Lucas is the top student in the class.	**5.** *worst*

topic		*n.*	**subject, theme, text** The topic of my project is: "Ways to preserve the environment."	
torment		*v.*	**badger, annoy, provoke, plague, torture, distress, pester, irritate** The bully tormented the small child.	*comfort, ease, aid, assist*
torrid		*adj.*	**sultry, tropical, scorching, sweltering** The Sahara is a torrid desert region.	*frigid, freezing*
torture	1.	*v.*	**abuse, torment, hurt** The kidnappers tortured their prisoner.	
	2.	*n.*	**agony, torment, anguish, suffering** The family went through torture during the war.	
toss	1.	*v.*	**throw, pitch, hurl, fling** He tossed the empty can into the trash.	*1. catch*
	2.	*v.*	**roll, lurch, heave, pitch, bob, sway** The boats tossed on the rough seas.	
tough	1.	*adj.*	**obstinate, stubborn, inflexible** Jose is a tough person to convince.	*1. easy, easygoing, mild, gentle*
	2.	*adj.*	**durable, strong, firm, sturdy** The tough cord held the parcel securely.	*2. brittle, fragile, weak*
	3.	*adj.*	**difficult, hard, strenuous, exhausting** Digging that flowerbed was a tough job.	*3. easy, simple*
	4.	*adj.*	**hard, sinewy, leathery** The steak is too tough to chew.	*4. tender, soft, succulent*
tour	1.	*n.*	**trip, excursion, journey, visit** They had a tour of Europe last summer.	
	2.	*v.*	**visit, explore, sightsee, travel around** The Jones family toured Europe by car.	
tourist		*n.*	**traveler, visitor, sightseer** Tourists usually visit the Eiffel Tower when they are in Paris.	
tournament		*n.*	**contest, competition, match, meet** The tennis tournament was held in June.	
trace	1.	*n.*	**sign, mark, impression, trail, indication, remains, record** The police could not find a trace of the burglars.	
	2.	*v.*	**hunt, track down, seek, find, look for** The courier company promised to trace the lost parcel.	*2. lose, misplace*
	3.	*v.*	**draw, sketch, outline** Ben traced the letters of the alphabet.	
trade	1.	*n.*	**commerce, business** The fur trade has declined.	
	2.	*n.*	**occupation, calling, profession, employment, business** Mr. Reed's trade is plumbing.	

	3.	*v.*	**exchange, deal, swap, barter** Ross wants to trade his car for a van. *n.* Will he get a good trade?	
	4.	*v.*	**do business with, deal, buy and sell** We trade with many nations.	
tradition	**1.**	*n.*	**practice, habit, custom** It is a tradition to wear red on Chinese New Year. *adj.* They had a traditional Polish wedding. *adv.* Traditionally, we eat turkey on Christmas Day.	**1.** *novelty, new idea*
	2.	*n.*	**legend, myth, folklore, fable, superstition** According to Greek tradition, gods and goddesses lived on Mt. Olympus.	**2.** *fact, true story*
tragic		*adj.*	**sad, dreadful, sorrowful, ill-fated** President John F. Kennedy and his brother Robert died tragic deaths. *n.* Their deaths were tragedies. *adv.* They were tragically assassinated.	*happy, joyous, comic, cheerful, pleasant*
train	**1.**	*n.*	**series, string, chain, sequence, succession** They have been dogged by a train of misfortunes.	
	2.	*v.*	**prepare, practice, drill** She trained for years to be a champion skater. *n.* Her coach is an excellent trainer.	
trait		*n.*	**quality, feature, characteristic, mark, attribute** Two good traits to have are kindness and dependability.	
traitor		*n.*	**renegade, betrayer, hypocrite, false friend, turncoat** A traitor is someone who betrays country or friend.	*patriot, supporter, defender, true friend*
tranquil		*adj.*	**calm, peaceful, quiet, still, placid, restful, undisturbed, serene** They lead a tranquil life in the country. *n.* They lead a life of tranquillity.	*rough, violent, tempestuous, disturbed, agitated*
transform		*v.*	**change, convert, turn, alter** The city transformed the parking lot into a park. *n.* What a transformation that was!	*maintain, keep, preserve*
transient	**1.**	*n.*	**traveler, migrant, drifter, visitor** Many farms hire transients at harvest time. *adj.* Transient workers move around the country looking for jobs.	**1.** *resident*

	2.	*adj.*	**transitory, brief, short-lived, passing, fleeting** Youth and beauty are transient.

2. *permanent, eternal, lasting, abiding*

transitory	*adj.*	**temporary, brief, passing, fleeting, short-lived, transient** She had a transitory loss of memory after the accident.

long, long-lived, lasting, durable, permanent, eternal

transparent	**1.**	*adj.*	**clear, lucid, see-through** Glass is transparent.
	2.	*adj.*	**sheer, translucent, gauzy, diaphanous** Her transparent dress was lined with silk.
	3.	*adj.*	**plain, apparent, obvious, evident** No one believed his transparent lie.

1. *opaque, muddy*

2. *opaque*

3. *vague, hidden, obscure, mysterious*

trap	**1.**	*n.*	**snare, ambush** The farmer set a trap for the fox. *v.* We trapped the mice in a mousetrap.
	2.	*n.*	**plot, intrigue, ruse, device** The detective's trap fooled the drug dealer.

trash	*n.*	**garbage, waste, rubbish, refuse, litter, debris, junk** Put that trash in the wastebasket.

valuables, treasure

travel	**1.**	*n.*	**journey, trip, voyage, tour, expedition** Marco Polo wrote fascinating stories about his travels to China. *n.* He was a great traveler.
	2.	*v.*	**journey, move, proceed, go, rove, tour** We will travel by sea on this trip. *n.* We are seasoned travelers.

treacherous	**1.**	*adj.*	**deceitful, unreliable, disloyal, undependable, unfaithful, false** A traitor is a treacherous person. *n.* Julius Caesar died because of the treachery of Brutus.
	2.	*adj.*	**unsafe, risky, hazardous, dangerous** Many accidents occur on this treacherous stretch of road.

1. *dependable, loyal, true, reliable, trustworthy*

2. *safe, reliable, secure*

treasure	**1.**	*n.*	**riches, wealth, loot** Divers found treasure in the sunken Spanish galleon.
	2.	*v.*	**value, esteem, cherish, prize, regard, care for, love** Ellie treasures her stamp collection.

1. *trash, garbage, junk*

2. *scorn, disregard*

treat	**1.**	*n.*	**pleasure, delight** The performance was a real treat for the audience.
	2.	*v.*	**handle, act toward, manage** This company treats its employees well. *n.* The employees are happy with their treatment.

treaty		*n.*	**contract, agreement, bargain, pact** The two nations signed a treaty to end the war.	

tremble		*v.*	**shake, quiver, shiver, quake, shudder** Oliver Twist trembled with fear as he stood before his cruel master.	*stay still, be stable, stay calm*

tremendous
1. *adj.* **frightful, appalling, horrifying**
   A tremendous earthquake hit San Francisco.
2. *adj.* **huge, enormous, vast, immense, gigantic, colossal, stupendous**
   We were awed by the tremendous size of the new stadium.
   2. tiny, minute, small, wee, miniature

trend
1. *n.* **leaning, drift, inclination, tendency**
   The trend today is toward healthy living.
2. *n.* **style, fashion, mode, vogue**
   Movie stars often set the trend in fashion.

tribute
1. *n.* **honor, respect, praise, esteem, gratitude, recognition**
   The student paid tribute to her teacher.
   1. dishonor, scorn, blame
2. *n.* **ransom, bribe, payment, toll, levy**
   The conquerors demanded tribute from the captured people.

trick
1. *n.* **ruse, deception, hoax, ploy, gimmick**
   The students played a trick on their teacher on April Fool's Day.
2. *n.* **feat, stunt, act, number**
   The magician performed new tricks.
3. *n.* **knack, art, technique, gift, skill**
   There is a trick to making good pastry.
4. *v.* **deceive, hoax, cheat, swindle, dupe, trap, bluff, fool, defraud**
   The salesperson tricked the teenager into buying the faulty car.

tricky
1. *adj.* **crafty, wily, deceitful, deceptive, foxy**
   The tricky politician won votes through false promises.
   1. straightforward, open, aboveboard
2. *adj.* **intricate, difficult, complicated**
   There are many tricky turns in the mountain roads.
   2. easy, safe, clear-cut

trim
1. *n.* **order, good condition, shape**
   The crew made certain the sailboat was in trim for the regatta.
   1. disorder, mess
2. *v.* **clip, cut, prune, shear, crop, lop**
   The gardener trimmed the hedge.
   2. lengthen, extend
3. *v.* **decorate, adorn, ornament**
   We trim the Christmas tree in December.
4. *adj.* **neat, orderly, tidy, spruce**
   The house was in trim condition.
   4. untidy, unkempt
5. *adj.* **slim, shapely, fit**
   Erin is trim because she exercises daily.
   5. shapeless, overweight, obese

trimming		*n.*	**decoration, ornament** The whole family hung trimmings on the huge Christmas tree.	
trip	1.	*n.*	**journey, voyage, tour, excursion** Liam makes many business trips.	
	2.	*v.*	**stumble, slip, fall, tumble** Cathy tripped over the rock and fell.	
triumph	1.	*n.*	**victory, conquest, success** The landing on the moon was one of the triumphs of modern science.	1. *loss, defeat, failure, setback*
	2.	*v.*	**conquer, win** Venus triumphed over Serena to win the tennis championship.	2. *lose*
triumphant		*adj.*	**victorious, successful, winning** The triumphant team celebrated all night long.	*unsuccessful, beaten, defeated*
trivial		*adj.*	**small, petty, unimportant, slight, insignificant, trifling, minor** He lost marks for trivial mistakes.	*important, serious, significant, major, exceptional*
trouble	1.	*n.*	**hardship, pain, suffering, misfortune, worry, distress, difficulty, misery** Mary never complains about her troubles.	1. *pleasure, delight, happiness, ease, joy, comfort*
	2.	*n.*	**sickness, ailment, disease** Uncle John has heart trouble.	2. *health*
	3.	*v.*	**worry, upset, perturb, concern, distress** The news of the plane crash troubled us. *adj.* Their troubled looks told us something was wrong.	3. *console, calm, relieve*
	4.	*v.*	**bother, annoy, pester, disturb, irritate** Don troubled us with his loud music.	4. *leave alone*
true	1.	*adj.*	**actual, genuine, real, accurate, authentic, correct** The true story of the accident was finally revealed.	1. *untrue, false, incorrect, fake, fictitious*
	2.	*adj.*	**reliable, sincere, dependable, faithful, loyal** Serge has always been a true friend.	2. *unreliable, insincere, unfaithful, disloyal*
truly	1.	*adv.*	**sincerely, genuinely, really** I'm truly grateful for your help.	
	2.	*adv.*	**certainly, indeed, absolutely, surely, positively, definitely** Matisse was truly a great artist.	
trust	1.	*n.*	**faith, hope, confidence, belief** Pinocchio put his trust in bad companions.	1. *doubt, distrust*
	2.	*v.*	**believe in, confide in, rely on, depend on** Pinocchio trusted the wrong people.	2. *mistrust, doubt, disbelieve, distrust*

trustworthy	*adj.*	**reliable, dependable, faithful, honest, truthful, conscientious, responsible** Parents should insist on trustworthy babysitters.	*undependable, unreliable, insincere,*
truthful	*adj.*	**reliable, exact, honest, candid, correct, accurate, sincere** Reporters should write truthful accounts of events.	*dishonest, false, inaccurate, untruthful*
try	1. *n.*	**attempt, trial, effort, endeavor** Take another try at the high jump.	
	2. *v.*	**attempt, tackle, undertake** Patsy tried skiing last winter.	*2. avoid, evade, reject, abandon*
turbulent	1. *adj.*	**violent, stormy, wild, fierce** Turbulent waves lashed the coast.	*1. calm, gentle, pacific, smooth*
	2. *adj.*	**noisy, restless, agitated, rowdy, boisterous, riotous** The police scattered the turbulent mob.	*2. quiet, orderly, peaceful*
turmoil	*n.*	**confusion, chaos, disorder, uproar, commotion** The town was in turmoil after the earthquake.	*order, peace, calm*
twirl	1. *n.*	**spin, whirl, turn, twist, revolution** The dancer made many rapid twirls. *v.* Heavenly bodies twirl through space.	
	2. *v.*	**coil, twist, wind, wrap, curl** Jane twirled the string around her finger.	*2. untie, unwind, remove*
twist	1. *n.*	**twirl, whirl, turn, spin** Give the top a twist.	
	2. *v.*	**turn, wind, coil, spin, twirl** The spider twisted the web around the helpless fly.	
	3. *v.*	**distort, contort** The victim's face twisted in pain.	
	4. *v.*	**curve, crook, bend, swerve, veer** The road twists to the right at the top of the hill.	
typical	1. *adj.*	**normal, regular, usual, ordinary, standard, conventional** A typical school day begins at nine o'clock. *adv.* The school day typically starts at nine o'clock.	*1. uncommon, unusual, strange, exceptional, extraordinary*
	2. *adj.*	**characteristic, like, expected** It is typical of Mike to be late.	*2. unexpected, unlike*
tyrant	*n.*	**dictator, despot, oppressor** A tyrant ruled the country for years. *n.* The people suffered under his tyranny.	

U

For many centuries, words containing *U* or *V* could be spelled with either letter. *Have* could be *haue*; *upon* might be *vpon*; *native* may appear as *natiue*.

Around 1800, *V* was established as a consonant and *U* as the fifth vowel. Since that time, these letters have not been interchanged.

ugly	1.	*adj.*	**unsightly, unpleasant, repulsive, hideous, revolting, loathsome** In the fairy tale, the ugly frog turned into a handsome prince.	**1.** *beautiful, lovely, gorgeous, attractive, handsome, comely*
	2.	*adj.*	**dangerous, threatening** The wrestler gave his opponent an ugly glare.	**2.** *mild, reasonable*
ultimate		*adj.*	**final, last, extreme, farthest, terminal** An Olympic gold medal is the ultimate achievement for an athlete.	*beginning, start, first, prior, preliminary, initial*
unable		*adj.*	**incapable, not able, unfit** The injured athlete was unable to complete the race.	*able, capable*
unanimous		*adj.*	**united, unified, collective, homogeneous** The jury came to a unanimous decision of "not guilty."	*divided, opposing, divergent, dissenting, discordant*
unappetizing		*adj.*	**uninviting, unpalatable, unappealing, unsavory** Rancid food is unappetizing.	*tempting, inviting, savory, appealing*
unbelievable		*adj.*	**inconceivable, preposterous, untenable, improbable** Years ago communication by e-mail was unbelievable.	*possible, probable, tenable, conceivable*
uncertain	1.	*adj.*	**doubtful, unsure, undecided, indefinite, dubious, unresolved** Sarah is uncertain about which university to attend.	**1.** *definite, secure, sure, certain, resolved*
	2.	*adj.*	**unsettled, changeable, unreliable, unpredictable** We canceled our trip because of the uncertain political situation in the region.	**2.** *settled, reliable, unchangeable, predictable*
uncommon		*adj.*	**rare, unusual, extraordinary, unique** In an uncommon act of charity, the miser donated money to the poor.	*common, usual, familiar, regular, normal, customary*
unconcerned		*adj.*	**disinterested, nonchalant, heedless, insouciant, indifferent, apathetic** We can no longer be unconcerned about preserving our environment.	*interested, keen, eager, zealous, concerned*
uncover		*v.*	**reveal, disclose, expose** The FBI uncovered a plot to assassinate the President.	*conceal, hide*
underhanded		*adj.*	**furtive, secret, surreptitious, sneaky, clandestine, sly** Criminals are involved in underhanded activities.	*aboveboard, open, honest, straightforward*

understand	1.	*v.*	**comprehend, catch, know, grasp, construe, perceive, fathom** I understand what the author is saying.	**1.** *misunderstand, mistake, misconstrue*
	2.	*v.*	**believe, hear, gather, assume** I understand Ben won a scholarship.	
understanding	1.	*n.*	**knowledge, perception, comprehension** This book is beyond my understanding.	**1.** *misunderstanding, misinterpretation*
	2.	*n.*	**agreement, common view** After months of negotiation, the two companies reached an understanding.	**2.** *stalemate, deadlock, impasse*
undertaking		*n.*	**venture, project, enterprise, task, endeavor** Space exploration is a costly undertaking.	
uneasy		*adj.*	**anxious, troubled, perturbed, upset, worried, nervous, agitated, unsettled** Reg is uneasy about the business contract he just signed. *n.* His uneasiness was evident in his inability to eat and sleep.	*composed, calm, collected*
unemployed		*adj.*	**jobless, out of work, inactive** Many unemployed people lined up to apply for jobs at the new plant.	*employed, at work, busy*
unequal		*adj.*	**uneven, irregular, unbalanced** Weigh scales must not be unequal.	*regular, balanced, even, equitable*
unequaled		*adj.*	**unmatched, matchless, supreme, unrivaled, unique, unparalleled** His swimming record remains unequaled.	*common, usual, frequent, many*
unethical		*adj.*	**shady, dishonorable, improper, unscrupulous** The used car dealer was charged for unethical business dealings.	*ethical, upright, honorable, scrupulous*
unexpected		*adj.*	**unforeseen, surprising, startling** Unexpected illness caused the singer to cancel the performance.	*predicted, foreseen, expected, anticipated*
unfasten		*v.*	**release, untie, undo, loose, disconnect, unhitch, unsnap** The crew unfastened the ship's ropes.	*tie, fasten, moor*
unfit	1.	*adj.*	**incompetent, inept, unable** Why is that dancer unfit to perform?	**1.** *competent, able, hale, sound*
	2.	*adj.*	**unsuitable, improper, inappropriate** The water is unfit for human consumption.	**2.** *correct, apt, suitable, proper*
unforeseen		*adj.*	**surprising, unexpected, startling, unpredicted, abrupt** The defeat of the champion was unforeseen.	*predicted, foreseen, expected, anticipated*

unforgettable		*adj.*	**notable, impressive, exceptional, extraordinary** The moon landing was an unforgettable event.	*forgettable, common, unimpressive,*
unfortunate		*adj.*	**unlucky, ill-fated, hapless** The acrobat had an unfortunate accident.	*fortunate, lucky*
unhappy		*adj.*	**sad, miserable, gloomy, dismal, dejected, distressed, sorrowful, melancholy, downhearted** The children are unhappy about the loss of their pet.	*cheerful, happy, joyful, merry, glad, jolly, ecstatic, lighthearted*
uniform	1.	*n.*	**costume, garb, attire** The band's uniform is colorful.	
	2.	*adj.*	**even, steady, regular, stable, constant, consistent** There is a uniform temperature throughout the building.	**2.** *uneven, irregular, varying, erratic, variable, inconsistent*
	3.	*adj.*	**equal, identical, alike, similar, correspondent** Those two packages are of uniform size.	**3.** *different, unlike, varied, varying*
unique	1.	*adj.*	**distinctive, unmatched, single, novel** Every single human being is unique.	**1.** *common, usual*
	2.	*adj.*	**rare, uncommon, unusual** Michelangelo had a unique talent.	**2.** *ordinary, everyday, common*
unite		*v.*	**join, combine, merge, associate, consolidate, amalgamate** The two companies united against their competitors.	*divide, separate, part, sunder*
unity		*n.*	**harmony, concord, agreement, accord** The new leader restored unity to the country.	*discord, dissension, conflict, contention*
universal	1.	*adj.*	**worldwide, global, catholic** There is universal concern for the environment.	**1.** *local, district, regional, urban, suburban*
	2.	*adj.*	**general, widespread, entire, extensive, comprehensive** The government's proposal met with universal approval.	**2.** *partial, limited, incomplete*
unkempt		*adj.*	**untidy, disorderly, tousled, slovenly, disheveled, rumpled, ill-kept, bedraggled** The tramp's unkempt appearance frightened the children.	*tidy, neat, orderly, well groomed*
unruly		*adj.*	**unmanageable, rowdy, uncontrollable** Police were called in to control the unruly mob at the rock concert.	*docile, well-behaved, orderly, obedient*
untidy		*adj.*	**messy, slovenly, unkempt** Steve was told to clean up his untidy room.	*tidy, neat*

uphold		*v.*	**maintain, support, back up, confirm, sustain, champion**	*confront, oppose, counter, resist, obstruct, contradict*
			Citizens are expected to uphold the law.	
upright	1.	*adj.*	**vertical, erect**	**1.** *horizontal*
			Upright pianos require less space than grand pianos.	
	2.	*adj.*	**virtuous, honest, fair, aboveboard, circumspect**	**2.** *dishonest, unfair, underhanded*
			It is best to deal with upright citizens.	
uprising		*n.*	**revolt, rebellion, riot, upheaval, revolution, insurrection**	*order, peace*
			The army was sent to quell the uprising.	
uproar		*n.*	**commotion, confusion, hubbub, clamor, disturbance**	*quiet, calm, order*
			The spectators were in an uproar over the umpire's unfair call.	
uproot		*v.*	**pull up, remove, extract, rip up, eradicate**	*maintain, preserve, take root*
			The tornado uprooted many trees.	
upset	1.	*v.*	**overturn, tilt, topple, tip over, knock over, capsize**	**1.** *right*
			Rough water upset the canoe.	
	2.	*v.*	**disturb, bother, fluster, perturb, agitate**	**2.** *please, calm, soothe, ease*
			News of the tragedy upset everyone.	
	3.	*v.*	**defeat, beat, overthrow, topple, conquer**	**3.** *lose, be defeated*
			The newcomer upset the favorite in the match.	
up-to-date		*adj.*	**fashionable, modern, stylish, in vogue, new, current**	*out-of-date, old-fashioned, antique, antiquated*
			Which car has the most up-to-date engineering?	
urge	1.	*n.*	**need, desire, impulse**	
			She stifled an urge to yawn.	
	2.	*v.*	**implore, beg, plead, entreat, coax**	**2.** *deter, discourage*
			I urge you to continue your education.	
	3.	*v.*	**drive, compel, press, push, force**	**3.** *withhold, block, inhibit*
			The general urged the troops into battle.	
urgent		*adj.*	**pressing, serious, vital, critical, pressing**	*trivial, insignificant, unimportant*
			The doctor received an urgent call for help.	
use	1.	*n.*	**utility, value, applicability, practicability**	**1.** *misuse, abuse, misapplication*
			The salesperson claimed the appliance could be put to many uses.	
	2.	*v.*	**employ, utilize, apply, expend, consume**	**2.** *discard, reject, refuse, neglect, waste*
			We used all our resources to build the tower.	

useful		adj.	helpful, valuable, advantageous, beneficial, serviceable It is useful to know some first aid.	useless, valueless, worthless
useless	1.	adj.	worthless There is a lot of useless junk in the attic.	1. useful, saleable
	2.	adj.	futile, fruitless, hopeless, in vain, pointless All rescue attempts were useless.	2. productive, useful, hopeful
usual	1.	adj.	ordinary, normal, common, everyday Insects are the usual carriers of pollen.	1. uncommon, unusual, abnormal
	2.	adj.	habitual, customary, traditional, conventional It is usual to bow as a greeting in Japan. adv. North Americans usually shake hands when they meet.	2. unconventional, extraordinary
utmost	1.	adj.	greatest, ultimate, most, maximum This news bulletin is of the utmost importance!	1. least, minimum
	2.	adj.	farthest, furthest, remotest, extreme Explorers probe the utmost regions of the world.	2. nearest, closest
utter	1.	adj.	complete, total, thorough, absolute, sheer, unqualified Utter joy was felt when the rescue team arrived. adv. The survivors were utterly exhausted.	1. incomplete, partial, limited
	2.	v.	speak, say, voice, tell, articulate, declare, announce, express, state The bully was heard to utter an apology.	2. remain silent

V

To the Romans, the numeral 5 was represented as *V*. Traders would show this amount by holding four fingers together with the thumb extended, to indicate *V* (5).

Winston Churchill made the *V* for "Victory" sign famous by holding his right hand high, with the first two fingers spread wide.

vacant		*adj.*	**empty, unoccupied, free, available** There is a vacant house next to ours. *n.* Is there a vacancy nearby?	*inhabited, filled, occupied, full, taken*

vacant   *adj.*   **empty, unoccupied, free, available**   *inhabited, filled, occupied, full, taken*
There is a vacant house next to ours.
n. Is there a vacancy nearby?

vague
1. *adj.* **uncertain, unsure, indefinite, obscure**   *1. definite, certain, sure, clear*
John's vague answer left everyone wondering.
2. *adj.* **dim, indistinct, hazy, faint**   *2. clear, distinct, well-defined*
The vague outline of a ship could be seen in the fog.

vain
1. *adj.* **conceited, egotistical, proud, arrogant**   *1. humble, modest, meek*
The vain actor spent hours getting ready for the party.
2. *adj.* **futile, useless, unsuccessful**   *2. effective, successful*
The lifeguard made a vain attempt to save the boy.

valiant   *adj.*   **brave, bold, daring, courageous, heroic, gallant, fearless, dauntless**   *cowardly, fearful*
The soldier received a medal for his valiant deed.
adv. The troops fought valiantly.

valid
1. *adj.* **proper, suitable, sound, genuine**   *1. improper, false, fictitious*
Do you have a valid excuse for being late?
2. *adj.* **legal, binding, lawful, legitimate, official**   *2. illegal, unlawful, invalid*
That contract is not valid without both signatures.

valor   *n.*   **courage, bravery, gallantry, heroism**   *cowardice, timidity, fear*
He received a medal for valor in the war.

value
1. *n.* **worth, importance**   *1. unimportance*
What value do you put on your time?
2. *n.* **price, cost, charge**
What is the value of this gold pen?
adj. It is a valuable pen.
3. *v.* **price, assess, appraise, estimate, compute, evaluate**
The owner valued his car at $20,000.
4. *v.* **prize, respect, treasure, cherish**   *4. disregard, scorn*
I value her friendship.

values   *n.*   **ideals, norms, standards, mores**
Children learn traditional values from their parents.

vandal   *n.*   **looter, raider, destroyer**
Vandals broke the windows.
v. They vandalized the building.
n. Vandalism is a continuing problem everywhere.

vanish   *v.*   **disappear, evaporate, dissolve**   *appear, materialize*
The magician waved his wand and the rabbit vanished!

vanquish	*v.*	**defeat, conquer, overpower, master, overcome, beat, crush, subdue** The army vanquished its enemies.	*surrender, yield, give in*
vapor	*n.*	**moisture, fog, mist, steam, condensation** The vapor from the shower clouded the bathroom mirror. *v.* The water vaporized.	
variety	1. *n.* 2. *n.*	**assortment, diversity, mixture** This store sells a wide variety of candies. **kind, sort, type, brand, category** Red Delicious is my favorite variety of apples.	1. *uniformity, similarity*
various	*adj.*	**many, several, numerous, diverse, differing** There are various ways to solve the problem.	*few*
vary	*v.*	**change, differ, alter, modify, fluctuate** The price of most things varies according to supply and demand.	*be steady, hold, remain*
vast	1. *adj.* 2. *adj.*	**huge, great, tremendous, mighty, immense, colossal, enormous** A vast crowd assembled in St. Peter's Square on Easter Sunday. **boundless, unlimited, immeasurable** The universe is vast.	1. *small, little, slight, tiny* 2. *limited, confined, restricted, finite*
vegetate	*v.*	**deteriorate, waste away, languish, stagnate, idle, loaf, laze, weaken** Many people vegetate in front of the television set all day.	*grow, participate, respond*
vehement	*adj.*	**intense, fierce, fiery, earnest, fervent, forceful** There are many vehement opponents of cruelty to animals. *adv.* They protest vehemently against cruelty to animals.	*indifferent, unconcerned*
veil	1. *n.* 2. *n.* 3. *v.*	**cover, cloud, screen, blanket** Veils of white mist hung over the valley. **face covering, head covering** The bride wore a veil of antique lace. **cover, hide, conceal, obscure, screen** Heavy smog often veils Los Angeles.	3. *expose, reveal, show, disclose*
velocity	*n.*	**speed, rate** Light travels at a velocity of 186,000 miles per second.	
vengeance	*n.*	**revenge, retribution, reprisal, retaliation** The tribe swore vengeance on the invaders.	*forgiveness, tolerance, pardon*

venture	*n.*	**endeavor, undertaking, enterprise, chance, risk, project, speculation** His venture in real estate proved successful. *v.* He ventured a large sum of money on the building.	*certainty*
verbal	*adj.*	**oral, spoken, vocal, unwritten** The two groups arrived at a verbal agreement. *adv.* They agreed verbally.	*written*
verdict	*n.*	**decision, judgment, finding, conclusion** The accused person waited anxiously for the jury's verdict.	
verify	*v.*	**confirm, support, guarantee, prove, vouch for, establish** Two witnesses verified the suspect's alibi.	*deny, contradict, dispute*
versatile	*adj.*	**resourceful, adaptable, able, expert, well-rounded, accomplished** The versatile performer can sing, dance, and act.	*limited*
versed	*adj.*	**familiar, trained, proficient, learned, skilled, able, accomplished** Jose is versed in five languages.	*awkward, ignorant, incompetent, unskilled, unfamiliar*
vertical	*adj.*	**erect, perpendicular, upright** The wallpaper has vertical stripes.	*horizontal*
veteran	1. *adj.*	**seasoned, experienced, weathered** The veteran performer got a standing ovation.	*1. amateur, unseasoned, inexperienced*
	2. *n.*	**war survivor, old-timer** Grandpa is a Vietnam War veteran.	
veto	1. *n.*	**refusal, prohibition, rejection, denial** The president's veto of the club's proposal angered the members.	*1. approval, sanction, endorsement*
	2. *v.*	**reject, deny, turn down, forbid, disallow, prohibit** The council vetoed our proposal for a new park.	*2. approve, endorse, allow, sanction*
vex	*v.*	**displease, annoy, anger, provoke, trouble, irritate, disturb** The protesters' loud heckling vexed the speaker.	*please, delight, satisfy*
vibrant	1. *adj.*	**vivid, lively, bright, brilliant, strong, intense, striking, glowing** The vibrant colors of the autumn leaves delighted the visitors.	*1. dull, flat, colorless, lifeless*

2. *adj.* **active, energetic, lively, vigorous**
She inspires her students with her vibrant personality.

2. insipid, lifeless, inactive, dull, slow, lethargic, phlegmatic

vibrate *v.* **quake, tremble, throb, quiver, sway**
The buildings vibrated when the earthquake struck.
n. The vibrations terrified the occupants.

vice **1.** *n.* **flaw, shortcoming, fault, failing, defect, weakness**
Dad's only vice is smoking.

1. strong point, talent, gift

2. *n.* **corruption, immorality, iniquity**
The police try to keep our cities free of vice.

2. virtue, morality, goodness

vicious **1.** *adj.* **spiteful, malicious, wicked, destructive**
Their vicious lies caused a lot of grief.

1. harmless, noble, virtuous

2. *adj.* **savage, brutal**
The dictator launched a vicious attack on his opponents.

2. gentle

victor *n.* **winner, champion, conqueror**
The victor acknowledged the crowd's cheers with a wave.
adj. He was victorious in three matches.

loser

victory *n.* **conquest, triumph, success, win**
The team was congratulated for its victory in the debate.

defeat, failure, loss

vie *v.* **contend, compete, fight, struggle, challenge, contest**
Two strong teams vied for the Rose Bowl.

share, cooperate

view **1.** *n.* **sight, scene, outlook, vista, panorama**
The view from the mountaintop is spectacular.

2. *n.* **opinion, feeling, belief, judgment**
It is my view that we need a new leader.

3. *v.* **see, look at, look on, survey, scan, examine, watch**
The press was invited to view the designer's new collection.
n. The reporter was an avid viewer.

vigilant *adj.* **watchful, alert, wary, observant**
The vigilant security guard nabbed the shoplifter.
n. Vigilance is a necessity in this job.

careless, negligent, inattentive

vigorous *adj.* **energetic, lively, robust, healthy, active, spirited, strong, forceful**
Grandfather is still vigorous although he is 85 years old.
adv. The workers vigorously protested against the new rules.

weak, lifeless, inactive, feeble

vile	1.	*adj.*	**nasty, odious, disgusting, bad, offensive, unpleasant, repulsive** Vile odors came from the chemical plant.	1. *pleasant, good, agreeable*
	2.	*adj.*	**filthy, obscene, gross, vulgar, coarse, despicable, sordid** Vile language is not appreciated.	2. *polite, cultured, acceptable, refined*
violence	1.	*n.*	**brutality, outrage, savagery** There have been outbreaks of violence in some parts of the country.	1. *mildness, peace*
	2.	*n.*	**force, might, fury, intensity, impact, rampage, onslaught** Many houses collapsed under the violence of the tornado.	2. *weakness, calm*
violent	1.	*adj.*	**strong, forceful, raging, furious, rough, turbulent, severe** Violent thunderstorms lashed the coast.	1. *weak, tranquil, calm*
	2.	*adj.*	**fierce, savage, brutal** He was told to control his violent temper.	2. *gentle, peaceful, easy-going*
visible	1.	*adj.*	**distinct, in view, clear, in sight** The enemy's camp was visible through the telescope.	1. *invisible, unobservable*
	2.	*adj.*	**evident, apparent, plain, obvious, noticeable** After a day's treatment there was a visible improvement in the patient. *adv.* The crowd was visibly shaken by the bad news.	2. *concealed, buried, hidden*
vision	1.	*n.*	**sight, eyesight** Pilots must have good vision.	1. *blindness*
	2.	*n.*	**foresight, insight** The founder of our school was a person with vision.	2. *hindsight*
	3.	*n.*	**ghost, spirit, phantom, fantasy, apparition, image, illusion** Many prophets claim to have seen visions.	
vista		*n.*	**outlook, view, perspective, prospect** College opens up new vistas of knowledge for many students.	
visual		*adj.*	**optical, visible, perceptible** Many visual learning aids are used in our school.	
visualize		*v.*	**picture, imagine, fancy, envision** We visualized her Italian village as Rosa described it.	
vital	1.	*adj.*	**important, urgent, critical, basic, pressing, serious, essential, chief** Preserving the environment is a vital issue today.	1. *trivial, superficial, unnecessary, unimportant*

	2.	*adj.*	**forceful, lively, strong, energetic, dynamic, vibrant** She is one of the most vital leaders we have had in years. *n.* Her vitality inspires everyone.	*2. listless, weak, dull, phlegmatic*

vivacious   *adj.*   **animated, active, lively, spirited, playful, vibrant**
We always enjoy her parties because she is such a vivacious host.

dull, uninteresting, lifeless, listless, phlegmatic

vivid

1. *adj.* **bright, brilliant, strong, intense, striking**
The vivid colors of the autumn foliage covered the hills.

1. dull, flat, colorless, lifeless

2. *adj.* **lively, vibrant, active**
The author has a vivid imagination.

2. dull, boring

3. *adj.* **distinct, clear, lifelike, realistic**
Parkash has vivid memories of his home in India.

3. dull, vague, nondescript

void

1. *n.* **blank, vacuum, emptiness, empty space**
The death of her husband left a void in her life.

2. *v.* **cancel, annul, reverse, rescind, break**
Dan voided his rental agreement when he didn't pay his rent.

2. validate, effect, bind, enforce

volunteer

1. *n.* **unpaid worker, helper**
Many volunteers help out at the hospital.
adj. The volunteer staff works in every department.

1. paid help, employee

2. *v.* **offer, step forward, enlist**
During the war, many young people volunteered to serve in the army.
adj. Their voluntary efforts were greatly appreciated.

2. force, compel, recur, conscript

voluptuous   *adj.*   **profuse, sumptuous, opulent, sensuous**
Voluptuous curves are appealing to some.

simple, plain, bare, sparse

voyage

1. *n.* **journey, cruise, trip, excursion, tour**
After their retirement, they went on a voyage around the world.

2. *v.* **travel, journey, cruise, visit**
They voyaged to many lands.

vulgar   *adj.*   **rude, uncouth, obscene, coarse, crude**
That's a very vulgar remark!
n. Such vulgarity is not appreciated.

polite, cultured, refined, tasteful

vulnerable   *adj.*   **susceptible, defenseless, unprotected, unguarded**
Without vaccination, we are vulnerable to measles.

protected, guarded, immune, impervious, invincible

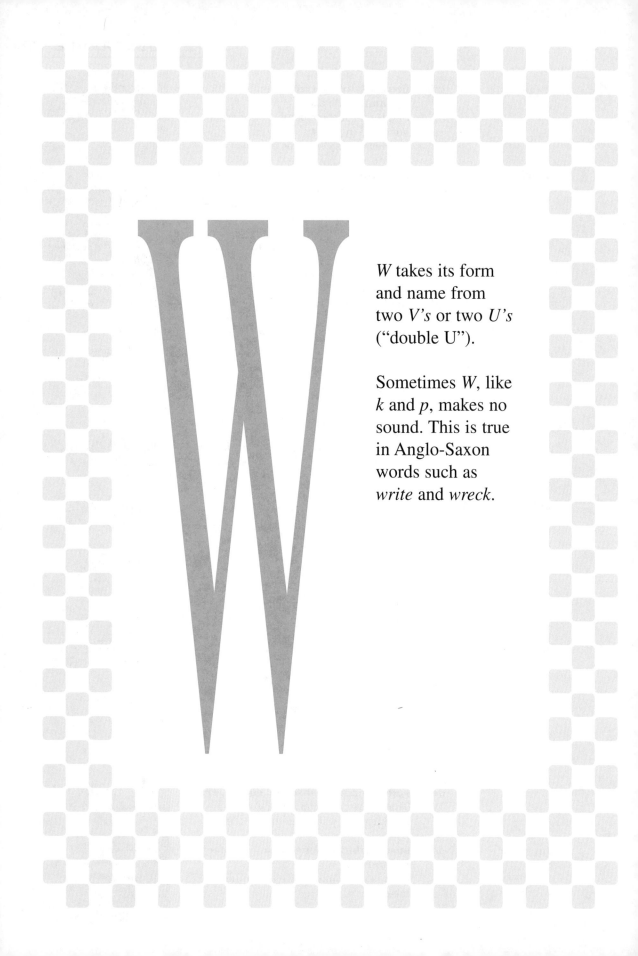

W takes its form and name from two *V's* or two *U's* ("double U").

Sometimes *W*, like *k* and *p*, makes no sound. This is true in Anglo-Saxon words such as *write* and *wreck*.

wages		*n.*	**pay, salary, earnings, income, remuneration** He makes good wages as a programmer.	
wail	1.	*n.*	**howl, whine, cry, shriek** The wail of the air raid sirens wakened the villagers.	1. *whisper, murmur*
	2.	*v.*	**cry, weep, howl, lament, sob, bawl** The baby wailed when she fell.	2. *laugh, smile*
wait	1.	*n.*	**stay, pause, delay, stop** Luke had a long wait for the bus.	
	2.	*v.*	**linger, remain, stay, tarry** I'll wait for five more minutes.	2. *leave, go*
	3.	*v.*	**look for, expect, watch for** He waits for the mail every day.	
	4.	*v.*	**serve, attend to** Jay waits on tables after school. *n.* He is a waiter.	
wake		*v.*	**arouse, awake, rouse, stir** Please wake me at six o'clock tomorrow.	
walk	1.	*v.*	**stroll, stride, saunter** Jim walked to the store.	1. *run*
	2.	*n.*	**stroll, hike, ramble, saunter** Pa and Ma went for a walk in the park.	
wander	1.	*v.*	**roam, ramble, saunter, meander** Joan and I wandered through the mall.	
	2.	*v.*	**stray, drift, digress** My mind wandered during the long, dull speech.	2. *settle, rest, anchor, focus*
wane		*v.*	**fade, weaken, decline, lessen, decrease, sink, subside** Her health waned after the operation. *adj.* We had to stop our gardening as we couldn't see in the waning light.	*increase, strengthen, wax, brighten*
want	1.	*n.*	**need, poverty, destitution, privation** We raised money for the people in want.	1. *abundance, plenty, wealth, affluence*
	2.	*v.*	**wish for, desire, crave, yearn for** My brother wants a ten-speed bicycle. *n.* His wants are always met.	
	3.	*v.*	**need, require, lack** This room wants a new coat of paint.	
war		*n.*	**conflict, combat, battle, confrontation** Many people died in the Vietnam War.	*peace*
warm	1.	*v.*	**heat, make hot** Let's warm the leftovers for lunch.	1. *cool, chill*
	2.	*adj.*	**tepid, lukewarm** Would you like some warm milk?	2. *cold, frozen*
	3.	*adj.*	**not cold, cosy, snug** Rona put on a warm coat before leaving. *adv.* She was wise to dress warmly.	3. *chilly*

	4.	*adj.*	**kind, tender, loving, friendly, sincere, pleasant, gracious, cheerful, cordial** The innkeeper gave us a warm welcome.	**4.** *unfriendly, unkind, aloof, hostile, cool*
warn		*v.*	**caution, advise, notify, inform, alert** We were warned of the coming storm. *n.* We canceled our fishing trip because of the storm warning. *adj.* We slowed the car when we saw a warning light flashing ahead.	
wary		*adj.*	**cautious, alert, careful, prudent** It is wise to be wary with strangers.	*unwary, rash, careless, reckless*
waste	1.	*n.*	**garbage, refuse, rubbish, trash, junk, debris** Our lakes and rivers are polluted by industrial waste.	**1.** *valuables*
	2.	*v.*	**squander, misuse, fritter, throw away** Don't waste your money on comics. *n.* Comics are a waste of money.	**2.** *save, preserve, hoard, economize, accumulate*
	3.	*v.*	**fade, weaken** Pei-Lin wasted away from cancer.	**3.** *strengthen, grow, develop*
wasteful		*adj.*	**extravagant, lavish, reckless** The wasteful man spends his money foolishly.	*thrifty, tight-fisted*
watch	1.	*n.*	**heed, attention, guard, supervision** Keep a close watch on the children.	**1.** *inattention, neglect*
	2.	*n.*	**timepiece, wristwatch, pocket watch** Does your watch keep good time?	
	3.	*v.*	**observe, see, look at, notice, survey, regard, gaze at, view** We watched the news on television.	**3.** *overlook, disregard, ignore*
	4.	*v.*	**be careful, take heed, be cautious, be on guard** Watch where you're going!	**4.** *be reckless, be rash, be careless*
watchful		*adj.*	**vigilant, alert, wary, careful, attentive, cautious** The security guard kept a watchful eye on the crowd.	*careless, negligent, heedless*
waver	1.	*v.*	**vacillate, hesitate, fluctuate** She wavered over which university to attend.	**1.** *be decisive, be certain*
	2.	*v.*	**flutter, flicker, falter, totter, quiver, tremble, shake** The suspect's voice wavered when the police questioned him. *adj.* The candle's wavering flame threw eerie shadows on the wall.	**2.** *steady, remain steady*
way	1.	*n.*	**route, road, direction, course** Please show me the way to the campsite.	
	2.	*n.*	**custom, manner, habit, style** Ramon has adapted to our way of life.	

3. *n.* **method, means, procedure, measure**
We have to find a way to raise funds for the trip.

wayward *adj.* **difficult, troublesome, unruly, willful, disobedient, rebellious**
Wise counseling has helped many wayward youths.

obedient, steady

weak
1. *adj.* **feeble, shaky, frail, delicate, wasted**
The sick child is too weak to stand.

1. strong, vigorous, sturdy, robust

2. *adj.* **unsound, flimsy, unstable**
The weak rung on the ladder broke when Bob stepped on it.

2. strong, sturdy

3. *adj.* **feeble, ineffective, ineffectual, timid**
The politician was voted out of office for being a weak leader.

3. strong, competent, able, assertive

4. *adj.* **diluted, thin, watered down**
The weak coffee tasted awful.

4. strong, concentrated

wealth
1. *n.* **money, riches, fortune, assets**
They made their wealth from oil.
adj. The wealthy family donated money for a new hospital.

1. poverty, want, need

2. *n.* **abundance, large quantity**
There is a wealth of talent in our school.

2. scarcity, shortage, dearth

weary *adj.* **tired, fatigued, exhausted**
The weary runner collapsed in a faint.
n. He was overcome by weariness.

fresh, lively, rested

website *n.* **location, a page, a series of pages, site**
Many businesses and institutions have websites on the Internet.

weep *v.* **sob, cry, shed tears**
Annette wept for joy at her wedding.

laugh, chuckle, giggle, smile

weird *adj.* **strange, peculiar, eerie, odd, mysterious, unearthly, uncanny**
People reported seeing weird flying objects.

normal, usual, common, natural

well
1. *n.* **water hole, spring, pool**
How deep is this well?

2. *v.* **gush, flow, stream, spurt, ooze**
Tears welled in her eyes when she heard the sad news.

3. *adj.* **healthy, strong, sound, vigorous**
Ben is well again after his operation.

3. ill, sick, ailing, weak, unwell

4. *adj.* **favorable, good, satisfactory, right**
I hope all is well with your family.

4. unfavorable, bad, unsatisfactory

5. *adv.* **intimately, personally**
Do you know her well?

6. *adv.* **thoroughly, completely, fully**
The recipe said to mix the batter well.

6. poorly, barely, scarcely

7. *adv.* **nicely, favorably, adequately, successfully**
David is doing well in school.

7. poorly, badly, inadequately

whim	*n.*	**notion, fancy, urge, impulse, quirk, caprice, inclination** On a whim, we decided to go to Paris.	*plan*
whole	*adj.*	**entire, complete, total, undivided** The greedy girl ate the whole box of chocolates.	*partial, incomplete*
wholehearted	*adj.*	**sincere, true, complete, earnest, enthusiastic, unreserved** The teacher gave his wholehearted support to our project.	*indifferent, lukewarm, half-hearted*
wholesome	1. *adj.*	**nutritious, healthy, nourishing, sound** A wholesome diet includes grains, vegetables, fruits, and milk.	*1. unwholesome, harmful, noxious*
	2. *adj.*	**decent, moral, clean, responsible, honest, worthy** The children were raised in a wholesome atmosphere.	*2. immoral, wicked, bad, degrading*
wicked	*adj.*	**sinful, evil, immoral, bad, corrupt, vile** Cinderella had a wicked stepmother.	*good, loving, kind*
wild	1. *n.*	**bush, wilderness, wasteland, jungle** Lions roamed in the wilds of Africa.	
	2. *adj.*	**untamed, savage, unbroken** The cowboy tamed the wild horse.	*2. tame, broken, civilized*
	3. *adj.*	**natural, desolate, rugged, bleak, wooded, forested, uncultivated** There are many wild areas in Canada's North.	*3. populated, inhabited, cultivated*
	4. *adj.*	**unruly, violent, disorderly, lawless, reckless, fanatical** A group of wild fans started a riot at the soccer game.	*4. orderly, law-abiding, well-behaved*
wily	*adj.*	**cunning, sly, crafty, scheming, tricky, shifty, crooked, shrewd** A wily car dealer cheated them.	*open, sincere, honest, straightforward*
win	1. *n.*	**conquest, victory, triumph, success** One more win and the Cup is ours! *v.* We won the game in overtime.	*1. defeat, loss*
	2. *v.*	**get, gain, achieve, capture, earn, secure, receive** Mario's kindness won our gratitude.	*2. lose*
wind	1. *v.*	**twist, turn, curve, bend, weave, meander, ramble, zigzag** The Mackenzie River winds northward to the Arctic Ocean. *adj.* The winding road is dangerous at night.	
	2. *v.*	**coil, twist, twine, roll, loop** Helen wound the yarn into a ball.	*2. unwind, unroll*

winner	*n.*	**champion, conqueror, victor** Ray was the winner in the golf game.	*loser*
winning	*adj.*	**attractive, charming, appealing, enchanting, pleasing, delightful, fascinating, captivating** The mayor flashed us a winning smile.	*repulsive, irritating, sickening, disgusting*
wisdom	*n.*	**judgment, sense, reason, knowledge, comprehension, prudence** King Solomon was known for his wisdom.	*foolishness, stupidity, folly*
wise	*adj.*	**intelligent, astute, profound, clever** The leader of the country is a wise person.	*foolish, stupid, silly*
wish	*v.*	**desire, crave, long, hope, hanker, yearn, want** Tom wished for a computer. *n.* His wish came true on his birthday.	
wistful	*adj.*	**pensive, sad, forlorn, sorrowful, melancholy, thoughtful, doleful** Jan had a wistful look as she left for camp. *adv.* She waved wistfully at her family.	*happy, joyous, exuberant*
wit	1. *n.*	**humor, fun** The comedian amused us with his wit.	
	2. *n.*	**intellect, brains, mind, sense** Cliff used his wits to earn some money.	**2.** *stupidity*
withdraw	1. *v.*	**recall, draw back, retreat, pull back** The general withdrew his troops from battle.	**1.** *advance, proceed*
	2. *v.*	**take out, remove** She withdrew some money from her bank account. *n.* She made the withdrawal from her bank account to buy a car.	**2.** *deposit, put in*
withdrawn	*adj.*	**shy, quiet, reserved, unfriendly, unsociable, uncommunicative** The child has been withdrawn since she lost her dog.	*friendly, open, sociable*
withhold	*v.*	**keep, retain, hold back** The witness withheld information from the police.	*give, provide*
without	1. *prep.*	**lacking, not having, deprived of** The survivors went without food until they were rescued.	**1.** *with*
	2. *adv.*	**outside, outer part** We painted the house within and without.	**2.** *inside*
withstand	*v.*	**resist, tolerate, bear, endure, suffer, cope with** It is difficult to withstand long, cold winters.	*submit, surrender*

witness	1.	*n.*	**onlooker, observer, spectator, eyewitness** Were you a witness to the attack?	
	2.	*v.*	**see, notice, observe, view, note** Mark witnessed the accident.	
witty		*adj.*	**clever, humorous, funny, amusing** Yang entertained us all night with his witty remarks.	*dull, serious, solemn*
woebegone		*adj.*	**despondent, depressed, dejected, sad, sorrowful, glum, downcast, somber** Her woebegone face told us something was wrong.	*happy, thrilled, glad, lighthearted, cheerful*
wonder	1.	*n.*	**amazement, astonishment, awe, surprise, fascination** When she saw the pictures of Mars, she was filled with wonder.	
	2.	*n.*	**marvel, miracle, sight, spectacle** Niagara Falls is a famous natural wonder.	
	3.	*v.*	**question, speculate** I wonder when we can travel to the moon.	
wonderful	1.	*adj.*	**incredible, marvelous, splendid, superb, striking, spectacular, amazing, remarkable** Modern science can do wonderful things.	*1. unimportant, ordinary, simple, banal, everyday*
	2.	*adj.*	**good, fine, great, terrific, superb, super, fabulous** We had a wonderful time at the party!	*2. bad, dreadful, horrid*
work	1.	*n.*	**job, labor, task, toil, effort** The work of building the Great Wall of China took many lives.	*1. leisure, relaxation, ease*
	2.	*n.*	**employment, job, trade, occupation, profession** She has been looking for work since she graduated.	*2. vacation, unemployment*
	3.	*n.*	**product, creation** The sculptor's works sell for a great deal of money.	
	4.	*v.*	**toil, labor** The employees worked long hours each day.	*4. rest, relax*
	5.	*v.*	**operate, perform, run, go, function** How does this machine work?	
worldwide		*adj.*	**global, universal** The Internet provides immediate worldwide communication.	*local, regional, neighboring*
worn		*adj.*	**shabby, tattered, threadbare, frayed** The worn clothes were discarded.	*new, fresh, unused*
worry	1.	*n.*	**trouble, care, anxiety, concern, problem, misery, despair** Simi was filled with worry over the test.	*1. assurance, calm, comfort, security*

	2.	*v.*	**torment, disturb, upset, trouble, vex, bother** Ed's poor health worries everyone.	*2. leave alone, please, reassure, comfort*
worth	1.	*n.*	**value, price, merit** What is the worth of your home?	
	2.	*n.*	**good, use, importance, benefit, value, merit** Is there any worth in reading fairy tales?	
worthless		*adj.*	**valueless, useless, good-for-nothing** Counterfeit money is worthless.	*valuable, precious, worthwhile, useful*
worthwhile		*adj.*	**valuable, useful, profitable, good, beneficial, worth the effort** The project to help the retired people proved worthwhile.	*worthless, useless, bad, trivial, pointless*
worthy		*adj.*	**deserving, valuable** Helping to save the environment is a worthy cause.	*worthless*
wrap	1.	*v.*	**cover, parcel, bundle** The butcher wrapped the steak in waxed paper.	*1. uncover, unwrap, open*
	2.	*v.*	**clothe, cover, swathe, shroud, cloak, envelop, enfold** I wrapped the baby in a warm blanket.	*2. uncover, unfold, unclothe*
wrath		*n.*	**anger, rage, ire, fury** The government incurred the wrath of the people with the new taxes.	*gentleness, kindness, mildness*
wreck	1.	*n.*	**ruin, derelict, mess, dilapidated structure** That vacant house is now a wreck.	
	2.	*v.*	**ruin, destroy, demolish, raze, level** The old school building was wrecked by a tornado.	*2. build, construct, preserve, restore, repair*
wretched	1.	*adj.*	**gloomy, shabby, miserable, forlorn, inferior** The slums of the city are wretched places.	*1. cheerful, affluent*
	2.	*adj.*	**poor, pitiful, unfortunate** The wretched people were forced from their homes.	*2. fortunate, lucky*
wrong	1.	*n.*	**crime, sin, wickedness, vice, transgression, misdeed, error** There are many wrongs in this world.	*1. justice, goodness, right, honesty, virtue*
	2.	*v.*	**hurt, harm, abuse, ill-treat** Carl wronged Sue when he lied about her.	*2. aid, assist, help*
	3.	*adj.*	**evil, wicked, unjust, unlawful, bad, immoral, sinful** It is wrong to steal.	*3. right, proper, suitable, fair, moral*
	4.	*adj.*	**incorrect, erroneous, false, mistaken** That's the wrong answer.	*4. right, proper, correct, accurate*

X came to us from the ancient Egyptian hieroglyphics via the ancient Greeks and Romans. Not many English words begin with *X*, but it is a versatile letter which always has intrigued us.

X can be used by itself to represent an unknown quantity. We solve equations to find *"X"* in algebra. *X* marks the spot on maps and diagrams. *X* names geometric angles and lines. It can be used as a personal signature by someone who cannot write. But best of all, it sends our kisses in cards and letters to loved ones.

x   *n.*   **unknown quantity, unknown**
Solve the equation to determine the value of x.

known quantity, known, given

Xerox   *v.*   **photocopy, reproduce, copy, photostat, duplicate**
It is illegal to Xerox copyrighted material.
n. I made a Xerox of my notes for Belinda.

originate, print, invent

Xmas   *n.*   **Christmas, Yule, Yuletide, the Nativity**
"Xmas" is the abbreviation for Christmas.

Y

Did you know that *Y* in English can be used as a consonant or as a vowel? As a vowel, *Y* replaces the sound of *I* in words such as *type* and *psychic*. It takes on the sound of *E* at the end of words such as *happy* and *happily.*

Y gets the credit for starting one of our most used words, *yes.*

yearly	*adv.*	**annually, once a year**	
		Petunias bloom yearly.	
		adj. The school holds a yearly concert.	
yearn	*v.*	**pine, long for, hanker, desire, crave**	*avoid, loathe*
		I yearn for the peace of the countryside.	
yell	*n.*	**shout, scream, bellow, holler, roar, cry**	*whisper, murmur*
		James gave a yell when he tripped over the stone.	
		v. People on the roller coaster yelled in excitement.	
yield	1. *v.*	**produce, supply, furnish, bear**	1. *deny, take away, refuse*
		Orchards yield fruit.	
		n. This orchard gives an excellent yield.	
	2. *v.*	**surrender, cede, give up, submit, give in, succumb**	2. *oppose, resist, fight*
		After a long struggle, the people yielded to the demands of the leader.	
	3. *v.*	**give way, come apart, bend, cave in**	3. *support, uphold*
		The shelf yielded under the weight of the books.	
young	1. *n.*	**offspring**	1. *parents*
		Animals protect their young.	
	2. *adj.*	**juvenile, youthful, childish**	2. *old, aged, elderly*
		The show is designed for young people.	
		n. This movie is suitable for the young.	
	3. *adj.*	**inexperienced, callow, green, immature**	3. *experienced, veteran, expert, mature*
		Young football players are coached by the veterans.	
youth	1. *n.*	**child, youngster, teenager, juvenile**	1. *adult, elderly person, elder, senior*
		The youths were commended for their bravery during the fire.	
	2. *n.*	**childhood, adolescence**	2. *old age, senility*
		The old friends shared memories of their youth.	
	3. *n.*	**younger generation, young, children**	3. *older generation, seniors*
		A country's youth is its future.	
youthful	*adj.*	**young, fresh**	*aged, old, mature, venerable, antiquated*
		The movie star was complimented for her youthful looks.	

Z's old English name was *izzard.* Americans call it *zee. Zed* is the Canadian name. It is the last consonant.

Z, because of its sound, is often used in cartoons and comics to represent snoozing and snoring: Z-Z-Z-Z-Z-Z.

zany		*adj.*	**wacky, funny, humorous, silly, madcap, slapstick, outlandish** The clown's zany antics amused us.	*serious, somber*
zap	1.	*v.*	**hit, strike** Sue zapped the ball over the fence.	
	2.	*v.*	**microwave, cook, reheat** Zap the leftovers and we'll eat quickly.	
zeal		*n.*	**ardor, fervor, passion, zest, gusto** The astronauts trained with zeal. *adj.* Miriam's zealous efforts paid off with a scholarship.	*indifference, apathy, reluctance, indolence*
zenith		*n.*	**top, pinnacle, summit, apex, height, climax, crest, crown** Elvis Presley reached the zenith of the recording industry.	*bottom, base, foundation, depth*
zero		*n.*	**nil, nothing, naught, none, zilch** The score is two to zero.	*something, anything*
zest	1.	*n.*	**tang, bite, spice, pungency, piquancy** Spices add zest to food. *adj.* This curry has a zestful taste.	1. *blandness, mildness*
	2.	*n.*	**relish, gusto, zeal, enjoyment, ardor, enthusiasm, fervor** Grandpa has such a zest for life.	2. *disgust, distaste, apathy, indifference*
zigzag		*adj.*	**crooked, askew, jagged, winding, rambling, meandering, indirect** We followed a zigzag course up the hill. *v.* Paths zigzagged through the woods.	*straight, direct, unswerving, parallel*
zilch		*n.*	**nothing, zero, nil, naught** Those actors received zilch for their efforts.	*something, anything*
zip		*v.*	**fasten, close, do up** Zip up your coat in this cold weather!	*unfasten, unzip, open, undo*
zone	1.	*n.*	**territory, district, area, region** The reporter was sent to the war zone.	
	2.	*n.*	**area, region, belt, band, latitude** Canada is in the north temperate zone.	
	3.	*v.*	**plan, set apart, restrict to, apportion** This land has been zoned for a park.	3. *leave unrestricted, leave open*
zoom	1.	*v.*	**speed, rush, hurry, bustle, race, fly, dash, hurtle** Race cars zoomed around the track.	1. *saunter, dawdle, crawl, creep*
	2.	*v.*	**climb, soar, rise, ascend** The show's ratings zoomed this season.	2. *crash, sink, fall, descend, plummet*